THE IRISH POET
AND THE
NATURAL WORLD

THE IRISH POET
AND THE
NATURAL WORLD

An Anthology of Verse in English
from the Tudors to the Romantics

Edited by
Andrew Carpenter and Lucy Collins

CORK UNIVERSITY PRESS

First published in 2014 by
Cork University Press
Youngline Industrial Estate
Pouladuff Road, Togher
Cork, Ireland

British Library Cataloguing in Publication Data
A CIP catalogue record for this book is available from the British Library.

ISBN-978–1-78205-064-3

Typeset by Burns Design
Printed in Malta by Gutenberg Press Ltd

In memory of
Margaret Collins (1925–2012)
and
Anne Isdell-Carpenter (1915–2010)

CONTENTS[1]

1 Where possible, three dates are given for each author: birth, date of first circulation of the work printed in this anthology and death.

Part II: 1690–1739

Part III: 1740–1769

Part V: 1800–1819

ACKNOWLEDGEMENTS

We would like to thank the staff of the following libraries and institutions who have been unfailingly helpful to us: Trinity College Dublin, University College Dublin, the National Library of Ireland, the Royal Irish Academy, the Gilbert Collection in the Pearse Street Library Dublin.

In addition, we thank the following for generously providing help of various kinds: Toby Barnard, Ray Bates, Charles Benson, Bernadette Cunningham, David Dickson, Éamonn de Búrca, Patrick Duffy, Frank Ferguson, Anne Fogarty, Raymond Gillespie, Jane Grogan, Margaret Kelleher, James Kelly, Máire Kennedy, Rolf and Magda Loeber, Linde Lunney, James McGuire, Cormac Ó Gráda, John Fischer, Hermann Real, Ian Campbell Ross, the late Tony Sweeney, Brendan Twomey, John Waters, James Woolley, Julia Wright and our colleagues in the School of English, Drama and Film at University College Dublin. We are grateful also to the staff at Cork University Press – particularly to Maria O'Donovan – and to the anonymous readers for the press whose reports were a great help in our revision of the Introduction.

We acknowledge, with thanks, permission to quote from materials in the possession of the Board of Trinity College Dublin, the Trustees of the National Library of Ireland, the Board of the British Library and the Council of the Royal Irish Academy.

NOTE ON THE TEXTS

The poems in this anthology are arranged chronologically so that the reader can appreciate the evolving relationship between Irish poets and the natural world from the late Tudor period to the Romantic.

Since we aim to present the reader with texts that are both true to their original sources and yet readable, we have retained the original capitalisation, spelling and lineation; proper names are given in their original forms. Obvious misprints have been silently corrected.

Some substantive changes have been made throughout: (1) the letters 'u' and 'v', 'i' and 'j' have been amended to conform with modern usage; (2) the word 'it's' meaning 'of it' has been changed to 'its'; (3) 'hir' is amended to 'her'; (4) the word 'least' is amended to its modern form 'lest' and (5) the words 'than' and 'then', often used interchangeably in the sixteenth and seventeenth centuries, are amended to their modern forms. The most considerable change, however, is in (6) punctuation. Until the nineteenth century, many authors expected the compositor in the printing house to supply the punctuation for the printed text; this was often done to a set formula. We have therefore made such changes as are necessary to make the texts intelligible. The sources of the texts are listed at the end of the volume.

Notes found in the original text are presented as footnotes, in angle brackets < >.

Many of the texts in this anthology are extracts from longer works. An omission is signalled by an ellipsis before the omission except when the omission is of lines before the first line printed here, in which case an ellipsis is printed at the beginning of the extract.

Line numbers are keyed to this printing of the texts.

Since it is more likely that the reader will dip into this book than read it from beginning to end, some references are explained more than once.

INTRODUCTION

The Irish Poet and the Natural World 1581–1819

Throughout history, man's relationship with the natural world has been central to his attempts to understand the meaning of life. Though the origins of modern ecocriticism lie in Romantic opposition to the destruction of nature by industrial advancement,[1] earlier texts reveal close emotional and practical connections to the non-human world, as well as a capacity to reflect on the implications of such interdependence. Works of literature offer unique insights into this relationship, exploring the diversity of responses – philosophical, scientific and spiritual – that man has made to his environment. Poetry is particularly suited to such a range of engagement, its linguistic richness and formal variety allowing the individual human subject – and the complex matrix of living things to which the poet gives utterance – intense and memorable expression. From pastoral allegory to geological treatise in verse, each poem illuminates the relationship between human and non-human worlds and demonstrates the enduring importance of this connection.

Wild nature, in the form of dramatic landscapes and extreme weather conditions, has always had an impact on the imagination of man. More recently, ecocritical perspectives on literature highlight the need to move beyond these representations to examine the impact of man's actions on all forms of life. The exploitation of natural resources and mistreatment of animals, together with the environmental problems generated by advances in agricultural methods and large-scale urban development, raise many questions about human responsibility towards the earth. In this anthology, therefore, as well as selecting poems of man's connection with the landscape and with animals, we have chosen texts that reveal the importance of his philosophical and scientific enquiry into nature in its broadest sense, and into the development of human understanding of the natural world. Mysterious natural phenomena are contemplated in these works, as is the complex interplay between the earth's resources and

1 Some of the earliest interventions in the study of literature and the environment took Romantic writers as their focus. Jonathan Bate's *Romantic Ecology: Wordsworth and the Environmental Tradition*, published in 1991, is a particularly significant early work. For a discussion of this phase of ecocritical development see Timothy Clark, *The Cambridge Introduction to Literature and the Environment* (Cambridge: Cambridge University Press, 2011).

human organisation; poems of spiritual enquiry appear alongside vivid descriptions of polluted urban landscapes and meditations on man's power to shape place.

Poems that examine the relationship between human and non-human worlds inevitably raise questions about collective or social identity. It is this sense of shared perspective that has been most thoroughly contested in the modern world as philosophers, theologians and poets have questioned the validity of the traditional, hierarchical view of man's place in the 'Great Chain of Being'. Few of the poets in this volume would have shared Alexander Pope's vision of an unproblematic 'we' responding to nature and the universe with shared insight and intention; instead the power of man over nature – or, indeed, that of nature over man – is mediated in varying ways throughout this anthology across a spectrum of practical, political, ethical and philosophical positions. In Ireland between the Tudor conquests and the Romantic period, these variations are especially complex, due to the layered – and sometimes merging – cultural and political dynamics of Gaelic Irish, Old English and New English communities living in and on the land. Individuals from the various tribal, linguistic or sectarian sections of Irish society held diverse attitudes towards the natural world around them; attitudes shaped by their differing intellectual, religious or ethical traditions and lived experience. Inevitably, and in particular due to the variance in language use, they expressed the dynamics of these relationships in distinctive ways. Since we are including only work in the English language in this volume, the range of these representations is necessarily circumscribed, and the perspective that is reflected in these pages is predominantly that of educated Protestants during the seventeenth, eighteenth and early nineteenth centuries.[2] The experience of significant social and political changes that took place throughout Ireland in these years shaped the work of the poets in this book in varying ways however. For those who identified closely with

2 Only about a dozen of the nearly one hundred poets in this volume are known to have been professed Catholics. For a wider selection of verse in English by Irish Catholics, see *Verse in English from Tudor and Stuart Ireland* and *Verse in English from Eighteenth-Century Ireland*, both edited by Andrew Carpenter (Cork: Cork University Press, 2003 and 1997). For verse in Irish, see Seán Ó Tuama and Thomas Kinsella, eds, *An Duanaire 1600–1900: Poems of the Dispossessed* (Dublin: Dolmen Press, 1981) and Mícheál Mac Craith's comprehensive 'Literature in Irish *c.*1550–1690' in Margaret Kelleher and Philip O'Leary, eds, *The Cambridge History of Irish Literature*, 2 vols. (Cambridge: Cambridge University Press, 2006) I, pp. 191–231.

Ireland, strong ties to place and community were the basis for observation. For those living in the country for a comparatively short time, the mood was often one of discovery or evaluation. Neither of these responses is exempt from political significance, revealing the natural world in Ireland as an important site for contested loyalties with links to community and family set against economic opportunity and desire for personal aggrandisement. These tensions have produced poems rich in detailed observation of the natural world, and resonant with an array of social meanings.

The remarkable variety of the work in this anthology is indicative of the complexity of its literary roots that extend from Irish language materials and the Bible to classical texts and nature poems in the English language. As Thomas Herron has suggested, the corpus of poetry in Irish alone between the fourteenth and the seventeenth centuries indicates the depth of an indigenous culture that engaged with, but was not merely derivative of, other European sources.[3] This in turn suggests that the representation of the natural world in Irish-language poetry reflected the changes in social perspective, as well as in political power, that were a feature of the centuries preceding this volume.[4] Long before the period covered by this anthology, the poets of the middle ages saw the hand of God in everything around them, in all natural phenomena, as well as in the human condition. For the medieval Irish monks and scribes, the natural world was a manifestation of divine perfection, and they often saw the tension between freedom and discipline as a tension between the freedom of nature and the discipline of the written culture within which they were working. Seamus Heaney, in an essay on early Irish nature poetry, notes the presence of both wildness and restraint in this material:

> On the one hand, there is the *pagus*, the pagan wilderness, green, full-throated, unrestrained; on the other hand there is the lined book, the Christian *disciplina*, the sense of a spiritual principle and a religious calling that transcends the almost carnal lushness of nature itself.[5]

3 Thomas Herron, 'Introduction: A Fragmented Renaissance' in Thomas Herron and Michael Potterton, eds, *Ireland in the Renaissance c.1540–1660* (Dublin: Four Courts Press, 2007), p. 34.

4 Many examples of this can be found in Thomas Kinsella's ground-breaking anthology of Irish-language poetry. See Ó Tuama and Kinsella, eds, *An Duanaire 1600–1900*.

5 Seamus Heaney, 'The God in the Tree' in Seán MacRéamoinn, ed., *The Pleasures of Gaelic Poetry* (London: Penguin Books, 1982), p. 26.

This relationship between a plentiful natural world and the restraint necessary for the construction of verse is both thematically and formally important to many of the poets in this anthology, though its earliest Irish resolution may lie in Irish-language poetry of the middle ages.[6] Other writings from the period explore the relationship between wildness and civilisation. In the medieval tale of *Buile Shuibhne*, for example, King Sweeney's angry reaction to the planned building of a church on his land leaves him doomed by the priest's curse to roam throughout Ireland, unable to find rest. In exile, Sweeney learns the difference between a natural landscape cultivated for man's use and one which remains wild.[7] This distinction remains an important one for the representation of nature by poets in Ireland, one that is indicative of the complex and changing political climate of the centuries before the collapse of the Gaelic order.

Questions of language and of literary tradition are particularly complex in the context of intellectual development in early modern Ireland. The Irish language was a vital point of continuity, both in oral and written forms; poets continued to celebrate the beauty of natural life in Ireland, but the collapse of the old social structures (*briseadh an tseangháthaimh*, as Dáithí Ó Bruadair termed it) and the exile into which so many Irish-speakers were forced during the seventeenth century, gave their verse a sense of cultural and physical loss that we do not find in English-language verse of the period. Yet though the poetic worlds of these two communities in Ireland – Irish-speaking and English-speaking – remained largely apart in the seventeenth century, many later works in this anthology reveal the impact that spoken Irish was to have on spoken English in Ireland. Murroghoh O'Connor's poem on Kerry and those in John Winstanley's anthologies of the mid-eighteenth century, among others, indicate in their phraseology, spelling or vocabulary some familiarity with spoken Irish.[8] While macaronic poems found in chapbooks and manuscripts show clearly how widespread was the Hibernian pronunciation later

6 Robin Flower, *The Irish Tradition* (Oxford: Oxford University Press, 1947) is still a useful guide to Irish-language writing in the medieval period.

7 Oona Frawley attributes this distinction to nostalgia for a lost life, which in turn she sees as a recurring element of bardic poetry. Oona Frawley, *Irish Pastoral: Nostalgia and Twentieth-Century Irish Literature* (Dublin: Irish Academic Press, 2005), p. 18.

8 At its simplest, this can be seen in the use of assonance or in rhymes such as take/speak and treat/yet. For an assessment of the pronunciation of seventeenth- and eighteenth-century Hiberno-English (or Irish-English), see Alan Bliss, *Spoken English in Ireland 1600–1740* (Dublin: Cadenus, 1979), pp. 186–94.

denounced by Thomas Sheridan the elocutionist,[9] such diction was exaggerated wildly in 'stage Irish' of the seventeenth and eighteenth centuries.[10] The only poem included in this anthology that demonstrates this extreme form of Hiberno-English (or Irish-English) is 'Lord Altham's Bull'. Though 'polite' writers whose English was influenced by the Irish language were not normally eager to demonstrate this fact, Ulster poets who spoke Ulster-Scots were proud to write in that dialect;[11] we have thought it necessary to 'translate' the poems by Samuel Thomson and Francis Boyle in this anthology.

During much of the period covered by this volume, Latin was studied systematically in Ireland and was one of its principal languages; 'in times when Irishmen were divided in their loyalties,' observed W. B. Stanford, 'their common respect for ancient Greece and Rome provided an intellectual and emotional link between them'.[12] However, after the Reformation, the English language became associated with incoming Protestants and the Latin language developed particular, sometimes contradictory, uses: since it was the language of the Catholic church, it was a vehicle for the expression of opposition to English Protestantism; but it was also, as the language of official documents in England, the medium for expressing allegiance to the English crown. More significantly, for this anthology, it retained its position in schools and universities on both sides of the sectarian divide (on the Continent as well as in Ireland) as the language of instruction; many poets first encountered poetry in the Latin or Greek languages and sought (or were trained) to emulate classical models. Familiarity with such texts was often indicative of the level

9 'Rules to be observed by the Natives of Ireland in order to attain a just Pronunciation of English', in Thomas Sheridan, *A Complete Dictionary of the English Language …* (London: Dilly, 1789), pp. lxxxvii–xci. For macaronic chapbook poems see Carpenter, ed., *Verse in English from Eighteenth-Century Ireland*, pp. 6–23 and references.

10 See Bliss, *Spoken English*, pp. 312–6 and Joep Leerssen, *Mere Irish and Fíor-Ghael: Studies in the Idea of Irish Nationality, its Development and Literary Expression Prior to the Nineteenth Century* (Cork: Cork University Press, 1996), pp. 88–129. Other useful texts on Hiberno-English include Markku Filppula, *The Grammar of Irish English: Language in Hibernian Style* (London: Routledge, 1999); P. W. Joyce, *English as We Speak it in Ireland* (Dublin: Gill, 1910) and Diarmaid Ó Muirithe, ed., *The English Language in Ireland* (Cork: Mercier, 1977).

11 The political statement being made here links Ulster with Scotland rather than with England or, indeed, with the rest of Ireland.

12 W. B. Stanford, *Ireland and the Classical Tradition* (Dublin: Irish Academic Press, 1976), p. 245. See also John Wilson Foster 'Encountering Traditions' in John Wilson Foster, ed., *Nature in Ireland: A Scientific and Cultural History* (Dublin: Lilliput, 1997), pp. 23–70 (p. 39).

of education that the poet had received. As late as the eighteenth century, the lack of a classical education was a source of self-consciousness for ordinary people.[13] Translations of classical texts were available in Ireland for schoolboys and for those not deemed worthy of education – a category that often included women. Strong-willed women, of course, resisted these limitations and their scholarly persistence yielded diverse intellectual dividends.[14] In this anthology, however, few of the poems written by women were derived from classical models. Among the early poets, Richard Stanihurst, Edmund Spenser and Payne Fisher most clearly demonstrate facility with classical materials, and among later ones Thomas Sheridan (who translated Persius for the schoolboys he taught), William Dunkin and Edmund Burke.

Equally significant to some of the poets in this book was the Bible as translated into English in the seventeenth century. In Biblical texts, heard so often that many settlers would have known them by heart, lay not only the justification for the plantation and settlement of Ireland but also explanations for natural phenomena. In this respect, however, one of the most influential texts of the period was *Topographiae Hiberniae* by the twelfth-century Norman Welshman, Giraldus Cambrensis (Gerald of Wales). In this text Ireland, an isolated island at the edge of Europe, was represented as a wild land inhabited by uncivilized, lazy and barbarous people, only redeemed by their incomparable skill at music. Though it was initially designed for readers of his own time, *Topographiae Hiberniae* was to remain, until the late seventeenth century, the standard justification for England's repeated attempts to conquer Ireland and stamp out the indigenous language and culture. The influence of Cambrensis can be seen in the work of Elizabethan writers such as Fynes Moryson, Edmund Spenser, Sir John Davies and Richard Beacon, and he was not fully answered or his prejudiced views refuted until John Lynch's *Cambrensis Eversus* of 1662.[15]

13 See Penelope Wilson, 'Classical Poetry and the Eighteenth-Century Reader' in Isabel Rivers, ed., *Books and their Readers in Eighteenth-Century England* (Leicester: Leicester University Press; New York: St Martin's Press, 1982), p. 70.

14 Irish examples of women poets from the seventeenth and eighteenth centuries include Mary Monck (*c.*1678–1715), Mary Barber (*c.*1685–1755) and Constantia Grierson (*c.*1705–32).

15 For extracts from the relevant texts, see Seamus Deane, Andrew Carpenter and Jonathan Williams, eds, *The Field Day Anthology of Irish Writing*, 3 vols. (Derry and London: Field Day and Faber, 1991), I, pp. 171–247.

If Cambrensis's negative view of the inhabitants of Ireland helped to persuade the empire-builders and planters of the early modern period of the morality of their actions, his highly favourable appraisal of Ireland's natural advantages was probably equally influential. According to his account, Ireland was an ideal place for settlement with ample opportunities for agricultural development. The land was, he wrote, 'fruitful and rich in its fertile soil and plentiful harvests. Crops abound in the fields, flocks on the mountains and wild animals in the woods…'.[16] He praised Ireland's rivers, lakes and seas, and described in detail the appearance and behaviour of the birds, beasts and reptiles found throughout the island. He also recounted stories of a talking wolf, a horse-like woman and a creature that was half-man and half-ox before detailing the contrary motions of the Irish Sea, the existence of wonderful wells and the miracles performed by various Irish saints. Though even Cambrensis himself admitted that some of his descriptions were fanciful, his book was widely consulted and the idea that Ireland was a potentially rich country inhabited by bestial barbarians became a commonly held belief among early modern planters and administrators.

Contested Territories: Political, Intellectual and Cultural Life from the Tudors to the Battle of the Boyne

The arrival in Ireland in the sixteenth and seventeenth centuries of the conquering armies and Protestant settlers of Tudor, Stuart and Commonwealth England – with their efficient ships, their armies, their legal structures and their concepts of the right to 'possess' land – was to change life in Ireland irrevocably and put an end to a world in which poets used the Irish language to celebrate changing seasons and the wildlife around them.[17] The newcomers imposed systems of enclosure and plantation on the untilled grazing land of Ireland, constructing stone-built farms and walled towns, and bringing mapmakers and lawyers with them to the land they colonized. Many who had traditionally tilled smallholdings were forced off the land, becoming landless 'cottiers', living by the roadside in thatched cabins made of

16 Gerald of Wales, *The History and Topography of Ireland*, trans. John J. O'Meara (Harmondsworth: Penguin, 1982), p. 34.

17 For translations of Early and Middle Irish poems on the seasons, the weather and blackbirds, see *Field Day* I, p. 346 and pp. 47–8.

mud, 'mostly without either chimney or window'[18] and moving around the countryside to find work.[19] The English settlers created very different living conditions to those that had existed before and the land they worked – and which they claimed to own – was walled or hedged against intruders. The traditional respect that the people of Ireland had shown for nature, and their willingness to live in harmony with it, was at odds with the settlers' urge to make Ireland productive and economically viable in a world increasingly dominated by trade and commerce. At the same time, poets and thinkers in Ireland as elsewhere began to construe nature – cultivated nature as well as wild nature – as an idealized space; a strategy that would have far-reaching effects, both politically and artistically.[20] If the poetry of early seventeenth-century England figured that country as Eden, it was a vision of a perfection based not only on the acquisition of new knowledge but also on expansionist aims: according to Chris Fitter the poetry of Protestant England at this time exhibited 'enthusiasm for paradisal holiness as overflowing beyond enclosed precincts, in sharp contrast with the *hortus conclusus* tradition and the Catholic reverence of sacred ground'.[21] In Ireland, where most of those writing verse in English acknowledged Protestant England as their motherland, these aims had both political and cultural manifestations;[22] to a greater or lesser extent, these shaped the lives and writings of those dwelling here.

There is no doubt that the complex intersection of literary traditions in Ireland places a significant emphasis on the formal authority of poetic texts as well as on the links between the newly created work and its poetic precursors. Accordingly, translation played an important role in the formation of poetic tastes throughout the late sixteenth and

18 Richard Twiss, *A Tour in Ireland in 1775* (London, 1776), p. 29.

19 The cabins of sods and thatch would, in time, return to the earth from which they had been made, leaving little or no trace on the landscape. See F. H. A. Aalen, Kevin Whelan and Matthew Stout, eds, *Atlas of the Irish Rural Landscape* (Cork: Cork University Press, 1997), p. 75.

20 Chris Fitter engages with these developments in his chapter on seventeenth-century English poetry in *Poetry, Space, Landscape: Towards a New Theory* (Cambridge: Cambridge University Press, 1995), pp. 233–315. Poems in this anthology depicting rural life as an idyll include those by John Cunningham, William Carr and James Stuart.

21 Fitter, *Poetry, Space, Landscape*, p. 236.

22 See the selections from Spenser below. In Dorothy Smith's 'The Shepherd's Jubilee' (1701), the flora and fauna of Ireland loyally welcome an English Lord Deputy into their earthly paradise – a paradise that had turned sour for the author of the 1641 'A Looking-Glasse of the World'.

seventeenth centuries. Richard Stanihurst's 'A Devise made by Virgil …' is indicative of the importance of the translator's art as a means of displaying creative talent; in this instance it also draws attention to Stanihurst's idiosyncratic rendering of the English language. In the work of later poets too – William Dunkin and John Leslie, for instance – one can see a complex interweaving of formal strategies and poetic material, suggesting the subtlety with which the representation of nature helped to shape the individual poet's sense of himself as a writer, and his particular response to the Irish environment. English nature poets of the seventeenth century evidenced their classical education through use of pastoral and georgic, and through their direct engagement with authors such as Horace, Pindar and, most especially, Virgil. By the eighteenth century, in Ireland as well as in England, these features show not so much the poet's background as a desire to cultivate readers appreciative of his intellectual sophistication and poetic sensitivity.[23]

The pastoral mode has obvious significance for any study of developments in the poetic representation of the natural world. In spite of the widespread use of the term, however, critics are divided on the issue of whether pastoral is historically delineated or a permanent mode within literary studies.[24] Annabel Patterson argues in favour of a pragmatic response: 'It is not what pastoral is that should matter to us… but how writers, artists and intellectuals of all persuasions have *used* pastoral for a range of functions and intentions that the *Eclogues* first articulated'.[25] This term therefore crystallises key debates on how attitudes to the countryside have developed, both historically and through literary representation. It also indicates the complex heritage of the pastoral mode, which reflects not only the idyllic lives of classical shepherds but the textual history from which they were

23 Individual poets such as Thomas Gray, Alexander Pope and James Thomson demonstrated their classical reading in letters and in textual annotation. A poet's library in the eighteenth century typically contained a good selection of classical texts, though this is no guarantee that they were read. See Wilson, 'Classical Poetry and the Eighteenth-Century Reader', p. 70.

24 Diverse definitions of pastoral emerge in the work of modern critics including Frank Kermode, Leo Marx, Renate Poggioli, Thomas G. Rosenmeyer and Raymond Williams. Paul Alpers comments on these and others in *What is Pastoral?* (Chicago and London: University of Chicago, 1996), pp. 10–11. Alpers himself draws particular attention to the relationship between the mode and its historical context, pp. 8–43.

25 Annabel Patterson, *Pastoral and Ideology: Virgil to Valery* (Berkeley and Los Angeles CA: University of California Press, 1987), p. 7.

formed – Virgil's innovative reworking of Theocritus' *Eclogues*.[26] It is pastoral's allegorical power that reveals the imaginative reach of the mode, and draws attention to its potential as a vehicle for political thought. Pastoral may be loosely described as the representation of country life in an idealised form, and must be distinguished from georgic with its purposeful emphasis on agricultural and rural topics. In contrast to the tensions that mark the georgic mode, the pastoral ideal privileged simplicity and ease, characteristics that were decisively eroded, from the seventeenth century onward, by the modernising of agricultural practices for economic gain. The sophistication of urban life was in fact built on the consumption of rural profits, yet these two environments were increasingly seen in opposition to one another, with the countryside construed as a place of innocence and retreat.[27] This contrast would later lead to the term 'pastoral' being attributed to any text that described the rural with implicit or explicit contrast to the urban.[28]

A significant concern for today's readers of such poems is the question of their ideological function. Raymond Williams is foremost among critics arguing that the idealized past of the pastoral represents a deliberate avoidance of the present inequities of land ownership.[29] Though Williams is writing of England, his point is even more significant in the Irish context. If one accepts this point of view, the pastoral mode becomes inextricably linked to cultural politics and exposes the complex dynamics of power at the heart of textual representation. Yet pastoral did not simply endorse seventeenth- and eighteenth-century hierarchies; indeed, in England, it often stood in opposition to courtly power and to the incursions of unchecked urban development. The question of temporality was an important one in

26 Timothy Saunders, in *Bucolic Ecology: Virgil's Eclogues and the Environmental Literary Tradition* (London: Duckworth, 2008) explores the relationship between bucolic song and the physical universe, drawing attention to the intertwining of the natural world with literary tradition.

27 Keith Thomas investigates this interdependence between rural and urban in *Man and the Natural World: Changing Attitudes in England 1500–1800* (London: Penguin, 1983), pp. 243–253.

28 Terry Gifford, *Pastoral* (London: Routledge, 1999), p. 2.

29 Raymond Williams, *The Country and the City* (Oxford: Oxford University Press, 1975). Patrick Duffy notes, '[w]hat became landscape, had simply been land, which had been appraised mainly in terms of its utility for agriculture or its opposite, wild and uncultivated nature'. Patrick J. Duffy, *Exploring the History and Heritage of Irish Landscapes* (Dublin: Four Courts Press, 2007), p. 164.

this respect. Ben Jonson, Alexander Pope and even the Irish-born Sir John Denham altered the retrospective power of the pastoral by locating their poems in the country estates – or at least in the well-ordered countryside – of their own day, aware of the political ramifications of this choice, and of the partial nature of the world these poems reconstruct.[30]

For readers of this anthology, transitions in space, rather than time, are of key importance. In the Irish context neither the rural–urban divide, nor party politics carried the same weight as they did for writers in England. In Ireland the dynamics of power operated more clearly on religious and social grounds and the retention or dispossession of lands became a key political concern, particularly after and during the imposition of the Restoration land settlements in the late seventeenth century. Yet, as Ken Hiltner has pointed out, many pastoral works 'concern themselves with literal landscapes'[31] and for these the descriptive power of language is especially important. In a similar way, the Irish language tradition of *dinnseanchas* (the naming of places) lies behind some of the poems in this anthology praising particular Irish locales. In the Irish context, this celebration of real places – including the views from them and the mythical stories associated with them – puts 'nature' back at the centre of pastoral and affirms the value of an aesthetic response to these works. This not only has the potential to reinvigorate close engagement with these texts, but also encourages critics to explore the capacity of the poetry to move beyond typical conceits towards individual realisations. In this anthology, such a strategy continues to attend to the importance of the Irish environment in the construction of political and social difference, but also invites readers to enjoy the particularity of these varied poetic representations.

The complex interweaving of political realities and aesthetic possibilities is nowhere more evident than in the work of Edmund Spenser. His project to replicate the English pastoral tradition in Ireland used classical modes of representation that could yet be shaped

30 Terry Gifford acknowledges this in the case of Pope's 'Windsor Forest'. Gifford, *Pastoral*, p. 32.

31 Ken Hiltner in his book *What Else is Pastoral?* re-opens the possibility of reading texts in this way: 'while not denying the political and allegorical character of much of Renaissance pastoral, my objective … is to make clear that a broad range of Renaissance pastoral works do indeed frequently concern themselves with literal landscapes …'. Ken Hiltner, *What Else is Pastoral? Renaissance Literature and the Environment* (New York: Cornell University Press, 2011), p. 68.

to the specifics of Irish landscape and environment. As well as creating a version of Ireland that would rival English representations of the time, Spenser, as a planter, was keen to situate Ireland as a vital and productive land. '[Y]t is yet a most bewtifull and sweete Countrie as any vnder heaven: seamed throughout with manie goodlie ryvers replenished with many sortes of fishe most aboundantlie … adorned with goodlie woodes fitte for buildings of howses and shipps so commodiouslie'.[32] Following on Giraldus Cambrensis, Spenser judged the inhabitants of Ireland and their 'barbaric' language and customs to stand in the way of the accomplishment of this imperial ideal. His prose work, like that of most other planters from the Elizabethan period, links the brutish character of the Irish to their failure to cultivate the land. But things could be amended – by force if necessary. Richard Beacon, his contemporary, argued that 'a commonwealth overgrown with a generall corruption of manners and thereby become savage, barbarous, and barren, like unto the wilde olive and figge tree' could yet be 'pruned' to obedience and civility by a skilful administrator.[33] Likewise it was possible to envisage a time when Ireland's wealth and natural resources could be harvested peacefully: Spenser himself argued that one way of separating the land from its current occupiers was to depopulate it of Irish-speakers and to starve the people to death.[34]

In his poetry, however, he broadened his perception and, in the extract from the 'Mutabilitie Cantos' of *The Faerie Queene* included in this book, allows the reader to see the physical landscape of Ireland as an extension of classical heaven, a suitable place for the contest between the current world order and the goddess Mutability – though the very presence of the native Irish could lead to the transformation of the country from a place 'of wealths and goodnesse' to an ill-favoured and threatening environment. In 'Colin Clouts Come Home Againe' the varied landscape around Spenser's castle at Kilcolman also becomes an allegorical setting for the action: real hills, mountains, rivers and streams are given symbolic meaning and the myths associated with them raised to classical status. The verse shows

32 Edmund Spenser, *A View of the Present State of Ireland*, ed. W. L. Renwick (London: Eric Partridge, 1934), pp. 25–6.

33 Richard Beacon, *Solon His Follie* (1594), eds. Vincent Carey and Clare Carroll (Binghamton NY: Medieval and Renaissance Texts and Studies, Vol. 154, 1996), p. 75.

34 Andrew Hadfield, *Edmund Spenser's Irish Experience: Wilde Fruit and Salvage Soyl* (Oxford: Oxford University Press, 1997), p. 108.

Spenser acknowledging the power of landscape as a physical space of action as well as a symbolic setting of universal significance. Critics are divided as to how Spenser expected his readers to interpret his use of the Irish landscape[35] but his unambiguous reference to Ireland's natural advantages as well as to its dangers – chiefly in the shape of its people – allowed these contradictions to assume important aesthetic as well as political resonance. The inclusion of that dialectic permitted Spenser to validate his own presence in Ireland at the same time as he indicated the personal and creative difficulties of this position.

Spenser's use of the pastoral mode affirmed its aesthetic emphasis yet allowed the discord that the pastoral conceals to shape the progress of his poem. In this respect the 'Mutabilitie Cantos' constitute an early example of the potential of this mode to present expected forms of address and description, while at the same time facilitating the individual vision of the poet. Even the Faun's glimpse of Diana bathing, a familiar treatment of the classical material, suggests the transgressive elements that shadow the presence of Elizabethan administrators, such as Spenser himself, in Ireland. The violent repercussions of this act hint at the political volatility of the countryside at this time, as Diana's curse turns the Irish landscape from a place of beauty to one ruled by wild and lawless elements. It is a pattern of imagery in accord with the words of Sir John Davies who linked the breaking of the soil for planting to the breaking of Ireland by war:

> For the good husbandman must first break the land before it can be made capable of good seed; and when it is thoroughly broken and manured, if he will not forthwith cast good seed into it, it will grow wild again and grow nothing but weed; so a barbarous country must first be broken by a war, before it will be capable of good government.[36]

35 See, *inter alia*, 'Spenser sets the Agenda' in Nicholas Canny, *Making Ireland British 1580–1650* (Oxford: Oxford University Press, 2001), pp. 1–58; Patricia Coughlan, ed., *Spenser and Ireland: an Interdisciplinary Perspective* (Cork: Cork University Press, 1989); Anne Fogarty, ed., *Spenser in Ireland: The Faerie Queene 1596–1996,* spec. issue of *Irish University Review* 26:2 (Autumn/Winter 1996); and Andrew Hadfield, *Edmund Spenser, A Life* (Oxford: Oxford University Press, 2012).

36 Sir John Davies, *A True Discovery of the True Causes Why Ireland was Never Entirely Subdued* ..., ed. James P. Myers Jr (Washington DC: Catholic University of America Press, 1988), pp. 71–2.

In addition, the imagery suggests that good husbandry is essential to any improvement of the condition of Ireland. In this scheme, civil strife is not a descent into disorder, but rather a necessary precursor to a more fitting imperial unity.

Though pastoral idealism suggests that the Irish landscapes of the period were rich with natural resources, ideas of mutability and of threatened chaos predominate in several of the poems of the seventeenth century included here. The political instabilities of the time find articulation in individual experiences that question the endurance of the human subject. The sea storm is thus a familiar trope, allowing this turmoil a poetic trajectory capable of resolution, when the storm-tossed boat finally reaches shore. In addition to this metaphorical potential, the close ties that many of these poets had to Ireland and England necessitated actual sea voyages, often fraught with danger, between the two islands. 'The Description of a Tempest', a powerful poem by the Irish Catholic lawyer Richard Bellings, depicts a journey from Wales across the turbulent Irish Sea. At first becalmed, the sailors' attempts to whistle up a storm are followed by extremely high winds, figured here – as in Milton's *Lycidas* – in terms of classical deities. Yet in the graphic depiction of the storm that follows, the stylised text gives way to the extremes of sensory experience:

> But when the winds these waves doe beare away,
> She hangs in ayre, and makes a little stay:
> But downe againe from such presumptuous height
> Shee's headling borne by her attractive weight
> Into the hollow of a gaping grave,
> Intomb'd of each side with a stately wave.

The subtle combination of poetic craft and innovation here reveals the ways in which these poets can think beyond the limitations of established form without excising the familiarity of these materials from the minds of readers.

While Bellings' poetic voyage is between 'my country' – Ireland – and the 'Cambrian shore', 'A Great Sea-Storm describ'd' by Richard Head is set on a fantastical journey in search of O Brazeel, an enchanted island off the shore of Ulster. The poem draws on some of the standard tropes of sea poems – the image of pregnancy to conjure up the fullness of wind and wave, for example – yet narrates an energetic narrative of adventure. The motion that informs the Bellings poem is rendered here in visual terms as the sea dwarfs the landscape of Wales, past which Head's ship is sailing when overtaken by the storm. For Head the best expression of the chaos of the storm is the disordered human response, in particular its auditory quality: the confusion of those on board and the 'rude tongues' of the sailors. Yet there is humour at the heart of the turmoil: 'The Ship a Vessel seem'd, and we Mackrell/Pickl'd in Brine, and in our Cabins lie'. The prayer for deliverance with which each poem ends marks the difference in seriousness between them. In being spared, Bellings has gained time for repentance; Head, in his turn, begs to be delivered from the necessity of prayer itself. These two poems, among others in this volume that depict seascapes, reveal the complex tonal variations involved in rendering this most untameable of natural zones.

The aesthetic of risk invoked by these poems, both in theme and idiom, is indicative of the instabilities inherent in cultural participation in seventeenth-century Ireland and in the fate of the publications produced. Few poetic texts remain from this period, so it is hard to infer the literary history from these limited examples. Those that do exist are more preoccupied with political upheaval and with the consequent breakdown of order, than with nature or the environment. The conditions of war not only had an impact on the survival rate of books and pamphlets, but also constrained the writing lives of those who produced them. Both Richard Nugent, who was from a prominent Old English family, and the anonymous author of 'A Looking-Glasse of the World', apparently a planter forced out by the 1641 rising, were driven from Ireland by political circumstance, and record the feelings of loss occasioned by this separation. Even those whose sojourn in Ireland had been comparatively short were capable of attachment to its natural beauty: this dispossessed planter was particularly enthusiastic about the animal, bird, insect and reptilian life he had observed in the land from which he had been expelled. Like John Derricke who had praised Irish hawks so enthusiastically two generations earlier, he could not help but express his admiration for the natural world in Ireland.

The Early Eighteenth Century: Literature and Landscaping

As the seventeenth and eighteenth centuries progressed – and particularly after the Restoration land settlements – English laws on land tenure took full effect in Ireland and the landscape changed wherever the land was fertile enough to make it worth enclosing.[37] Roads were built and bogs were drained, while mapped, manured and cultivated lands were exploited to provide crops and livestock for sale. Planned estate villages replaced haphazard and temporary settlement. Wildlife became the 'property' of landlords, and markets and money replaced traditional ways of living in communities. The poems of Laurence Whyte from the 1740s mourn the demise of old social structures and agricultural practices, as well as established ties of kindred; they curse rack-renting landlords and grasping agents whose practices led to the deterioration of smallholdings. The incoming English planters and landlords were fired not only with the need to make money out of Ireland but also with Protestant zeal to accomplish God's work by subduing the land and its inhabitants – at least those inhabitants who clung obstinately to the old ways, the old language and, above all, the old Catholic religion. Thus by the late seventeenth century, the Irish countryside had become a cultural battleground between English and Irish, Protestant and Catholic, new ideas and old values.

In spite of these contesting worldviews, the eighteenth century proved a peaceful one in Ireland. This, together with economic and technological advancement, made it a period of remarkable richness for the publishing and reading of poetry. The end of the Williamite wars, combined with a relaxation of book trade restrictions and the growth of a middle-class readership in Dublin, offered notable opportunities for the growth of publishing and printing industries in Ireland. At the beginning of this period the market for cheap reprints of English texts far exceeded that for indigenous poetry, but the range of verse written and printed in Ireland grew as the century progressed.[38] Among this Irish-produced material were not only poems responding to the country's natural beauty and the growing interest –

37 Aalen, Whelan and Stout, eds, *Atlas of the Irish Rural Landscape*, pp. 134–205.

38 See Raymond Gillespie and Andrew Hadfield, eds, *The Oxford History of the Irish Book: Volume III, The Irish Book in English 1550–1800* (Oxford: Oxford University Press, 2006) – particularly the essays by Toby Barnard, Andrew Carpenter, Raymond Gillespie and Colm Lennon.

on the part of those who now owned her agricultural or mineral resources – in their exploitation, but also texts reflecting on the close interrelationship between human experience and the non-human environment. Poems with subjects as various as birds, the fishing industry and the discovery of gold mines, reveal not only the imaginative range of their creators, but also the complex relationship between the natural world and human social and political formations in this period.

Given the increasingly close relationship between English-speaking Ireland and England during the century after the Battle of the Boyne, it is hardly surprising that there are close affinities between the kinds of poems being written in the two cultures. Some of those reflecting on the natural world were working with generic modes of writing – the poem praising the patron's estate, for instance – rather than engaging with the political dimensions of the changing landscape in Ireland. English poetry of the time offers important interpretations of classical modes: Pope chose Virgil as the basis for his *Pastorals* (1709), while John Dyer's *Grongar Hill* (1726) was a re-working of the Pindaric Ode. Dyer would later turn to the georgic for his ambitious four-part poem, *The Fleece* (1757) which harnessed the experiential and instructional powers of verse; these were later exploited with equal vigour by the Irish poet Charles Boyd in his 1809 'A Georgic of Modern Husbandry'. English and classical poetry were both widely read in eighteenth-century Ireland and Irish poets tended to absorb the same influences as their English counterparts.[39] Some Irish poems from the period adhered to classical or English models so closely that they can be said to have little that is distinctively Irish about them, and these have not found a place in this anthology. Others, such as James Ward's 'Phoenix Park', substantially reworked a classical model to suit the Irish context and in so doing shed important light on the way Irish poets chose to see their environment. Most Irish poets writing in English at this time were published in London as well as Dublin and their work shows both how close the two cultures could be, as well as how distinctively they might differ. Individual works by

39 See Lesa Ní Mhunghaile, 'Bilingualism, Print Culture in Irish and the Public Sphere, 1700–*c.*1830' in James Kelly and Ciarán Mac Murchaidh, eds., *Irish and English: Essays on the Irish Linguistic and Cultural Frontier, 1600–1900* (Dublin: Four Courts Press, 2012), pp. 218–42. In the same volume, Liam Mac Mathuna's article 'Verisimilitude or Subversion? Probing the Interaction of English and Irish in Selected Warrants and Macaronic Verse in the Eighteenth Century' (pp. 116–40) explores the use of macaronic verse in English/Irish for comic effect.

Irish poets were appreciated by their English counterparts, as was the case for Henry Brooke's *Universal Beauty* (1735). Cultural mobility offered opportunities, but complicated the reception of poems too: while there was a considerable amount of common ground between the two countries in terms of literary taste, their preferences were not identical. Idiosyncratic treatments of nature and of place – particularly Irish ones – were sometimes intended for a specific audience and were accompanied by details only appreciated by a knowing reader.

Among the poems selected here, it is in James Delacourt's poem 'To Mr Thomson, on his Seasons' (1734) that the direct influence of an English poet on an Irish one is most clearly expressed. Delacourt, an eccentric figure, saw Thomson's *The Seasons* (1730) as a way of reawakening Irish poetic representations of nature, arguing that it was in response to Thomson's treatment of the natural world, that 'the Irish harp [is] new-strung once more'. His expression of a national cultural identity is an interesting feature for this time: rather than eliding the differences between English and Irish poets, Delacourt sought to define the latter, first with a druidic motif, then with descriptions of bogland and the bittern's cry. It is significant that Thomson's *The Seasons* is what Terry Gifford calls a 'complete pastoral' – one that idealizes a series of landscapes in turn, thus suggesting the value of differentiated environments.[40] This retention of the specificity of an Irish landscape and history is resonant in the work of other poets too and, towards the end of the eighteenth century – in William H. Drummond's 'Hibernia' or William Drennan's 'To Ireland', for instance – is often associated with the cultivation of a national poetic identity. The extent to which nature is identified with those poets keenest to represent her is another interesting element of Delacourt's poem. If 'Thomson is another name for nature now', whom would one consider to be Thomson's Irish counterpart – the mid-eighteenth century poet against whose work other poetry of the Irish natural world could be judged? Perhaps William Dunkin, Laurence Whyte or Samuel Shepherd could be seen in this light or, a generation later, John Leslie or Oliver Goldsmith. The last of these might prove an illustrative figure in this respect, his chequered career highlighting the range of possibilities open to Irish-born poets, as well as indicating the complexity of the relationships forged between English and Irish

40 Gifford, *Pastoral*, p. 47.

cultures and traditions. Later again, poets such as William Drummond and James Orr used a range of techniques drawn from topographical modes, together with ideas from moral philosophy, to explore not only man's relationship to nature in Ireland, but also his awareness of the attention that must be brought to bear on its representation.

Irish poets wrote about places other than Ireland, however. The close connections between Ireland and Scotland during the eighteenth century are reflected in James Arbuckle's 'Glotta' (1721); the poem was written while Arbuckle was a university student in Glasgow, shortly before he returned to Dublin.[41] Though this hymn to the River Clyde is in the mode of the European river poem,[42] it situates itself in a tradition of English-language pastoral verse, making reference to what were considered the classic poems of the genre, John Denham's 'Cooper's Hill' (1642) and Alexander Pope's 'Windsor Forest' (1713). Such a dialogue with key topographical poems is an important feature of Irish and Scottish verse of the time, showing that those writing what was essentially local verse presented themselves as being on equal terms with poets of international significance. In keeping with this strategy, the opening declaration of 'Glotta' echoes the practices of poets such as Pope and Ambrose Phillips in its combination of praise of both place and patron. The early emphasis of the poem is on immortalising the featured landscape in words, so that the act of representation itself – and the immunity from decay it presents – proves of key concern. Conversely, though, it is the enduring attraction of place that Arbuckle chooses to emphasise at a key moment in the poem: 'The Muse would sing, when Glasgow she surveys,/But Glasgow's Beauty shall outlast her lays'. This oscillation between assertions of the primacy of nature and of art can be found throughout the poem. The 'transplantation' of classical models permits the poet to use them with attention and innovation, to represent his environment more truly by tracing nature 'to her hidden Springs'. These 'hidden springs' are primarily natural laws, to which every aspect of the phenomenal world may be linked, and Arbuckle's

41 In an 1894 essay 'Ulster Poets and Poetry', D. J. O'Donoghue complains of Arbuckle's appropriation by the 'Scotch', as demonstrated by Chalmers' inclusion of him in his biographical dictionary, 'saying he was born in Glasgow, though Arbuckle was a most patriotic Irishman' (O'Donoghue, p. 22).

42 For details of the river poem in the English context, see Robert Arnold Aubin, *Topographical Poetry in XVIII-Century England* (New York: Modern Language Association of America, 1966), pp. 377–85.

enquiries here prove indicative of his larger interest in moral philosophy.

Poems written by Irish poets while abroad, such as those by Arbuckle, Swift and James Eyre Weekes in this anthology, can highlight a writer's engagement with the multiple cultures that have created the environment in which he finds himself. The most obvious example of such an engagement at this time is that of Jonathan Swift whose famous London poem, 'A Description of a City Shower' (1710), reflects not only his familiarity with classical and literary models – through his education in Ireland and his experiences as Sir William's Temple's secretary in England – but also the writer's urge to draw meaning from the experience of a chaotic urban space. As Carole Fabricant has pointed out, Swift transformed the concrete features of his environment into a symbolical depiction of his society;[43] for him, a description of the landscape of London life was a potent – and witty – way of showing up the failures and self-deceptions of its society. He was, as Irvin Ehrenpreis puts it, 'the Irishman showing off his familiarity with the English scene' and also the satirist showing up man's inability to deal with such basic environmental concerns as the disposal of waste.[44] This complexity inflects the relationship between speaker and reader in the poem. So the 'Careful Observers' at the opening of this poem are both those within the poem noting changes in the weather (later made redundant by the overwhelming aspect of its signs) and readers interpreting the coded text. Here the portents of change – the subdued cat, the painful corns – are quickly matched by less subtle indicators – such as the 'double stink' of the sewer, which registers the physical impact of environmental mismanagement. The rain, when it comes, is so mixed with dirt as to preoccupy the poet, whose coat, and text, is now a conglomeration of stains, of syllables, beats and pauses. Yet, as Ehrenpreis points out, this is a poem of warm familiarity with, as much as a satire on, urban life, and the vigour and amusement with which Swift wrote of London's inhabitants reveals his easy intimacy with

43 Carole Fabricant, *Swift's Landscape* (South Bend IN: University of Notre Dame Press, 1995), p. 3.

44 Irvin Ehrenpreis, *Swift, the Man, his Works and the Age*, 3 vols (London: Methuen, 1967–83), II (1967), p. 384.

this environment.[45] Animal and vegetable matter is never far from the city space, and the final six lines of the poem first map the path of the torrent from Smithfield to Holborn Bridge, then detail the material brought with it; the 'Dung, Guts and Blood', the 'Drown'd Puppies', 'Dead Cats' and 'Turnip-Tops'. Though those living in the city may think that they avoid direct engagement with nature, they cannot resist its forces. Likewise, as a mock georgic, this poem's textual precursors course through its length. The dialogue that Swift establishes is not with Virgil's original text, however, but with Dryden's translations of it.[46] Thus the poem not only depicts an environment but itself becomes one – one where the poetic expectations of the reader are broken down into a vision of nothing less than excremental, urban chaos.

Swift's obsession with waste, and with the structures provided to manage it, records the significance of natural processes even in a man-made environment. Cities were growing rapidly throughout eighteenth-century Europe. Paris and London were famously polluted but this anthology also contains several poems referring to the unpleasant state of Dublin at the time.[47] An anonymous poem 'The Upper Gallery' refers to broken sewers and filthy streets in Dubl[illegible] the untreated sewage that Swift noted streaming out of London flowe[illegible] to the sea and John Winstanley reminds his friend the Revd Mr----- that the sea water he is quaffing, presumably in Dublin Bay, contain[illegible] effluvia of various unpleasant kinds from cities all over the world. Dublin was also noted for its polluted air and the Corkman James Eyre Weekes depicts urban smog with superb skill in his poem 'On the late fog', written in London in 1762. Another poet unsympathetic to city life was William Webb who, in 1805, described Dublin as a 'concourse' of 'clouded dust', 'clattering noise' and 'sad stone wall[s]. He also deplored 'City taste' whose 'meddling hand' was adorning suburban gardens with inappropriate Chinese bridges and 'old-new Gothick nick-nack[s]'.

The rise of urban living was of course far more significant in the English than in the Irish context: by the end of the seventeenth century around one-sixth of England's population had spent at least part of

45 In his analysis of 'A Description of a City Shower', Ehrenpreis argues that the poem is a travesty of Dryden's practice of combining couplets, triplets and alexandrines in both his translations and his original work. *Swift: The Man, his Works and the Age*, II, pp. 385–6. In this respect the London setting is aptly suited to an aesthetic confrontation.

46 Ehrenpreis, *Swift*, II, p. 385.

47 See Fabricant, *Swift's Landscape*, pp. 24–93.

their lives in London and metropolitan perspectives inflected English literary production in important ways.[48] For poets in Dublin, the distance between urban and rural experiences was not so great,[49] and the tension between the natural and the artificial is only occasionally the chief concern of Irish poets, principally in poems that consider aspects of the city's infrastructure in both its practical and leisured manifestations. Included in this volume is 'The Bason', a poem on the Dublin reservoir, built in the 1720s to manage the city's water supply in an efficient and hygienic manner. In this unusual, though not especially accomplished, poem – published in 1727 and attributed to Charles Coffey – details of engineering emerge uncertainly in an Augustan style: 'Thence num'rous Tubes or leaden Pipes be spread,/And thro' the City every where be led;/…/*Celia* shall owe her Washes all to thee,/And *Myra* be indebted for her Tea'. What is instructive, though, is the way in which the parterres and walks constructed around the reservoir – spaces engineered for leisure – assume the aesthetic qualities of the classical landscape, complete with wood nymphs frequenting the planted hawthorns. This scene can be seamlessly integrated, poetically as well as practically, with the River Dodder that supplied the water for this project, so that the natural and the man-made merge. Few poems elsewhere in the volume deal as explicitly with engineered civic spaces as Coffey does here, though Thomas Newburgh's 'The Beau Walk, in Stephen's Green' (1758) combines the privileges of the fashionable city stroll with a Swiftian eye for 'dirt-bespattering' vehicles and animal detritus.

The seventeenth and eighteenth centuries were the period in which public gardens became important social spaces both in England and in Ireland. St Stephen's Green had been first laid out in the 1660s and in the century that followed several similar public parks were opened. Among the most significant of these was the pleasure garden at the Rotunda, planned by surgeon and midwife Bartholomew Mosse to raise money for Dublin's new Lying-in Hospital.[50] Modelled on London's Vauxhall Gardens, the Rotunda grounds rivalled the Beau

48 Fitter, *Poetry, Space, Landscape*, p. 239.

49 This proximity is demonstrated in works such as John Winstanley's 'A Poem Upon Daisy …' (*c.*1720), featuring the journey of a cow from Swords to Stonybatter, and Gerald Fitzgerald's 'The Academic Sportsman' (1773) which depicts scholars from Trinity College walking to the Dublin mountains for a day's shooting.

50 Ian Campbell Ross, ed., *Public Virtue, Public Love: The Early Years of the Dublin Lying-in Hospital, The Rotunda* (Dublin, O'Brien Press, 1986), pp. 20–25.

Walk in St Stephen's Green in elegance and popularity. Private gardens were also an attraction, and many living in the most prosperous parts of the city took pleasure in cultivating their own. Swift's garden in the liberties of St Patrick's was a focus of interest for the Dean and his friends, and a point of connection between Swift and Pope, whose garden at Twickenham expressed important changes in landscaping taste.[51] Swift also took an interest in the gardens of Sir Arthur and Lady Acheson in County Armagh. Landowners and their ladies alike were actively engaged in the aesthetic aspects of garden design, and sometimes equally concerned with a garden's potential for producing plants for both culinary and medicinal use.[52]

The most significant area of horticultural design and improvement in Ireland was associated with suburban estates like Patrick Delany's 'Delville' near Dublin and country estates like those in County Cavan celebrated by Wetenhall Wilkes. Improving landlords reflected the ethics of the georgic, in which active stewardship of the land was an essential part of man's relationship with his environment. By contrast, those owners who rented out their lands did not see themselves as 'farmers' but as 'gentry' who could live closer to the pastoral idyll, enjoying the tranquillity of rural remoteness without the rigours of labour. The 'country house' poem, a part of the English poetic tradition since the Renaissance, occupies an unusual position in the Irish context. In England the boom in country house building occurred between the mid-sixteenth and mid-seventeenth centuries when wealth from court positions or from commercial enterprises in the country itself supported extravagant building and landscaping projects. In Ireland, most substantial country houses were built a hundred years later and by immigrants rather than those born and bred on Irish land. In the fifty years following the end of the Williamite war, more than 160 new country houses were built in Ireland, and many others were remodelled.[53] Though for a decade or more after the war there remained ambiguity concerning the fate of Catholic-owned land,

51 Edward Malins and the Knight of Glin, *Lost Demesnes: Irish Landscape Gardening 1660–1845* (London: Barrie and Jenkins, 1976), pp. 31–52 and Joseph McMinn, *Jonathan Swift and the Arts* (Newark NJ: University of Delaware Press, 2010), pp. 51–80.

52 Toby Barnard, *Making the Grand Figure: Lives and Possessions in Ireland, 1641–1770* (New Haven CT: Yale University Press), pp. 197–209.

53 Rolf Loeber and Livia Hurley, 'The Architecture of Irish Country Houses 1691–1739: Continuity and Innovation' in Raymond Gillespie and R. F. Foster, eds, *Irish Provincial Cultures in the Long Eighteenth Century* (Dublin: Four Courts Press, 2012), p. 201.

eventually around half a million acres was granted to Irish and English Protestants.

Peace was, of course, a necessary prerequisite for the improvement of land and the constant warfare in seventeenth-century Ireland made any development in gardening or estate management extremely difficult: 'I observed that the best sorts of flowers and fruits are much rarer in Ireland than in England,' wrote Fynes Moryson in his *Itinerary* of 1617, 'for Ireland being oft troubled with rebellions ... the inhabitants take less pleasure to till their grounds or plant trees [being] content to live for the day'.[54] It was not only peace, but also prosperity, that proved essential to this kind of cultivation, and this was the preserve of the few. So it was that while the new, Protestant middle class in eighteenth-century Ireland was constructing hot houses for melons and having asparagus plants sent down from horticultural suppliers in Dublin, poor Catholics were being forced off the land into makeshift roadside cabins beside which they grew a few potatoes for their own use. Between the two extremes were tenant farmers, increasingly obliged to cultivate cash-producing crops in order to pay rent and tithes. Against this backdrop, gardening for pleasure could be seen as a luxury pastime, but could equally be judged an indicator of stability and good stewardship: 'improving' Protestant landlords sought to introduce productive (or exotic) trees and plants to Ireland, and in doing so, to further the holy work of civilizing the country.[55]

A peaceful Ireland – and one where previously uncultivated land was being allocated and mapped – offered promising terrain to those with money and inclination enough to become landscapers, and the creation of an appropriate relationship between the house and its setting became an important matter for seventeenth and eighteenth century architects.[56] Irish landscaping took its cues from English styles, which in turn often reflected Dutch and French elements. Differing tastes might be linked to shifts in political power, with new incumbents lamenting the disorder and low standards of their predecessors, who lacked 'anything that may speak of a genteel and wise economy'.[57] In their turn, displaced Catholic Irish or Old English

54 Quoted in Constantia Maxwell, *Country and Town in Ireland under the Georges* (London: George G. Harrap & Company, 1940), p. 98.

55 Barnard, *Making the Grand Figure*, pp. 197–202.

56 Barnard, *Making the Grand Figure*, p. 188.

57 Quoted in Barnard, *Making the Grand Figure*, p. 189.

criticized the greed of their successors. Those who did improve their estates maximized the impression of power, with avenues, parterres and hedges creating elaborate visual patterns. However, as the eighteenth century progressed, providing facilities for leisure became as important as constructing terraces from which guests could admire the formal garden, and the increasingly popular country sport of hunting required such amenities as deerparks and grouse moors. Country picnics, together with the more elaborate pastimes of playing at being cottars or sailors, contributed to the fashion for ornamental lakes, canals, water features or *cottages ornées*'.[58] While formal landscaping emphasized control, more naturalistic, picturesque techniques grew in popularity during this period. Though untamed nature took longer to be appreciated in Ireland than in England – primarily because of its association with the lawlessness of land beyond the Pale – the new, less formal, designs for estates were being taken up as early as the 1730s, and those demesnes that maintained older styles seemed dated to observers. By the 1780s, younger generations expressed impatience at the work of their forebears, in spite of the elaborate investment that these represented. Philip Luckcombe described the seat of Mr Francis Mathew at Thomastown, County Tipperary in these disdainful terms:

> The whole park is thrown into squares and parallelograms, with numerous avenues fenced and planted; where, if a hillock dared to interpose its little head, it was cut off as an excrescence, or at least cut through that the roads might be everywhere as level, as they are straight … I could not help wishing that instead of torturing the place to the plan, they had accommodated the plan to the place.[59]

Naturalism changed the relationship between architecture and landscape in significant ways. It had the effect, Stephen Daniels argues, of at once softening the impression of property and strengthening it, by composing the entire landscape as a picture to be appreciated by

58 Duffy, *Exploring the History and Heritage of Irish Landscapes*, p. 89. Little material evidence of seventeenth- and eighteenth-century Irish gardens remains; scholarship largely reflects projected designs and planned improvements. In either case, lavish schemes were the preserve of the wealthiest landowners only.

59 Quoted in Maxwell, *Country and Town in Ireland*, pp. 99–100.

the landowner.[60] The most striking examples of poems detailing landed estates in Ireland occur in the middle decades of the eighteenth century, from the 1730s to the 1760s, and most are lengthy poems celebrating the beauty of the house and lands, and the fine character of the owner. Frequently an appeal to patronage, the formulaic approach to this mode of writing is hardly surprising, though some poets – in particular Wetenhall Wilkes – offer vivid detail. 'Bellville', published in 1741 but articulating the improvements previously made by the Fleming family on their Cavan estate, shows Wilkes's technique to advantage in its praise of the formal design achievements. The poem opens by describing the house as though viewed from its hallway: the 'well til'd Hall', 'lofty Stair-case' and 'sumptuous Parlour' are approvingly noted. The success of the poem, though, lies in its treatment of the spatial elements of the grounds and the delicate balance between landscape and planted detail that shapes the rest of the verses. From the parterres with their perfectly combined flowers, the eye follows tall hedges towards the fountain, but is then diverted to take in the fort, and further, the deer park and breeding space for game birds. The shell-covered grotto, among the fashions of garden design at that time, contains mirrored panels to reflect the beauties of the surrounding landscape.[61] This self-conscious piece of construction creates a parallel to the poem itself: arranged in couplets, its stanzaic pattern is shaped to accommodate the material being observed and reflects the logic of perception. Encompassed within this orderly description is a glimpse of the sublime landscape that will play such an important role in Romantic experience:

> Convey me, Goddess, to the Eastern Side,
> Where an huge Mountain boasts Romantic Pride;
> Whose bulging Brows in wildest order rise
> Rude, Chaos-like, and seem to prop the Skies.
> Th' unequal, craggy Masses hang; and hence
> The spangled Rocks reflect an awful Glance.

60 Stephen Daniels, 'The Political Iconography of Woodland in Later Georgian England' in Denis Cosgrove and Stephen Daniels, eds, *The Iconography of Landscape* (Cambridge: Cambridge University Press, 1988), p. 45.

61 In his *Tour in Ireland in 1752*, Bishop Pococke mentions the fashion for summer houses and grottos decorated with shells and statuary. See Maxwell, *Country and Town in Ireland*, p. 101 and Malins and Glin, *Lost Demesnes*, pp. 41–3.

This intrusion of wildness on the perfect arrangement of the estate is both a shift in mood and part of the effect. This poem, like so many of its English counterparts reveals the extent to which design encompasses the control of the natural world and the human response to it.

Control of an entirely different kind was exhibited earlier in Thomas Sheridan's 'A Description of Doctor Delany's Villa' (1724). Reputedly the first example of modern garden design in Ireland, the grounds at Delville were said to compress considerable beauty into a small space.[62] Mary Delany provides a great deal of detail in her letters on the design and planting, and comments too on the naturalism achieved:

> in the middle, sloping from the terrace, every way, are the fields, or rather paddocks, where our deer and our cows are kept, and the rurality of it is wonderfully pretty. These fields are planted in a *wild way* with *forest trees and with bushes* that look so naturally you would not imagine it to be a work of art.[63]

Sheridan's is a compact poem where Wilkes's is extensive, and the amused irony of tone in this work contrasts with the unalloyed praise that such descriptive poems usually convey, emphasizing the intimacy between poet and addressee. In seemingly direct contradiction to Addison's dictum 'a spacious horizon is the image of liberty',[64] the opening four lines encapsulate the poem's containment of mode and purpose perfectly:

> Would you that Delville I describe?
> Believe me, Sir, I would not gibe;
> For who would be Satirical
> Upon a Thing so very small?

62 Mary Delany's letters reveal both the compact and varied character of the garden at Delville. Though small, its features involved a good deal of expense, satirized by Swift in his poem 'An Epistle upon an Epistle' (1729): 'But you forsooth, your *All* must squander,/On that poor Spot, call'd Del-Ville, yonder:/And when you've been at vast Expences/In Whims, Parterres, Canals and Fences …'. *The Poems of Jonathan Swift*, 3 vols, ed. Harold Williams (Oxford: Clarendon Press, 1966), II, pp. 476–77.

63 Mary Delany in a letter to her sister, July 19, 1744. *The Autobiography and Correspondence of Mary Granville, Mrs Delany*, 6 vols, ed. Lady Llanover (London: Richard Bentley, 1861) II, pp. 315–16.

64 Joseph Addison. *The Spectator*. No. 412, Monday, June 21, 1712.

Alluding to the inherent pressure to commemorate the grand house in verse, Sheridan immediately reveals how the character of the description is expressed in the form chosen for it, here in the contracted, riddling opening lines. The compression of its varied features – 'Windows, and Doors, and Rooms, and Stairs,/And Hills, and Dales, and Woods and Fields' – telescopes the built environment, natural features and their resources into one undifferentiated list and expresses in four lines what a poem such as 'Bellville' takes two hundred to unfold. In a Lilliputian moment (though Swift's *Gulliver's Travels* would not appear for a further two years) Sheridan likens the rivulet to a tear and trees to a head of lettuce. The final witty twist explains the poem's miniature trope in suitably economical fashion: 'In short, in all your boasted Seat, /There's nothing but yourself that's Great'.

After Swift: Nature and Sensibility

For Swift and his circle the mock-heroic mode represented an important poetic innovation in the Irish context.[65] It realised the satirical potential of verse, highlighting criticism of human folly – something not done before in English verse printed in Ireland. This was political writing at its most acute, with its combination of the use of classical materials and unrestrained comment on the follies of contemporaries, both handled with wit and control. Poetry by women of the period – Mary Barber, for example – shared this wit and lightness of touch, but within the formal classical structures we find acute human observation. This reflects a rise in the poetry of sensibility during the mid-eighteenth century, a development which placed the experiencing human at the centre of poetic representation. Preceding the Romantic preoccupation with emotion and thought, poetry of sensibility emphasised the realities of human engagement with the natural world and saw the fate of the two as connected. This sense of connection is an important dimension of the latter part of the eighteenth century; it heightens the level of personal interaction with

65 Besides Sheridan and Patrick Delany, Swift's circle included Mary Barber, William Dunkin, Constantia Grierson and Laetitia Pilkington. All but Grierson are represented in this volume. See Andrew Carpenter, 'Poetry in English, 1690–1800: from the Williamite Wars to the Act of Union' in Kelleher and O'Leary, eds, *The Cambridge History of Literature*, I, pp. 282–319.

the non-human world and emphasises the moral and political effects of such an emotional response.

A heightened awareness of the dependence of man on his environment was at no time more evident than during periods of unusual weather, when the influence of nature over the welfare of man was particularly clearly expressed. Fluctuating weather was a feature of almost all eighteenth-century topographical poetry, though for many of the most prominent English poets, such as Denham and Thomson, the weather was not felt, but rather observed.[66] The impact of weather on the island of Ireland can be traced through the poems in this anthology, from the seventeenth-century tempests of Bellings and Fisher to the 'balmy gales' of William Hartsonge's 'Lines written at the rocks of Kilcarrick' (1804). Ireland's climate features significantly in work that represents the resources of the country and from this perspective it has important economic and political significance too: the impact of the weather on agricultural production, and in turn on aspects of trade and economic legislation appears frequently in these pages. Hardship is often linked to challenging weather conditions and, though the period between 1450 and 1850 is often referred to as the 'Little Ice Age', it was in the years 1739–1741 that Ireland experienced some of the most severe weather conditions ever recorded in the country.

The Great Frost, as it later became known, caused unprecedented disturbance in Ireland's ecology: lakes and rivers were frozen, potato crops and grain harvests were ruined, and livestock and humans perished from hunger and disease. This devastation of the natural world was accompanied by upheaval in civic life, including the break up of rural communities and an increase in crime and social unrest. It was a combination of circumstances that would, to a large extent, be repeated in the Great Famine of 1845–9, though the longer duration of the latter disaster – and its particular demographic implications – would have more enduring social and political effects.

Surprisingly, the extraordinary climatic conditions that prevailed in Ireland for eighteenth months from the end of 1739 – and the disastrous famine that followed – though documented in David

66 Bridget Keegan, in her essay 'Snowstorms, Shipwrecks, and Scorching Heat: The Climates of Eighteenth-Century Labouring-Class Locodescriptive Poetry' differentiates poets for whom the weather is seen from those for whom it is felt. She argues that for labouring-class poets such as John Clare, Mary Collier, Stephen Duck and Mary Leapor, the weather was an experience that highlighted human vulnerability.

Dickson's book *Arctic Ireland* (1997) have largely been forgotten.[67] The famine was probably as serious as that of the nineteenth century though its political and social implications were far less widely reported or commented on. The famines of the late 1720s are more frequently cited than that of 1739–41, possibly because the earlier famine gave rise to Swift's famous pamphlet, *A Modest Proposal*. Yet poets like Dunkin show with unflinching clarity the devastating impact of the climatic conditions of 1739–41 on both human and non-human environments, as well as the challenge these circumstances presented to existing human perceptions of the relationship between man and nature in Ireland.[68] Though they did not engage with the political implications of the disasters in the way that Swift did in 1729 or poets of the Great Famine did in the late 1840s,[69] they were conscious of the many facets of the crisis, and the difficulties this presented for the act of representation itself. Some poets writing of the 1739–41 frost and famine drew on established poetic conventions for representing natural disaster while others offered innovative descriptions of diverse conditions. William Dunkin's 'The Frosty Winters of Ireland', a poem of close to 130 lines, first written in Latin and then in English, exemplifies a combination of these approaches, vividly representing the bitter extremity of this Irish natural disaster in language reminiscent of the classics. Instead of the 'Heaven' of fair weather and a plentiful harvest comes the vengeful cold, severe enough to arrest rivers mid-flow: 'Beneath the glassy gulph/Fishes benumb'd, and lazy sea-calves freeze/In crystal coalition with the deep'. The beauty of this description does not lessen the horror for the human observer; indeed it increases the sense that nature's power exceeds not only human intervention but human understanding too. Winter's 'frigid womb' brings forth not life, but the deathliness of unproductive seed – a deathliness matched by the failing plants and trees, by dying birds and insects.

67 James Kelly's recent essay 'Coping with Crisis: The Response to the Famine of 1740–41', *Eighteenth-Century Ireland – Iris an Dá Chultúr*, Vol. 27 (2012) notes the limited evidence of a public response to this crisis.

68 Cormac Ó Gráda and Diarmaid Ó Muirithe have noted the scarcity of texts in Irish relating to this event, though this was the language of most of the victims. They published five Irish language poems on the famine of 1740–41, together with translations and commentary, in *Eire–Ireland* 45:3/4 (Fall/Winter 2010), pp. 1–22.

69 See Chris Morash, ed., *The Hungry Voice: The Poetry of the Irish Famine* (Dublin: Irish Academic Press, 1989).

A different approach to the disaster was taken by Thomas Hallie Delamayne in his poem 'To Francis Bindon Esq'. In addressing an artist and instructing him on what to include in his painting ('O'er the froz'd North, I'd stretch a sheet of snow'), Delamayne draws attention both to the power and responsibility of representation, and indicates the need to confront the true horror of these conditions: 'And Man, athirst, scarce lift the ax to cleave/A moist subsistence from the hardened wave'. The artistic trope also facilitates a range of visual detail, from which the scale of the disaster and the complexity of the relationship between the humans and their environment can be clearly inferred. The emotional distance created by this scheme gives its social commentary additional weight and heightens the reader's horror as the arrested lives of the dead are revealed in the thaw.

The power and unpredictability of nature are graphically described in these scenes, and the extent to which not only the prosperity but the dignity of human life is dependent on working with nature becomes horribly clear. In Ireland as elsewhere in Europe, however, man's relationship with the natural world underwent profound change during the period with which this anthology is concerned.[70] The seventeenth century was the era of the polymath, in which the study of philosophy, religion and science mingled without the need for specialist training. This approach persisted – at least in the minds of those printing encyclopaedias for the book-buying middle classes – as late as the 1770s when Goldsmith's eight volume *A History of the Earth and Animated Nature* suggested that the entire field of knowledge was capable of mastery by a well-educated man. This approach to learning led to diverse views on the intellectual foundations for the study of nature and responses to the weather – that most volatile of natural manifestions – aptly demonstrated this divergence. Until the mid-eighteenth century in Ireland, these responses could still be loosely divided into three kinds: the first a superstitious belief in the wonders and horrors of nature; the second, understanding of the weather as a manifestation of divine pleasure or retribution; and third, the scientific study of Irish weather instituted by members of the Dublin Philosophical Society – particularly St George Ashe and William Molyneux – in the 1680s and continued intermittently thereafter.[71]

70 See Keith Thomas, *Man and the Natural World, passim.*

71 K. Theodore Hoppen, *The Common Scientist in the Seventeenth Century: A Study of the Dublin Philosophical Society 1683–1708* (London: Routledge and Kegan Paul, 1970), pp. 131–36.

As John Wilson Foster has remarked, the development of natural philosophy in Ireland was closely linked to figures of the Protestant faith, which influenced their strong rejection of any attribution of natural phenomena to supernatural causes.[72] In spite of this, however, superstitious beliefs persisted in Gaelic Ireland, emphasising the cultural differences between these groups.[73]

The process of gathering observations, such as that undertaken by the members of the Dublin Philosophical Society, was designed to uncover the laws of nature, which were not seen as distinct from God's agency but rather evidence of both his forethought and his miraculous actions. The faithful should be encouraged to read in the Book of Nature:

> which the Lord hath spread open before us, therein describing unto us those invisible things of His eternal Power and God-head … the Heaven, the Aire the Earth and Waters, every Creature in these being a several leaf or page: every part of each Creature, quality or created virtue in each, be a several line.[74]

Maren-Sofie Røstvig has noted that from the seventeenth century onward there 'developed a tendency to consider God as immanent rather than transcendent', encouraging those with a 'contemplative disposition' to seek a life of retirement in nature.[75] Thus the pastoral characteristics of retreat were combined with scientific enquiry as narratives of observation become part of a larger scholarly endeavour, often generated by provincial gentry and clergymen who already had strong antiquarian interests – Richard Edgeworth, Richard Barton and

72 Foster, 'Encountering Traditions', p. 56. Many Protestant figures maintained strong links with English intellectual circles; they travelled widely and many did at least a proportion of their work abroad. The Dublin Philosophical Society was founded in 1683, but both before and after that time there were Anglo-Irish members of the Royal Society of London, including William Petty (1623–87), mathematician, inventor and surveyor, William Molyneux (1656–98), natural philosopher and astronomer, and Narcissus Marsh (1638–1713), the founder of Marsh's library in Dublin. See also Helena C. G. Chesney, 'Enlightenment and Education', in Foster, ed., *Nature in Ireland*, pp. 367–386.

73 Alexandra Walsham, *The Reformation of the Landscape: Religion, Identity and Memory in Early Modern Britain and Ireland* (Oxford: Oxford University Press, 2011), pp. 368–74.

74 Quoted in Walsham, *Reformation of the Landscape*, pp. 331–2.

75 Quoted in Hiltner, *What Else is Pastoral?*, p. 80.

Bishop Edward Synge being exemplary of these categories.[76] Yet Francis Bacon had been in favour of the separation of scientific and religious approaches, a conviction that may have resulted in the privatisation of religious feeling about nature, rather than its elimination altogether. Affinity with place offered legitimacy to the systematic study of nature; these projects proceeded on a firm regional basis, seeking to differentiate between places rather than to trace similarities.[77] In this respect particular human communities were closely linked to the geographical and to the implications of dwelling in place. As noted above, echoes of the Irish-language *dinnseanchas* or the poetry of place can be detected, even in those Irish poets who only wrote in English.

Two poems from the mid-eighteenth century specifically address the intersection between philosophy and science. The first, a poem simply entitled 'Philosophy' by Henry Jones, a bricklayer by trade, meditates on the wonders of new scientific discovery. Instead of altering poetic form to meet this new challenge, however, Jones continues to invoke the Muse and her classical counterparts when describing a phenomenon such as electricity. For this poet, as for so many of the 'natural philosophers' of the time, scientific developments did not contradict God's law but instead supported the view of an ordered and created universe. The relationship of science to nature was more complicated however. Though science and nature share many characteristics, the poet expresses the relationship between the two as a contested one: 'Lo! here the Magnet's Magic charms the sight,/ And fills the soul with wonder and delight,/In her, coy Nature turns her face aside,/And mocks th'enquiring Sages learned Pride'. It

76 See David Fleming, 'Cycles, Seasons and the Everyday in mid-eighteenth-century Provincial Ireland' in Gillespie and Foster, eds, *Irish Provincial Cultures* (Dublin: Four Courts Press, 2012), p. 136 and Jan Golinski, 'Time, Talk, and the Weather in Eighteenth-Century Britain' in Sarah Strauss and Benjamin S. Orlove, eds, *Weather, Climate, Culture* (Oxford: Berg Publishers, 2003), p. 78.

77 The most significant early attempt to describe the different parts of Ireland took place in 1682 when William Molyneux, planning to make a map of Ireland complete with topographical descriptions, sent a sheet of queries to scholars living in all parts of the island. The plan for an Irish atlas came to nothing and much of the material collected was eventually burned. Hoppen, *Common Scientist*, pp. 21–22. See also J. H. Andrews, *Shapes of Ireland: Maps and their Makers 1564–1839* (Dublin: Geography Publications, 1997); K. Theodore Hoppen, ed., *Papers of the Dublin Philosophical Society 1683–1709* (Dublin: Irish Manuscripts Commission, 2007) and Richard Sharpe, ed., *Roderick O'Flaherty's Letters 1696–1709: To William Molyneux, Edward Lhwyd and Samuel Molyneux* (Dublin: Royal Irish Academy, 2013), pp. 81–84.

is the apparent contradictions in science that most interest the poet. 'Coy Nature' is not happy to see science unravelling her mysterious attributes even if the result is that man understands these phenomena more fully.

Richard Barton introduced a similar theme in his 1759 work, 'A Physico-Poetical Essay'. This text, which presents in poetic form the contents of Barton's 1751 lectures in natural philosophy, reveals not only how scientific knowledge may be applied to local wonders but also how it can find memorable poetic form. The poem is 'for the use of those, who not having the leisure to read the larger work in prose, may by means of verse, not only see, but easily retain in memory, the main Truths of that Book'. Barton emphasizes how suitable poetic form is for imparting 'philosophy' and science, citing as forebears not only Lucretius but also Thomas Hobbes whose description of 'the wonders of the Peak of Derby' had cost him 'a Latin Description of some hundred Hexameter lines'. Writing on Lough Neagh, a subject of lifelong interest to him, Barton presents nature as a subject that must invoke a long view from man since its patterns of change can take thousands of years to be understood:

> For once a verdant tree, e'er Noah's time,
> It grew a Cedar, in some distant Clime;
> Brought to IERNE, by the gen'ral flood,
> Low sunk in earth, long lay the fragrant wood;
> Till losing vegetation's pliant tine,
> The stiffen'd fibres harden'd into stone.

Comparing the significance of Lough Neagh with that of other major scientific or archaeological sites such as those in Egypt and Italy, Barton goes on to explain the processes of change the wood undergoes: 'Crystalline subtle steams pervade the pores,/And fine effluvia of metallic ores'. In many ways this poem is only part of a larger text, however. At intervals Barton inserts long footnotes explaining the science in detail; he also refers readers to his lectures for further explication, indicating the importance of intertextuality in the handling of scientific material. Though the first formal geological investigations at the Giant's Causeway had been carried out by the Dublin Philosophical Society between the years 1683 and 1708, significant – and sometimes acrimonious – debates on the origin and nature of the basalt of the Antrim coast took place from the 1750s onwards: Barton's poem appeared at an important early stage in these studies.

The Late Eighteenth Century: The Land and its Animal Life

Alongside the developing scientific and philosophical enquiries of the latter end of the eighteenth century, the politics of land ownership and management was of growing concern. In the Irish context, as Lawrence Whyte made so graphically clear in 'Deoch an Dorois', the problem lay in landlordism and a system of short-term rents. Tenant farmers had no incentive to improve their land, since to do so would encourage the landlord to raise the rent. Equally, the pressure to find cash for his rent and tithes meant the land must be efficiently farmed – once the tenant fell behind with his rent, he could be evicted. As the anonymous author of 'Ierne' put it, Irish tenant farmers '[a]re ill repaid for all their labouring Gains./But *Tithes* and *Tallies* grind their wretched lot,/And drive the famish'd Hinds from Cot to Cot.'

One of the best known statements on this subject is Oliver Goldsmith's 'The Deserted Village' (1770), a poem that exemplifies the complex overlap between Irish and English cultures during this time: though the village Goldsmith was writing about is often thought to be Lissoy, County Westmeath, where Goldsmith spent his childhood, it is likely that Goldsmith drew on his knowledge of the fate of similar villages in England, the country he lived in for most of his adult life. Perhaps the most important dimension of this poem is the close connection it makes between nature and community through its description of the beauties of remembered landscape. Brook and hill frame scenes of village life: cottage, farm, mill and church are the built and cultivated spaces within which the 'labouring swain' and 'bashful virgin' live and prosper. The destruction of this community has a clearly identified cause: the rapacious landlord who has taken over multiple landholdings, working some and allowing others to fall into neglect. Uncultivated land, in this scheme, shows not only the neglect of man but also the social inequalities that destroy harmonious living:

> Ill fares the land, to hastening ills a prey,
> Where wealth accumulates, and men decay;
> Princes and lords may flourish, or may fade;

A breath can make them, as a breath has made;
But a bold peasantry, their country's pride,
When once destroyed, can never be supplied.

'Hibernia' (1797), a poem by William Hamilton Drummond, which first appeared anonymously in the Belfast radical newspaper *The Northern Star*, calls attention to the countryside again. In this case it is the idealised state of Ireland that is threatened by mismanagement – not because of a rapacious landlord but because of lack of peace and harmony. Drummond expects his reader to share his understanding of Ireland as an island fortunate in its abundant natural resources but lacking in political direction. He declares his 'patriotic ire' early in the poem, and sees a call for a rule of peace and justice for Ireland as the purpose of his writing. He explores the way in which the island's topographical features work in harmony with its natural assets to shape the history of the island and the virtue of its people. Drummond clearly saw a union between Britain and Ireland as the best way for Ireland to realise her full potential yet he took no account of the natural cycles of development and decline, such as those Roy Foster has noted in respect of Ulster's transition from a place synonymous with wild nature and Gaelic identity in 1600, to one of industry and strong ties to Britain in the early decades of the nineteenth century.[78] In this way he placed the conventions of both the classical poem and the topographical account at the service of a political message.

Goldsmith and Drummond, two poets with very different backgrounds and ideological positions, and placed at either end of this twenty-year period, call attention to the renewed political importance of a country's natural resources. Around this time, poems of sustained attention to areas of particular natural beauty in Ireland suggest that specific landscapes considered attractive to visitors were also acquiring greater significance. The representation of Killarney, for instance, engages in important ways with how such landscapes are framed for the viewer or tourist. Killarney is the subject of many eighteenth-century poems, two of which are included in this anthology. The first of these, by Joseph Atkinson, dates from 1769 and evokes – somewhat self-consciously – a sublime landscape in keeping with the Romantic ideal: 'See from afar the alp-like mountains rise/To fill the mind with grandeur and surprise!' For Luke Gibbons, the Burkean

78 R. F. Foster, *Modern Ireland: 1600–1972* (London: Penguin Books, 1988), pp. 15–35.

sublime has specifically political overtones here, linked as it is to the identification of Killarney with Lord Kenmare.[79] As one of the few large Catholic landowners to retain their lands after the Williamite confiscations, Kenmare's ability to maintain control over the population around Killarney was crucial to the security of the area. The threat of instability, which is both political and aesthetic, links the Gothic to the topographical: both address the limits of representation, and here the suggestion of unexplained events may in fact allude to the incipient Catholic violence of the time.[80] Agrarian violence is, perhaps not surprisingly, hardly ever referred to in eighteenth-century Irish poems in English. Like the cabins of cottiers at the roadside, the fact that, at various times in the period, armed gangs roamed the countryside intent on damaging the crops, livestock and property of landlords was not a subject on which poets chose to dwell.

The climax of Atkinson's 'Killarny' is the hunt and capture of a wild stag, an instance of the extent to which the natural world and human motives for its exploitation became entwined in late-eighteenth century verse; poets from different walks of life, increasingly troubled by violence, tried to explore the relationship between human and animal lives. Atkinson presented the pleasures of the chase as an integral part of a rich and timeless landscape of Killarney but, although the excitement of the hunt can be traced in the texture of the poem's language, at its climax the perspective moves closer to that of the animal, and the terror the stag is experiencing becomes palpable for the reader:

> See, the Stag trembles—for his conscious fate;—
> Where is there rest! Or any safe retreat!
> In vain below—the furious chase to shun!
> Up the steep mountains 'tis as vain to run!

Atkinson thus allows us some empathy with the stag, while not condemning the practice of hunting entirely. He bids the pursuers not to kill the animal but to release him back into the woods '[a]mongst his wild companions free to live'; yet his plea for clemency is made

79 Luke Gibbons, 'Topographies of Terror: Killarney and the Politics of the Sublime', *The South Atlantic Quarterly* 95:1 (Winter 1996), pp. 23–44.

80 Gibbons, 'Topographies of Terror', p. 31. Julia M. Wright discusses the role of the Gothic in her exploration of Drennan's 'Glendalloch' in '"Thy Branching Words": Radical History and Education in Drennan's Verse' (unpublished paper).

as much on the grounds of future human pleasure as with the welfare of the animal in mind: 'He to your sons a future chase may give'. A later version of the poem (1798) saw the ladies who had been watching the chase adorn the antlers of the captured stag with a ribbon in one of the most ambiguous gestures in eighteenth-century Irish poetry.

The equivocal relationship between human and animal worlds had long been a subject for literary and artistic representation in Ireland, and it seem likely that, behind it, lay memories of the widely-read texts of Cambrensis, Davies and Spenser in which the boundaries between animal and human life in Ireland were deliberately blurred to emphasise the 'barbarous' nature of the Irish people. Other texts may have reached even further back into Irish literary history: John Derricke's praise of the falcons of Ireland is linked to the importance of hunting birds in late medieval Ireland and, quite possibly, to a lingering memory of the significance of the bird in Irish language texts. As early as the seventeenth century, though, the close relationship between human and animal worlds was certainly implied: the complete version of 'A Looking-Glasse of the World' (1644) contains sixty-five stanzas on animals, birds, reptiles and insects and nearly as many listing the different trades and callings of men.

It was in the eighteenth century, however, that the interdependence of man and animal began to be recognised, first in poems that praised the beauty of domestic and farm animals. Included among these is Winstanley's poem on Daisy the cow:

> A cherry red her shining Coat adorns,
> Her Head, black Eyes, sleek Face, and stately Horns;
> Her Body's comely, plump, both deep and round;
> With Legs and Hoofs, strong, straight, and smooth, and sound.

The economic imperatives that underpinned the control of animals did not suppress further reflection on the matter, however, and by mid-century – due to a complex intersection of ethical and scientific enquiries – poets began to examine the relationship with a more critical eye, considering the exploitative attitude that many humans adopted towards animals and its implications for their professed religious belief and for issues of social justice, especially in the context of race and gender. Many works in this anthology sought to shed new light on the lives of animals by individualizing their experiences and drawing inferences about their place in the world. Laetitia Pilkington's extraordinary 1725 poem, 'The Petition of the Birds', gives early voice to the experience of birds killed for sport, a strategy echoed sixty-five years later in the pseudonymously published 'Lamentation of *Cara Pluma*' in which a female pheasant who has lost her mate addresses a Belfast gunmaker who had supplied the instrument that had just killed her 'husband'. Similarly, James Henderson's 'The Woodcock' (1784), undermines the sport of game shooting, which he describes as a 'vulgar pleasure, and the sport of boys', and sets it against the beauty and tranquillity of life in nature. The irony inherent in the poet's praise for the 'youth of spirit…/…famous with the gun!' soon becomes clear: 'Stir not, O woodcock, though the stars appear,/Or fly not that way, for the fowler fear'. Increasingly the wanton destruction by humans of other living creatures came under scrutiny in these poems, and many adopted a hostile attitude not only to blood sports but also to bull baiting and cock fighting. As well as being progressive in their political attitudes, these works were often innovative in form and technique.

The different kinds of readership suggested by these poems indicate both the cultural visibility of blood sports in Ireland and the range of positions that could be adopted in relation to them. Poems that feature animals as the central focus for their discussion present greater stylistic challenges, however, and the poems in this book show the rich variety that this practice encompasses. 'Lord Altham's Bull' is an anonymous poem based around the sport of bull baiting, which was still common in Ireland in the late eighteenth century. Its strong narrative momentum reveals the excitement of these sports and the attraction they held for ordinary Irish men and women. Each stanza begins with four short lines, moving the action of the poem along in alternately rhyming lines – the use of both full and half rhymes encapsulating the swerving energies of the chase. Longer sections of prose patter allow the narrative of the tale, its many characters and rich variety of comment, to be developed more freely. The first person narration, together with the idiomatic language that facilitates the vivid humour of the piece, offers a particular perspective on a shared activity, while the journey of the bull down a series of Dublin streets creates a natural momentum for the story and exposes the bull to the human callousness for which he later takes revenge.

The irrepressible vigour of this poem, and its disregard for the welfare of the animal it depicts, can be contrasted with another anonymous poem from the same period, 'The Cock'. Here a very different form signals the gravity of the treatment of cockfighting. With regular seven-beat lines and alternating rhyme, the bravery of the bird and his natural desire to protect his young is first invoked, before the human power to distort these qualities emerges:

> Men, miscall'd, of brutal feelings,
>   Who in bar'brous sports delight,
> Joy to make more gen'rous creatures
>   Join in fierce, unnatural fight.

While making its disgust at those who enjoy these inhumane pursuits clear, the poem combines several other interesting features. The spectacular appearance of the cock with 'steel'd martial weapons' on his legs leads to a reference to Chaucer: these elements heighten the reader's sense of an animal removed from the natural habitat depicted at the opening of the poem. Another interesting dimension is the juxtaposition of the singular and collective entities in the poem. Contrary to the normal current of representation, it is the animal that is seen as the singular figure: the cock is individualized, the humans in the poem remain 'the gaping croud', 'the madd'ning rabble'. Bidding the muse leave the scene of depravity, the anonymous poet – like others of the period – highlights the ways in which the poetic process mediates, and takes responsibility for mediating, the ethical judgements of its readers. This has important ramifications for how we might interpret the focus on animal rights that emerges here. The clearest political connection that might be suggested by these poems is a link to the abolitionist cause, which indicates the importance of ethical issues surrounding the treatment of both animals and slaves at this time.[81]

Towards the end of the eighteenth century, identity politics became an important consideration for readers. It is not surprising that during this time greater attention was paid to the identity of poets themselves: in the last quarter of the eighteenth century and into the nineteenth, the first anthologies self-consciously devoted to Irish poetry were published. Samuel Whyte's *The Shamrock: or Hibernian Cresses*

81 David Perkins, in his essay 'Animal Rights and "Auguries of Innocence"', *Blake: An Illustrated Quarterly* 33 (1999) argues that to read animals in such poems as metaphors weakens their power of protest and is 'another mode of exploitation' (pp. 8–9). See also Chen Hong, 'To Set the Wild Free: Changing Images of Animals in English Poetry of the Pre-Romantic and Romantic Periods', *Interdisciplinary Studies in Literature and Environment*, 13:2 (Summer 2006), pp. 129–149.

(1772) claimed to be the first anthology exclusively of poems 'of native growth': 'The English have had their Collections; so have the Scotch; and both have enriched their publications with Gems from Ireland. We know nothing before, of this nature, undertaken amongst us'.[82] More famous was a series of collections edited by Joshua Edkins. The 1801 volume of his anthology differed from earlier volumes being 'exclusively composed of poetry strictly and purely Irish'.[83] Another positive dimension of this publication, suggested the editor, was that it was 'with one or two exceptions, composed intirely of Poems which now for the first time, see the light; and the Editor can say, with confidence, that he, alone, is the cause of the major part of them appearing at all'.[84] This perceived need to rescue poetic texts from oblivion, and the difficulties of doing so, were expressed by other editors too. John Anketell, in the note to his subscribers that prefaces his 1793 *Poems on Several Subjects*, details the struggle to extract subscriptions from individuals including Lord Clonmell, who 'assured me, without blushing, that he "had taken an oath never to read a line of poetry"'. This need to identify poets as Irish, and to seek support for their publication, would be important to the new elements of literary nationalism that would follow the Union.

Romanticism: the Union and Afterwards

Advances in agricultural science gathered pace in England throughout the eighteenth century as rationality rather than superstition began to shape man's relationship to nature. In Ireland these changes were slower and more variable, a pattern not only affected by the uneven development of philosophical and social thought, but by the dynamics of political and economic power, the slow development of urban centres and the lack of an extensive industrial revolution of the type experienced in England.[85] Despite attempts by the Dublin Society to

82 Samuel Whyte, *The Shamrock: or Hibernian Cresses. A Collection of Poems, Songs, Epigrams, &c. Latin as well as English, the Original Production of Ireland* (Dublin 1772), pp. iv–v.

83 Joshua Edkins, *A Collection of Poems, Mostly Original, By Several Hands* (Dublin, 1801), p. viii.

84 Edkins, *Collection of Poems*, p. vii.

85 The development of Belfast is noted in James Orr's 'Fort Hill' (1804), as are the signs of the linen industry.

improve farming methods, Ireland's ancient farming practices retained their cyclical patterns: in different parts of the country varying systems of crop rotation were in operation, while a transhumance was practiced by dairy farmers with access to mountain slopes where cattle were grazed during the summer months, reserving the more fertile, low-lying fields for crops.[86] Thus it is hardly unexpected for poets familiar with traditional poetic models to choose the georgic as a mode by which to combine reflection on the natural world with political and economic commentary. Throughout the eighteenth century many English poets were inspired by Dryden's 1697 translation of Virgil's *Georgics* including Ambrose Phillips, Christopher Smart and John Dyer. In the Irish context Charles Boyd's 'A Georgic of Modern Husbandry' (1809) is the most extraordinary of such works in its application of direct agricultural instruction to rural life. Himself a translator of Virgil, Boyd had a deep familiarity with his classical model, and in this respect he upheld Joseph Addison's view that the georgic 'should not be delivered with the simplicity of a plowman, but with the address of a poet'.[87] Yet it is Boyd's experience of real farming in County Wicklow that gives his long poem its attractiveness. Some sections of Boyd's georgic are very direct in their advice:

> Always in cribs, in yard or pasture, lay
> With Winter vegetables, nicest hay.
> Nothing more profitable is than this,
> You gain a third part, instantly, by fleece,
> Of what they cost, and sell for twice as much
> At least ...

Other parts of the poem are more meditative: 'Mild Autumn now prepares her changing hues/For artist's pencil and for poets muse'. This combined appreciation of both the most practical and the most aesthetic aspects of the natural world is interesting for this period too, in that it invests this most functional of modes with a Romantic sensibility.

The power of landscape to accumulate meanings is an important dimension of the topographical poem too, defined by Dr Johnson as

86 Fleming, 'Cycles, Seasons and the Everyday', p. 135.

87 Joseph Addison, 'An Essay on Virgil's Georgics', *The Work of Joseph Addison*. Vol. 2. (Philadelphia MD: J. B. Lippincott & Co, 1883), p. 380.

'a species of composition … of which the fundamental subject is some particular landscape, to be poetically described, with the addition of such embellishment as may be supplied by historical retrospection or incidental meditation'.[88] For Irish poets the opportunity to use the landscape as a way of making sense of the past offered suggestive possibilities at a time of revolutionary renewal. If the implication of Dyer's 'Grongar Hill' (1726) was that 'morals inhere in the landscape',[89] then the role of the poet in interpreting moral messages latent in nature is legitimated, and the topographical mode can come to suggest transformative possibilities as much as continuing harmony. This use of the landscape as a vehicle for particular thoughts and convictions is raised by John Barrell:

> In this poetry the landscape becomes a theatre where the poet's own moral reflections are acted out; where the objects do not so much give rise to the reflections, as the ready-made and waiting reflections justify the inclusion of this or that object in the poem.[90]

The particularity of the landscape is of special importance in the context of this choice and it is not surprising that most of the topographical poems in this anthology feature landscapes of renown such as those of Killarney, Glendalough and the Giant's Causeway. Earlier English examples of this mode, such as Sir John Denham's 'Cooper's Hill' (1642) and Edmund Waller's 'On St James's Park' (1661), invest natural features with political meaning but in the Irish context it was not until late in the eighteenth century that the potential for such a reading of landscape emerged.

As John Waters remarks, topographical poetry is associated, through particularity of place, with ideas of regional and national formation.[91] In this respect it calls attention to the human gaze – the subject who is observing and interpreting the landscape and, to an

88 Johnson, quoted in John Wilson Foster, 'The Topographical Tradition in Anglo-Irish Poetry', in *Colonial Consequences: Essays in Irish Literature and Culture* (Dublin: Lilliput Press, 1991), pp. 9–29.

89 Spacks, *Eighteenth-Century Poetry*, p. 43.

90 John Barrell, *The Idea of Landscape and the Sense of Place 1730–1840: An Approach to the Poetry of John Clare* (Cambridge: Cambridge University Press, 1972), p. 35.

91 John Waters,'Topographical Poetry and the Politics of Culture in Ireland, 1772–1820', in Ghislaine McDayter, Guinn Batten and Barry Milligan, eds, *Romantic Generations: Essays in Honor of Robert F. Gleckner* (London: Associated University Presses, 2001), p. 233.

extent, controlling it. Though in the topographical mode the perspective from which the land is viewed, and the generic features used, are both suggestive of harmonious intention, landscape is inevitably marked by modifications in land use and the changing seasons, and to observe these alterations is to part irrevocably from the ideal or the picturesque, which sought to minimise the consequences of agricultural industrialisation.[92] In keeping with this development Irish Romanticism tended to focus on the wild places of Ireland – the Powerscourt waterfall, the Giant's Causeway and the lakes of Killarney particularly – and the emotions they evoked. As Luke Gibbons has pointed out, the late-eighteenth century tourist might be exposed to an extra frisson of fear at the fact that the people who lived in these wild and 'uncivilized' places might well be rebelling against the settled community.[93] Thus the stability of topographical representation can sometimes be seen, paradoxically, as revelatory of underlying instabilities.[94] In keeping with this doubleness of perspective, there is a merging of technique in a number of poems in this anthology where the survey of topographical features is interwoven with individual response, intensifying the movement from the symbolic to the particular that is a significant dimension of loco-descriptive poetry. Thus from the early years of the nineteenth century, landscape poetry became less a representation of a static scene and more a reflection of the poet's personal perspective, in keeping with the increasing focus on sensibility that is a hallmark of English Romantic poetry.

Ireland's relationship to the Romantic movement is a complex one, and has been the subject of considerable re-evaluation in recent decades.[95] Earlier critics of Romanticism have tended to see the British Isles as a single cultural entity, ignoring both the particularity of literary production in Ireland during these decades, and the extent to which the distinct regions of Ireland, Scotland and Wales had an imaginative impact on English writers:

92 Ann Bermingham, *Landscape and Ideology: The English Rustic Tradition, 1740–1860* (Berkeley CA: University of California Press, 1986), p. 75.

93 Luke Gibbons, 'Topographies of Terror', pp. 23–44.

94 Waters, 'Topographical Poetry', p. 230.

95 For recent publications in this area see work by Claire Connolly, Ina Ferris, Luke Gibbons, Jim Kelly, Jane Moore, Christina Morin, Murray Pittock and Julia Wright.

> English literature, so-called, constitutes itself in the late eighteenth and early nineteenth centuries through the systematic imitation, appropriation, and political neutralization of antiquarian and nationalist literary developments in Scotland, Ireland, and Wales.[96]

But the nationalist views of Irish poets writing in English at this time were not neutralized or silenced; on the contrary, their love of the Irish countryside and their retelling of Irish legends in specific Irish settings suggests a strengthening of nationalist views after the Union, despite the threat of Napoleonic invasion. Irish Romanticism was not only linked to the Enlightenment ethos of human progress but also deeply affected by political events.[97] The Union led to more self-consciousness about what it was to be Irish, and ideas of voice and the framing of narrative drew attention to this issue.

James Orr's 'Fort-Hill' (1804) is fittingly experiential in emphasis. It chooses as its focus the most eye-catching of natural and built features: the roaring cataract and the dome of the church. In this way the poem implicitly contemplates the fullest range of human interaction with landscape: what is far away and what is close at hand. 'Fort-Hill' offers a sensory approach to the appreciation of landscape and, like Boyd's 'Georgic', an awareness that pleasure in nature can be indulged when the hard work of cultivation is complete; aesthetic achievement is the natural reward for the craft of making, for the farmer as it is for the poet. The observed landscape in Orr's poem is both a detailed naturalistic observation ('boats on the silver lake', 'conic hay-cocks') and a summoning of the metaphorical world of 'nymphs and the mead-mowing hinds'. Yet what is demonstrated most clearly here is that it is the shift in language that is the crucial one. Classical figures may indicate real-life farm labourers, but the vocabulary chosen to describe them sets the generic expectations clearly. Yet in spite of the beauty, and its celebration, references to the military history of the fort suggest a fear of violence, and provide a subtle link to Orr's involvement in the 1798 rebellion. A rather different fear, one far more in keeping with traditional Romantic concerns of loss of youth and hope, frames the accomplished rhythms of William Tighe's 'Lines Addressed to the

96 Katie Trumpener, *Bardic Nationalisms: The Romantic Novel and the British Empire* (Princeton NJ: Princeton University Press, 1997), p. xi.

97 In specific studies of Irish literature, Romantic elements are judged to appear – after some half-century's delay – in the work of James Clarence Mangan or in early W. B. Yeats.

River at Rosanna in the County of Wicklow' (1808). The opening lines of this poem contemplate the repeated depletion and renewal of the stream over the years that the speaker has known it, and in doing so set the cycles of nature in opposition to those of man, whose physical being is not capable of such rejuvenation. The notice that Tighe takes of the minutiae of the natural world is indicative of a new attentiveness to be found in the poetry of the period more generally, and the beauty and particularity of observed nature here signals a shift towards a more sensitive reading of the non-human world, such as that to be found in the work of Sydney Owenson in this volume.

The increased concentration on the power of the visual had a lasting effect on those who travelled to experience the power of landscape. The cult of the picturesque in Ireland exerted an important shaping force on modern tourism, which in turn determined how the landscape was conceptualised both by visitors to Ireland, and by those that lived there.[98]

> The Irish landscape, whether in the form of the savage sublime, the picturesque, or the straightforwardly scenic from which the traces of a disastrous history had been removed or aggregated into the theme-parks, also helped to situate this endearing abnormality as something that could be visited and consumed as a tonic for metropolitan weariness.[99]

For the stranger visiting Ireland there is often a tendency to disregard political realities, a refusal to engage with the socio-political, and a corresponding emphasis on the purity of topographical observation. This marks a separation of spheres that the modern reader may consider to be false: an assumption that there is little direct connection between the condition of the land, and the condition of its people. In these instances, and especially in the period immediately following the Act of Union in 1801, the relationship between the strange and the

98 Foster, 'Topographical Tradition', p. 21. See also Eóin Flannery, 'Ireland of the Welcomes: Colonialism, Tourism and the Irish Landscape', in Christine Cusick, ed., *Out of the Earth: Ecocritical Readings of Irish Texts* (Cork: Cork University Press, 2010), pp. 85–107. William H. A. Williams, *Tourism, Landscape, and the Irish Character* (Madison WN: University of Wisconsin Press, 2008) and *Creating Irish Tourism: The First Century, 1750–1850* (London/New York: Anthem Press, 2010).

99 Seamus Deane, *Strange Country: Modernity and Nationhood in Irish Writing Since 1790* (Oxford: Clarendon Press, 1997), p. 148.

familiar was especially potent.[100] English readers, used to seeing the Irish as 'Other', as irretrievably wild and difficult, were now faced with the prospect that they were in fact 'the same' – part of the same nation and requiring to be accepted on those terms.[101] The difficulties that English writers and travellers had in accepting this dynamic can be traced in the writing of the time, and the poems record the views of both topography and the management of land in Ireland as distinctively different from what was encountered in England or on the continent; these things needed to be recorded in different terms.

Though Richard Pococke's controversial *Tour in Ireland* (1752) and Arthur Young's three tours between 1776 and 1778 were known to eighteenth-century visitors to Ireland, more practical guidebooks were produced from the 1780s onwards, many of them in Ireland.[102] The development of this commercial literature was a prescient move as the early decades of the nineteenth century were marked by a considerable increase in travel; Claire Connolly notes the regular trips engaged in by writers and artists of the time and the corresponding increase in the significance of the journey motif in the novels of the period.[103] Ultimately, though, war would make travel to Europe difficult in the later Romantic period and railways would make travel to Ireland seem easier. These, among other factors, caused visitors of all kinds – including poets – to re-evaluate their relationship with the Irish countryside through which they passed.[104]

But perhaps the most significant factor in any such re-evaluation was the Great Famine of the 1840s. The collapse of the potato crop in Ireland and the enormous human suffering that arose from this natural disaster meant that the relationship between man and nature, and between man and man, changed irrevocably in Ireland within a few

100 Jefferson Holdridge argues that 'the allegory of union between Englishness (mirrored in the ordered, harmonious landscape of the beautiful) and Irishness (mirrored in the ruined or wild landscape of the sublime) says as much about individual consciousness as it does about public history'. Jefferson Holdridge, 'Dark Outlines, Grey Stone: Nature, Home and the Foreign in Lady Morgan's *The Wild Irish Girl* and William Carleton's *The Black Prophet*' in Cusick, ed., *Out of the Earth*, p. 20.

101 See Ina Ferris, *The Romantic National Tale and the Question of Ireland* (Cambridge: Cambridge University Press, 2002).

102 Foster, 'Topographical Tradition', p. 22.

103 Claire Connolly, *A Cultural History of the Irish Novel, 1790–1829* (Cambridge: Cambridge University Press, 2012), p. 52.

104 Fiona Stafford, 'England, Ireland, Scotland, Wales' in Nicholas Roe, ed., *Romanticism* (Oxford: Oxford University Press), p. 114.

years of the appearance of the last poem in this anthology. The Famine forcefully demonstrates the powerful intersection between the worlds of nature and politics that can be observed in so many of these poems. It raises, too, the challenges to representation that such a significant historical event can offer. And it prompts poets, from the middle of the nineteenth century onward, to reconsider how to address one of the most significant of Irish relationships, that between man and the natural environment.[105]

This anthology, then, seeks to present the reader with a reflection of the extraordinarily varied way in which Irish poets responded to their environment over a period of two hundred and fifty years, between the end of the middle ages and the generation before the Famine. The political events which seem to have most effect on the people of Ireland during this time – the wars and land settlements of the seventeenth century, the penal era, the 1798 rising, the Act of Union, and the call for Catholic emancipation – remain, mostly, in the background of these poems. So do the interactions between the cultures and lives of the various communities inhabiting the island of Ireland. Yet the importance of defining the self in relation to its environment remains a crucial concern for these poets, and the specific Irishness of people and place – whether perceived as a threat or as a state to be desired – lies behind many of the poems in this book. This attentiveness to the non-human world offers fascinating insights to the twenty-first century reader exploring the diversity of poetry in Ireland over the past five centuries.

105 See Morash, ed., *The Hungry Voice* and Crowley, Smyth and Murphy, eds, *Atlas of the Great Irish Famine* (Cork: Cork University Press, 2012).

SELECT BIBLIOGRAPHY

Aalen, F. H. A., Kevin Whelan and Matthew Stout eds, *Atlas of the Irish Rural Landscape* (Cork: Cork University Press, 1997).

Addison, Joseph, 'An Essay on Virgil's Georgics', *The Work of Joseph Addison*, 2 vols (Philadelphia PA: J. B. Lippincott & Co, 1883).

___, *The Spectator*. No. 412, Monday, June 21, 1712.

Alpers, Paul, *What is Pastoral?* (Chicago and London: University of Chicago Press, 1996).

Andrews, J. H., *Shapes of Ireland: Maps and their Makers 1564–1839* (Dublin: Geography Publications, 1997).

Aubin, Robert Arnold, *Topographical Poetry in XVIII-Century England* (New York: Modern Language Association of America, 1966).

Barnard, Toby, *Improving Ireland? Projectors, Prophets and Profiteers 1641–1786* (Dublin: Four Courts Press, 2008).

___, *Making the Grand Figure: Lives and Possessions in Ireland, 1641–1770* (New Haven CT: Yale University Press, 2004).

Barrell, John, *The Idea of Landscape and the Sense of Place 1730–1840: An Approach to the Poetry of John Clare* (Cambridge: Cambridge University Press, 1972).

Bate, Jonathan, *Romantic Ecology: Wordsworth and the Environmental Tradition* (London: Routledge, 1991).

Beacon, Richard, *Solon His Follie, or A Political Discourse Touching the Reformation of Commonweals Conquered, Declined, or Corrupted* (1594), eds Vincent Carey and Clare Carroll (Binghamton NY: Medieval and Renaissance Texts and Studies, Vol. 154, 1996).

Bell, Jonathan and Mervyn Watson, *A History of Irish Farming 1750–1950* (Dublin: Four Courts, 2008).

Bermingham, Ann, *Landscape and Ideology: The English Rustic Tradition, 1740–1860* (Berkeley CA: University of California Press, 1986).

___, 'System, Order, and Abstraction: The Politics of English Landscape Drawing around 1795' in W. J. T. Mitchell, ed., *Landscape and Power* (Chicago: University of Chicago Press, 2002), pp. 77–102.

Bliss, Alan, *Spoken English in Ireland 1600–1740* (Dublin: Cadenus, 1979).

Canny, Nicholas, *Making Ireland British 1580–1650* (Oxford: Oxford University Press, 2001).

Carpenter, Andrew, 'Poetry in English, 1690–1800: From the Williamite Wars to the Act of Union' in Margaret Kelleher and Philip O'Leary, eds, *The Cambridge History of Irish Literature*, 2 vols (Cambridge: Cambridge University Press, 2006), I, pp. 282–319.

___, *Verse in English from Eighteenth-Century Ireland* (Cork: Cork University Press, 1997).

___, *Verse in English from Tudor and Stuart Ireland* (Cork: Cork University Press, 2003).

Chesney, Helena C. G., 'Enlightenment and Education' in John Wilson Foster, ed., *Nature in Ireland: A Scientific and Cultural History* (Dublin: Lilliput Press, 1997), pp. 367–386.

Clark, Timothy, *The Cambridge Introduction to Literature and the Environment* (Cambridge: Cambridge University Press, 2011).

Collins, Lucy, 'The Frosty Winters of Ireland: Poems of Climate Crisis 1739–41', *Irish Ecocriticism,* spec. issue of *Journal of Ecocriticism* 5:2 (2013), pp.1–11.

Connolly, Claire, *A Cultural History of the Irish Novel, 1790–1829* (Cambridge: Cambridge University Press, 2012).

Coughlan, Patricia, ed., *Spenser and Ireland: An Interdisciplinary Perspective* (Cork: Cork University Press, 1989).

Crowley, John, William J. Smyth and Mike Murphy, eds, *Atlas of the Great Irish Famine* (Cork: Cork University Press, 2012).

Daniels, Stephen, 'The Political Iconography of Woodland in Later Georgian England' in Denis Cosgrove and Stephen Daniels, eds, *The Iconography of Landscape* (Cambridge: Cambridge University Press, 1988), pp. 43–82.

Daston, Lorraine and Katharine Park, *Wonders and the Order of Nature 1150–1750* (New York: Zone Books, 2001).

Davies, Sir John, *A True Discovery of the True Causes Why Ireland was Never Entirely Subdued ...*, ed. James P. Myers Jr (Washington DC: Catholic University of America Press, 1988).

Deane, Seamus, Andrew Carpenter and Jonathan Williams, eds, *The Field Day Anthology of Irish Writing*, 3 vols (Derry and London: Field Day and Faber, 1991).

Deane, Seamus, *Strange Country: Modernity and Nationhood in Irish Writing Since 1790* (Oxford: Clarendon Press, 1997).

Delany, Mary, *The Autobiography and Correspondence of Mary Granville, Mrs Delany*, 6 vols, ed. Lady Llanover (London: Richard Bentley, 1861).

Dickson, David, *Arctic Ireland* (Belfast: White Row Press, 1997).

___, *New Foundations: Ireland 1660–1800*, 2nd edition (Dublin: Irish Academic Press, 2000).

___, '1740–41 Famine' in John Crowley, William J. Smyth and Mike Murphy, eds, *Atlas of the Great Irish Famine* (Cork: Cork University Press, 2012), pp. 23–27.

Duffy, Patrick J., *Exploring the History and Heritage of Irish Landscapes* (Dublin: Four Courts Press, 2007).

Edkins, Joshua, *A Collection of Poems, Mostly Original, By Several Hands* (Dublin, 1801).

Ehrenpreis, Irvin, *Swift: The Man, his Works and the Age*, 3 vols (London: Methuen, 1967–83).

Fabricant, Carole, *Swift's Landscape*, 2nd edition (South Bend IN: University of Notre Dame Press, 1995).

Fairer, David, *English Poetry of the Eighteenth Century 1700–1789* (London: Pearson, 2003).

Ferris, Ina, *The Romantic National Tale and the Question of Ireland* (Cambridge: Cambridge University Press, 2002).

Filppula, Markku, *The Grammar of Irish English: Language in Hibernian Style* (London: Routledge, 1999).

Fitter, Chris, *Poetry, Space, Landscape: Towards a New Theory* (Cambridge: Cambridge University Press, 1995).

Flannery, Eóin, 'Ireland of the Welcomes: Colonialism, Tourism and the Irish Landscape' in Christine Cusick, ed., *Out of the Earth: Ecocritical Readings of Irish Texts* (Cork: Cork University Press, 2010), pp. 85–107.

Fleming, David, 'Cycles, Seasons and the Everyday in mid-eighteenth-century Provincial Ireland' in Raymond Gillespie and R. F. Foster, eds, *Irish Provincial Cultures in the Long Eighteenth Century* (Dublin: Four Courts Press, 2012), pp. 133–154.

Flower, Robin, *The Irish Tradition* (Oxford: Oxford University Press, 1947).

Fogarty, Anne, ed., *Spenser in Ireland: The Faerie Queene 1596–1996,* spec. issue of *Irish University Review* 26:2 (Autumn/Winter 1996).

Foster, John Wilson, 'Encountering Traditions' in John Wilson Foster, ed., *Nature in Ireland: A Scientific and Cultural History* (Dublin: Lilliput Press, 1997), pp. 23–70.

___, 'The Topographical Tradition in Anglo–Irish Poetry' in John Wilson Foster, *Colonial Consequences: Essays in Irish Literature and Culture* (Dublin: Lilliput Press, 1991), pp. 9–29.

Foster, R. F., *Modern Ireland: 1600–1972* (London: Penguin Books, 1988).

Frawley, Oona, *Irish Pastoral: Nostalgia and Twentieth-Century Irish Literature* (Dublin: Irish Academic Press, 2005).

Gerald of Wales, *The History and Topography of Ireland*, trans. John J. O'Meara (Harmondsworth: Penguin Books, 1982).

Gibbons, Luke, 'Topographies of Terror: Killarney and the Politics of the Sublime', *The South Atlantic Quarterly* 95:1 (Winter 1996), pp. 23–44.

Gifford, Terry, *Pastoral* (London: Routledge, 1999).

Gillespie, Raymond, *Seventeenth-Century Ireland: Making Ireland Modern* (Dublin: Gill and Macmillan, 2006).

Gillespie, Raymond and Andrew Hadfield, eds, *The Oxford History of the Irish Book: Volume III, The Irish Book in English 1550–1800* (Oxford: Oxford University Press, 2006).

Golinski, Jan, 'Time, Talk, and the Weather in Eighteenth-Century Britain' in Sarah Strauss and Benjamin S. Orlove, eds, *Weather, Climate, Culture* (Oxford: Berg Publishers, 2003), pp. 17–38.

Grogan, Jane, *Exemplary Spenser: Visual and Poetic Pedagogy in 'The Faerie Queene'* (Burlington V1: Ashgate 2009).

Hadfield, Andrew, *Edmund Spenser, A Life* (Oxford: Oxford University Press, 2012).

___, *Edmund Spenser's Irish Experience: Wilde Fruit and Salvage Soyl* (Oxford: Oxford University Press, 1997).

Harris, Jason and Keith Sidwell, 'Introduction: Ireland and Romanitas' in Jason Harris and Keith Sidwell, eds, *Making Ireland Roman: Irish Neo-Latin Writers and the Republic of Letters* (Cork: Cork University Press, 2009), pp. 1–13.

Heaney, Seamus, 'The God in the Tree' in Seán MacRéamoinn, ed., *The Pleasures of Gaelic Poetry* (London: Penguin Books 1982), pp. 25–34.

Herron, Thomas, 'Introduction: A Fragmented Renaissance' in Thomas Herron and Michael Potterton, eds, *Ireland in the Renaissance c.1540–1660* (Dublin: Four Courts Press, 2007), pp. 19–39.

Hiltner, Ken, *What Else is Pastoral? Renaissance Literature and the Environment* (New York: Cornell University Press, 2011).

Holdridge, Jefferson, 'Dark Outlines, Grey Stone: Nature, Home and the Foreign in Lady Morgan's *The Wild Irish Girl* and William Carleton's *The Black Prophet*' in Christine Cusick, ed., *Out of the Earth: Ecocritical Readings of Irish Texts* (Cork: Cork University Press, 2010), pp. 20–35.

Hong, Chen, 'To Set the Wild Free: Changing Images of Animals in English Poetry of the Pre-Romantic and Romantic Periods', *Interdisciplinary Studies in Literature and Environment*, 13:2 (Summer 2006), pp. 129–149.

Hoppen, K. Theodore, *The Common Scientist in the Seventeenth Century: A Study of the Dublin Philosophical Society 1683–1708* (London: Routledge and Kegan Paul, 1970).

___, ed., *Papers of the Dublin Philosophical Society 1683–1709* (Dublin: Irish Manuscripts Commission, 2007).

Hunt, John Dixon, *The Figure in the Landscape: Poetry, Painting and Gardening during the Eighteenth Century* (Baltimore MD: Johns Hopkins University Press, 1976).

Ingold, Tim, 'Footprints through the weather-world: walking, breathing, knowing', *Journal of the Royal Anthropological Institute* (2010), pp. 121–139.

Joyce, P. W., *English as We Speak it in Ireland* (Dublin: Gill, 1910).

Keegan, Bridget, 'Snowstorms, Shipwrecks, and Scorching Heat: The Climates of Eighteenth-Century Laboring-Class Locodescriptive Poetry', *Interdisciplinary Studies in Literature and Environment*, 10:1 (Winter 2003), pp. 75–96.

Kelleher, Margaret and Philip O'Leary, eds, *The Cambridge History of Irish Literature*, 2 vols (Cambridge: Cambridge University Press, 2006).

Kelly, James, 'Coping with Crisis: The Response to the Famine of 1740–41', *Eighteenth-Century Ireland—Iris an Dá Chultúr*, Vol. 27 (2012), pp. 99–122.

Kelly, James and Ciarán Mac Murchaidh, eds, *Irish and English: Essays on the Irish Linguistic and Cultural Frontier 1600–1900* (Dublin: Four Courts Press, 2012).

Kermode, Frank, *English Pastoral Poetry: From the Beginnings to Marvell* (New York: Norton, 1972 [1952]).

Leerssen, Joep, *Mere Irish and Fíor-Ghael: Studies in the Idea of Irish Nationality, its Development and Literary Expression Prior to the Nineteenth Century* (Cork: Cork University Press, 1996).

Loeber, Rolf and Livia Hurley, 'The Architecture of Irish Country Houses, 1691–1739: Continuity and Innovation' in Raymond Gillespie and R. F. Foster, eds, *Irish Provincial Cultures in the Long Eighteenth Century* (Dublin: Four Courts Press, 2012), pp. 201–219.

Low, Anthony, *The Georgic Revolution* (Princeton NJ: Princeton University Press, 1985).

Mac Craith, Mícheál, 'Literature in Irish *c.*1550–1690' in Margaret Kelleher and Philip O'Leary, eds, *The Cambridge History of Irish Literature*, 2 vols (Cambridge: Cambridge University Press, 2006), I, pp. 191–231.

McLysaght, Edward, *Irish Life in the Seventeenth Century* (Dublin: Irish University Press, 1969).

Mac Mathuna, Liam, 'Verisimilitude or Subversion? Probing the Interaction of English and Irish in Selected Warrants and Macaronic Verse in the Eighteenth Century' in James Kelly and Ciarán Mac Murchaidh, eds, *Irish and English: Essays on the Irish Linguistic and Cultural Frontier, 1600–1900* (Dublin: Four Courts Press, 2012), pp. 116–40.

McMinn, Joseph, *Jonathan Swift and the Arts* (Newark NJ: University of Delaware Press, 2010).

McWilliams, Brendan, 'The Kingdom of the Air: The Progress of Meteorology' in John Wilson Foster, ed., *Nature in Ireland: A Scientific and Cultural History* (Dublin: Lilliput Press, 1997), pp. 115–132.

Malins, Edward and the Knight of Glin, *Lost Demesnes: Irish Landscape Gardening 1660–1845* (London: Barrie and Jenkins, 1976).

Marx, Leo, *The Machine in the Garden: Technology and the Pastoral Ideal in America* (New York: Oxford University Press, 1964).

Maxwell, Constantia, *Country and Town in Ireland under the Georges* (London: George G. Harrap and Company, 1940).

Mitchell, Frank, *The Irish Landscape* (London: Collins, 1976).

Mitchell, W. J. T., 'Imperial Landscape' in W. J. T. Mitchell, ed., *Landscape and Power* (Chicago: University of Chicago Press, 2002), pp. 5–34.

Morash, Chris, ed., *The Hungry Voice: The Poetry of the Irish Famine* (Dublin: Irish Academic Press, 1989).

Montaño, John Patrick, *The Roots of English Colonialism in Ireland* (Cambridge: Cambridge University Press, 2011).

Moriarty, Christopher, 'The Early Naturalists' in John Wilson Foster, ed., *Nature in Ireland: A Scientific and Cultural History* (Dublin: Lilliput Press, 1997), pp. 71–90.

Ní Mhunghaile, Lesa, 'Bilingualism, Print Culture in Irish and the Public Sphere, 1700–*c.*1830' in James Kelly and Ciarán Mac Murchaidh, eds, *Irish and English: Essays on the Irish Linguistic and Cultural Frontier, 1600–1900* (Dublin: Four Courts Press, 2012), pp. 218–42.

O'Donoghue, D. J., 'Ulster Poets and Poetry', *Ulster Journal of Archaeology*. Second Series, 1:1 (Sept 1894), pp. 20–22.

Ó Gráda, Cormac and Diarmaid Ó Muirithe, 'The Famine of 1740–41: Representations in Gaelic Poetry', *Eire-Ireland* 45:3/4 (Fall/Winter 2010), pp. 1–22.

O'Halloran, Clare, *Golden Ages and Barbarous Nations: Antiquarian Debate and Cultural Politics in Ireland c.1750–1800* (Cork: Cork University Press, 2004).

O'Kane, Finola, *Ireland and the Picturesque: Design, Landscape Painting and Tourism 1700–1840* (London and New Haven: Yale University Press, 2013).

O'Kane, Finola, *Landscape Design in Eighteenth-Century Ireland: Mixing Foreign Trees with the Natives* (Cork: Cork University Press, 2004).

O'Kelly, Patrick, *The Eudoxologist: or an ethicographical survey of the western parts of Ireland* (Dublin: for the author, 1812).

Ó Muirithe, Diarmaid, ed., *The English Language in Ireland* (Cork: Mercier, 1977).

Ó Tuama, Seán and Thomas Kinsella, eds, *An Duanaire 1600–1900: Poems of the Dispossessed* (Dublin: Dolmen Press, 1981).

Palmer, Patricia, *Language and Conquest in Early Modern Ireland* (Cambridge: Cambridge University Press, 2001).

Patterson, Annabel, *Pastoral and Ideology: Virgil to Valery* (Berkeley and Los Angeles CA: University of California Press, 1987).

Peake, Charles, ed., *Poetry of the Landscape and the Night: Two Eighteenth-century Traditions* (London: Edward Arnold, 1967).

Perkins, David, 'Animal Rights and "Auguries of Innocence"', *Blake: An Illustrated Quarterly*, 33 (1999), pp. 4–11.

Poggioli, Renato, *The Oaten Flute: Essays on Pastoral Poetry and the Pastoral Ideal* (Cambridge MA: Harvard University Press, 1975).

Reed, Arden, *Romantic Weather: The Climates of Coleridge and Baudelaire* (Hanover and London: University Press of New England, 1983).

Rosenmeyer, Thomas G., *The Green Cabinet: Theocritus and the European Pastoral Lyric* (Berkeley and Los Angeles CA: University of California Press, 1969).

Ross, Ian Campbell, ed., *Public Virtue, Public Love: The Early Years of the Dublin Lying-in Hospital, The Rotunda* (Dublin: O'Brien Press, 1986).

Saunders, Timothy, *Bucolic Ecology: Virgil's Eclogues and the Environmental Literary Tradition* (London: Duckworth, 2008).

Sharpe, Richard, ed., *Roderick O'Flaherty's Letters 1696–1709: To William Molyneux, Edward Lhwyd and Samuel Molyneux* (Dublin: Royal Irish Academy, 2013).

Sheridan, Thomas, *A Complete Dictionary of the English Language* … (London: Dilly, 1789).

Spacks, Patricia Meyer, *Reading Eighteenth-Century Poetry* (Oxford: Blackwell, 2009).

Spenser, Edmund, *A View of the Present State of Ireland*, ed. W. L. Renwick (Oxford: Clarendon Press, 1970).

Stafford, Fiona, 'England, Ireland, Scotland, Wales' in Nicholas Roe, ed., *Romanticism* (Oxford: Oxford University Press), pp. 114–25.

Stanford, W. B., *Ireland and the Classical Tradition* (Dublin: Irish Academic Press, 1976).

Strauss, Sarah and Benjamin S. Orlove, eds, *Weather, Climate, Culture* (Oxford: Berg Publishers, 2003).

Swift, Jonathan, *The Poems of Jonathan Swift*, 3 vols, ed. Harold Williams (Oxford: Clarendon Press, 1966).

Thomas, Keith, *Man and the Natural World: Changing Attitudes in England 1500–1800* (London: Penguin Books, 1983).

Trumpener, Katie, *Bardic Nationalisms: The Romantic Novel and the British Empire* (Princeton NJ: Princeton University Press, 1997).

Twiss, Richard, *A Tour in Ireland in 1775* (London, 1776).

Vancouver, Charles, *General View of the Agriculture of Hampshire* (London, 1813).

Walsham, Alexandra, *The Reformation of the Landscape: Religion, Identity and Memory in Early Modern Britain and Ireland* (Oxford: Oxford University Press, 2011).

Waters, John, 'Topographical Poetry and the Politics of Culture in Ireland, 1772–1820' in Ghislaine McDayter, Guinn Batten and Barry Milligan, eds, *Romantic Generations: Essays in Honor of Robert F. Gleckner* (London: Associated University Presses, 2001), pp. 221–244.

Whyte, Samuel, *The Shamrock: or Hibernian Cresses. A Collection of Poems, Songs, Epigrams, &c. Latin as well as English, the Original Production of Ireland* (Dublin, 1772).

Williams, Raymond, *The Country and the City* (Oxford: Oxford University Press, 1975).

Williams, William H. A., *Creating Irish Tourism: The First Century, 1750–1850* (London and New York: Anthem Press, 2010).

___, *Tourism, Landscape, and the Irish Character* (Madison WN: University of Wisconsin Press, 2008).

Wilson, Penelope, 'Classical Poetry and the Eighteenth-Century Reader' in Isabel Rivers, ed., *Books and their Readers in Eighteenth-Century England* (Leicester: Leicester University Press; New York: St Martin's Press, 1982), pp. 69–96.

Wright, Julia, '"Thy Branching Words": Radical History and Education in Drennan's Verse' (unpublished paper).

Woods, C. J., *Travellers' Accounts as Source-Material for Irish Historians* (Dublin: Four Courts Press, 2009).

Wyse Jackson, Patrick N., 'Fluctuations in Fortune: Three Hundred Years of Irish Geology' in John Wilson Foster, ed., *Nature in Ireland: A Scientific and Cultural History* (Dublin: Lilliput Press, 1997), pp. 91–114.

PRELUDE

This Nymph of Ireland, is at all poynts like a yong wenche that hath the greene sicknes[1] for want of occupying. She is very fayre of visage, and hath a smooth skinn of tender grasse. Indeed she is somewhat freckled (as the Irish are) some partes darker than other. Her flesh is of a softe and delicat mould of earthe, and her blew vaynes trayling through every part of her like ryvoletts. She hath one master vayne called the Shanon, which passeth quite through her, and if it were not for one knot (one mayne rocke) it were navigable from head to foot.[2] She hath three other vaynes called the sisters, the Seuer, the Noyer & the Barrow,[3] which rysing at one spring, trayle through her middle partes, and joine together in theyr going out. Her bones are of polished marble, the grey marble, the blacke, the redd, and the speckled, so fayre for building that their houses shew like colledges, and being polished, is most rarely embelished. Her breasts are round hillockes of milk-yeelding grasse, and that so fertile, that they contend with the vallyes. And betwixt her leggs (for Ireland is full of havens), she hath an open harbour, but not much frequented. She hath had goodly tresses of hayre *arboribusqu' comae*,[4] but the iron mills, like a sharpe toothed combe, have notted & poled her much, and in her champion partes[5] she hath not so much as will cover her nakedness. Of complexion she is very temperate, never too hott, nor too could, and hath a sweet breath of favonian[6] winde. She is of a gentle nature. If the anger of heaven be agaynst her, she will not bluster and storme, but she will weepe many dayes together, and (alas) this last summer she did so water her plants, that the grasse and blade was so bedewed, that it became unprofitable, and threatens a scarcity. Neyther is she frosenharted, the last frost was not so extreame here as it was reported to be in England. It is nowe since she was drawne out of the wombe

1 A form of anemia, now known as chlorosis, suffered mainly by girls at puberty; the cure normally recommended was sexual activity ('occupying') followed by childbirth.

2 There were several rocky obstructions to navigation on the Shannon in the seventeenth century.

3 The rivers Suir, Nore and Barrow.

4 of trees and foliage.

5 open countryside. The reference is to deforestation in early modern Ireland due to the demand for charcoal used in the smelting of iron.

6 westerly.

of rebellion about sixteen yeares, by'r lady nineteen,[7] and yet she wants a husband, she is not embraced, she is not hedged and diched, there is noo quicksett[8] putt into her.

from Luke Gernon's 'A Discourse of Ireland' (1620)

7 The Earl of Tyrone had submitted to English crown forces in 1603.

8 cuttings of whitethorn set in the ground to form hedges.

PART I
1580–1689

JOHN DERRICKE
(*fl.* 1575-**1581**)

The title page to *The Image of Irelande*, printed in London in 1581, states that the impressive woodcuts of life in Elizabethan Ireland it contains – as well, presumably as the long poem that precedes them – were 'made and devised by Ihon Derricke, Anno 1578'. Nothing definite is known about this John Derricke, but it seems likely that, whoever he was, he accompanied Sir Henry Sidney during his second period as Lord Deputy of Ireland (1575–78) as Sidney moved around the country putting down rebellion against the English crown with an iron hand.

The verse in *The Image of Irelande*, from which the following extract comes, is not easy on the modern ear – partly because it is in couplets of unfamiliar 'fourteeners' – and partly because it is slow-moving, repetitious and prejudiced. However it contains the first description in English verse of the birds, beasts and landscape of Ireland and, as such, belongs in this book. Derricke mixed extravagant praise of Ireland's natural resources – clearly designed to entice settlers from England to Ireland – with ferociously anti-catholic rhetoric directed at the native Irish. His particular vituperation, in the side-notes as well as in the text itself, was directed at Sidney's main antagonist, Rory Og O More and his followers – the 'wild Irish Woodkarns' or kerns (Ir. *ceithearn*, a footsoldier). But Derricke's appreciation of natural life in Ireland and his admiration for the craft of falconry as practised in the country illuminate the following passages.

from: The First Part of the Image of Irelande

And havyng now the lothsome goulf
   of deepe Dispair well paste,[1]
We did approche *Thelysiane* feelds
   of comfort at the laste,
Where all the Crewe of heavenly Dames
   with one consent beganne
To sit them doune, and on my cause
   advisedly to scanne.[2]

1 With the exceptions listed in the 'Note on the Text', Derricke's spelling has been retained, though his punctuation has been modernized. In this selection from the early part of this long poem, the poet has passed through the 'lothsome' gulf of deep despair (engendered by contemplating the 'pestiferous' native Irish) towards the paradise of the Elysian Fields, where he will be able to compose his poem. He is accompanied by three goddesses, Invention, Memory and 'pleasant Conveyance' (conveyance = the art of communicating) who have been deputed by 'a royal God' to assist him in his versifying – because, without these three, 'what soever a man doeth is altogether unsaverie'. He explains in a side-note: <The aucthour (author) at last through many daies travail obtaineth the Porte and Haven of reste, where his three foresaid companions Invention, Memorie and Conveighaunce, consultyng together, agree and conclude that he should entreat upon (write about) the Irishe soile and inhabitauntes of the same, with the fertilitie of the ground.>

2 carefully to examine what I was planning to do.

In whiche high court of Parlament[3]
it was concluded on,
That of the famous Irishe soile,
I should enlarge upon.
And lest thereof in any parte[4]
I might relate a misse,[5]
By reason of the longitude,
or latitude, there is[6]
A goodly brave Piramides[7]
erected passyng high,
From whence all corners of the lande
I might at large discrie;[8]
From whence I did behold and see
most noble flowyng streames,[9]
Fit for the Marchantes of the worlde
to saile from forraine Realmes,
Wherein were sondry store of beastes
in waters that doe live,
To whom their proper names I am
unable for to give.
Yet were thei suche as doe maintaine
and serve for common wealth,
By yeeldyng plentie to the soile,
where store of people dwelth.
Yea, suche and suche (if credit may
be given unto me then),
As doe refreshe the hongrie soule,
and serve the use of man;

3 discussion or debate.

4 <Marke the preparation made for the aucthour, leste peradventure he might relate aught amisse, and, so by false discoverie of thynges therein contained, ronne in danger of reprofe (run in danger of reproof), whereunto the nature of the Caviller is passyngly addicted.>

5 i.e. relate amiss, make a mistake.

6 i.e. that is there (in Ireland).

7 pyramid – an imagined, high vantage point (to provide the equivalent of an aerial view of Ireland).

8 discover everything by observation.

9 <By these flowyng stremes are ment the goodlie Havens and Rivers through every parte of Irelande, most famous for marchantes, in whiche rivers also are store, change and choise of all fine and delicate fishes, and that in most abondant sort, a notable pleasure and necessarie commoditie for a common wealthe, and this is the firste parte concernyng the waters.>

All whiche I sawe abondantlie,
  aloofe where I did stande,
But farre more braver things than those[10]
  upon the stable lande.
I there beheld how evrie parte,
  and percell[11] was convaide,
With hills and woods and champion ground,
  most artificial laid.[12]
The hills directly ronnyng forth,
  and turnyng in again,[13]
Muche like a sort of croked mates,
  and overtwhartyng menne.
The woodes above and neath those hills,[14]
  some twenty miles in length,
Rounde compaste with a shakyng bogge,
  a forte of passyng strength,[15]
From whence a certaine fire is drawne
  to sheeld from Winters colde,
Whereas Poh Morishe hides hymself
  as in a fenced holde….

No beast that noyeth[16] mortall man,
  is procreated theare:
It brynges forthe no Lion feare,[17]
  not yet the rav'nyng Beare.
No beastes (I saie) whiche do possesse,

10 <As the Rivers of Irelande are notable famous for the varietie of all manner of fisshes, given in moste plentifull maner, so is the lande farre more renowmed (renowned) for her situation, pleasant ayre operation, and goodly store of all maner of cattel behofefull (behooveful, necessary) for the lande, and for all kinde of wildfoule for pleasure and profite of man, as in the discourse thereof shall spedely be set out.>

11 percell = parcel, a quantity of land; convaide = sustained, supported.

12 champion ground = open country; artificial laid = skilfully laid out.

13 i.e. hills of Ireland lie in straight ranges – but they also curve back on themselves like fellows with bent backs or men who are trying to obstruct you (overtwhartyng = overthwarting).

14 <The description of the woods of Ireland.>

15 This quatrain suggests that there are extensive woods on and around the hills, beyond which are dangerous bogs; winter fuel (turf) is taken from these bogs, but they also provide sanctuary for *Poh Morishe* (Rory Og O More), as safe there as if he were in a defended stronghold.

16 annoyeth.

17 fearsome.

one jote of crewell kinde,[18]
Excepte the Wolfe that nosome is,[19]
in Irishe soile I find.
But as for other sortes of beastes,[20]
delightyng mortall eye:
Therein consistes her chefest[21] praise,
who maie it here denye?
First for gallant stouryng Steede,[22]
mans help at all assaies,[23]
And next for Neate,[24] whereby his life,
is lengthned sondrie waies[25] ….

And now as touchyng featherd Foules,[26]
and birdes of eche degree,
The nomber doeth extende so farre,
that tis too hard for me
The multitude thereof to knowe,
or shewe in plaine prospecte,
Because I am no God at all,
my cunnyng hath defecte.[27]
Of haukes which retaining sondry names[28]
the Countrie store doeth breede,
Whose names if Pacience will abide,[29]
in order shall proceede.
The Goshauke[30] first of the Crewe,
deserves to have the name,
The Faucon next for high attemptes,

18 i.e. savage by nature; 'jote' = jot.

19 nosome = noisome, troublesome. <Greate store of wolves in Irelande.>

20 <Irelande replenished with all kinde of necessarie and profitable cattel.>

21 chiefest.

22 gallant = gallantry; a 'stouryng Steede' is a brave horse suitable for battle.

23 assays, trials.

24 cow or calf.

25 in sundry (various) ways.

26 <Plentie of all kinde of wildefoule in Irelande whatsoever maie be named.>

27 i.e. my knowledge is defective.

28 <Ireland hath great store of hawks bred in it.>

29 i.e. if you will be patient.

30 goshawk = a large, short-winged hawk. <The names of the hawks that are bred in Ireland with their estimations orderly which are in the number seven.>

in glorie and in fame.
The Tarcel[31] then ensueth on,
good reason tis that he
For fliying haukes in Ireland next
the Faucon plaste should bee.
The Tarcel gentles[32] course is nexte,
the fourth peer of the lande,
Combined to the Faucon with
a lovers freendly bande.
The pretie Marlion[33] is the fifth,
to her the Sparhauke nexte,
And then the Jacke and Musket[34] laste,
by whom the birds are vexte.
These are the Haukes whiche cheefly breed
in fertile Irishe grounde,
Whose matche for flight and speedie wyng[35]
elswhere be hardly founde.
(And to conclude) of feathered foules,
there breeds the cheef of all,
A mighty foule, a goodlie birde,
whom men do Eagle call.[36]
This builde her neast in highest toppe
of all the Oken tree,[37]
Or in the craftiest place, whereof
in Irelande many bee:
Not in the bounds of Englishe pale,
whiche is a civill place,[38]
But in the Devills Arse,[39] a Peake

31 A tercel is a male peregrine falcon.

32 Tercel-gentle is another name for a type of male falcon.

33 A merlin is a kind of small falcon; sparhawk = sparrowhawk.

34 musket = the male sparrowhawk; 'jack' is another name for it. Both are trained to attack and 'vex' other birds.

35 <The Irish hawks peerless for speediness of wing.>

36 <Many eagles in Ireland.>

37 This builds her nest at the very top of oak trees.

38 Elizabethan writers constantly compared the civilized 'Pale' (i.e. the eastern part of Ireland, mostly under English control) with the wild, barbarous remainder of the island.

39 'The Devil's Arse' is a phrase normally used to refer to a cave in the Peak District in northern England – but is here used of some wild place in Ireland. 'Peake' is the top of the mountain.

where Rebells most imbrace.[40]
For as this foule[41] and all the reste
are wilde by Nature's kinde,
So do thei kepe in wildest Nokes,[42]
and there men do them finde.
For like to like the Proverbe saith,
the Leoparde with the Beare,
Doth live in midest of desarts rude,
and none doeth other feare.[43]
For as the Irishe Karne[44] be wilde,
in maners and in fashion,
So doe these foules[45] enhabite, with
that crooked generation.
Yet when as thei are taken yong
(though wilde thei be by kinde),[46]
Enstructed through the Fauconer's lure,
by triall good I finde
That thei doe come as twere at becke,
and when as thei[47] doe call,
She scarce will stint on twige or bowe,
till on his fiste she fall.[48]
Thus thei obey their tutors hestes[49]
and doe degenerate[50]
From wildness that belonged to
their forepossessed state. …

40 embrace, congregate.

41 i.e. the eagle.

42 nooks, hiding places in remote parts of Ireland.

43 i.e. neither fears the other; the quatrain embellishes the old proverb 'like will to like', widely quoted in sixteenth-century England. rude = uncivilized.

44 kern, (Ir. *ceithearn*, a footsoldier).

45 i.e. young eagles.

46 i.e. by nature.

47 i.e. the eagle-handlers.

48 i.e. the bird does not stop or rest on a twig or a bough but flies on until she comes to rest ('falls') on the wrist of her handler. This is a rare reference to hunting with trained eagles in Ireland.

49 behests, commands.

50 lose the qualities normal to a wild bird, i.e. they are tamed.

RICHARD STANIHURST
(1547–**1582**–1618)

Richard Stanihurst is the most interesting and significant Irish-born poet writing in English before Swift. His family was prominent in the Old English community in Dublin, and Stanihurst was educated in Kilkenny, at Oxford and at the Inns of Court in London. (There was no university in Ireland when Stanihurst was young.) When he returned to Ireland, Stanihurst was tutor to the children of the eleventh earl of Kildare. He wrote both prose and verse in English and in Latin; his English work includes accounts of Ireland, translations from Latin verse and original verse. He eventually became a catholic priest and a respected practitioner of alchemy.

Stanihurst had strong views on how the English language should be pronounced and written and the fact that he followed his own theories on spelling in his verse makes it difficult for modern readers. Even his contemporaries mocked his way of writing English; however, Stanihurst combined the scholar's knowledge of the English language with the poet's enthusiasm for it and created striking effects by mixing words from the world of the epic with words from the street and by boldly employing nouns as verbs and verbs as nouns in a way later exploited by Lewis Carroll and James Joyce. Though some critics have thought that Stanihurst must have meant his verse to be comic, his scholarly prefaces show that he was trying to open up a new way of writing English verse, and that he saw this as a scholarly exercise in the highest humanist tradition. The poem that follows is the earliest of many Irish poems in English describing ordinary people's reaction to extreme cold.

A Devise made by Virgil … Englished.
[*A River hard frozen*]

Theare chariots doe travayle, wheare late the great argosye sayled:[1]
By reason of the river knit with a frostye soder.
Wheare the great hulck floated, theare now thee cartwheele is hagling:
Thee water hard curded with the chil ysye rinet.
Where skut's furth launched, theare now the great wayn is entred:
When the river frized by reason of the weather.

1 A rough paraphrase of the text might run as follows: 'Because the river is knit together by the solder of the frost, chariots travel where recently a great fleet sailed; where the great, heavy ship used to float is now hacked and mangled with cartwheels. The river is curdled, as it were, by the cold ice. Where trading-boats were launched before, great heavy carts rumble since the river is frozen. Because the water is so firmly congealed, there are now cheerful carmen where mariners used to row. Now the carter treats the place where people used to sail as an alleyway – turned like this because of the chill of the winter. Now haywains and horse-drawn vehicles travel where the navy used to go, their new-found pathway defined by the frost. Carts get used to going in parts where ships normally pass because the moisture that's always there is now icebound. Oxen are tethered in their stalls where ships usually go because the water can't flow. Where little coastal sailing boats normally belong, lots of cart wheels crash around; it is winter's excesses that have brought about these strange happenings. The water that used to support a ship now supports cartwheels; the freezing weather makes the water gather firmly together. Where the rudder used to steer, the goad now pokes the oxen; the winter's cold makes the river as hard as a rock.'

Wheare rowed earst mariners, theare nowe godye carman abydeth,
Thee flud, congealed stiflye, relats the reason.
Now the place of sayling is turnd to a carter his entrye,
This change thee winters chillines hoarye bredeth.
Now wayns and chariots are drawne, wheare navye dyd harrow:
This new found passadge frostines hoarye shaped.
Wheare barcks have passed, with cart's that parcel is haunted:
From woonted moysture for that ice heeld the water.
Wheare stems have traversd, there have oxen traced in headstal:
By reason yse knitting thee water heeld froe floing.
Wheare the flye boat coasted, theare cart wheels clustred ar hobling
This new strange passadge winter his hoarnes habled.
Earst the flud, upbearing thee ship, now the cartwheele upholdeth.
When water is ioygned firmlye with hoarye weather.
Whear ruther steered, thee goad theare poaked hath oxen:
Thee winters coldnesse thee river hardlye roching.

EDMUND SPENSER
(*c*.1552–*c*.**1595**–1599)

Edmund Spenser spent most of his adult life in Ireland as Secretary to the Lord Deputy, Lord Grey. Almost everything he wrote after 1580, including most of *The Faerie Queene*, all of Colin Clouts *Come Home Againe* and the *Epithalamion*, was written in Ireland and he used the country as a setting in these poems. Ireland is seen as both friendly and welcoming (in *Colin Clout* and the *Epithalamion*) and as wild, untamed and frightening. Spenser seeks to explain these apparently irreconcilable perceptions of the Irish countryside in the following passage from the 'Mutability Cantos' of *The Faerie Queene.*

The main event of the Mutability Cantos is a grand trial – presided over by 'Nature' – at which the claims of the present world order, represented by the existing gods, are challenged by the upstart goddess Mutability, who wishes to supplant Jove as chief of the heavenly hierarchy and make change rather than stasis the ruling principle of the universe. Spenser chose to set this trial in the mountains of north County Cork, near his Castle at Kilcolman. The local rivers become nymphs attending the goddess Cynthia (or Diana) and their physical characteristics (i.e. the large rocks in the river bed of the River Bregoge and the fact that the Awbeg river (which Spenser calls the 'Mulla') appears to dry up in the summer) are 'explained' as having been caused by the spiteful reaction of Cynthia/Diana when she finds out that the god Faunus has seen her naked. The roughness of the natural world around Spenser in real life is seen to have been caused by the anger of the goddess – which anger has also turned what was once the paradise of the Irish countryside into a land of wolves and thieves.

from: The Faerie Queene
from: The Mutabilitie Cantos
[Book VII, Canto VI, stanzas 36–55]

... Eftsoones[1] the time and place appointed were,
Where all, both heavenly Powers, & earthly wights,[2]
Before great Natures presence should appeare,
For triall of their Titles and best Rights:
That was, to weet,[3] upon the highest hights
Of *Arlo-hill*[4] (Who knowes not *Arlo-hill*?)
That is the highest head (in all mens sights)
Of my old father *Mole*,[5] whom Shepheards quill
Renowned hath with hymnes fit for a rurall skill.[6]

1 soon afterwards.

2 creatures.

3 in fact.

4 Galtymore, the highest peak in the mountain range near Spenser's estate.

5 Spenser called the Ballyhoura and Galtee mountain ranges 'Old Father Mole'.

6 The reference is to Spenser himself, shepherd/narrator of *Colin Clouts Come Home Againe.*

And, were it not ill fitting for this file,[7]
To sing of hilles & woods, mongst warres & Knights,[8]
I would abate the sternenesse of my stile,
Mongst these sterne stounds[9] to mingle soft delights;
And tell how Arlo through Dianaes spights[10]
(Beeing of old the best and fairest Hill
That was in all this holy-Islands hights)
Was made the most unpleasant, and most ill.
Meane while, ô *Clio*, lend *Calliope* thy quill.[11]

Whylome,[12] when *IRELAND* florished in fame
Of wealths and goodnesse, far above the rest
Of all that beare the *British* Islands name,
The Gods then us'd (for pleasure and for rest)
Oft to resort there-to, when seem'd them best:
But none of all there-in more pleasure found,
Then *Cynthia*; that is soveraine Queene profest[13]
Of woods and forrests, which therein abound,
Sprinkled with wholsom waters, more than most on ground.

But mongst them all, as fittest for her game,[14]
Either for chace of beasts with hound or boawe,
Or for to shroude in shade from *Phoebus* flame,
Or bathe in fountaines that doe freshly flowe,
Or[15] from high hilles, or from the dales belowe,
She chose this *Arlo*; where shee did resort
With all her Nymphes enranged on a rowe,
With whom the woody Gods did oft consort:
For, with the Nymphes, the Satyres[16] love to play & sport.

7 tale.

8 The main subjects of *The Faerie Queene* are chivalry and feats of valour.

9 grim moments.

10 spite. Spenser will tell how Arlo, once called the fairest hill in holy Ireland, was transformed by the spite of Diana, classical goddess of hunting, into the most unpleasant.

11 The classical muses of history and of epic poetry.

12 in former times.

13 acknowledged.

14 recreation.

15 either.

16 Goat-footed, half-human creatures of classical mythology, addicted to sensual pleasures. Here they play and sport with Diana's nymphs – goddesses of streams and trees.

Amongst the which, there was a Nymph that hight
Molanna;[17] daughter of old father *Mole*,
And sister unto *Mulla*,[18] faire and bright:
Unto whose bed false Bregog whylome stole,[19]
That Shepheard *Colin* dearely did condole,[20]
And made her lucklesse loves well knowne to be.
But this *Molanna*, were she not so shole,[21]
Were no lesse faire and beautifull then shee:
Yet as she is, a fairer flood[22] may no man see.

For, first, she springs out of two marble Rocks,
On which, a grove of Oakes high mounted growes,
That as a girlond seemes to deck the locks
Of som faire Bride, brought forth with pompous showes
Out of her bowre, that many flowers strowes:[23]
So, through the flowry Dales she tumbling downe,
Through many woods, and shady coverts flowes
(That on each side her silver channell crowne)
Till to the Plaine she come, whose Valleyes shee doth
drowne.[24]

In her sweet streames, *Diana* used oft
(After her sweatie chace and toilesome play)
To bathe her selfe; and after, on the soft
And downy grasse, her dainty limbes to lay

17 A nymph by the name of Molanna. This is the name Spenser gave to the Behenna river, a shallow, rocky river that rises in the mountains near his estate.

18 The Awbeg river.

19 Spenser refers to the myth he told in *Colin Clouts Come Home Againe*. The Bregoge river flows around what used to be Spenser's land and joins the Awbeg river (Mulla). The Bregoge used to appear to dry up in the summer; in fact, the water flowed underground and rose again farther down its course to join the larger river. Spenser plays upon this natural phenomenon in a fanciful love-story about the two rivers. The Allo (now known as the Blackwater and the larger river into which all these smaller ones eventually flow) is cast as the husband eventually intended by 'Old Father Mole' (the mountains) for his daughter Mulla. Her lover, Bregoge, outwits Father Mole by intertwining with Mulla before either river gets to the Blackwater.

20 earnestly lamented.

21 shallow.

22 river.

23 i.e. brought forth ceremoniously from her flower-strewn bower.

24 flow through.

In covert[25] shade, where none behold her may:
For, much she hated sight of living eye.
Foolish God *Faunus*,[26] though full many a day
He saw her clad, yet longed foolishly
To see her naked mongst her Nymphes in privity.[27]

No way he found to compasse[28] his desire,
But to corrupt *Molanna*, this her maid,
Her to discover for some secret hire:[29]
So, her with flattering words he first assaid;[30]
And after, pleasing gifts for her purvaid,
Queene-apples,[31] and red Cherries from the tree,
With which he her allured and betraid,
To tell what time he might her Lady see
When she her selfe did bathe, that he might secret bee.

There-to hee promist, if shee would him pleasure
With this small boone, to quit[32] her with a better;
To weet, that where-as shee had out of measure
Long lov'd the *Fanchin*, who by nought did set her,[33]
That he would undertake, for this to get her
To be his Loue, and of him liked well:
Besides all which, he vow'd to be her debter
For many moe[34] good turnes than he would tell;
The least of which, this little pleasure should excell. …

Molanna helps Faunus hide so that he sees Diana naked, but he is caught and chased by Diana and her nymphs.

25 secluded.

26 Spenser has invented the name (cf. 'faun') for this reworking of the classical story of Diana and Actæon.

27 privacy.

28 accomplish.

29 to reveal her (Diana) for some secret bribe.

30 tried.

31 crabapples.

32 repay.

33 i.e. since, for a long time, she had been deeply in love with the river Funsheon – another tributary of the river Blackwater – who cared nothing for her…

34 more.

So they him follow'd till they weary were;
When, back returning to *Molann'* againe,
They, by commaund'ment of *Diana*, there
Her whelm'd with stones.[35] Yet *Faunus* (for her paine)
Of her beloved *Fanchin* did obtaine,
That her he would receive unto his bed.
So now her waves passe through a pleasant Plaine,
Till with the *Fanchin* she her selfe doe wed,
And (both combin'd) themselves in one faire river spred.

Nath'lesse, *Diana*, full of indignation,
Thence-forth abandond her delicious brooke;
In whose sweet streame, before that bad occasion,
So much delight to bathe her limbes she tooke:
Ne onely her, but also quite forsooke
All those faire forrests about *Arlo* hid,
And all that Mountaine, which doth over-looke
The richest champian that may else be rid,[36]
And the faire *Shure*,[37] in which are thousand Salmons bred.

Them all, and all that she so deare did way,[38]
Thence-forth she left; and parting from the place,
There-on an heavy haplesse curse did lay,
To weet,[39] that Wolves, where she was wont to space,[40]
Should harbour'd be, and all those Woods deface,
And Thieves should rob and spoile that Coast[41] around.
Since which, those Woods, and all that goodly Chase,[42]
Doth to this day with Wolves and Thieves abound:
Which too-too true that lands in-dwellers[43] since have
found.

35 The river is still shallow and rocky.

36 The richest countryside which might, otherwise, be cleared.

37 The river Suir.

38 weigh, esteem.

39 that is.

40 roam.

41 land.

42 hunting ground.

43 inhabitants.

RICHARD NUGENT
(*fl.*1604)

Richard Nugent was a member of a prominent Old English family based in County Westmeath.[1] His only published work was a sonnet sequence, *Rich: Nugents Cynthia. Containing direfull sonnets, madrigalls, and passionate intercourses, describing his repudiate affections expressed in loves owne language* (London, 1604) which concerns his rejection by the Irish 'Cynthia'. The poet, spurned, left Ireland for London and, in the sonnet that follows, expressed his feelings for the land he was forced to leave.

Fare-well sweete Isle

Fare-well sweete Isle, within whose pleasant Bowres
I first received life and living ayre;
Fare-well the soile, where grew those heav'nly flowres
Which bravely decke the face of my fierce faire;[2]
Fare-well the place, whence I beheld the towres
With pale aspect, where her I saw repaire;
Fare-well ye floods, encreased by those showres
Wherewith mine eyes did entertaine despaire;
Fare-well cleare lake, which of art made the glasse[3]
To rarest beautie, of mine ill the roote,
When she vouchsafes upon thy shores to passe,
Blessing thy happie sand with thy[4] faire foote;
Fare-well faire *Cynthia*, whose unkind consent
Hath caus'd mine everlasting banishment.

1 For information on Nugent, as well as a full critical assessment of his sonnet sequence, see Anne Fogarty's introduction to *Cynthia by Richard Nugent* ed. Angelina Lynch (Dublin, Four Courts Press, 2010).

2 The paradox is typical of Petrarchan love poetry; it is the lady's behaviour that the poet sees as 'fierce'.

3 This passage suggests that the surface of the lake – acting like an artificial (or hand-made) mirror – reflects the lady's beauty (the cause of the poet's ills) when she condescends to walk past it.

4 A misprint for 'her'.

ANONYMOUS
(1622)

In September 1621, thousands of starlings ('stares') did battle with each other over Cork city, thoroughly alarming the citizens. The ballad that commemorated the event suggested that this unnatural event was a sign of divine displeasure and urged Cork's citizens to repent of their evil ways (ll. 107–8).

from: A Battell of Birds

most strangly fought in Ireland, upon the eight day of September last, 1621, where neere unto the Citty of Corke, by the river Lee, we are gathered together such a multytude of Stares, or Starlings, as the like for number, was never seene in any age ...

Marke well, Gods wonderous workes, and see,
what things therein declared be,
Such things as may with trembling feare,
fright all the world, the same to heare:
or like to these, which heere I tell,
no man alive remembreth well.

The eight day of September last,
which made all Ireland much agast:
Were seene (neere Corke) such flights of Birds,
whose numbers, cannot well by words,
counted be: for greater store,
as never seene, nor knowne before.

The flights, so many legions seem'd,
as thousand thousands they were deem'd,
All [soaring] up, along the skye,
as if the battle were on hie:
in multytudes, without compare,
which like black clowds, made dim the are.[1]

First from the easterne skyes apeared,
A flight [of] Stares, which greatly feared
The p[eo]ple there the same to see,
as like could not remembred be:

1 air.

for they in war[like] squadrons flew,
as if they others would persue.

And as this flight, thus hovering lay,
prepared all in battle ray:
From out the west, another came,
as great in number as the same,
and there oppos'd in warlike might,
themselves against the other flight.

Whereas these Stares, or starling Birds,
for want of Helmetts, Glaves and Swords,
They used their Tallents, Bills, and Bekaes,[2]
and such a battle undertakes:
that trembling feare and terror brought,
to all which saw this battle fought.

For first, the Easterne flight sat downe,
with chattering noyes upon the ground,
As if they challenged, all the rest,
to meete and fight even brest to brest,

where presently was heard from farre,
the same like chattering sound of warre.

And there upon the westerne flight,
downe by the easterne Birds did light,
Where after they a while had set,[3]
together in their Birdlike chat,
they all upon asudaine[4] rose,
and each the other did oppose.

2 helmets, gloves, swords, talons, bills and beaks.

3 sat.

4 a sudden.

from: *The second part …*

And filling thus the Azure skie
with these their troupes up mounted hie,
They seem'd more thick, than moats ith Sunne;[5]
a dreadfull battle there begun:
and in their kind more strongly fought,
then can immagen'd be by thought.

Thousands of thousands, on a heape,
upon the others backes did leape,
With all their forced strengths and might,
To put their Bird-like foes to flight:
and as it were in battle ray,
long time they kept them, thus in play.

To fight this battle in the ayre,
their bills and beakes their weapons were,
Which they performed in such a sort,
as makes me doubtfull to report:
that silly[6] Birds should thus arise,
and fight so fircely in the skyes.

But so it was and strange withall,
that Birds should thus at discord fall,
And never cease, till they had slaine,
thousands, starke dead upon the plaine:
where people tooke them up in feare,
a thing most strange to see and heare.

With broken wings, some fell to ground,
and some poore silly Birds were found,
With eyes pickt out, struck downe halfe dead,
and some no braines left in their head,
but battered forth, and kil'd out right,
most strangly in this ayery fight.

5 than motes of dust in (a ray of) sun.

6 deserving of compassion or sympathy.

Yet long with loud and chattering cryes,
each company gainst other flyes:
With bloody beakes, remorselesse still,
their fethered foes to maine or kill,
where whilst this battle did remaine
their bodies fell like dropes of raine.

Thousands were to the Citty borne,
with wounded limbes, and bodies torne:
For all the fields were overspread,
with mangled starlings that lay dead,
in bloud and feathers strang to se,[7]
which men tooke up aboundantly.

It was a wonder to explaine,
the number of them hurt and slaine,
And being a wonder let it rest,
the Lord above he knoweth best:
what these poore creatures did intend,
when thus to battle they did bend.

But such a battle nere was fought,
by silly Birds which have no thought:
In doing ill, nor any mind,
to worke contrary to their kind,
but yet as nature gave them life,
so here they strangly fell at strife.

What now for trueth is publisht forth
esteeme it as a newes of worth:
And by the wonder of their dayes,
learne to leave off all wicked wayes,
for sure it is that God it sent,
that of our sinnes we should repent.

7 strange to see.

RICHARD BELLINGS
(*c.*1598–**1624**–1677)

Richard Bellings, one of the most prominent catholic lawyers of seventeenth-century Ireland, was born into a well-established family which owned estates in counties Wicklow and Kildare. He went to London as a young man to be educated at Lincoln's Inn and later played a central role in Irish political life in the 1640s, becoming secretary to the confederate supreme council. In the poem that follows, Bellings – like Milton in 'Lycidas' – brings the classical gods to a turbulent Irish Sea.

The Description of a Tempest

Bound for my countrey[1] from the Cambrian[2] shore,
I cut the deepe;[3] the Mariners implore,
With whistling prayer, the winde growne too milde,
To hasten to beget their sayles with childe.[4]
The humble Sea, as of our ship afraid,
Pale, breathlesse, prostrate at our feet, is laid.
The morne, scarse out of bed, did blush to see
Her rude beholders so unmannerly.[5]
She scarse had blusht, when she began to hide
Her rosie cheekes, like to a tender Bride.
To sute[6] Aurora, all the heavens put on
A mournfull vayle of black, as shee had done,
And gave the garments to the Sea they wore,
Wherewith it growes more blew[7] now than before.
This stage being set, the lightnings tapers were,[8]
The drumms such thunder as afright each ear.
Upon this summons great King *Eolus*,[9]
Attended on by *Nothus* and *Zephirus*,[10]

1 Ireland.

2 Welsh.

3 i.e. I pass through the sea.

4 i.e. the sailors are 'whistling for the wind'.

5 i.e. the morning blushed to see the sailors behaving in such an unruly fashion.

6 = suit, harmonize with, fit in with (the mood of). Aurora was the Roman goddess of the dawn.

7 i.e. blue.

8 Before the advent of electricity, stages were lit with tapers.

9 god of the winds in classical mythology.

10 the south wind (*recte* 'Notus') and the west wind.

Enters, and where the King his steps doth place,
The waves do swell, trod with so proud a grace.
He was to speake, but opening of his mouth,
The boisterous winde did blow so hard at South,
I could not heare, but as the rest told me,
He spoke the prologue for a tragedie.
Behold huge mountaines in the watry maine,
That lately was a smooth and liquid plaine,
Ore which our Sea-drunke Barque doth reeling ride.
She must obey, but knowes not to which tyde;
For still she plowes that rugged mutinous place,
All skillful Pilots call the breaking race.[11]
A while ambition bare her up so hie,
Her proud discoloured flagg doth touch the skie;
But when the winds these waves doe beare away,[12]
She hangs in ayre, and makes a little stay:
But downe againe from such presumptuous height
Shee's headlong borne by her attractive weight[13]
Into the hollow of a gaping grave,
Intomb'd of each side with a stately wave.
Downe poure these billows from their height of pride:
Our Barque receives them in at every side.
But when they finde no place where to remaine,
The scuddle holes[14] do let them out againe.
At length, as Castles where no force can finde
A conquest, by assault are undermin'd,
So in our Barque, whose walls no waves could breake,
We do discover a most trayterous leake.
To this, though much our hopes do now decline,
We do oppose the Pump,[15] our countermine:[16]

11 a strong, rushing current of water which, in this case, is topped by breaking waves.

12 move away.

13 i.e. drawn down by the force of gravity.

14 scuppers.

15 i.e. although our hopes are dashed, we use the ship's pump to counter the effect of the leak.

16 i.e. our way of outwitting the enemy. A countermine was a subterranean passage constructed by the defenders of a fortress under attack to intercept a tunnel made by the besiegers.

That midway breakes,[17] whereat our Master cryes
All hope is past, the Seas must close our eyes;
And to augment death's hideous show the more,
We in the poope[18] can scarse discerne the prore;[19]
Such ugly mists had overcast the ayre,
That heaven, I thought, had meant we should despayre.
But in the last act of this Tragedie,
Behold, our great God's all-discerning eye
Caused in an instant these thick mists disband;
The winds are calm'd, and we at Skerries land.

Dread ruler of the floods, whose powerful will
Each thing that hath a being must fulfill,
Whose hand markes forth the end of each man's dayes,
And steers our humane[20] ship in unknown wayes;
To thee, great guide, the incense[21] I present:
Thou gav'st me time to live, and to repent.

17 i.e. half-way through the operation of pumping the ship, the pump itself breaks.

18 the high deck at the stern of the ship.

19 prow.

20 human.

21 i.e. this poem.

LADY ANN SOUTHWELL
(1571–*c.***1626**–1636)

Lady Ann Southwell (née Harris) and her first husband Thomas Southwell came to Ireland early in the seventeenth century as planters. They lived for many years at Poulnelong Castle in County Cork and developed a wide circle of friends and acquaintances. Lady Southwell's lively intellect and her grasp of contemporary neo-Platonism appears in the ambitious (and ambiguous) mock elegy below, in which she shows a delight in word-play and a fascination with complex ideas about the nature of the universe. The Countess of Londonderry, whose soul is the subject of the poem, had been a maid of honour to Queen Elizabeth in her youth. When Lady Londonderry really died in 1627, Lady Southwell wrote 'An Epitaph' on her and referred to this poem as recently written, so it can probably be dated about 1626.[1] The text is taken from a manuscript.

from: An Elegie written by the Lady A: S: to the Countesse of London Derrye.
supposeinge hir to be dead by hir long silence

Since thou, fayre soule, art warbling[2] to a spheare
from whose resultances theise quickned weere,[3]
since thou hast layd that downy couch[4] aside
of lillyes, violletts, and roseall[5] pride,
and lockt in marble chests that tapestrye
that did adorne the worlds epitome
soe safe that doubt it selfe can never thinke
fortune or fate hath power to make a chinke;[6]
since thou, for state, hath raisd thy state soe farr,[7]

1 For recent work on Lady Ann Southwell, see Marie-Louise Coolahan, *Women, Writing and Language in Early Modern Ireland* (Oxford, Oxford University Press, 2010) pp. 181–90 and references.

2 A term from falconry meaning to cross the wings together over the back. Neo-Platonism asserts the high origins of the human soul and concerns itself with ways in which that soul may return to its eternal home. In this case, the soul of the countess is imagined rising, physically, through the skies to heaven.

3 i.e. since you are winging your way to the heavens, from the debris of which your body was created ...

4 i.e. the body – in which your soul has been resting ...

5 roseate, rose-coloured.

6 This complex quatrain seems to mean: and you have locked in a marble vault that physical manifestation of the world (your body) so safely that it has no further power to harm the integrity of the spirit.

7 'state' can mean the mode of existence of a spiritual being. The line is thus a play on words, and the couplet means, roughly: since you, because of your high rank [presumably high spiritual rank], have raised your spiritual self far up above the circular vault of the skies to a wide heaven ...

to a large heaven from a vaute circular,
because the thronginge virtues in thy brest
could not have roome enough in such a chest,
what need hast thou theise blotted Lines[8] should tell
soules must againe take rise, from whence they fell,
from paradice, and that this earths darke wombe
is but a wardrobe till the day of do[o]me
to keepe those wormes, that on hir[9] bosomes bredd,
till tyme, and death, bee both extermined?
Yet in thy passage, fayre soule, let me know
what things thou saw'st in riseinge from below?
Whether that Cynthia, regent of the flood,[10]
will[11] in her Orbe admitt of mortall brood?
Whether the 12 Signes serve the Sun for state,
or elce confine him to the Zodiaque,[12]
and force him retrograde to bee the nurse
(whoe circularly glides his oblique course)
of Alma Mater,[13] or unfreeze the wombe
of Madam Tellus[14] —wch elce Proves a tombe?[15]
Whether the starrs be Knobbs uppon the spheres?
Or shredds compos'd of Phœbus goulden hayres?

8 i.e. this poem.

9 her; i.e. that graves on this earth are no more than places to keep bodies (where worms breed) until time and death both come to an end. For similar imagery, see the sermons of John Donne (1624).

10 The passage which follows assumes a knowledge of the Ptolemaic system of the universe in which a series of concentric spheres, punctured by the holes of different sizes through which shone sun, moon, planets and stars, were constantly moving, each in its own way, around the earth. As the countess's soul passes through the spheres on its way to the distant heavens, it gets a chance to see what happens on each level. The first level encountered is that of Cynthia, the moon, who, personified as a goddess, controls the tides (the flood). The question is, are there men on the moon or, at least on the moon's sphere?

11 MS reads 'wth'.

12 The signs of the Zodiac are based on the patterns of stars. The question is whether the sun is independent of (and hierarchically superior to) the stars or subservient to them.

13 The ancient Romans gave this name, 'the white mother' to the nurturing goddesses, particularly Ceres. Here it is applied to a sign of the zodiac through which the sun has to pass on an oblique course so that, like a nurse, he can give life to the earth.

14 goddess of the earth.

15 i.e. the earth would be a tomb if it were not warmed by the sun and if the seasons did not pass.

Or whether th'Ayre be as a cloudy sive?[16]
The starrs be holes through wch the good soules drive?
Whether that Saturne that the 6 out topps[17]
sitt ever eatinge of the bratts of Opps,[18]
whose jealousye is like a Sea of Gall[19]
unto his owne proves periodicall?[20]
But as a glideinge star whoe falls to earth
or lovers thoughts, soe soules ascend theyr birth,
wch makes mee thinke, that thyne had noe one notion,
of those true elements, by whose true motion
all things have life, and death;[21] but if thyne eyne[22]
should fix a while uppon the Christalline,[23]
thy hungrye eye, that never could before,
see, but by fayth, and faythfully adore,
should stay, to marke the threefould Hierarchye,[24]
differinge in state, not in fælicitye
how they in order, 'bout Jehova move,
in severall offices, but wth one love,
and, from his hand, doe hand in hand come downe,
till the last hand doe heads of mortalls crowne.[25]
Fayne would I know from some that have beene there
what state or shape cælestiall bodyes beare?[26]

16 sieve.

17 At the time this poem was written, it was thought that there were six planets of which Saturn was the most distant from earth.

18 In classical mythology, the god Saturn was in the habit of devouring the children born to him by his wife Ops, though she did manage, according to some legends, to save some of her children, including Jupiter, Neptune and Pluto, from their father.

19 See Job 16. 13.

20 The reference is to the regular movements of the planet Saturn.

21 Lady Londonderry's soul (unlike earthly 'things'), is not subject to death.

22 eyes.

23 i.e. upon the highest level of the heavens where, according to Ptolemy, a crystal sphere existed between the *primum mobile* and the firmament.

24 According to Dionysius the Areopagite, there are three divisions of angels, each one comprising three orders. Angels live in the highest levels of heaven, around Jehovah: but they also descend to earth to perform tasks such as crowning kings (line 60).

25 By the doctrine of the Divine Right of Kings, earthly monarchs were crowned by God's angels.

26 Another key question of the age: what type of bodies will the righteous have in heaven?

For Man, to heaven, hath throwne a waxen ball,
in wch hee thinks h'hath gott true formes of all,
and, from the forge howse of his fantasie,
hee creates new, and spins out destinye.
And thus, theise prowd wormes, wrapt in lothsome rags,
shutt heavens idea upp, in letherne baggs.[27]
Now since in heaven are many ladyes more,
that blinde devotion busyely implore,
Good Lady, freind, or rather lovely Dame,
if yow be gone from out this clayie frame,
tell what yow know, whether th' Saynts adoration
will stoope to thinke on dusty procreation.
And if they will not, they are fooles (perdye)[28]
that pray to them, and robb the Trinitye;[29]
The Angells joy in o[u]r good conversation,
yet see us not, but by reverberation,[30]
And if they could, thow[31] s[ain]ts as cleere eies have,
if downe yow looke to earth, then to the grave,
tis but a Landkipp,[32] more, to looke to Hell;
in viewinge it, what strange thinges may yow tell? ...

27 A wax ball would take an image imprinted on it, so these lines could be paraphrased: man has created a heaven out of his own fantasies and, 'prowd worme' that he is, has shut up what he knows of the perfections of heaven ('Heavens idea') in leathern bags, i.e. books.

28 By God! certainly.

29 Criticism of adherents of the Roman Catholic Church who pray to saints and so 'robb the Trinitye' (i.e. God himself) of prayers.

30 reflection. What kind of 'bodies' angels had, and whether they, saints and departed souls had senses as we understand them, were subjects of heated debate in the seventeenth century.

31 though.

32 landscape.

ANONYMOUS
(*c.*1636)

The setting for this very early hunting song is the countryside of Fingal, north of Dublin, and the location for the meet of huntsmen and hounds is Howth Castle, the seat of the St Lawrence family, Lords of Howth. Since those named in the first stanza were active in the 1630s, the song clearly dates from that period. The earliest written text, however, is a scribal copy of the mid-eighteenth century. Since the song had been sung for a hundred years before it was captured on paper, it is not surprising that its metrical pattern had become muddled and some of its words garbled in transmission. The text has been lightly edited for this printing. Though the song is in English, the influence of the Irish language can be seen in the use of assonance rather than end-rhyme in places. Some words are also spelled to indicate Hiberno-English pronunciation.

Ye merry Boyes all that live in Fingaule

Ye merry Boyes all that live in Fingaule
I will tell you a Tale, how a Hare catch't a fall.
There was Michael St Lawrence and Patrick Aspoor,
Robbin Hod-goor, and Jacky Radmoor.
With Robbin Hilliard (with his gay little Grey)
And Stephen Ash-pole, a gay merry Boy.

They met on a Day in St Lawrences[1] Hall,
Where he gave 'em hot waters, good meat, and strong Ale.
And one ting more may be said for his fame,
For his Sport he ventur'd his Ey and his Arm.

There was St Lawrence's Scutty,[2] and her Daughter Betty,
Short cropt curryd[3] Iron, and Merry-hunting Don,
Ho[d]goiers Hector's a Gay Gray-hound,
Hee'l take three Yards at every Bound,
And tho' he had a blemish upon one Eye,
It was hard for all that to give him the go-by.[4]

1 <The Ld. of Hoths.> The head of the family in the 1630s was Nicholas St Lawrence, 23rd Lord Howth.

2 These are names of hunting dogs.

3 combed.

4 not to include him.

They went over the Ditches with their Dogs and Bitches,
They spar'd not to beat Bear,[5] Barley and wheat.
Last out of some Bryars, they got their Desires,
There started a Hare, that runned most rare[6]
Which set 'em a barking with all their train,
Till the merry light Hare was very ny Slain.

But in a fine Mead, she being almost spent,
She made her last Will, ay[7] and Testament;[8]
Cropt Curr, with thee, says she, I will not stay,
Nor with true running Cutty, that show'd such fair play,
But to thee, brave Hector, I yeild up my Leef;
And so Hector bore her and ended the Streef.[9]

Then Hodgier came in to bear up the Hare
His Breeches fell down, and his Ars it was bare,
But Patrick Ash pole he spoke a bold word,
He woud go to Baldoyle[10] to see what the Town coud afford.

And when the Boys came to the gay Town,
They got salt pork and Yellow Ba-coon,[11]
Which they then just cut down from the smoke.
And Patrick Ash pole play'd a very good Cook,
He slash'd it, and wash'd it, and I[12] know not what,
But[13] not one bit he left on't but 'twas all he Eat.

5 barley. To beat is to move noisily through the fields to scare out game.

6 exceptionally well.

7 MS reads: 'EE'.

8 The belief that a hare makes a will as it dies and gives permission to a particular dog to kill it is of ancient origin.

9 strife.

10 MS reads: 'Baldoit.' Baldoyle is a town in Fingal, not far from Howth.

11 An indication of the conservative pronunciation of Hiberno-English in seventeenth-century Fingal. Richard Stanihurst had noted in 1577 that, in Wexford (where the pronunciation of English was very similar to that of Fingal), 'most commonly in wordes of two sillables, they give the last the accent.' (Raphaell Holinshed, *The Firste Volume of the Chronicles of England, Scotlande, and Irelande* (London, 1577) f.31*r*, col.1).

12 MS reads: 'EE'.

13 Conjectural reading: MS reads: 'Mut'.

The Drink it was good and so was the Bread,
They took off their Liquors till they were all Red,[14]
And when they had done they sang the Hares Knell,
And if I had more,[15] faith more I wou'd tell.

14 i.e. red in the face. 'Took off' means drank eagerly.

15 i.e. (presumably) more liquor.

ANONYMOUS
(1644)

Though this strange poem was printed in London, it is strongly linked with events in Ireland and was almost certainly written in Ireland by a Protestant English planter who had been forced out of his 'happie state' and 'setled place' in Ireland during the 1641 Rising. The poet/planter, who had clearly been committed to building up his herd and raising cattle for live export, used the 'Complaint' which precedes the poem proper to bewail the 'grievous smart' he suffered when 'the Countrey' rose up against him and his farm was taken from him. The poem itself is a reflection (or mirror) of the world as a whole and was probably written before the 'Complaint'. Since there is mention of wren-boys (whose mid-winter activities were common in Ireland at this time), of a harp, of fishing boats going to England, France and Spain, and of the otter by its Irish name (water-dogge = Ir. *Madra uisce*), the poem was clearly written by someone living in Ireland – though the presence of moles and unicorns (neither of which was to be found in Ireland) shows that poet intended his poem to mirror the entire world rather than just the country where he had been plundered. Despite its lumbering style and basic prosody, the poem is of considerable interest for the poet's attitudes towards nearly one hundred species of birds, fish and animals and, at the end of the poem, for the brief accounts of about sixty trades and professions – all of which would have been practised in English settler communities in Ireland in the 1630s.

from: A Looking-Glasse of the World, or, the Plundred Man in Ireland:

His voyage, his observation of the Beasts of the Field, of the Fishes of the Sea, of the Fowls of the Aire, of the Severall Professions of Men, &c.

The Complaint

Who can that hears or sees but bear a part
To help to bewaile our grievous smart?
Being lately blessed with perfect health,
An also endued with store of wealth,
Nothing afraid our happie state
Should change by any untimely fate:
Our people from the fields come runne,
To bring us news we were undone.
The countrey up against us rises,
Making our goods theire lawfull prize.
Often we trotted from Market to Faire,
And for good beast no money we spare,
To adde to our flood,[1] our herd, our flock,

1 (probably) = flote, a herd of cattle.

That now we were come into a brave stock;[2]
Each year great droves[3] we could well affoard,
Of fatted good Beeves to send a ship-board.
First went[4] our fat, and after our leane,
Next at our Selves they draw their Skeene;[5]
Our Market being spoiled thus on the Land,
And troubles increase as thick as the sand,
Some catcheth the pickax for the hard ground,
Some shovle and spade to make the trench round;
Some constrained to carry the barrow,
While others the house top watch with the sparrow.[6]
To tell all our Grief I mean not here,
Fearing lest some should let fall a teare;
Yet to think upon our settled place,
Whence we were thrust with foul disgrace,
This makes our heart with sorrow spring,
That have heard their mocks and libels sing;
But give such leave in height of their pride
Unto their own ruine fast to ride.
And all that doth against Gods Truth stand,
May fall as ship wrackt on the sand.
God end these troubles, and send peace,
That our estates and friends may increase;
Happily to live, comfortably to die,
On the wings of Faith to God to flie.

2 i.e. we had built up a fine herd of livestock.

3 Herds of cattle driven to the port for export by the drover.

4 i.e. the first victims of the rebels were our fat cattle. The line carries echoes of Jacob's dream of the fat and lean cattle in Genesis 41.

5 Ir. *scian*, dagger, long knife.

6 These lines describe the English settlers defending themselves – digging trenches with pickaxes, shovels and spades, and keeping watch for attackers.

from: A Looking-Glasse of the World:
or,
The Plundred Mans voiage

The Earth is made both firm and sure,
To Man and his heirs for to endure;
With all things moving in wood or field,
Their service unto man doth yeeld.

The stately Horse both swift and strong,
Is guided with a leather thong:
In warre, in peace, seek the world round,
A more usefull creature is not found.

The Cow I can hardly reaise,[7]
How in few words I should her praise;
Of her we find meat for babes and men,
God grant we never want her then.

The Sheep for profit not the least,
But may compare with any beast,
For every yeer a fleece doth spring,
Makes Spinners and Carders[8] merrily sing.

The Goat doth crop the tender tree,
Wherefore keep from thy Nurcerie:[9]
Yet good is both their flesh and milk,
Their skin for gloves well sowe[10] with silk.

The Hogges delight is in the mire,
Bestowe on him a ring of wire,
That he may weare it in his nose,
And will not be proud thereof I suppose.

7 A seventeenth-century spelling of 'rise' – here meaning to arouse oneself to a higher level of feeling or expression.

8 A carder was one who prepared wool for spinning by combing it with a metal comb or 'card'.

9 i.e. where young trees and plants are raised.

10 sewn.

The Dogge waits at his masters heels
When he doth walk abroad the fields:
And when that honest men do rest,
He takes a thief then by the brest.

The Cat doth watch by the wheat mow,
To keep away those we not allow;
As Rat and Mouse with their vermin breed,
That destroys our corn for bread and feed …

[There follow stanzas devoted to wild creatures of all kinds, from the lion to the snail.]

The Frogge that lives in meadow green,
Sometimes more black then yellow seen:
Though the Frog alters with the weather
Let not mens minds change with a feather.[11]

The swelling Toad each man doth fear,
His poisoning breath for to come neer:
But if the Toad be dead and drie,
In the head more pearl saies then I.[12]

The Spider to make threed[13] doth use,
And sets her web in the light to chuse:
Her living chiefly herein lies,
By catching of the heedlesse flies.

Of all the kind of wormes that be,
The Silk-worme chiefest in degree:
For Kings and Queens do think no scorn,
Their work upon them to be worn.

11 i.e. with a puff of wind or for a light or insignificant reason.

12 Many people in the seventeenth century wore amulets or rings containing a toad-shaped stone called a 'toadstone'. Though toads (and the breath of toads) were thought to be poisonous, it was also believed that 'toadstones' could be retrieved from the heads of dead toads. Pain from a bite or sting from any venomous creature was alleviated if the wound was rubbed with a toadstone. See Shakespeare's *As You Like It*, II, 1.

13 thread.

The Louce the quick eye doth espie,
Where he lies couchant[14] secretly:
By chance makes many a stout man shugge,[15]
Well as the begger cloth'd in a patch'd rugge.

In the raging Seas and restlesse floods,
God hath provided for our goods;
Such great varieties of fish,
As any heart of man can wish.

The Oyster without bone or claw,
Commonly we eat them raw;
And chuse them for a breakfast fine,
Being well washt with a cup of wine.

The Crab and Lobster with many feet,
Upon the ground not accounted fleet;[16]
Yet at feasting tables comes in the crowd,
And for daintie dishes are allow'd.

The Sturgeon, Saman, and the Ling,[17]
The Flounder, Plaise, and the Whiting;[18]
These after the Fishers-boat doth dance,
And into *England*, *Spaine*, and *France*.

With the Whale what creature can compare,
For greatnesse in earth, water, or aire?
Man unto man wondring tells
What monsters in the Sea there dwels.

The Sprat and Herring in number great,
We do provide for speciall meat,

14 Lying down. The term comes from heraldry.

15 To shog or shug is to rouse someone from sleep by inflicting pain.

16 swift or nimble.

17 sturgeon, salmon and ling, a sea fish not unlike cod.

18 The placing of emphasis on the second syllable of 'whiting' suggests Hiberno-English pronunciation.

Against the Spring, and time of Lent;
For to eat flesh some have been shent.[19]

The Pike, the Breame, the Roach, the Dace,[20]
The Ele the mud is his chief place;
These are deceived by baited hooks,
Beware Youth of wanton womens looks.

The Otter or the water-dogge,[21]
That lives in rivers, ponds, and bogge,
His tyrannie many a fish doth feel,
For himself is provided a trap of steel.

[There follow stanzas on every kind of bird and insect.]

The Veldenere,[22] Blackbird, and Thrush,
Makes Musick upon every bush:
They sing as well to the churle, or clown,[23]
As he that weares a velvet gowne.

The Lark with joy when it is day,
Up towards Heaven doth take her way:
So should our thoughts first in the morning,
For sleep is but to death a warning …

What commendation with us men,
Which do destroy the little Wren,
Making a sport their lives to spill,
When they are free from doing ill.[24] …

The Waspe loves sweet things as his life,
Yet oft deare byes it with great strife:

19 unwilling. Some Protestants (like all Catholics) were forbidden to eat meat in Lent – which is why sprat and herring were stored (usually in brine) to be eaten in Lent.

20 fresh-water fish.

21 Cf. Ir. *Madra uisce*: 'water dog' or otter.

22 fieldfare – a species of thrush.

23 Both words mean a rustic or low-born peasant.

24 The Irish custom of catching and killing a wren on St Stephen's Day.

The Bee sometimes in fight overcomes,
Robs Orchards and Shops of Pears and Plums.

[There follow stanzas devoted to humans following a multitude of professions and callings from the Goldsmith and the Grosser (who stocks 'out-landish spice') to the Physitian, the Painter (who 'shapeth the Lyon, with Bull and Beare' – presumably on inn signs), the Chimney-sweeper (who uses a holly bush to clean chimneys) and the Barbar (with his 'washball sweet'). The sequence begins with a remarkably non-hierarchical stanza on the human condition.]

The Bud and Blossome on the tree,
So come into the world do we;
By Gods all-disposing power,
Some in tent, and some in tower.

The Gentleman that lives by his Lands,
And sets to work many poore mens hands:
Churlish conditions, he hates them all,
He is courteous, kind, and liberall ...

The Pedler comes with his pack ats back,
Saying, Dame what now do you lack?
See choice of Needles, Pins, Points,[25] and Laces,
And for your little girles I have Bongraces.[26]...

The Printer paper and Inke he finds,
To print the thoughts of many minds:
One age to let another know,
What things hath hapned here belowe ....

Now come three Sergeants to arrest our bones,
And carrie them between hard stones:
Age, Sicknesse, Death, with his sting,
Remember always of this thing.

FINIS

25 Tagged pieces of ribbon or cord used for fastening shoes and clothing.

26 Broad-brimmed hats.

PAYNE FISHER
(1616–**1645**–1693)

Payne Fisher was born in Dorset and educated at both Oxford and Cambridge. Though he enlisted in the army raised by Charles I to fight against the Scots, Fisher changed sides and abandoned the royalists after the king's forces were defeated at Marston Moor in July 1644. When he came to Ireland in July 1645, it was as commanding officer of a small force of troops apparently attached to the Scottish covenanter army led by General Robert Monro. After his adventures in Ireland, Fisher settled in London where he became a successful poet and was appointed poet laureate to Cromwell. His large output includes much verse in Latin and many panegyric poems. At the Restoration, Fisher changed sides again and he is said to have ended his days in poverty. The light-hearted verse letter that follows gives a vivid description of the effects of a rough, overnight voyage on Lough Neagh – the largest lake in Ireland, over seventeen miles in length – on the young officer and his soldiers. The text is taken from a manuscript.

On a dangerous Voyage twixt Mazarine and Montjoy[1]

To my hono^{re}d Freind Ma^{jor} G. L.

Wee had now weighed up our Anchors and hoist sayles,
Whiles Heavens serener breath in whisp'ring gales
Sighed forth our Farwell and, loath to dismisse
Such Freinds, did court us with a parting Kisse.

But oh! this Truce turn'd Tragicall, and Heat
Which we presum'd a Fortune, proved our Fate.
For now the windes gan mutine,[2] and grow wild
Oth' sudden, which before seem'd reconciled.
The wrinckled Ocean gan to loure[3] and shewe
Hir supercilious anger in hir browe.
The Billowes playd at Bandy,[4] and toss't our Barke
Above the clouds, which mounted like a Larke.
The Surges dasht the Heavens as thoe they ment
To wash the face o'th' cloudy Firmament,
And make't more cleare; and truely it made us stare
To see the Water mingle with the Aire.

1 The baronies of Massareene are on the shores of Lough Neagh, as is Mountjoy.

2 mutiny.

3 lour, look dark and threatening (normally only used of gathering storm clouds).

4 a way of playing tennis that is no longer known or practised.

Old Fry that carried a Tempest in his looks,[5] now grew
Madd, and more blustring than those Windes that blew.
You'd think the Boatmen wilde to heare 'um hoope;
This haules out Larboard, t'other flancks the Poope:[6]
That, ha[u]les the Bowling[7] which was scarce made fast
Before a counter-gust ore'whelmd both Mast
And Maine-Yard both;[8] not leaveing us scarce sheet[9]
Enoughe to wipe those teares wee shed to see'it.
Both Card and Compasse faild.[10] The Pilot now
Could doe noe more then hee hat holds the ploughe.
The Master was in his dumpes: the Seamen stood
Like senselesse stones, or statues made of wood.
Our Rudder too (the Bridle of our Shipp)
Quite broak in twaine lay tumbled in the Deepe.
Soe that the Vessell did at Randon[11] run
Threatning hir owne and our destruction.

Thus Fate and Feare beseiged us round about,
That Hope could not get in nor danger out.
Wee cry'ed for succors and lookt every way,
But still the more wee lookt, the lesse wee sawe.
Oft we Implored the windes: but they such noise
And murmuring made, they would not heare our voice.
Oft wee Invokd the Nimphes,[12] but they, poore Elves,
In this sad Pickle could scarce healp them selves.

5 MS reads 'loaks'. Old Fry must be someone known to the poet and the recipient of the poem.

6 Larboard (now known as Port) was the name given to the left side of a ship, the side opposite from starboard. When the stern of a ship is higher than the rest of her because there are cabins there, that area is known as the poop. The poet implies that the crew did not know what they were doing, one placing the ship so that its larboard side was broadside to the gale, another turning the ship so that the wind was at her stern.

7 bowline, a rope designed to keep the sail steady.

8 The main yard is the spar, attached to the main mast, which supports the main sail.

9 sail.

10 A card was a circular piece of stiff board on which were marked the 32 points of the compass.

11 random.

12 The goddesses of the ocean or (in this case) the lough.

Often wee takt[13] about but found how Crosse
The Current, and how vaine our labour was.
Wee fathomed[14] oft but saw no ground was neere,
Noe ground[15] wee saw, alas, but of dispayre.

And now within us did a storme arise
More feirce; whiles from the floudgate of our eyes
The fluent teares fell downe, like showers of Raine,
Striveing to mixe their Water with the Maine.[16]
Our Teares did swell the Tide! Our Sighes each sayle,
Our cryes might cleave the clouds, yet could not quell
The roaring Sea which, car[e]lesse of our moane,
Drowned all cryes and clamors in hir owne.

At length, nights sable Curtaines being undrawne,
The Infant-day appeared in hir first dawne.
The clouds with it began to looke more cleare,
The Sea more calme. Wee now arose to cheere
Our fainting spirits, and to each other speake
A generall joy. Some crept from of[f] the deck,
Some from the Plancks; and all like wormes at last
Crawld from their Crooked Holes, the Storme being past.
The Weather-beate[n] Souldiers who the night did supp
Were all growne Mawe-sick,[17] and did cast it up.
Those Bannick-eating[18] Blew-capps[19] too that deale
In noe other Dialect, then Haver-Meale[20]
Did now disgorge their geere[21] up: with which motion
And workeing of the Waves lookt like a Potion.[22]

13 tacked.

14 took soundings of the depth of the water with a fathom-line.

15 reason, basis (echo, with a double meaning from the previous line).

16 the sea – here the water of the lough.

17 sick in the stomach.

18 Bannock was a cake made of oatmeal or barley mixed with water and cooked on a griddle.

19 The Scots traditionally wore blue caps or bonnets.

20 haver-meal = oatmeal; dialect (here) = local food; oatmeal is the typical, traditional food of the Scots.

21 the rubbish in their stomachs.

22 a dose of liquid medicine.

One spawld,[23] another purged[24] and being inclined
To a loose disease was troubled with the wind.

And truely the wind did trouble most, and there
Was scarce one 'mong us all, but had his share.
Some, voyd of sense, grew giddy; these forgott
Themselves, and took the Bark for Charon's Boat.[25]
Another was soe smear'd with pitch, you might
Had you not knowne him, sweare hee had beene a sprite.[26]
Some sprawling on the Decks were trodden on,
And soe dissfigurd that they scarce were knowne.
Some broak their shancks, some noses, and but few
But either had his head broak or his browe.
In fine, all finely handled were, and such
As seemd to have the least harme, had too much.

Thus Sir, you see how all night long wee weare
Turmoild, and tosst betweene hope and dispayre:
Till pittying Neptune[27] with his Trident did
Calme and controule those blustr'ing winds, which chid,[28]
Retired back to their cavernes, and noe more
Did dare molest us, till wee came a shoare.

23 to spall = to sprawl, stagger or stumble.

24 emptied his bowels.

25 i.e. the boat which conveyed souls of the departed to Hades, in classical mythology.

26 spirit.

27 God of the seas.

28 reprimanded.

JOHN PERROT
(*fl.***1659**–1671)

John Perrot was a convinced Quaker who probably came to Ireland from England in the middle of the seventeenth century. He was a colourful and eccentric figure whose many pamphlets show him to have been, for substantial periods of his life, unbalanced. As an active Quaker, he was imprisoned in Kilkenny, Waterford, Limerick and Dublin as well as in England and on the Continent. In 1656, Perrot set out on a mission to Rome to convert the pope to Quakerism, as a result of which he was questioned by the inquisition and imprisoned in 'The Rome-prison of Mad-men' for a period. He also spent time in the leper colony in Venice. He eventually died in poverty in Jamaica in about 1671. The following text comes from one of Perrot's long visionary poems.

from: A Song for that Assembly[1]

... Thus said the Lord, *Hear*, *Man*, and I'l *demand*,
Who round the *swelling Seas* hath fixt *dry Land*?
Who's he that maketh ev'ry *Fish's way*?
And, who doth *bar* the *Night*, and *open Day*?
Who hath created *Wonders* in the *Deep*?
And who feeds *Worms* which in her bottom *creep*?
Where's *he* who by his *Wisdoms* words or *wishes*,
That's able t'answer me among the *Fishes*?
The *Lempits spaun*,[2] what Man hath seen to *tell*?
And how gain'd she her Cov'ring of a *Shell*?
Who gave *her strength* fast to the *Rock to cleave*,
That no Fish *else* of *life* can her *bereave*?[3]
Can Man this *secret* unseal and unlock,
Whether another *substance* than the *Rock*
Doth she *feed on*? let him in *Wisdom* speak,
What *Instrument* hath she *the Rock* to *break*?
Who knows the *Spaun* which *Cockles & Musles* shed,
And what's the *substance* wherewith it is *fed*?
Who knows *the time* of their Natures *conception*,
And when's the *moment* brought unto *Perfection*?
Who leads the *Wrinckles*[4] over *Mountains* high
Of *craggy Rocks*, which in the *Oceans* lye?

1 'That Assembly' is 'The Congregation in the Valley of Megiddon'.

2 the spawn of the limpet.

3 deprive.

4 winkles, periwinkles.

Who built the *House* which she *bears* on her *back*,
Wherein she's hid, as in a *sealed* Sack?
Her *one Scale* opens and shuts; it's her *Door*,
Wherewith she seals *salt moysture* up in *store*,
That when the *Ebb* her Lodge to *Air* doth *give*,
Till *Flood* returns, she hath enough to *live*.[5]
Was it by *Art* of Wise *Princes or Kings*,
Or, who gave to the *flying Fish* her *wings*?
Which when pursu'd by other *Fishes* great,
That would her *Life destroy*, and *Body eat*,
Therewith in ev'ry *Chase*, *Life* to *defend*,
Doth out of *Natures* Element *ascend*?
Who gave the *Dolphin* her dear *tender Love*,
And made her *swiftest*, which in *Seas* do move?
Who made *two Fishes* Weapons for to *wear*,
Whereby they *swim*, dreadful with *Sword* and *Spear*;
Though being *little*, and in substance *small*,
Yet are a *Terrour* to the mighty *Whale*?
Who makes the *Oyster* gape with *ardent heat*
In *Summer-time*, as if she wanted *meat*?
And whilst yet thus her *shells* stand *open wide*,
Who taught the *Crab-fish* to draw near *her side*,
And with his *claw* a *Stone* therein to *put*,
Whereby to save *her life*, she cannot *shut*,
And thus is made the other *Fishes Bait*,
Which, for the same, takes time to *watch* and *wait*?
Who gave some Fishes *fins*, others *walking leggs*,
And makes some *spaun*, and others to *lay Eggs*?
Who hatches *Tortles Eggs* hid in the *Sand*,
And who sustains their *Life* by Sea and Land?
Who of a *Seed* hath made thee *flesh* and *bone*,
And whereof made I every *precious Stone*?
Of what's compos'd *Earth*, *Trees and ev'ry Plant*?
And which was *first*, *LIGHT*, or the *ADAMANT*?[6]

5 i.e. when the retreating tide exposes her shell to the air, she has enough salt moisture (in her shell) to survive until the tide returns.

6 Adamant is the mineral corundum; however, in the ancient and early modern worlds, the term was used to refer to a hard rock; or it might be a lodestone or magnet. Here it seems to mean the universe as a whole.

Who answers? What, can Man *reveal* to me
The *substance* whereof I compos'd the *Bee*?
Who knows his *Art* which makes the *Honey-comb*?
And, who made *Man* before a *Woman's Womb*?
What's the *Infusion*, who can it *resemble*,
Which at the *Cock's-Crow* makes the *Lyon tremble*?[7]
The same which fills the *Elephant* with *fear*,
When that a *Mouse* before him doth *appear*.
Who taught *Jack-halls*[8] to hunt the *Lyon's prey*,
And *Pilot-fish*, to lead the *Shark* her way?
One knows the *thing*, which to all flesh seems *strange*,
How that *Camelion* her self doth *change*
Into *all Colours*, perfect *White* excepted,
Which by the *Law* for *Man's meat* is rejected.[9]
I bend th'exalted *flames* of *Phœbus* low,[10]
Autumn[11] to usher *Winter's birth* of Snow,
Her *Travel*,[12] as a *Vest*, on Earth doth spread,
Wherein the Night-steps of *Wild-beasts* are read;
Which though the *girdings*[13] of the *Night* conceals,
Day dawned, printed *Lines* to Man *reveals*.
Though *Lions roar*, and *Wolves* do *howl* and *bark*,
Panther, with them I sent to *Noah's Ark*;
A golden thrid[14] I've given with *clear sight*,
To measure the *blind Bats* and *Screech-Owls* flight,
The *Moles* dark paths, a *Laborynth* obscure,
Yet *scrutal*[15] *Worm* doth comprehend it sure ...

7 The lion is said to tremble when it hears a cock crow. The question is, what man-made potion or liquid has the same power?

8 jackals.

9 The chameleon is a lizard-like creature that changes its colour to suit its environment. It is one of the animals labelled as 'unclean' in Lev. 11:30 and therefore something the Jews were forbidden to eat.

10 i.e. God also controls the sun and the seasons.

11 i.e. in the autumn.

12 travail, i.e. winter's action of giving 'birth' to the snow. The word also means the action of travelling.

13 the girdling. The line means that the night-time movements of wild beasts are revealed in the early-morning snow.

14 an (imaginary) thread.

15 an apparently unrecorded word connected with 'scrutiny'; so = scrutinous, searching.

…Who gave the *Wren* her *treble Voice* to sing,
Consorting[16] *Musick* with the *Timbrel*[17] *string*;
And in *much Joy*, sav'd from an *evil chance*,
Makes her *in Summer* in Vine branches *dance*?
The *Red-breast's* shril Notes singing on a *Rock*,
Sounds as a *Shepherd piping* to his *Flock*;
Who gave the *love* which she *bears* in her *breast*,
And *Innocency* for a seat of *rest*?
Who makes the *Thrush* in *Spring-time* to rejoyce,
And gifted her with a *loud chanting Voice*? ...
Who [18]*Black-birds* whistle, which makes *Woods* to ring?
Sweet *Valleys* eccho whilst yet she doth *sing*,
In *Deserts*; who from under *shadows* mute
Raiseth her *Voice* to sing unto the *Lute*?
Who fills the *Nightingale* with *Harmony*,
Her Tune *transcending* all in *Air* that fly?
Who strain'd her *seven strings* unto perfect *tryal*?
Which makes *the Musick* on her well set *Vyal*;[19]
Who makes the *Lark* ascend with *out-stretcht wing*,
A Song of *Melody* on high *to sing*?
Who hath her *Organ* unto *sweet Notes* bound,
And *blows* the *Bellows* for her *Pipe* to sound?
And who hath given unto the *Turtle-Dove*
Her mind of *Chastity* and *pure Love*,
And made her of her *Mate*, so dear a *Lover*,
That chusing *ONE*, she'l never chuse *Another*? ...

16 playing music together.

17 A tambourine-like percussion instrument.

18 i.e. who creates the blackbird's whistle?

19 A viol could have up to seven strings.

KATHERINE PHILIPS
(1632–**1662**–1664)

Katherine Philips, who was born in London of Welsh extraction, became known in England and Wales during the 1650s as a wit and as a poet. She came to Dublin in 1662 and soon attached herself to the court, becoming friendly with the new Lord Lieutenant, the Duke of Ormond, and joining the circle of poets in and around Dublin Castle. Members of this group gave each other mock classical names: Lady Elizabeth Boyle was 'Celimena' for example, Lady Mary Cavendish 'Policrite', Lady Anne Boyle 'Valeria', Sir Edward Dering 'Silvander' and Katherine Philips 'Orinda', known to her admirers, then and ever since, as 'the matchless Orinda'.[1]

Katherine Philips's most famous Dublin achievement was her translation of Corneille's tragedy, *La mort de Pompée* which was staged in the new theatre in Smock Alley.[2] Some of Philips's verse also found its way out of her circle and into the hands of the Dublin bookseller Samuel Dancer who, without permission, included three of her poems – including that which follows – in his *Poems by Several Persons of Quality and Refined Wits* (Dublin, 1663).

The Irish Greyhound[3]

Behold this Creature's form and State,
Which Nature therefore did create;
That to the World might be exprest
That miene[4] there can be in a Beast,
And that we in this shape might find
A Lyon of another kind.
For this Heroick Dog does seem
In Majesty to Rival him,
And yet vouchsafes to Man to shew
Both service and submission too.
By which we this distinction have
That Beast is fierce, but this is brave:

1 *Letters from Orinda to Poliarchus* (London, 1705). The volume contains many detailed observations on literary activity in Dublin between June 1662 and June 1663.

2 For a reconstruction of the first night of *Pompey*, see Christopher Morash, *A History of Irish Theatre 1601–2000* (Cambridge, Cambridge University Press, 2002), pp. 21–9.

3 The dog celebrated here – probably the property of Philips's friend, Lord Orrery – was an example of the very large and very ancient breed of wolfhounds owned by the Irish aristocracy in the early modern period. These dogs nearly died out after the extinction of wolves in Ireland in the eighteenth century but the breed was revived and refined in the nineteenth century. The term 'greyhound' is now used to describe a different breed of dog.

4 mien, strength and beauty of appearance.

This Dog hath so himself subdu'd
That Hunger can not make him rude.[5]
And his behaviour does confess,
True Courage dwells with Gentleness:
With sternest Wolves he dares engage,
And Acts on them succesful rage.
Yet too much Curtesie may chance
To put him out of Countenance.
And when in his opposers' blood
Fortune does make his virtue good,[6]
This Creature from an Act so brave
Growes not more sullen, but more grave.
He would Man's Guard be, not his sport;
Believing he hath ventur'd for 't;[7]
But yet no blood or[8] shed or spent
Can ever make him Insolent.
Few Men of him to doe great things have learn'd,
Or when th'are done, to be so unconcern'd.

5 rough, violent.

6 i.e. when fortune has brought him success …

7 i.e. dared to undertake dangerous tasks for it.

8 either.

SIR WILLIAM TEMPLE
(1628–*c.***1663**–1699)

Sir William Temple and his sister Martha were brought up in Dublin where their father, Sir John Temple, was Master of the Rolls. After time at Cambridge and on the continent, Sir William returned to Ireland for much of the 1650s, living on his estate near Carlow; he was elected MP for Carlow in the Irish parliament of 1661. His sister Martha married Sir Thomas Giffard in Dublin in 1662 but he died a week later and she lived out the remainder of her life in her brother's household – a domineering presence, according to Jonathan Swift, Temple's secretary. The Temple household moved to England in 1663.

Sir William was the most famous diplomat of his age and also a writer of discernment and taste whose essays on many subjects – gardening, poetry and grief as well as economics and political theory – are justly regarded as among the best of the age. His political memoirs are also famous, but his verse is neglected. This ingenious poem may well have been written in Ireland.

On my Lady Giffard's Loory[1]

Of all the questions which the curious raise
Either in search of knowledge or of praise,
None seem so much perplexed or so nice[2]
As where to find the seat of paradise.
But who could once that happy region name,
From whence the fair and charming Loory came?
To end this doubt would give the best advice,
For this was sure the bird of paradise.
Such radiant colours from no tainted air,
Such notes and humour from no lands of care,
Such unknown smells could from no common earth,
From no known climate could receive a birth:
For he alone in these alive outvy'd
All the perfumes with which the phoenix died.

About a gentle turtle's was the size,[3]
The sweetest shape that e'er surprized eyes.
A longish hawked bill, and yellow brown,
A slick black velvet cap upon the crown.

1 lory, a brilliant, parrot-like bird found in south-east Asia.

2 difficult to decide.

3 i.e. the size of a turtle dove.

His back a scarlet mantle cover'd o'er,
One purple sploach[4] upon his neck he wore.
His jetty eyes were circled all with flame;
His swelling breast was, with his back, the same.
All down his belly a deep violet hue
Was gently shaded to an azure blue.
His spreading wings were green, to brown inclin'd,
But with a sweet pale straw-colour were lin'd.
His tail, above was purples mixt with green,
Under, a colour such as ne'er was seen;
When like a fan it spread, a mixture bold
Of green and yellow, grideline[5] and gold.
Thus by fond nature was he drest more gay
Than eastern kings in all their rich array;
For feather much, as well, as flower, outvies
In softness silk, in colour mortal dyes.

But none his beauty with his humour dare,
Nor can his body with his soul compare.
If that was wonder, this was prodigy;
They differ'd as the finest earth and sky.
If ever any reasonable soul
Harbour'd in shape of either brute or fowl,
This was the mansion; metamorphosy
Gain'd here the credit lost in poetry.[6]
No passion moving in a human breast
Was plainer seen, or livelier exprest.
No wit or learning, eloquence or song,
Acknowledg'd kindness, or complain'd of wrong,
With accents half so feeling, as his notes:
Look how he rages, now again he doats;
Brave like the eagle, meek as is the dove,
Jealous as men, like women does he love.
With bill he wounds you sudden as a dart,
Then, nibbling, asks you pardon from his heart.

4 splotch, patch of colour.

5 gridelin, the name of a colour, a pale purple or grey violet; sometimes, a pale red.

6 i.e. Ovid's poetic *Metamorphoses* are unbelievable compared to this transformation.

He calls you back if e'er you go away,
He thanks you if you are so kind to stay.
When you return, with exultation high
He raises notes that almost pierce the sky,
But all in such a language, that we guest,
Though he spoke ours, he found his own the best.

Such a badeen[7] ne'er came upon the stage,
So droll, so monkey in his play and rage;
Sprawling upon his back, and pitching pyes,[8]
Twirling his head, and flurring at the flies.[9]
A thousand tricks and postures would he show,
Then rise so pleased both with himself and you,
That the amaz'd beholders could not say
Whether the bird was happier, or they.

With a soft brush was tipt his wanton tongue,
He lapt his water like a tiger young:[10]
His lady's teeth with this he prick'd and pruned;
With this a thousand various notes he tun'd.
A chagrin[11] fine cover'd his little feet,
Which to wild airs would in wild measures meet.
With these he took you by the hand, his prey
With these he seiz'd, with these he hopt away.
With these held up he made his bold defence,
The arms of safety, love, and violence.

With all these charms Loory endow'd and drest,
Forsaking climates with such creatures blest,
From eastern regions and remotest strands
Flew to the gentle Artemisa's hands;[12]
And, when from thence he gave the fatal start,
Went to the gentle Artemisa's heart;

7 a clown.

8 meaning unclear – competing [in chattering] with magpies?

9 to flurr is to fly up or to fly with whirring or fluttering wings.

10 The lory has bristles on its tongue – and in this is more like an animal than a bird.

11 shagreen, a type of untanned leather with a rough granular surface often dyed green.

12 In Greek mythology, Artemisa was the daughter of Zeus and Leto and the twin sister of Apollo. Here it is a fanciful, classical name for Lady Giffard.

Fed with her hands, and perch'd upon her head,
From her lips water'd, nested in her bed;
Nurst with her cares, preserved with her fears,
And now, alas! embalmed with her tears.
But sure among the griefs that plead just cause,
This needs must be acquitted by the laws:
For never could be greater passion,
Concernment, jealousy, for mistress shown,
Content in presence, and at parting grief;
Trouble in absence, by return relief;
Such application, that he was i'th'end
Company, lover, play-fellow, and friend.

Could I but hope or live one man to find
As much above the rest of human-kind
As this above the race of all that fly,
Long should I live, contented should I die.
Had such a creature heretofore appear'd
When to such various Gods were altars rear'd,
Who came transformed down in twenty shapes
For entertainment, love, revenge, or rapes:
Loory would then have Mercury been thought,[13]
And of him sacred images been wrought:
For between him sure was sufficient odds,
And all th'Egyptian, Gothic, Indian Gods:
Nay, with more reason had he been ador'd
Than Gods that perjur'd, Goddesses that whor'd:
Yet such the greatest nations chose or found,
And rais'd the highest plant from lowest ground.

13 Mercury was the winged messenger god of the classical world.

AMBROSE WHITE
(*fl.*1665)

Almanacs were very popular in seventeenth-century Ireland, though they were so heavily used that few have survived. The astronomical information they contained was calculated for the town in which they were printed, and the body of the almanac contained information likely to be useful to those living in the area – the phases of the moon and the dates of fairs, for instance.

Ambrose White was the first significant publisher of almanacs in Restoration Dublin (Doctor Whalley and Andrew Cumsty being the others). White's 'Astrological Almanack' for Dublin for 1665 is packed with useful advice that reminds one how rural Dublin was at the time: 'To preserve thy health, rise early and walk the fields, especially by running waters. Breakfast: Clarified Whey, Scurvey Grass, Ale and Wormwood Beer'; and 'Cut down timber in the Old of the Moon, and it will not be so subject to rend, nor crack, nor be Worm-eaten'. It is also clear that astrological and astronomical prognostications were as important, for the husbandmen of the day, as long-range weather forecasts. Each month of the almanac's advice was preceded by an appropriate verse.

Verses for the year and for each month of 1665

from: *An Almanack and Prognostication for the year of our Lord 1665 ... calculated according to Art and referred to the Horizon of the Ancient and Renowned City of DUBLIN*

'Tis you bright Stars, that in the fearful Sea[1]
Do guide the Pilot through his purpos'd way;
'Tis your direction that doth commerce give
With all those Men that through the World do live.

January 1665

Make much of them that labour sore.
Love well thy Wife, relieve the poor
To bed betimes, for being there,
It will both Wood and Candle spare.

February 1665

Spend not thy time in fruitless wooing,
Be sure to keep the Plough a going,
For thou wilt find they self more able,
By a Plough going than a Cradle.

1 These introductory verses appear next to the general title. Subsequent verses are printed before each month's entry.

March 1665
Now Sea and Land do will and wish,
For sparing Flesh to feed on Fish,[2]
If Fish be scant and fruit of trees,
Supply that want with Butter and Cheese.

April 1665
Let Cisley look well to her Dairy,
That Cheese be not tough nor Butter hairy[3]
For though some count her office meanly,
It is a fine thing to be cleanly.

May 1665
Rise early now this Month of May
And walk the fields that be so gay,
To hear the Cuckow chant his lay,
The Nightingale and popping Jay.[4]

June 1665
Whilst husband looks abroad what lacks,
Let Wife at home be mending sacks,
Though Ladies they may tear and rend,
Good Huswives make shift and mend.[5]

July 1665
July thou art guilty of much evil,
Thy Hea-cocks make Men & Maids uncivil,
Better no Hay were, yea, nor no Horses,
Than that Maids should be Whores, and after turn nurses.[6]

2 The eating of meat was forbidden during Lent.

3 There are several references to the finding of hairs in butter in texts from seventeenth-century Ireland; this verse suggests that hairs might fall from the heads of dairymaids during the long and tedious business of churning butter by hand. (Irish butter churns were often held firm between the thighs).

4 The popinjay or green woodpecker.

5 The distinction is between fine rich 'ladies' who destroy clothes and hardworking, lower-class 'housewives' who mend them, and know how to make do with what they have.

6 The references are to sexual encounters in the fields during the season of hay-making.

August 1665
Now with all hands your Harvest ply,
Cut down your Oats, reap Wheat & Rie,
Hook up your Pease, Mow down your Barly,
And ply thy work both late and early.

September 1665
Let Wife not gad, but keep at home,
For gadding Wife is worse than none,
Though man the best Husband be alive,
If Wife be bad, he scarce can thrive.

October 1665
If weather serve, thy business ply,
Be sure let not Plough idle lie,
For to get wealth is not amiss,
To use all means that lawful is.

November 1665
To quicken thy spirits and make thy self merry,
Drink now and then a cup of sherry,
But do not make it a common trade,
Lest things abused the worst are made.

December 1665
And to conclude this good old year,
Invite thy neighbours to good cheer,
Let Gates and Doores wide open be,
That rich and poor may enter free,
Let not the Cook or Butler rest,
And hang such churles as will not feast.

RICHARD HEAD
(*c*.1637– **1674**–1686)

Richard Head, one of the most colourful writers of the Irish Restoration period, was born in the North of Ireland. His father was killed in the Rising of 1641 after which the family fled from Carrickfergus to Belfast and on to Devon. Head apparently attended Oxford but left without a degree and became a bookseller in London. He returned to Ireland in about 1660 and wrote an indecent play, *Hic et Ubique or The Humours of Dublin* which was, apparently, performed in a tavern in Dublin. The text of the play, published in 1663, is of great interest for its representation of spoken Hiberno-English and for its extensive, if satirical, portrayal of Dublin characters. Head went on to write the first substantial pornographic novel in English (set mostly in Ireland), *The Miss Display'd* (1673) and many peculiar works of fiction as well as jest books and mock travel books. His most famous book was the semi-autobiographical, *The English Rogue described in the life of Meriton Latroon, a witty extravagant* (1665). Head was an inveterate gambler and seems to have lived as racy and reckless life as his fictional characters. The verse that follows comes from his extraordinary fictional account of the discovery of O Brazeel, an enchanted island off the coast of Ireland. He himself is said to have drowned during a crossing to the Isle of Wight.

A Great Sea-Storm describ'd
which hapned in the discovery of O Brazeel, commonly called the Inchanted Island.

Nothing but *Air* and *Water* is in sight,
And each 'gainst t'other did its force unite.
The blustring Winds let loose did raging fly,
And made the *Water* seem to scale the *Sky*.
Much like to *Libertines* let loose, will know
No Law to guide them, but astray will go.

The Sea, to swell her teeming Womb, brings forth
Wave after *Wave*, and each of greater Birth:
Waves grow to *Surges*, *Surges Billows* turn;
The *Ocean* is all *Tympany*;[1] the *Urn*
Of *Water* is a *Brimmer*;[2] *Neptune* drinks
So full a Cup, it overflows the brinks:
Insulting *Waves*, how durst ye proudly dash
At *Heav'n*, as though its cloudy face you'd wash!

1 A puffed up swelling.

2 A tankard or goblet filled to the brim.

What, is the lower *Water* fully bent
To mix with that above the *Firmament*?[3]
Or by *Invasion* does it go about
To put the Element of *Fire* quite out?[4]

The Sea roll'd up in *Mountains*: O! 'tis such,
That *Penmen-maur's* a Wart,[5] if't be so much.
Which fall again into such hollow *Vales*,
I thought I'd crost the Sea by *Land* o're *Wales*.[6]
And then to add confusion to the *Seas*,
The Sailers speak such *Babel* words as these:
Hale in Main-Bowlin, Mizen Tack-aboard;[7]
A *Language* like a *Storm* to be abhor'd.
I know not which was loudest, their rude Tongues,
Or the big Winds with their whole Cards[8] of Lungs.
So hideous was the noise, that one might well
Fancy himself to be with Souls in Hell,
But that the Torments differ; those Souls are
Punisht with *Fire*, but these with *Water* here.

Our *Helm*, that should our *floating Castle*[9] sway,
We lasht it up, lest it should run away.
Our Ship now under Water seems to Sail,
Like a Toast drown'd within a Tub of Ale.[10]

3 A reference to the Ptolemaic world view which asserted that the earth was the centre of the universe; rain occurred when the waters that were above the sky or 'firmament' overflowed.

4 This line echoes one in 'An Anatomie of the World: the First Anniversary' by John Donne (1573–1631): 'The Element of fire is quite put out.' In the Ptolemaic world view, the earth was surrounded by fire.

5 i.e. the mountainous waves are so huge that they make the real mountains of North Wales (including Penmenmaur) look like an insignificant excrescence.

6 This seems to mean that the poet thinks he has been tossed right over Wales by the waves.

7 These are orders to the seamen to haul in the ropes attached to the sides of the main sail and to bring aboard the ropes attached to the sails on the mast towards the stern.

8 This seems to mean that the winds possessed 'lungs' that could overpower (or 'trump' as in a game of cards) the shouts of the sailors.

9 The ship – so called here because the stern, rising high above the water, could look like a castle.

10 Some drinkers in seventeenth-century England and Ireland used to put a nutmeg, sugar and a piece of toasted bread into a mug of ale.

Our tatter'd Sails did all hang down in pieces,
Like hedge that's hung with Rags, and Beggars fleeces.[11]
Our Tackling crack't,[12] as if it had been made
To assist the *Fidlers*, not the *Boat-swains* Trade.

We pumpt the Ship, but to as little end,
As to repent, yet never to amend:
For all the Water we pumpt out with pain,
The *Sea* with scorn returns, and more again.

The *Guns* on board, design'd for our defence,
Heav'n thundred so, it almost scar'd them thence.
And yet to *Heav'n* for this give thanks we may,
But for its *Lightning* we had had no *day*.

Drinking Salt-water now the Clouds grew sick,
And spewd it down upon our heads so thick,
That 'twixt the low and upper Seas that fell,
The *Ship* a *Vessel* seem'd, and we *Mackrell*
Pickl'd in Brine, and in our Cabins lie,
Souc't up therein for Immortality.[13]

The fear of being drowned, made us wish
Our selves transpeciated[14] into Fish.
Indeed this fear did so possess each one,
All look't like *Shotten-Herring*, or *Poor-John*.[15]
Nay, of our saving there was so much doubt,
The *Pilots* faith began to tack about;
And had he perisht in this doubtful Fit,
His Conscience sure with the same Ship had split;

11 sheepskin rugs.

12 The ropes and other ship's tackle made a cracking sound – as tense with pressure as the strings of a fiddle.

13 i.e. the ship seemed like a tub in which mackerel were pickled – and we, lying soaked in our cabins, seemed destined to die like soused mackerel.

14 change our species from human to fish.

15 A 'shotten' herring is one weakened after spawning and a 'Poor-John' was a type of small cod that had been dried and salted.

For which way into Heav'n his Soul could steer,
Star-board or *Lar-board*, that still cryes *No Neer*?[16]
But we were in great Danger, you will say,
If Seamen once begin to kneel, and pray.
What *Holy Church* ne're could, the *Seas* have done,
Made Seamen buckle to devotion;
And force from them their *Litany*, whilst thus
They whimper out, *Good Lord, deliver us*:
So I pray too, *Good Lord deliver me*
Hence forth from being taught to pray at Sea.

16 Starboard is the right side of a ship and larboard (since 1844 called 'port') the left side of a ship. 'No neer' was an order to the helmsman to keep the ship close to the wind (*The New Practical Navigator*, London, 1807). The ship would be likely to capsize if allowed to swing broadside to the wind.

EDMUND ARWAKER
(*c.*1655–**1686**–*c.*1710)

Edmund Arwaker was educated at Kilkenny College and Trinity College Dublin, and was ordained into the Church of Ireland. He was chaplain to the Duke of Ormond and, later, archdeacon of Armagh. Arwaker was not only the most prolific Irish poet of his age but probably the worst. One of the less absurd offerings from his pen is a poem of enthusiastic greeting for the invention of a device for distilling sea water and so making it drinkable – an invention which, it was thought, would greatly improve life on board ship, and so enable the British to conquer the most distant nations. The poem exudes the frightening optimism that often accompanies man's attempts to 'correct' nature (line 12).

from: Fons Perennis:
A poem on the excellent and useful invention of making sea-water fresh

… You[1] the Twin-Charms of Youth and Beauty give,
A Bliss that few are willing to out-live.[2]
In those soft Streams, distilling from the Sea,
To whose first Knowledge you prepar'd the Way,
The Rough-dull Skin grows smooth and clear as they.
The Sea thus happily improv'd by you,
Does ev'ry day a rising *Venus* shew. …
No more our Ladies to the *Spaw*[3] shall go,
Who to your Streams may greater Blessings owe. …

… The Sailer now to farthest Shores may go,
Since in his Road[4] these *lasting Fountains* flow;
The Sea, corrected by this wondrous Pow'r,
Preserves those now whom it destroy'd before:
No more with Thirst the Feav'rish Sea-man dyes,
The Briny Waves afford him fresh Supplies.
The mighty *Boyle*[5] does by his pow'rful Art,

1 i.e. the distilled sea water.

2 to live without.

3 spa (pronounced 'spaw' in the seventeenth and eighteenth centuries).

4 road = any way from one place to another; it refers, here, to the sea over which the ship passes.

5 The Hon. Robert Boyle (1627–91), son of the great earl of Cork and the most famous Irish scientist of his day, who gave the invention his blessing.

The Ocean to a Well of Life convert;
Whose fame had *Israel's* thirsty Monarch heard,
He had these Springs to *Bethel's* Well preferr'd;
And their Diviner Vertue had (if known)
Excus'd the Risque he made *three Worthies* run:[6]
Had these in *Naaman's* Days been understood,
Jordan's famed Stream had scarce been thought so Good;
Nor wou'd their Influence, more truely Great,
Require he shou'd the Healing Bath repeat.[7]
Boyle, our good Angel, stirs the Sov'reign Pool,
That makes the Hydropic-Leprous[8] Seamen whole,
And now, who first shall put to Sea, they strive,
Since safer there, than on the Shore they live;
And, when to Coasts remote they boldly steer,
Proclaim the Worth of their Preserver there. …

6 II Samuel 23 tells the story of three mighty men who broke through the ranks of the encircling Philistines to bring King David water from the well of Bethlehem. He did not drink the water but offered it to God saying: 'Is not this the blood of the men that went in jeopardy of their lives?'

7 The prophet Elisha instructed Naaman, who wanted to be cured of his leprosy, to bathe himself seven times in the river Jordan. Naaman did so and was healed. II Kings 5.

8 having an insatiable thirst and afflicted with leprosy.

PART II
1690–1739

NAHUM TATE
(1652–**1696**–1715)

Nahum Tate, the son of the poet Faithfull Teate, was born in Dublin. He changed his name from Teate to Tate when he was at Trinity College, from which he graduated in 1672. He later moved to London where he knew all the literary figures of the day and collaborated with Dryden on the second part of *Absalom and Achitophel* (1682). Tate made a living as a poet and dramatist and became Poet Laureate in 1692.

In an interesting and underrated collection of poems, *Miscellanea Sacra: or, Poems on Divine & Moral Subjects Vol I*, Tate explores religious themes with sensitivity and skill. In the poem below, he draws sobering conclusions about mortality from his contemplation of a human skeleton, inviting the reader to admire, with him, 'Nature's Skill' in the construction of the living human body of which the skeleton is a bare reminder.

Upon the Sight of an Anatomy[1]

1

Nay, start not at that *Skeleton*,
'Tis your own Picture which you shun;
Alive it did resemble Thee,
And thou, when dead, like that shalt be:
Converse with it, and you will say,
You cannot better spend the Day;
You little think how you'll admire
The Language of those *Bones* and *Wire*.

2

The *Tongue* is gone, but yet each Joint
Reads Lectures, and can speak to th'Point.
When all your Moralists are read,
You'll find no Tutors like the Dead.

3

If in Truth's Paths those *Feet* have trod,
'Tis all one whether, bare or shod:
If us'd to travel to the Door
Of the Afflicted Sick and Poor,

1 A human skeleton with the bones wired together – used for anatomy classes in medical schools.

Though to the Dance they were estrang'd,
And ne'er their own rude Motion chang'd;[2]
Those Feet, now wing'd, may upwards fly,
And tread the Palace of the Sky.

4

Those *Hands*, if ne'er with Murther stain'd,
Nor fill'd with Wealth unjustly gain'd,
Nor greedily at Honours graspt,
But to the *Poor-Man*'s Cry unclaspt;
It matters not, if in the Myne
They delv'd, or did with Rubies shine.

5

Here grew the *Lips*, and in that Place,
Where now appears a vacant space,
Was fix'd the *Tongue*, an Organ, still
Employ'd extreamly well or ill;
I know not if it cou'd retort,
If vers'd i'th'Language of the Court;
But this I safely can aver,
That if it was no Flatterer;
If it traduc'd no Man's Repute,[3]
But, where it cou'd not Praise, was Mute:
If no false Promises it made,
If it sung Anthems, if it Pray'd,
'Twas a blest *Tongue*, and will prevail
When Wit and Eloquence shall fail.

6

If Wise as *Socrates*, that *Skull*,
Had ever been, 'tis now as dull
As *Mydas*'s;[4] or if its Wit
To that of *Mydas* did submit
'Tis now as full of Plot and Skill,

2 i.e. even if they were never accustomed to dancing, and never moved elegantly.

3 i.e. if it did not slander anyone.

4 Socrates was famed for his wisdom, Midas for his stupid request that everything he touched might be turned to gold, and Machiavelli for his political scheming.

As is the Head of *Matchiavel*:
Proud Laurels once might shade that Brow,
Where not so much as Hair grows now.

7

Prime Instances of Nature's Skill,
The *Eyes*, did once those Hollows fill:
Were they quick-sighted, sparkling, clear,
(As those of Hawks and Eagles are,)
Or say they did with Moisture swim,
And were distorted, blear'd, and dim;
Yet if they were from Envy free,
Nor lov'd to gaze on Vanity;
If none with scorn they did behold,
With no lascivious Glances rowl'd:
Those Eyes, more bright and piercing grown,
Shall view the Great Creator's Throne;
They shall behold th'*Invisible*,
And on Eternal Glories dwell.

8

See! not the least Remains appear
To shew where Nature plac'd the *Ear*!
Who knows if it were Musical,
Or could not judge of Sounds at all?
Yet if it were to Council bent,[5]
To Caution and Reproof attent,
When the shrill Trump shall rouse the Dead,
And others hear their Sentence read;
That Ear shall with these Sounds be blest;
Well done, and *Enter into Rest*.

5 i.e. if it listened to wise advice.

GEORGE WILKINS
(1674–**1699**–?)

George Wilkins was born in Lisburn, County Antrim and educated at Trinity College Dublin. He was ordained into the Church of Ireland and eventually became rector of Blaris, a parish on the border between the counties of Antrim and Down. In February 1724, while holding this living, Wilkins preached the sermon at the funeral of Sir John Rawdon, father of the first Earl Moira – presumably his patron at the time. *The Chace of the Stagg*, written when Wilkins was a young man, is an impressive example of early Dublin verse printing; it is also a lively and entertaining piece that contains accounts of feasting, lovemaking and stag hunting on a large (presumably) Irish estate and is the first substantial Irish poem in English on the 'noble' art of stag-hunting. It also contains a rare description of a storm over the land rather than at sea. Since the poem was dedicated to Mary Somerset, Duchess of Ormond (1665–1733), Wilkins was presumably hoping that it would bring him some ecclesiastical preferment, but there is no record of this.

from: The Chace of the Stagg: a descriptionary poem

... At length, a mighty Stagg that sleeping lay
Ore-heard the noise, and found it bent[1] his way,
Arose, and staring round him listning stood
With prickt up ears, to catch the sound that rode
Upon the breezes that towards him flew,
Which instinct taught him did his Life persue;
He shoke himself, then starting from his Lodge,
He issu's forth among the Men and Dogs,
Swift as a bolt that from the Clouds breaks forth
Or hasty Tempests from the stormy North,
A gliding Swallow cannot pass more free
Or move the grass with gentler touch than he;
Scarce can the course of nimble footed sight
Keep equal pace with his impetuous flight;
All now observe him bounding o'er the Mead,
Snuffing the air, and tossing up his head
He bears away.[2] ————
His armed brow and Stately neck he shews;
Turning he views, and gazes on his foes;

1 i.e. was coming. The poet has earlier described the huntsmen and hounds setting out for the hunt and the baying of the hounds.

2 i.e. changes direction. The half-line rules in lines 17 and 24 are in the original printing.

Like two old Trees his lofty horns appear,
Whose wide extended Arms themselves do rear
Above the rest, and overlook the Wood
As if to shield the Forrest where they stood….

But see[3] ————
What adverse chance on all our pleasure waits;
The shiny Glory of the day retreats;
Big-bellied Clouds come marching up apace,
And all the beauties of the Sun deface;
In long array, charged front to front[4] they low'r,
And thro' their airy Empire justling scow'r;
The labouring hulks their folded doors do rend,
And, like torn Bombs, fraught with dire mischief send
Bolts, and red lightnings darting from above.[5]
Folded in sheets, and curling thro' the Grove,
Quick thro' the sky the nimble Lightning shone,
'Tis here—'tis there,—and everywhere,—and gone,—
Encountring Whirlwinds[6] rattle along the Air,
And struggling Tempests make promiscuous[7] War;
The splintering Oaks cleft by the Thunder fly,
And huge extended trunks spread o're the champain[8] lye
To sheltring Covert Beasts for succour run,
But far away by the wild tempest blown,
They sidling strive, and bear against the blast,[9]
Like tacking Ships by adverse winds opprest.
Large pelting hail in dashing Showers falls,
And bouncing o're the Plain along it rolls;
O're the rough Lake the broken whirlwinds sweep,
Furrowing its face and plowing up the deep.

3 This passage comes towards the end of the poem as the huntsmen are returning home having killed the stag.

4 i.e. in a long line, as if in military formation and ready to attack.

5 i.e. it is as if heavily laden ships of burden were bursting open doors in their sides and sending down harmful [thunder-]bolts like damaged shells, and darting red lightning from above.

6 winds whirling from opposite directions – 'counter' to each other.

7 random. i.e. violent winds struggle against each other indiscriminately.

8 field, ground.

9 i.e. they strive not to be blown sideways, and they lean against the wind.

Th'enchaft[10] billows surge with surly roar,
And with white frothy anger lash the shore;
And now the pleasure of the day is lost,
The Chace is broke, their noble pastime crost; …

10 (figuratively) heated.

DOROTHY SMITH
(*fl.*1701)

The arrival in Dublin of the new Lord Lieutenant of Ireland, Laurence Hyde first earl of Rochester (1642–1711), in September 1701 was marked by the appearance in print of two poems of welcome by otherwise unknown Dublin poets, Dorothy Smith and Bartholomew Williams. Williams's Pindaric ode celebrating the occasion is extraordinary – full of infelicitous images and awkward vocabulary. Dorothy Smith's poem, on the other hand, though it contains some surprising images, is fresh and lively in its depiction of Nature's imagined response to the arrival of the Lord Lieutenant. Her dedication to Lord Rochester, however, contains the following peculiar passage:

> … And if there be [in the poem] any Newness of Thought, or Softness of Expression, worthy your Notice; 'tis all the Authress cou'd have Aim'd at: Let Elevation and Sublimity, be the Praise of Men's Ætherial Fancy, Our Sex are content to creep below, with Tenderness and Purity; which indeed, is the peculiar Nature of Pastoral Verse. To be low and Artless is a Beauty, when we wou'd make Nature Shine out. Which way, I have followed as near as I cou'd, and have rather chose to write after this manner, because, Pastorals are more suitable to a Womans Feeble and Enervate Muse … (Sig A4v)

Despite her assertions of lowness, artlessness, feebleness and enervation, modern readers will find Mrs Smith's poem entertaining, imaginative and energetic – though its imagery is eccentric, its logic muddled and its prosody irregular. The poem is a long one and the passages that follow have been chosen because they are among the most lively. The text contains, even for its time, an unusually high number of initial capital letters.

from: The Shepherds JUBILEE or, a Pastoral Welcome,

To his excellency the Earl of Rochester, etc. on his arrival in Ireland, written by Mrs Dorothy Smith.

… Look round! How all Things now begin to smile,
Since his Arrival on our Happy Isle!
See, How Creation's Face Enlivn'd seems!
And Pregnant Earth with Fair Abundance Teems.
See, see, the Plains, and Groves New Liveries wear!
And Second Spring Through all the Fields appear.[1]
An Universal Joy in Nature's seen;
The Vales are Spangl'd, and the Mountains green.
The Gurgling Brooks and Sprouting Fountains Play,
While Tumbling Rivers, Swell with Joy the Sea.

1 a poetic liberty since Lord Rochester arrived in the month of September.

The Whistling Winds breath forth their Softest Airs,
And ev'ry Leaf its Jocund Sympathy declares.
The Browzing Herds their Lowing Mirth display;
While on the steepy Cliffs, the Frisking Lambkins Play.
The Chearful Birds too, with Unskilful Notes
Assemble all, and stretch their warbling Throats.
The Liquid Fry[2] above the Liffee leap,
Bask in the Sun, and strive to quit the Deep.
Behold *Aurora*! Clad in all her Radiant Beams;
And Sable Night, with dusky Twilight Gleams!
    Come, Shepherds come; Your Pipes and Voices Raise,
    To Glad the Great Enliv'ner of your Lays.[3]

The Mournful Swans, that Haunt the Loughs and Springs,
Their Ditty's Change, and clap their Joyful Wings.
Progne,[4] no longer Chirps upon the Chimney Tops,
But Trills below, and through the hedges Hops.
Nay, Philome[5] forgets her wonted Strains,
And not in Juggings,[6] on her Thorn complains,
But Soars aloft, and like the Lark in Air,
Chants her sweet Carrols forth, to charm the Ear.
The dismal Raven, and the Birds of Night
No more, with Discord now, the Dying Fright.
Their Dire ungrateful Screams, to Tunes are turn'd,
And Songs are sung, where Lovers Rag'd and Mourn'd.
Thy Presence, has these Wonders wrought, and more!
All Nature owns, thy Influencing Pow'r;
Yields to thy Will, and takes from thence her Charms;
While thy Creation, Nature's self Alarms.
    Come Shepherds, come; Your Pipes and Voices Raise,
    To Glad the Great Creator of your Lays.

2 young fish.

3 The echoic refrain suggests that Mrs Smith was familiar with Spenser's 'Epithalamium'.

4 a poetic name for a swallow.

5 the nightingale.

6 jugging = (of a nightingale or other songbird) to utter a sound like 'jug'.

The very Forrest too, Regales your Sense,[7]
And now, at thy Approach, Sends Tribute thence.
The Bramble, Thorn, wild Jessamin,[8] and Rose,
The Fragrant Honours of the Wood disclose.
Oaks Gum Distil,[9] and Fir-trees Balm[10] afford,
And spreading Palms, with Racy[11] Wines are Stor'd.[12]
Poplars and Cedars bend their Leafy Heads;
While Blooming Lillies, spring[13] in Marshy Beds.
Nay, all the Flowry wildness of the Ground,
Opens to thee, and spreads its Odors round.
Courting thy Smell, to take with them Repast;[14]
A Treat is furnish'd out, at Natures Cost.
For thou'rt the only Friend, the welcome Swain,
The Fields, the Birds and Spring wou'd Entertain.
   Come, shepherds, come; Your Pipes and Voices Raise,
   To Glad the Sovereign Lord of all your Lays.

For thee, the Satyrs[15] and the Woodland Fawns
Make Holyday, through all the Verdant Lawns.
For thee the Nerieds,[16] and the water Gods,
Sport on the Banks, and Revel on the Floods.
In Rings, for thee, Dryads[17] and Faires [*sic*] Dance,
And by their Nightly Mirth, thy Fame Advance.
   Come Shepherds, come, Your Pipes and Voices raise
   To Glad the Great Restorer of your Lays.

7 i.e. provides your senses with a feast.

8 jasmine, a climbing shrub with fragrant, white flowers.

9 Probably a reference to the oil or gum distilled from the acorns of the oak tree.

10 aromatic resin naturally secreted by fir trees.

11 A 'racy' wine is one with a distinctively strong, piquant taste or odour.

12 There were palm trees in seventeenth-century England and Ireland, and a fermented drink was made from palm juice in eighteenth-century England; but the word also carries Biblical resonance.

13 i.e. spring into growth.

14 food, a meal. This extraordinary passage seems to mean that the woods are using their choicest aromas to entice the Lord Lieutenant to join them in a feast – he being (lines following) the only friend to nature that the natural world would entertain.

15 goat-footed demi-gods of the woods in classical mythology.

16 goddesses of the river and sea in classical mythology.

17 mythological nymphs who live in trees, particularly oak trees.

Then Sing, ye Winds, and play the Rustling Trees,
Laugh all ye Brooks; and Smile ye swelling Seas,
Bloom all ye Meads, and spread your Flowry Scene;
Sweat[18] all ye Woods, and show your Vernal Green.
Revel ye water-Gods, and Bask ye scaly Fry;
Bubble each Spring, until your Fountain's Dry.
Low all ye Herds, and Bleat ye Tripping Flocks;
Pipe all ye Swains, and Eccho all ye Rocks.
Chant all ye Birds, and fill the Earth with Glee;
For this is Nature's Glorious Jubilee.
  Come, Shepherds, come; Your Pipes and Voices Raise,
  To Glad the Great Maintainer of your Lays.

As Green the Trees, as Trees the Fields Adorn,
As Mast[19] the Oak, as Bearded Ears the Corn,
As Dates the Palm-Tree, or as Sloes the Thorn,
As Moon the Night, or Sun the Risi[n]g Morn.
So does his Virtue all his Actions Grace,
And by Transparence[20] Gloss his Noble Race.
  Come, Shepherds, come; Your Pipes and Voices Raise,
  To Glad the Great Preserver of your Lays. …

… While ranging Bees, Riffle Melliflous Flow'rs,
And Heav'n delights in Incense, Earth in Showr's,
While Finny Fish are to the Deep confin'd,
And Corn and Seas are Ruffl'd by the Wind,
While the full Bowl's the Bacchanalian's Joy,
While Men are Fickle, and the Women coy;
Let Great Alexis[21] Praise, the Woods Declare,
And ev'ry Tree, his Branching Virtues bear. …

… Lean Dearth a Stranger to our Huts shall be,
And we no more, Wars Devastation See.

18 The implication is that the green leaves are the 'sweat' produced by trees in the spring.

19 The fruit of beech, oak, chestnut, and other woodland trees, especially when used as food for pigs.

20 This seems to suggest that the fact that his lordship's qualities can be seen through his actions helps the poet understand the nobility of his background.

21 i.e. let the woods declare their praise of the great Lord Rochester.

Your Milky Kine,[22] shall come Safe home at Night;
And at your Doors, unlade their sweepy[23] Freight.
Goats on the Summets, shall securely Feed,
And Fleecy Flocks, no Prowling Spoilers Dread. …

… On this Occasion, from all Parts Resort,
And to Alexis, Pay your Rural Court.
Cull all the Gardens, and the Blooming Fields;
And bring the Choicest Flow'rs that Autumn yields.
Rob ev'ry Bank, and Ravish ev'ry Bed
To make a Garland for Alexis Head.
Collect *Hyblæan*[24] Sweets to Scent the Air,
And thus a Solemn Festival Prepare.
A Table Spread, with *Ceres*[25] Blessings Crown'd;
And let, with Luscious Plenty, Mirth Abound.
Bring Ripn'd Fruits, and Baskets Load
With Rustick Dainties, for Delight and Food.
The Peach, the Apricock, and Pear Provide,
And turn the Nect'rines on their Tempting side.
Filberts[26] and Chestnuts of a Nut-Brown Hue,
And Sloes that have not lost their Frosty Blue.
Squeeze the swell'd Grape, and Press the Juicy Plumb,
Until the Sprightly Bev'rage Flowing come;
Then, Bumpers fill, of what shall please you Best;
And let *Alexis* Health Proclaim the Feast.
In Beechen Bowls[27] Carouse, and Quaff around
The Chearful Juice; till All, in Joy, are Drown'd,
And his Repeated Name, the Plains Resound.
Come, Shepherds, come; Your Pipes and Voices Raise
To Pay the Tuneful Tribute of your Lays. …

22 cows.

23 characterized by sweeping movement or form. The reference seems to be to the swaying udders full of milk.

24 of honey.

25 Ceres was the Roman goddess of pastoral pursuits and crop-growing, but it is worth noting that this poem appeared at the time of autumnal festivals of 'Harvest Home' in the settler community.

26 hazel nuts.

27 madders (Ir. *meadar*).

JONATHAN SWIFT
(1667–**1710**–1745)

Though Swift was born and educated in Ireland – and indeed, passed most of his life the country – he liked to think of himself as an Englishman and visited London for extended periods in the first years of the eighteenth century. During these years, he tried his hand at several different forms of writing, including the imitation of Virgil's Georgics that follows. The poem, which first appeared in *The Tatler* in October 1710, was much admired by Swift's friends and – as he made clear when writing to Esther Johnson ('Stella') in Dublin – by Swift himself. The 'city' in which the poem is set is London.

A Description of a City Shower

Careful Observers may foretell the Hour
(By sure Prognosticks) when to dread a Show'r:
While Rain depends,[1] the pensive Cat gives o'er
Her Frolicks, and pursues her Tail no more.
Returning Home at Night, you'll find the Sink[2]
Strike your offended Sense with double Stink.
If you be wise, then go not far to Dine,
You'll spend in Coach-hire more than save in Wine.
A coming Show'r your shooting Corns presage,[3]
Old Aches[4] throb, your hollow Tooth will rage.
Sauntring in Coffee-house is *Dulman* seen;
He damns the Climate and complains of Spleen.

Mean while the South, rising with dabbled Wings,
A Sable Cloud a-thwart the Welkin[5] flings,
That swill'd more Liquor than it could contain,
And, like a Drunkard, gives it up again.
Brisk *Susan* whips her Linen from the Rope,
While the first drizzling Show'r is born aslope:

1 is imminent.

2 sewer (beneath the house) or cesspool (often in the garden).

3 i.e. shooting pains in your corns (hard growths on the toes) indicate that the shower is coming.

4 Pronounced, in the early eighteenth century, as a disyllable: 'aitches'.

5 the sky; the couplet means that a dark cloud, arising from the rain-soaked south, covers the sky.

Such is that Sprinkling which some careless Quean[6]
Flirts[7] on you from her Mop, but not so clean:
You fly, invoke the Gods; then turning, stop
To rail; she singing, still whirls on her Mop.
Not yet the Dust had shun'd th'unequal Strife,
But, aided by the Wind, fought still for Life;
And wafted with its Foe by violent Gust,
'Twas doubtful which was Rain and which was Dust.
Ah! where must needy Poet seek for Aid,
When Dust and Rain at once his Coat invade;
His only Coat, where Dust confus'd with Rain
Roughen the Nap,[8] and leave a mingled Stain.

Now in contiguous[9] Drops the Flood comes down,
Threat'ning with Deluge this *Devoted*[10] town.
To Shops in Crouds the daggled[11] females fly,
Pretend to cheapen goods,[12] but nothing buy.
The Templar[13] spruce, while ev'ry Spout's abroach,[14]
Stays till 'tis fair, yet seems to call a Coach.
The tucked-up Sempstress walks with hasty Strides,
While Streams run down her oil'd Umbrella's Sides.
Here various Kinds, by various Fortunes led,
Commence Acquaintance underneath a Shed.
Triumphant Tories and desponding Whigs[15]
Forget their Fewds, and join to save their Wigs.
Box'd in a Chair[16] the Beau impatient sits,
While Spouts run clattering o'er the Roof by Fits,

6 hussey, housemaid.

7 flicks.

8 the surface of the cloth.

9 continuous.

10 doomed.

11 sprinkled.

12 i.e. to bargain for goods.

13 law student.

14 streaming with water – like a cask that has been broached.

15 The Earl of Oxford's Tory ministry had ousted the Whig government a few weeks before this poem appeared.

16 sedan chair.

And ever and anon with frightful Din
The Leather sounds; he trembles from within.
So when *Troy* Chair-men bore the Wooden Steed,
Pregnant with *Greeks* impatient to be freed,
(Those Bully *Greeks*, who, as the Moderns do,
Instead of paying Chair-men, run them thro'),
Laoco'n struck the Outside with his Spear,
And each imprison'd Hero quaked for Fear.[17]

Now from all Parts the swelling Kennels[18] flow,
And bear their Trophies with them as they go:
Filth of all Hues and Odours seem to tell
What Street they sail'd from, by their Sight and Smell.
They, as each Torrent drives, with rapid Force,
From *Smithfield* or St. *Pulchre's*[19] shape their Course,
And in huge Confluent join at *Snow-Hill* Ridge,
Fall from the *Conduit*[20] prone to *Holborn-Bridge*.
Sweepings from Butchers Stalls, Dung, Guts, and Blood,
Drown'd Puppies, stinking Sprats, all drench'd in Mud,
Dead Cats, and Turnip-Tops come tumbling down the Flood.[21]

17 For the story of the Trojan horse and Laocoön, see Virgil's *Æneid* II, 40–56.

18 gutters.

19 St Sepulchre's Church in Holborn was next to Smithfield, the London meat market; rubbish and offal from the market was thrown into the gutters that flowed into the notorious Fleet Ditch which itself joined a filthy watercourse called Snow Hill stream. Holborn Bridge spanned Fleet Ditch.

20 The Great Conduit was a man-made underground channel that brought drinking water from Tyburn into the city of London.

21 Swift wrote a note explaining that he intended the last three lines of the poem – deliberately rhymed as a triplet and in 'licentious' six-stressed Alexandrines – to be seen as parody of the lazily-written verse of the time. However, modern critics view the lines as powerful and effective.

THOMAS PARNELL
(1679–**1713**–1718)

Thomas Parnell was born in Dublin, educated at Trinity College and ordained into the Church of Ireland. In 1706, he was appointed archdeacon of Clogher and in 1716 became vicar of Finglas, near Dublin. He visited London frequently and became friendly with Swift, Pope and other members of the Scriblerus Club. Alexander Pope, who edited Parnell's verse for publication after his death, described the poem that follows as one of 'the most beautiful things I have ever read' (*The Correspondence of Alexander Pope* ed. George Sherburn (Oxford: Clarendon Press, 1956), I, 396).

from: Health, an Eclogue

Now early Shepherds o'er the Meadow pass,
And print long Foot-steps in the glittering Grass;
The Cows neglectful of their Pasture stand,
By turns obsequious to the Milker's Hand. …

Here wafted o'er by mild *Etesian*[1] Air,
Thou Country *Goddess*, beauteous *Health*! repair;
Here let my Breast thro' quiv'ring Trees inhale
Thy rosy Blessings with the Morning Gale.[2]
What are the Fields, or Flow'rs, or all I see?
Ah! tastless all, if not enjoy'd with thee.

Joy to my Soul! I feel the *Goddess* nigh,
The Face of Nature cheers as well as I;
O'er the flat Green refreshing Breezes run,
The smiling Dazies blow[3] beneath the Sun,
The Brooks run purling down with silver Waves,
The planted Lanes rejoice with dancing Leaves,
The chirping Birds from all the Compass rove
To tempt the tuneful Echoes of the Grove:

1 The 'Etesian' winds are the winds that (in Mediterranean countries) blow from the northwest for about forty days every summer; they are thought to give relief from the summer heat.

2 i.e. a gentle breeze.

3 flower.

High sunny Summits, deeply shaded Dales,
Thick Mossy Banks, and flow'ry winding Vales,
With various Prospect[4] gratify the Sight,
And scatter fix'd Attention in Delight.

Come, Country *Goddess*, come, nor thou suffice,
But bring thy Mountain-Sister, *Exercise*.
Call'd by thy lively Voice, she turns her Pace,
Her winding Horn[5] proclaims the finish'd Chace;
She mounts the Rocks, she skims the level Plain,
Dogs, Hawks, and Horses, crowd her early Train;
Her hardy Face repels the tanning Wind,
And Lines and Meshes[6] loosely float behind.
All these as Means of Toil the Feeble see,
But these are helps to Pleasure join'd with thee.

Let *Sloth* lye softning 'till high Noon in Down,
Or lolling fan her in the sult'ry Town,
Unnerv'd with Rest; and turn[7] her own Disease,
Or foster others in luxurious Ease:
I mount the Courser,[8] call the deep mouth'd Hounds,
The Fox unkennell'd flies to covert Grounds;
I lead where Stags thro' tangled Thickets tread,
And shake the Saplings with their branching Head;
I make the Faulcons wing their airy Way,
And soar to seize, or stooping strike their Prey;
To snare the Fish I fix the luring Bait;
To wound the Fowl I load the Gun with Fate.
'Tis thus thro' change of Exercise I range,
And Strength and Pleasure rise from ev'ry Change.
Here beautious Health for all the Year remain,
When the next comes, I'll charm thee thus again.

4 differing vistas, views.

5 The hunting horn being blown or 'winded' as air is forced through it.

6 i.e. snares for catching wild animals and birds.

7 alter, amend.

8 stallion, powerful horse.

Oh come, thou *Goddess* of my rural Song,
And bring thy Daughter, calm *Content*, along,
Dame of the ruddy Cheek and laughing Eye,
From whose bright Presence Clouds of Sorrow fly:
For her I mow my Walks, I platt my Bow'rs,[9]
Clip my low Hedges, and support my Flow'rs;
To welcome her, this Summer Seat I drest,
And here I court her when she comes to Rest;
When she from Exercise to learned Ease
Shall change again, and teach the Change to please. …

9 i.e. intertwine the branches of growing shrubs to make bowers.

JAMES WARD
(1691–**1718**–1736)

James Ward was a contemporary of Swift's friend Thomas Sheridan, both at school in Dublin and at Trinity College, from which both men graduated in 1711. Like Sheridan, Ward was ordained into the Church of Ireland and he eventually (1726) became Dean of Cloyne. As Ward makes clear, his poem on Dublin's great public park, the Phoenix Park, was heavily influenced by two earlier topographical poems, 'Cooper's Hill' by the (Dublin-born) Sir John Denham (1643) and Alexander Pope's 'Windsor Forest' (1713). The following extracts are intended to give an idea of the scope of this first substantial example of a topographical poem set in Ireland.

from: *Phoenix* Park[1]

... Shall *Cooper's-hill* majestick rise in Rhyme
Strong as its Basis, as its Brow sublime,
Shall *Windsor* Forrest win immortal Praise,
It self outlasting in its Poets Lays,
And thou, O *Phoenix* Park! remain so long
Unknown to Fame, and unadorn'd in Song? ...

What Scene more lovely, and more form'd for Bliss,
What more deserves the Muse's Strain than this?
Where more can boundless Nature please, and where
In Shapes more various, and more sweet appear?

Now when the Centre of the Wood is found,
With goodly Trees a spacious Circle bound,
I stop my wandring—while on ev'ry Side,
Glades op'ning to the Eye, the Grove divide,
To distant Objects stretch my lengthen'd View,
And make each pleasing Prospect charm anew. ...

Deep in the Vale old *Liffy* rolls his Tides,
Romantick Prospects crown his rev'rend Sides;[2]
Now thro' wild Grotts, and pendant Woods[3] he strays,
And ravish'd at the Sight, his Course delays,

1 Phoenix Park, to the west of Dublin, was laid out as a public park in the reign of Charles II.

2 Phoenix Park was larger in the seventeenth century than it is today and the Liffey then flowed through – rather than as it flows today, alongside – the park.

3 i.e. through wild grottos and past low-hanging trees.

Silent and calm—now with impetuous Shock
Pours his swift Torrent down the steepy Rock;
The tumbling Waters thro' airy Channels flow,
And loudly roaring, smoak, and foam below.

Fast by his Banks stands, high above the Plain,
A Fabrick rais'd in peaceful *Charles*'s reign,[4]
Where vet'ran Bands, discharg'd from War, retire,
Feeble their Limbs, extinct their martial Fire:
I hear methinks, I hear the gallant Train,[5]
Recount the Wonders of each past Campaign:
Conquests, and Triumphs in my Bosom roll,
And *Britain*'s Glory fills my wid'ning Soul:
Here blest with Plenty, and maintain'd at Ease,
They boast th'Adventures of their youthful Days;
Repeat exhausted Dangers o'er again,
And sigh to speak of faithful Comrades slain.
Silent the list'ning Audience sit around,
Weep at the Tale, and view the Witness Wound:
What mighty Things each for his Country wrought
Each tells,—and all how bravely *Marlbro*' fought.[6]

There, o'er wide Plains, my lab'ring Sight extends,
And fails itself e'er the long Landskape ends:
Where Flocks around the rural Cottage seen,
Brouze the young Buds, or graze the tufted Green;
And Fields bespread with golden Crops appear,
Ensuring Plenty for the following Year. ...

There the broad Ocean spreads his Waves around,
With anchor'd Fleets a faithful Harbour crown'd:
By whose kind Aid we num'rous Blessings share,
In Peace our Riches, and our Strength in War.
While thus retir'd, I on the City look,

4 The Royal Hospital at Kilmainham, founded to provide a home for retired soldiers, had been completed in 1674, during the reign of Charles II.

5 group of people, in this case of old soldiers.

6 John Churchill (1650–1722), duke of Marlborough, commander of the English and Dutch forces during the War of the Spanish Succession (1704–13).

A Groupe of Buildings in a Cloud of Smoak;
(Where various Domes for various Uses made,
Religion, Revels, Luxury, and Trade;
All undistinguish'd in one Mass appear,
And widely diff'ring are united here);
I learn her Vice and Follies to despise,
And love that Heav'n which in the Country lies.
The Sun in his Meridian mounted high,
Now warns me to the covert Bow'r to fly;
Where Trees officious croud about my Head,
And twisted Woodbine forms a fragrant Shade.
No noisy Ax thro' all the Grove resounds,
No cruel Steel the living Branches wounds:
Rev'rend in Age the wide-spread Beech appears,
The lofty Oak lives his long Date of Years.

Here careless on some mossy Bank reclin'd,
Lull'd by the murm'ring Stream, and whistling Wind;
Nor poys'nous Asp I fear, nor savage Beast,
That wretched Swains in other Lands infest:
Fir'd with the Love of Song, my Voice I raise,
And woo the Muses to my Country's Praise.

JOHN WINSTANLEY(?)
(1677–**1718**–1750)

Ringsend, now a suburb of Dublin, was a rather rough seaside village in the early-eighteenth century, cut off from the city at high tide. However it boasted fine taverns and a good beach and was a favourite place for excursions from Dublin – particularly for women who hoped that stroking the captive dolphin, Jenny, would bring them an easy childbirth and good luck. It is not clear whether the bantering burlesque that follows – first published in January 1718 at the request of Jenny's 'lamenters' – was the work of John Winstanley himself or of one of his poetaster friends. It is one of the entertaining Dublin poems later included in his anthology *Poems Written Occasionally by John Winstanley ... interspers'd with many others ... by Several Ingenious Hands* (Dublin, 1742).

An ELEGY on the much lamented Death of JENNY the FISH, who departed this Life at *Ring's-End* the 19th of *January*, 1718

If Ladies weep when petted Lap-dogs die,
And Birds expiring make the Misses cry;
What Grief may be expected in the Town,
When it is told, that *Rings-end Jenny's* gone?
Long *Puppet-Shews*[1] deserted were by Wits;
She was the sole Amusement of our *Citts*;[2]
But, *now she's gone*, their chief Diversion's fled,
And Time, like *Jenny*, on their Hands lies dead.
We deem'd (delighted with the earthly Scene)
She would, with us, a longer Space remain:
Howe'er, at first, her Landing on our Shore,
We dreaded; now her Exit we deplore.
No sure Presage of Evil, as we thought,
But rather Blessing to our *Isle* she brought.
A *happy Omen* to our Coasts she came,
Her leaving us too soon, is all in her we blame.
To guard us from *Rebellion* and *Invasion*
She came, nor left us while there was Occasion:
As Evils some strange Monsters have pursu'd,
So others oft appear in Lands for Good.

1 A popular street entertainment in eighteenth-century Dublin
2 city-dwellers.

How much did stroaking *Jenny*'s back dispose
To *Easy Birth*, and help the *Mother*'s Throws?[3]
Let those her *Virtues*, who have try'd, proclaim,
And Infants yet unborn shall praise her Name.
In love to Human-kind she landed here,
Against the last, (a bad Child-bearing Year.)
Oh! never may the like return again!
For *Jenny* best of *Midwives*, never can.
Had *Jenny* on *Egyptian* Coast appear'd,
In ancient Times they had her Form rever'd;
Rais'd Fanes[4] in Honour; great *Lucina*'s[5] Name,
Had only now the Second been in Fame.
Their *Dogs* and *Cats* no more had been obey'd;
So fine a *Fish* had their Devotion sway'd.
So soft! so sleek! so beautifully plump!
Nine foot, at least, in length from Nose to Rump:
Spotted it's Skin, reflecting to the Eye,
The Green and Azure of the Sea and Sky;
Divinely mixt; no Bird or Beast e'er shew'd,
A Neck so finely turn'd all Mouths allow'd.
Much Comfort *Females* by her Death have lost;
But you it's *Keepers* may lament it most:
Much *Profit Jenny* to her Namesake brought,[6]
Who, for the Morrow, had no need of Thought,
While *Jenny* liv'd; for th' ready pence came in,
As constant as the Morrow did begin.
What Crouds of *Citts* and Coaches throng'd the Door?
My *L—d M—r* at his *Levy* had not more:[7]
Yet let not too much Grief your Hearts invade,
Nor while the *Skin* remains despair of Trade;
Tho' of the Life the Body be bereft,
There's all that charm'd the Eyes of People left.

3 throes.

4 temples. The Egyptians were famous for apotheosizing cats and dogs.

5 The goddess of childbirth in Roman religion and myth.

6 Presumably the name of the 'keeper' of the dolphin was also Jenny.

7 The Lord Mayor of Dublin held an annual 'levee' or reception to which many citizens were invited.

One great Advantage have Spectators too,
The shyest, without Fear, may touch it now,
Not as before, may view each Part on't nigh,
And to the full indulge their Curiosity.
Nor *Jilts* have you, to take your *Cully*'s Treat,
A less Pretence;[8] the *Skin*'s a Wonder yet;
You[9] are it's nearest *Emblem* we can find,
Less did it prey on Fish, than You Mankind.[10]
She earned her Bread, repaid her *Keeper*'s Cost,
But whatsoe'er is *spent on you*, is lost.
Ah! had you all, instead of *Jenny* gone,
And *Providence* reliev'd the injur'd Town!
But cease to mourn, She shall not be forgot,
Nor while her *Skin* remains, her *Mem'ry* rot.
Perhaps, in time it may be *Jenny*'s doom,
T'adorn some *Virtuoso*'s curious Room:[11]
Or (worthy of a more exalted Fame)
To some new *Constellation*, give the Name.

EPITAPH:
On JENNY the FISH.

The *Waters* bore me, next the Earth did share,
My Life, I now am mounted in the Air:
Thorough *three Elements* already past,
It will be well, if I escape the *last*.

8 i.e. nor do you, young whores, have any less reason to accept the offer of an outing (to go and see Jenny's skin) from your foolish menfriends.

9 jilts.

10 i.e. Jenny (when alive) preyed less on fish than you, young whores, do on men.

11 Collectors of natural curiosities ('virtuosi') would often set aside a room for their display.

JOHN WINSTANLEY(?)
(1677–*c.***1720**–1750)

The 'rich' family behind this poem was that of the Right Hon. Robert Rochford (1652–1727), Speaker of the Irish House of Commons and Lord Chief Baron of the Irish Exchequer; he was a wealthy man who owned a mansion at Gaulstown, Co. Westmeath and a house at Newpark, near Swords, Co. Dublin. His two sons George (1683–1730) and John (1692–1771) were both Members of the Irish Parliament and were friends of Jonathan Swift.

Stonybatter was, at the time of this poem, a settlement on the lane running from the village of Cabra to the city of Dublin. Fields and gardens lay on either side of it – though the fact that the Dublin butchers' abattoirs were close by may give this poem a subtle twist. At the end of the earlier poem 'Mully of Mountown', referred to in line 12, the beautiful Mully is slaughtered for meat.

The poem is impossible to date though it was not printed until 1742 when it appeared in Winstanley's anthology of *Poems*.

A Poem
Upon *Daisy*, being brought back from New Park to Stonybatter

How dull, how faded *New Park* Meadows seem!
And *Stonybatter* Fields how gay, how green!
Should this the Wonder prove of *Nymph* or *Swain*;
Tell them, that *Daisy*'s quitted *New Park* Plain,
In *Stonybatter* flow'ry Meads to graze again.

Most lovely *Daisy*! sprung of *lovely Race*!
(For many a Charm thy Mother, *Lovely*, grace)
A cherry red her shining Coat adorns,
Her Head, black Eyes, sleek Face, and stately Horns;
Her Body's comely, plump, both deep and round;
With Legs and Hoofs, strong, streight, and smooth,
and sound:
Nor *Mountown Mully*,[1] fam'd for Beauty rare,
For Teats and Udders can with her compare:
Then, from her Breath, a spicy Odour flows,
Perfuming all around, where'er she goes.

1 'Mully of Mountown', a poem by William King (1663–1712) celebrating a 'beauteous' and much-loved cow belonging to Judge Upton of Mountown near Dublin, was often reprinted following its first appearance in 1704.

Had *Jove* seen *Lovely*, when a *Bull* he turn'd,
Not for *Europa*, but for her, he'd burn'd;[2]
Neglected *Ïo*, ne'er had made such Stir,
But jealous *Juno* run horn mad[3] on her.
Forgive me, *Daisy*! I a while digress,
Tho' *Lovely*'s Fame be great, thine is no less;
Thy Beauties too, anon shall grace my Song,
Tho' she, and *New Park*, yet my Verse prolong.

New Park! by Nature a delightful Seat,
By Art improv'd; and the design'd Retreat
Of a rich *Family*, both *good*, and *great*:
Who, if they oft'ner but retired there,
Would make that pleasant Place the better Fare;
Meat wou'd the Kitchen fill, the Cellar Wine:
The Parlour with bright Side-board daily shine;
The House with chearful honest friends abound;
And all with Pleasure, Mirth, and Joy be crown'd;
There, jovially they'd spend each circling Day:
The *Men* with *Mirth*, and *Wine*, the *Lady's Tea*;
Nor Babling Tongue reveal whate'er they do, or say.
Their *Tea-Table* should then become my Theme:
Not grac'd with *Scandal*, but with *Lovely*'s Fame,
Her *Honey-butter*, and her *Sugar-Cream*.

But *Gallstown*'s lov'd Improvements so much please,
That there they choose to spend the Summer Days;
The pleasant Gardens there, the fine Canal,
The spacious *Walks*, delightful as the *Mall*,[4]
The shady *Groves*, the lovely *Plains* and *Fields*,
And almost all that Art or Nature yields,
So long delight that *New Park* seems to mourn
It's want of Entertaining in it's Turn.

2 The god Jupiter turned himself into as bull to be able to seduce Europa and, in another story, he turned the priestess Ïo (whom he loved) into a long-suffering heifer to protect her from the wrath of his wife, Juno.

3 Maddened by being cuckolded.

4 A gravel walk in the centre of Sackville (now O'Connell) Street, Dublin.

Rough are the Walks, and fading all the trees,
Nor seldom quiver with a sprightly Breeze;
Feint *Echos* sound throughout the *empty Dome*,
As vainly calling for the *Master* home.
Poor *Tirlogh*[5] says, the *Cows* repining seem,
Nor can he whistle to divert their Spleen;
Nor *Oonagh* on her falt'ring Tongue prevail,
To chant one Song to please them o'er the Pail;
What grieves her more too, is (as I hear say)
That *Lovely*'s Milk now set the common way,[6]
Nor e'er put by, (as us'd) for *Cream* for *Tea*:
Howe'er, one minds the Cows, and one the Churn,
And both devoutly wish their *Lord*'s Return:
As th' other Servants do too, I dare say,
But them I mind not, as not in my Way:
My chief design being only *Daisy*'s Praise,
Tho' mourning *New Park* claim'd these doleful Lays.

Daisy! my worthy, my delightful Theme!
(For oft I've tasted, and shall taste thy *Cream*)
Long may thy swelling *Udders* spring with *Milk*;
Late, very late, the merry *Milk Maid* Bilk;[7]
But ready still, both Morn' and Ev'ning stand
With running Teats to meet *brisk Molly*'s Hand:
And *Molly*, in Return (as 'tis but meet)
Shall still take care to keep her *Vessels* sweet;
Her *Dairy* clean, her *Milk* from lavish Waste,
From all *Domestick Thieves* devouring Taste;
That arrant *Thief*, the bold voracious *Cat*,
That covets *Cream*, tho' cloyed with *Mouse* and *Rat*,
But *Puss* ('tis true) is dead, so there's no fear of that.

5 Turlough and Oonagh are here used as typical proper names for Irish farmworkers.

6 i.e. not kept apart from that of the other cows.

7 give her the slip. The line seems to mean that Daisy has recently refused to produce any milk for the ordinary milkmaid. She will, however (as the next couplet makes clear) produce milk for Molly.

Ah! *Molly*! *Molly*! much, (let me advise)
Thy glorious *Fame* for *Cream* and *Butter* Prize:[8]
For what avails the *China* rich and fine,
The burnish'd *Plate*, that on *Tea-tables* shine,
The various Sorts of costly, foreign *Tea*,
As *Green*, *Imperial*, *Hyson*, or *Bohea*,[9]
If thy *domestick Banquet* fail to feast,
With most substantial *Food*, the hungry *Guest*:
If thy delicious *Butter*, nicely spread
On many a thin-slic'd Piece of whitest Bread,
Thy sweetest *Cream*, do not the Table grace,
The rest, (to me) but fill an empty Space;
Is all but glitter, all a mere *Slop-bowl*;
Thy *Cream*, thy *Butter*, charm the *Poet*'s Soul;
Shall make thy *Fame*, thro' neighb'ring Houses ring,
And my glib Tongue thy lasting Praises sing.

8 The final paragraph is addressed, rather surprisingly, to Molly the milkmaid rather than Daisy the cow.

9 Four different kinds of tea available in Dublin at the time.

JAMES ARBUCKLE
(*c.*1700–**1721**–*c.*1747)

James Arbuckle came from Belfast. Like many young Irishmen from the dissenting tradition, he went to the University of Glasgow (rather than to the old-fashioned, Anglican-oriented Trinity College Dublin), where he made a name for himself as a writer of verse and political activist. He settled in Dublin in about 1722 and became prominent in the circle around Viscount Molesworth, adopting the pseudonym 'Hibernicus' in his paper *The Dublin Weekly Journal*. He gained a reputation as a moral philosopher and took an active part in the broadsheet culture of Dublin in the 1720s and '30s, involving himself with Swift, Delany and Dunkin. Arbuckle was a cripple and, as such, cruelly satirized by his enemies. This early poem describing the landscape and natural wealth of the Clyde valley, and referring to the study of natural science in Glasgow, was inscribed to James Brydges, first Duke of Chandos, Earl and Marquess of Carnarvon (d. 1744).

from: Glotta:[1] a Poem:

Sacred, O *Glotta*, be the following Strains;
Thy flow'ry Borders, and thy pleasing Plains,
Inspire the Muse. *Carnarvon*, present be;
I Sing of *Glotta*, and I Sing to thee;
Whose late appearance in these *Northern* Climes
Is thus reflected back in *Northern* Rhimes.

Windsor's fair Forest[2] in the Poet's Lays
Its verdant Beauties far and wide displays;
Nor length of Time can change the beauteous Scene,
Become Immortal in the Godlike Strain.
Ev'n Trees long since decay'd, in Verse arise,
And wave for ever in fictitious Skies.
Oh! did my Breast with equal Ardor glow,
So *Glotta's* Flood should in my Numbers flow.
Not *Cooper's*-Hill[3] more Graceful should appear,

1 An early name for the Scottish River Clyde, possibly derived from the name 'Clota' in Tacitus's account of Roman Britain. The title page of 'Glotta' refers to Arbuckle as 'A Student of the University'.

2 Alexander's Pope's poem 'Windsor Forest' (1713).

3 Sir John Denham's poem.

Nor lovely *Loddon's*[4] Christal Waves more clear.
Tho' *Thames* in five Degrees of better Skies,
Nearer the Sun, and Royal *BRUNSWICK* lies,[5]
Tho' fair *Augusta's Towrs* his Banks adorn,
And plenty boasts an unexhausted Horn,
Our *Glotta* yet with justice lays her Claim
To share his Beauty, tho' not Wealth and Fame.
Here Nature's Charms in gay Confusion rise,
Not less delightful, while they give surprize. …

The Muse would sing, when *Glasgow* she surveys,
But *Glasgow's* Beauty shall outlast her lays. …

Oh, How my Breast with Ardent Wishes glows!
The Muses now their lov'd Retreat[6] disclose,
With pious Care preserving still in Bloom
Transplanted hither, th'Arts of *Greece* and *Rome*.
Here in long Mazes of abstracted Thought
Thy Footsteps, Truth, the learned Tribe have sought.
Our virtuous Youth the generous Chase pursue,
Improving Antient Arts, or searching new:
Not idly resting in the show of Things,
But tracing Nature to her hidden Springs.[7]
Yon' radiant Host of rolling Orbs above,
How vast their Circles, and how swift they move,
What Pow'r directs their everlasting Line,
By Turns to seek the Centre, or decline,
What Second-Cause Heav'n's high Commands performs
In shatt'ring Tempests, and convulsive Storms,
When in an awful Gloom the Clouds arise,
Blue Light'nings flash, and Thunders burst the Skies;
Why cold the fluid Element restores

4 The river Lodden is a tributary of the Thames.

5 i.e. though the Thames is five degrees (of latitude) closer to the sun than the Clyde. 'Royal Brunswick' is George I, one of whose titles was Duke of Brunswick-Lüneburg. 'Augusta'= London.

6 i.e. the University of Glasgow.

7 This liberal study of 'natural science' was probably undertaken by Arbuckle and his fellow students in student coteries and clubs rather than as part of the official university curriculum.

A harder Substance, yet of wider Pores.
Or what more nearly touches Human-kind,
The Pow'rs and Nature of Immortal Mind,
Which only conscious of its Being, knows
Th'Eternal Sourse from whence that Being flows.
How Laws their Force and Sanctity obtain,
How far they reach, and what they should restrain.
Whence flow the Rules the Good and Just obey,
And how themselves all Virtue's Arts repay.
Happy Pursuits that bring serene Delight,
Endear past Labours, and to new invite. …

O happy *Glotta*, such a Realm to boast;
A Realm unless by thee supported, lost, …
Thy plenteous Flood a scaly Breed supplies;
And Seas produce the Gold the land denies.
An hundred Nations by thy Bounty live
And in return their Wealth to *Britain* give.
See! how in Shoals the finny Squadrons sail,
Their numbers dreadful to the Tyrant *Whale*.
Thro' the green Wave the sparkling *Herring* springs,
The Surface breaking into Silver Rings.
The broad-back'd *Cod* his scarlet Gills displays,
Devours his Neighbours, and usurps the Seas.
Couch'd on the Deep, a horrid Monster lies
The *Seal*, and barks to silent Rocks and Skies.
In vain their number, and their Strength in vain
Can Fraud oppose, or Industry restrain:
Caught in the Net, a certain Prey they lie,
Or by the Hook's dissembling Bounty die.
Ev'n deeper yet, our Luxury pursues
The slumbring *Oyster* in its peaceful Ooze.
Delicious Morsel! what, alas! avail
Thy lucid Globe, and close indented Mail?
But what is losing such a Life as thine,
If in a Crown the ripen'd Drop[8] shall shine;

8 A pearl.

Or on *Belinda's* panting Bosom shown,
Enslave a Thousand Hearts, besides her own?[9]
Repine not we, tho' barb'rous Nations boast
Exaustless Riches in a Golden Coast;
Since in our Floods are lodg'd those precious Stores,
That join both Worlds, and make their Products ours.
These Blessings Heav'n, and Liberty bestow;
And such thy happy Portion, *Glotta* now. …

9 A reference to the main female character in Alexander Pope's *The Rape of the Lock* (1714).

JONATHAN SWIFT (1667–1745) and WILLIAM DUNKIN (1705–1765) (1723)

In 1723, after the death of Vanessa Van Homrigh (whose violent attachment to Swift had been the cause of much gossip and of considerable embarrassment to him), Swift took a long journey, alone, to the south and west of Ireland. In the course of this expedition, he wrote a poem in Latin on the rocky seascape in the barony of Carbery in west County Cork. When the poem was first printed, in Swift's *Works* in 1735, it was accompanied by a translation by William Dunkin, at the time still a student at Trinity College Dublin. Dunkin went on to become a clergyman in the Church of Ireland and a well-known schoolmaster. He also became a friend of Swift and one of the witnesses to his will. He was a fine poet in Latin and in English, and was famously praised as such by Swift. The translation that follows is one of the few poems of the age purporting to describe the wild west of Ireland – later to become the focus for so much sentiment and so much verse. Swift's poem and Dunkin's translation both belong firmly in the classical tradition, however.

Carbery Rocks in the County of Cork, Ireland

Lo! from the Top of yonder Cliff, that shrouds
Its airy Head amidst the azure Clouds,
Hangs a huge Fragment;[1] destitute of props
Prone on the Waves the rocky Ruin drops.
With hoarse Rebuff the swelling Seas rebound,
From Shore to Shore the Rocks return the Sound:
The dreadful Murmur Heav'n's high Convex cleaves,
And *Neptune*[2] shrinks beneath his Subject Waves;
For, long the whirling Winds and beating Tides
Had scoop'd a Vault into its nether Sides.
Now yields the Base, the Summits nod, now urge
Their headlong Course, and lash the sounding Surge.
Not louder Noise could shake the guilty World,
When *Jove* heap'd Mountains upon Mountains hurl'd,
Retorting *Pelion*[3] from his dread abode,
To crush Earth's rebel Sons beneath the Load.

1 Possibly a reference to the ruined Iron Age promontory fort on Sherkin Island, just off the mainland of County Cork and within the barony of Carbery – or to an imaginary ruin.

2 classical god of the sea.

3 The reference is to the classical mythological story in which Jove or Jupiter, king of the gods, threw Mount Pelion (a mountain in Thessaly) down from the heavens to crush the earthly giants who had tried to rebel against him. The giants had previously piled Mount Pelion on top of Mount Ossa to try and reach the heavens and overthrow the gods. Retorting = throwing the mountain back to crush those who had offended him.

OFT too with hideous yawn the Cavern wide
Presents an Orifice on either Side,
A dismal Orifice from Sea to Sea
Extended, pervious to the God of Day:[4]
Uncouthly joyn'd, the Rocks stupendous form
An Arch, the Ruin of a future Storm:
High on the Cliff their Nests the *Woodquests*[5] make,
And Sea calves stable in the oozy Lake.[6]

BUT when bleak Winter with her sullen Train
Awakes the Winds, to vex the watry Plain;
When o'er the craggy Steep without Controul,
Big with the Blast, the raging Billows rowl;
Not Towns beleaguer'd, not the flaming Brand
Darted from Heav'n by *Jove's* avenging Hand,
Oft as on impious Men his Wrath he pours,
Humbles their Pride, and blasts their gilded Tow'rs,
Equal the Tumult of this wild Uproar:
Waves rush o'er Waves, rebellows[7] Shore to Shore.
The neighb'ring Race,[8] tho' wont to brave the Shocks,
Of angry Seas, and run along the Rocks,
Now pale with Terror, while the Ocean foams,
Fly far and wide, nor trust their native Homes.

THE Goats, while pendent[9] from the Mountain top
The wither'd Herb improvident[10] they crop,
Wash'd down the Precipice with sudden Sweep,
Leave their sweet Lives beneath th' unfathom'd Deep.

THE frighted Fisher with desponding Eyes,
Tho safe, yet trembling in the Harbour lies,
Nor hoping to behold the Skies serene,
Wearies with Vows the Monarch of the Main.

4 allowing the daylight to penetrate it.

5 wood-pigeons.

6 i.e. young seals live in the seaweed-filled water below.

7 re-echoes.

8 native inhabitants.

9 hanging as if suspended.

10 heedless or unaware of the danger.

THOMAS SHERIDAN
(1687–**1724**–1738)

Thomas Sheridan, one of the most famous Dublin schoolmasters of the eighteenth century, was born in County Cavan. He was educated at Trinity College, Dublin and ordained into the Church of Ireland; he was a close friend of Jonathan Swift and an important member of the circle surrounding the dean. In the affectionate but ironic poem that follows – 'ironic' since Delville was in reality a spacious building on fairly extensive grounds – Sheridan describes the 'country house' at Glasnevin, near Dublin, on which Dr Patrick Delany (1685–1768), mutual friend of Swift and Sheridan, spent so much more than he could afford.

A Description of Doctor Delany's Villa

Would you that *Delville*[1] I describe?
Believe me, Sir, I would not gibe;
For who would be Satirical
Upon a Thing so very small?

You scarce upon the Borders enter,
Before you're at the very Centre.
A single Crow can make it Night,
When o'er your Farm he takes his Flight;
Yet in this narrow Compass, we
Observe a vast Variety;
Both Walks, Walls, Meadows and Parterres,[2]
Windows, and Doors, and Rooms, and Stairs,
And Hills, and Dales, and Woods and Fields,
And Hay, and Grass, and Corn it yields;
All to your Haggard[3] brought so cheap in,
Without the Mowing or the Reaping.
A Razour, tho' to say't I'm loath,
Wou'd shave you and your Meadows both.

1 The name Delville is a shortening of 'Heldeville', the name Swift gave to the house when it was jointly tenanted by Delany and his TCD friend, Dr Richard Helsham. Under the influence of Alexander Pope, the gardens at Delville were laid out in the latest Dutch fashion creating one of Ireland's earliest naturalistic gardens.

2 ornamental parts of the garden, containing flowerbeds.

3 a yard where hay or straw is stacked.

Tho' small's the Farm, yet here's a House
Full large to entertain a Mouse,

But where a Rat is dreaded more
Than savage *Caledonian*[4] Boar;
For, if 'tis enter'd by a Rat,
There is no Room to bring a Cat.

A little Riv'let seems to steal
Down thro' a Thing you call a Vale
Like Tears along a wrinkled Cheek,
Like Rain along a Blade of Leek;
And this you call your sweet *Meander*,
Which might be suck'd up by a Gander,
Could he but force his nestling Bill
To scoop the Channel of the Rill.
I'm sure you'd make a mighty Clutter,
Were it as big as City Gutter.

Next come I to your Kitchen-Garden,
Where one poor Mouse wou'd fare but hard in;
And round this Garden is a Walk,
No longer than a Taylor's Chalk:[5]
Thus I compute what Space is in it,
A Snail creeps round it in a Minute.

One Lettice makes a shift to squeeze
Up thro' a Tuft you call your Trees;
And once a Year a single Rose
Peeps from the Bud, but never blows;[6]
In vain then you expect its Bloom!
It cannot blow for want of Room.

In short, in all your boasted Seat,
There's nothing but yourself that's Great.

4 Scottish.

5 i.e. no longer than could be made by a tailor using his chalk (for marking cloth).

6 come into bloom.

THOMAS SHERIDAN(?)
(1687–**1725**–1738)

The first appearance of this entertaining poem is in a broadside printed by Sarah Harding in Dublin in 1725. It was subsequently fathered on Swift (by Elrington Ball in *Swift's Verse*, 1929), but is now thought to have been the work of Thomas Sheridan – an attack on his enemy Dick Tighe. The poem with the (arguably more suitable) title 'The Case of Man' re-appeared in the 1751 miscellany *Poems Written Occasionally by the Late John Winstanley A.M.L.D., F.S.T.C.D. Interspers'd with many Others, By Several Ingenious Hands*. Vol II, (Published by his Son [George Winstanley] Dublin, S. Powell for the Editor, 1751), pp. 158–62.

from: To the Honourable Mr D. T.[1]

What strange Disorder often springs,
From very light and trivial Things!
Which makes Philosophers conjecture,
They are from Providence a Lecture,
To check our Vanity and Pride,
And many other Faults beside:
This gave the first Creation Rise
Of *Maggots*, *Insects*, *Worms*, and *Flies*,
Of *Bugs*, *Wasps*, *Midges*, *Mice*, and *Rats*,
And *barking Curs*, and *spit-fire Cats*;
That, strive to shun 'em where you will,
There's one or t'other at you still:
No *Man* escapes insidious Vermin,
From Coat of Frize,[2] to royal Ermin;
From the low Joint-stool, to the Throne,
These Plagues of *Egypt*[3] favour none.
And now to point the several Ways,
Such Trifles have such Pow'r to teize:

1 Almost certainly a reference to Richard (Dick) Tighe, the man who (by telling Lord Carteret that Sheridan had preached a sermon on a text arguably insulting to the Queen), caused him to lose a valuable church living. Swift and Sheridan both wrote poems attacking Tighe.

2 Frieze is a coarse, woollen cloth and a joint-stool (l. 15) a simple, three-legged stool.

3 The ten plagues inflicted on the people of Egypt to persuade them to release the Jews from bondage are described in the book of Exodus chapters 5–11.

The lurking *Maggot* in your Meat,
Destroys your Appetite to eat.

Proceed to Bed, that Place of Rest:
Lay down your Head, and do your best,
One little skipping, sorry *Flea*,
Can chase the God of *Sleep* away.

The *Bug*, that Spawn of rotten Wood,[4]
Not only sucks, but taints your Blood.
At length you seize the worthless Prize,
You squeeze, he bursts, and bursting, dies;
But still a greater Curse you find,
So strong a Stink he leaves behind.

The crawling *Louse* assails you next,
You grope, and grope, you fret, you're vext;
This little Speck of Sweat and Dirt,
Altho' it cannot greatly hurt,
Yet still it makes you scratch and shrug,
As much as the adherent *Bug*.[5]

If none of these, a *Rat* or *Cat*,
Or nibbling *Mouse*, or buzzing *Gnat*,
May come as you're supinely laid,
And break the Peace which Sleep has made;
So slight an Accident destroys
The greatest of all human Joys!

If to the Fields you walk for Air,
What num'rous Squadrons meet you there,
Flies of all Sorts and Hues you see,
From ev'ry Ditch, and ev'ry Tree;

4 Until late in the eighteenth century, the Aristotelian belief that maggots wer 'spontaneously generated' in rotten meat persisted: this passage suggests that *Cime. lectularius*, the bed-bug or house-bug, a blood-sucking hemipterous insect found in bedsteads and other furniture (that emits an offensive smell when touched), was generated spontaneously in rotten wood.

5 i.e. the bed-bug.

Like Dust in Clouds, or powd'ring Hail,
Your Face on all Sides they assail;
Eyes, *Cheeks*, *Brows*, *Lips*, *and Chin*, and *Nose*,
Are all attack'd by swarming Foes;
You tap them with your Hands in vain,
No sooner off, but on again:
Such are the Plagues of human Life,
Doom'd ever thus to live in Strife,
With Things so much beneath our Care,
To wage an everlasting War. …

LAETITIA PILKINGTON
(*c*.1708–**1725**–1750)

Laetitia Pilkington is best known for her highly entertaining three-volume *Memoirs of Laetitia Pilkington* (1748–54). In addition to its revelations about her own unconventional life, Mrs Pilkington's *Memoirs* contains what is, in effect, the first biography of Swift. Embedded in the text are many of her own poems and some by her friends; the one below was written before the acrimonious separation and divorce between Laetitia and her clergyman-poet husband, Matthew Pilkington.

The Petition of the Birds

to Mr Pilkington on his return from shooting.

Ah Shepherd, gentle Shepherd! spare
Us plum'd Inhabitants of Air
That hop, and inoffensive rove
From Tree to Tree, from Grove to Grove;
What Phrensy has possess'd your Mind?
To be destructive of your Kind?
Admire not[1] if we Kindred Claim,
Our sep'rate Natures are the same;
To each of us thou ow'st a Part
To grace thy Person, Head, or Heart;
The chaste, the fond, the tender *Dove*
Inspires thy Breast with purest Love;
The tow'ring *Eagle* claims a Part
In thy courageous, gen'rous Heart;
On thee the *Finch* bestow'd a Voice
To bid the raptur'd Soul rejoice;
The *Hawk* has giv'n thee Eyes so bright,
They kindle Love and soft Delight;
Thy snowy Hue and graceful Mien,
May in the stately *Swan* be seen;
The *Robin*'s Plumes afford the red,
Which thy soft Lips and Cheeks bespread;
Thy filial Piety and Truth,
The *Stork* bestow'd to crown thy Youth.
Did we these sev'ral Gifts bestow
To give Perfection to a Foe?

1 i.e. do not be surprised.

Did we so many Virtues give,
To thee, too fierce to let us live?
Suspend your Rage, and every Grove,
Shall echo Songs of grateful Love.
Let Pity soothe and sway your Mind,
And be the Phoenix of Mankind.

Mr B-------R
(*fl.*1726)

Though this poem was not published until 1742, it was written when Lord Carteret was Lord Lieutenant of Ireland between 1724 and 1730. The author was possibly a Mr Belcher, holder of minor offices in Dublin Castle and probably the same man as the 'Secretary Belchier' to whom 'The Villa' (see below under 1754) was dedicated. Ortolans are attractive small birds – buntings – regarded as a delicacy for the table; in the eighteenth century, they were often reared in cages before being sent to the kitchen.

On the Ortolans
For Lady Carteret.

Go my sweet Ortolans, it is decreed,
That at the Castle you must forthwith bleed,
And there among the Rarities be seen,
To entertain our Vice-Roy and his Queen:
Go then, my Birds, your Lives with pleasure yield,
And prove yourselves the choicest of the Field;
It is more Honour for you thus to die,
Than live in Prison, or away to fly.
The Muse, regarded by them, has prevail'd,
And now they go as fast as Ship e'er sailed;
Not dreading any thing they haste along,
And twittle to themselves a kind of Song:
Arrived, safe they readily become
Victims, in honour to their native Home,
And strive at Court acceptable to prove,
Who're sent as Pledges of the Muse's Love.
Let then the Cook, by his nice Skill and Art,
Do Justice to them both in ev'ry part;
And for it worthily deserve the Praise,
Much more than *Cotswold* Poet does the Bayes.[1]

1 The reference is probably to Ambrose Philips, whose rather precious poetry was much ridiculed. Philips, who was born in Shropshire – not far from the Cotswolds in the southern part of central England – came to Ireland in 1724 as secretary to Hugh Boulter, Archbishop of Armagh; he stayed on as a member of the Irish parliament until the 1740s and was well known in and around Dublin Castle.

MURROGHOH O'CONNOR
(*fl.***1726**)

In 1719, there appeared in Dublin and London a strange poem entitled *A Pastoral In Imitation of the First Eclogue of Virgil: Inscrib'd to the Provost, Fellows, and Scholars of Trinity College, Dublin, by Murroghoh O Connor of Aughanagraun*. The poet (whose first name is spelt differently in each printing of his verses) had rented a farm from the university and the poem sets out his side of a disagreement between landlord and tenant; but it also contains much information on farming in early eighteenth century Kerry and includes interesting comments on the natural landscape: O'Connor's farm is described as having 'a lovely prospect of the strand' though bogs and rocks 'deform that spot of earth'; he and his friends eat scollops and edible seaweed ('Slewcawn') and occasionally have their nets broken by porpoises which they call 'sea hogs' (Ir. *muc mara.*) The poem was reprinted in Dublin in 1726 in a volume containing three other poems on O'Connor and his woes, as well as the poem that follows, praising the scenery and quality of life in county Kerry; this is the first Irish-printed 'landscape' poem to extol the beauties of the West of Ireland.

from: The County of Kerry. A Poem

Sure there are poets who did never dream,
On Brandon hill,[1] nor taste the gentle stream,
Which from the glitt'ring summit daily flows:
And the bright pebbles in its fair bosom shews:
From thy clear height I take my lofty flight,
Which opens all the country to my sight:
Both rocks and woods are from thy prospect seen,
Blake[2] in the winter, in the summer green:
Where e'er I turn'd my eyes new scenes appear,
Adorn'd with all the blessings of the year:
On one side Dingle forms a goodly bay,
Well known to mariners that cross the sea.
Tho' choice of wines are wreck'd upon the coast,
It can of a much nobler liquor boast;
Bulcawn,[3] that strong support to sons of earth,
Can elevate the soul to nobler mirth;

1 Mount Brandon. <An high hill in Kerry remarkable for a bright stone, which by the reflection of the sun shews at a great distance the time of the day.>

2 bleak, pale, bare of vegetation.

3 strong liquor or whiskey. Ir. *balcán*, strong person.

Milesian Bards[4] are by its force inspir'd,
When from the labours of the day retir'd:
The Indies here pour out sufficient store,
Of all their riches on this distant shore:[5]
Lough-Layn[6] the next sweet object of my sight,
Can add new wonders and my verse invite;
Smooth are thy waters and thy fountains deep,
Whilst precious stones upon the bottom sleep;[7]
Stones, that give lustre in the dead of night,
Out-shine the stars in their apparent light;
Here pearls intermix'd with common sand,
Neglected lye upon the bord'ring strand.[8]
With such our lord[9] in foreign courts appear'd,
To polish them he no expences spar'd;
Admir'd by all for such a costly dress,
They thought him king, nor cou'd they think him less.
And thou smooth Leawn, which by its borders flows,
And guards Ross castle 'gainst our monarch's foes;
Thy gentle stream deserves uncommon praise,
Which thro' the winding valleys gladly strays; ...

What land can such a store of jewels boast,
As daily shine upon our plenteous coast:
Rome in her grandeur, never cou'd produce,
Such stones as we in common houses use;

4 Milesius was the mythological ancestor of the Gaelic Irish race, so the adjective is used to distinguish those descended from the founders of the race from all later invaders.

5 A reference (as at line 13 above) to goods washed ashore from vessels wrecked off the Kerry coast.

6 Lough Leane or the Lower Lake. <A lough remarkable for a number of precious stones, which shine very much by night, and it is imagin'd by all People that there's a Carbuncle concealed in it.>

7 When describing Lough Leane, Charles Smith wrote: 'The common people hereabouts have a strange romantic notion of their seeing in fair weather, what they call a carbuncle at the bottom of this lake, in a particular part of it.' In a note to this passage, he doubts 'whether there be such a stone subsisting in nature or not'. Charles Smith, *The antient and present state of the county of Kerry. …* (Dublin, 1756), p. 124.

8 Smith noted that pearls had been found in both the Lower Lake and in the river Lane or Laune. For a full account of the pearl fisheries of Ireland, see John Lucey, *The Irish Pearl: a cultural, social and economic history* (Bray, Co. Wicklow, 2005).

9 Lord Kenmare.

Her Gothick structures and her marble domes.
Were far inferior to our Kerry stones;[10]
Lexshnaw[11] thou goodly pile for ever blest,
No monarch ever such a seat possest;
Plenty for ever dwells within thy walls,
Each day an ox beneath the hatchet falls;
Whole herds of deer upon thy mountains stray,
Thy ponds abounding with the finny frey;
Surrounded with the springs of gentle Fale,
The winding Cashin and the lympid Geal;[12]
Plenty and peace in ev'ry house abound,
Such happiness can no where else be found;
I who desire to live an easy life,
Absent from faction and remote from strife;
In Kerry only must expect to find,
Those lasting blessings sought by human kind.

10 Marble from quarries in Kerry is a famously durable and beautiful building material.

11 The now demolished castle at Lixnaw, near Listowel, was the seat of the Earls of Kerry.

12 The rivers Feale, Cashin and Galey (together with the river Brick) flow past or near Lixnaw.

CHARLES COFFEY(?)
(1700–**1727**–1745)

Charles Coffey is best known for his ballad operas and was the first dramatist to incorporate Irish songs into English-language libretti for the Dublin and London stages.[1] He is said to have been a schoolmaster in Dublin and to have been a friend of the Irish actress Peg Woffington. Some time in the 1730s, Coffey moved from Dublin to London where he was active – but not spectacularly successful – in dramatic circles. The poem that follows is attributed to Coffey by a contemporary in one of the copies in the National Library of Ireland. Though it is not of much poetic merit, it is one of the few surviving poetic accounts of an artificially created 'natural' recreational space – in this case around the reservoir designed to supply Dublin with water – in an eighteenth-century Irish urban environment.

Canto I of 'The Bason' describes Apollo chasing Dodor i.e. Dodona or the River Dodder, a tributary of the Liffey that rises in the Dublin Mountains and flows through the southern suburbs of Dublin. Canto II tells how, to escape the god, Dodona collapsed and dissolved into 'A shining Fluid sliding o'er the Green'. In the passage that follows (from Canto III) a disconcerted (and grammatically inept) Apollo prophesies the future of the place where Dodona had escaped him. The Bason (which survived until the nineteenth century) was surrounded by an elegant tree-lined walk and enclosed by a boundary wall. In these extracts, Apollo is speaking.

from: The Bason:
a poem inscrib'd to Samuel Burton[2] Esq., in Three Cantos

from: Canto III

'A Stately City then for Arts renown'd,
This Isle's Metropolis, with Blessings crown'd;
In thy salubrious Waters rich shall be,
And chiefly owe their Beings all to thee.
Near this fair Town, for thy auspicious Sake,
A wide capacious Bason shall they make;
Where thy clear Streams continually shall glide,
From which the Aqueducts shall be supply'd:
Thence num'rous Tubes or leaden Pipes be spread,
And thro' the City every where be led;
Thro' which for Use the chrystal Liquid flows
In purling Rills complaining as it goes;
Celia shall owe her Washes all to thee,
And *Myra* be indebted for her Tea:
Thus every one shall taste thy bounteous Stream,
And hence perpetuate sweet *Dodor*'s Name.

1 See Frank Llewelyn Harrison, 'Music, Poetry and Polity in the Age of Swift', *Eighteenth-Century Ireland* I (1986), 37–63, particularly pp. 49–62.

2 1687–1733. Banker, MP for Sligo and alderman of Dublin.

Around thy Banks shall lovely Prospects rise,
To gratify each Sense, and charm the Eyes;
Beauteous Parterres shall terminate the Sight,
Whose Walks shall yield unspeakable Delight;
On either Side young Hamadryades[3] shall
With verdant Quicks[4] make up an od'rous Wall;
And interspers'd throughout the whole appear,
Inimitable Beauty every where. …

Thy native Virtues shall attract the Fair,
While Crowds of Youths attendant will appear.
Sweet Consorts[5] weekly shall thy Bosom charm,
Whose heavenly Airs shall ev'ry Virgin warm:
Thy gliding Streams their Murmurs shall forbear,
A softer Melody than theirs to hear.
The Notes all whisper'd by the gentle Breeze,
Shall dying sigh amidst the trembling Trees.
The hov'ring Lark shall thro' the Branches sing,
And warbling in the Air expand the Wing.
The sprightly Airs shall round the Scions play,
And *Doder*'s Banks resound the cheerful Lay.' …

3 wood-nymphs.

4 hawthorns.

5 concerts.

MARY BARBER
(*c.*1685–**1728**–1755)

Mary Barber, the wife of a Dublin woollen draper, was an active and accomplished poet. She was a member of Swift's Dublin circle in the 1730s and acted on his behalf with publishers in London. Many of her poems spring from domestic activities. It is not clear which of Mrs Barber's country friends owned gardens fit to be described as 'your Versailles'; however the poem that follows is notable for containing (at lines 45-52) the earliest poetic description of the Northern Lights or *aurora borealis* as seen in Ireland.

Written from Dublin to a Lady in the Country

A Wretch, in smoaky *Dublin* pent,
Who rarely sees the Firmament,
You graciously invite, to view
The Sun's enliv'ning Rays with you;
To change the Town for flow'ry Meads,
And sing beneath the sylvan Shades.

You're kind in vain—it will not be—
Retirement was deny'd to me;
Doom'd by inexorable Fate,
To pass thro' crouded Scenes I hate.
O with what Joy could I survey
The rising, glorious Source of Day!
Attend the Shepherd's fleecy Care,
Transported with the vernal Air,
Behold the Meadow's painted Pride,
Or see the limpid Waters glide;
Survey the distant, shaded Hills,
And, pensive, hear the murm'ring Rills.

Thro' your *Versailles*[1] with Pleasure rove,
Admire the Gardens, and the Grove;
See Nature's bounteous Hand adorn
The blushing Peach, and blooming Thorn;
Behold the Birds distend their Throats,
And hear their wild, melodious Notes.

1 The gardens at the palace of Versailles, laid out by Andre le Notre on the instructions of Louis XIV between 1662 and 1700, were the most famous pleasure gardens in the world.

Delighted, thro' your Pastures roam,
Or see the Kine[2] come lowing home;
Whose od'rous Breaths a Joy impart,
That sooths the Sense, and glads the Heart;
With pleasure view the frothing Pails,
And silent hear the creaking Rails;[3]
See whistling Hinds[4] attend their Ploughs,
Who never hear of broken Vows;
Where no Ambition to be great,
E'er taught the Nymph, or Swain, deceit.

Thus thro' the Day, delighted, run;
Then raptur'd view the setting Sun;
The rich, diffusive God behold,
On distant Mountains pouring Gold,
Gilding the beauteous, rising Spire,
While Crystal Windows glow with Fire;
Gaze, till he quit the *Western* Skies,
And long to see his Sister rise;
Prefer the silent, silver Moon
To the too radiant, noisy Noon.

Or *Northward* turn, with new Delight,
To mark what Triumphs wait the Night;
When Shepherds think the Heaven's foreshow
Some dire Commotions here below;
When Light the human Form assumes,
And Champions meet with nodding Plumes,
With Silver Streamers, wide unfurl'd,
And gleaming Spears amaze the World.

Thence to the higher Heav'ns I soar,
And the great Architect adore;
Behold what Worlds are hung in Air,
And view Ten Thousand Empires there;
Then prostrate to JEHOVA fall,
Who into Being spake them all.

2 cows.

3 The corkcrake or 'landrail' has a distinctive, rasping call.

4 farm workers, rustics.

MATTHEW PILKINGTON
(1701–**1731**–1774)

The diminutive Matthew Pilkington is better known today as the estranged husband of the fast-living poet Laetitia Pilkington than for his own substantial accomplishments as classical scholar, poet and art historian. He was born in County Offaly and, after graduating from Trinity College, was ordained into the Church of Ireland and married Laetitia in 1725. The Pilkingtons were aspiring poets and early in their married life were valued members of the circle surrounding Dean Swift – a circle which included Mary Barber, Constantia Grierson and Patrick Delany. Within a few years, however, Matthew offended both Swift and Pope, and when he and Laetitia involved themselves in a very public and very acrimonious divorce, fashionable society shunned them both. Laetitia went on to compose a risqué three-volume memoir while Matthew redeemed himself by writing what became the standard work on the lives of the world's painters, *The Gentleman's and Connoisseur's Dictionary of Painters* (1770). He was also a poet of considerable skill as his *Poems on Several Occasions* (1731) demonstrates.

The Bee

In tenui Labor. Virg.[1]

To yonder newly-open'd Rose,
Whose Leaves the Morning's Blush disclose,
How swift that prudent *Insect* flies,
Who oft in Beds of Fragrance lies;
And now the dewy Drop devours
That soft Impearls the blowing Flow'rs!
He now on Wings of *Zephyrs*[2] rides,
Then, smooth in airy Circles glides,
And tastes whatever *Nature* yields
In fragrant Gardens, Groves or Fields.

That Vi'let Bank—, how sweet it smells!
How long on ev'ry Bloom he dwells—!
The *Primrose* now he makes his Prey,
And steals the *Cowslip*'s Sweets away.

Cease —, artful Plund'rer —, spoil no more
These Blossoms of their balmy Store,

1 'The subject of my labour a small one …' Virgil, *Georgics* IV, 6. This section of the *Georgics* is about bees.

2 Zephyr was the west wind in classical mythology.

Which Nature taught them to produce,
For nobler Man's Delight and Use:
Nay —, rather Plunder — since we find
No Traces of the Theft behind.

But now, why nimbly do'st thou rise,
And lightly Skim before my Eyes?
And why thy Tender Pinions spread,
To humm, and wanton round my Head?
What swells thy little Heart to Rage?
Rash *Fool*! what prompts thee to engage
With Man, so far surpassing thee?
Why do'st thou whet thy Sting at me?
When thou in *Woodbine*[3] Bow'rs did'st play,
Or in the *Rose* embosom'd lay,
Or thro' the scented Allys flew
Where Vi'lets breathed, or Lillies grew,
Did I thy harmless Joys molest?
Did I with Terror fill thy Breast?
Did e'er I chace thee round the Bow'r
For sweets, the Spoils of many a Flow'r?
And wilt thou, vain, ungrateful Thing!
At me direct thy poison'd *Sting*?
Fly hence—to lonely Desarts fly—,
And wilt thou still persist—, then die—.
And now, thy silken Wings I seize,
These silken Wings no more shall teize,
Nor shall they, smooth, thy Body bear
Along the Bosom of the Air;
But thus—, torn off—, thro' Tempests go,
The Sport of all the Winds that blow:
And next, thy *Head* shall cease to cleave
To thee, so indiscreetly brave:
The Sting, that wont to give us Pain,
I thus —, for ever render vain,
And thou a nameless Carcase art,

3 honeysuckle.

Despoil'd of ev'ry harmful Part.
'Tis done —, and now methinks I find
Compassion working in my Mind;
A tender Pity swells my Breast,
Too late, alas! to thee exprest:
These Eyes, which Death's cold Hand hath seal'd,
How dim they seem! with Darkness veil'd!
These Limbs, which knew to form so well,
With curious Art the waxen Cell,
And there reserve its Treasures rare,
That might with *Hybla*[4] Sweets compare,
Now stiff —, there, piteous Object, lie,
O Life! How swiftly do'st thou fly!

A Moment since, and thou coud'st Rove
Thro' Orchard, Meadow, Lawn, or Grove,
Delighted in the Sunshine play,
And Float along the lucid Ray;
Or skim the dimply Stream, and roam
Far distant from thy Straw-built Home;
Yet now thy little *Spirit*'s fled,
And thou art number'd with the Dead;
Alas! how small a space supplies
The *Insect*, and the *King* that dies!

By so severe, so hard a fate,
Was *Pompey*[5] strip'd of all his State,
Like thee a headless Corse[6] was made,
No Sigh, no Tear, no Honour paid.

Forgive, ah gentle *Shade*, forgive
That Hand, by which you cease to Live;
That Hand shall soon a Tomb prepare,
And place your injur'd Body there;
That Hand the sweetest Flow'rs shall bring,

4 A region of Sicily, famous in antiquity for the quality of its honey.

5 Pompey the Great (106BC–48BC), one of the original triumvirate that ruled Rome. After his assassination in Egypt, his head was cut off and sent to his rival, Caesar.

6 corpse.

The lov'liest Daughters of the Spring,
The *Pancy*[7] gay, the *Vi'let* blue,
And *Roses* of celestial Hue,
Carnations sweet, of various dye,
And Tulips, form'd to please the Eye,
And ev'ry fragrant op'ning Bloom,
Shall breathe its Odours round thy Tomb:
And I, too conscious of my Crime,
Shall make thee Live to future Time.

7 pansy.

JAMES BELCHER(?)
(*fl.*1726–**1732**)

This poem first appeared as an anonymous broadsheet in Dublin in 1732 (Foxon 163); on the only known copy of this printing (now in the Huntington Library) an early owner has inscribed 'By Ia. Belcher Esqr'. If this is correct, the poet is the same man as the author of 'On the Ortolans' of *c.*1726 and, according to Professor James Woolley, of several other poems in the 1742 anthology edited by John Winstanley (*Poems written Occasionally* …), where this poem is reprinted.

Several items in Winstanley's anthology (as well as in that published by his son, George, in 1751) concern man's relationship with animals; pet cats seem to have been regularly picked upon for cruel treatment.

A Cat may look upon a King

An Epistolary Poem on
The Loss of the Ears of a favourite Female Cat

Thou Enemy, who e'er thou art,
Thy Actions show thy harden'd Heart;
To serve a fav'rite CAT so base!
To spoil the Beauty of her Face!
The Muse, did she thy Name but know,
Would lash thee well and shame thee too.

Had'st thou for *Shingles* wanted cure,
And bled her in the Tail,[1] besure,
Thou might'st have been excus'd for that,
But to cut both Ears off the cat!

Out of meer Mischief and Ill Nature,
To so deserving a dear Creature,
Is an unpardonable thing:
A CAT may look upon a King.

Or had she *Catterwawling* went,
Or in thy Pantry once been pent,[2]
Thou might'st, perhaps, had Reason great,
In such a Manner her to treat:
But, to be cruel and unkind,

1 Shingles (*herpes zoster*) was only clinically identified in the nineteenth century. At the time of this poem, the term covered various skin ailments, one cure for which involved the use of cat's blood.

2 shut up.

To one, not rav'nously inclin'd,
Who nurs'd at that time *Kittens* three,
No Punishment's enough for thee.

Tho' no *Advertisement* can find thee,
Or *Law* to good Behaviour bind thee:
Yet in Revenge these *Curses* take,
From *Puss*, who is provok'd to spake.[3]

May'st thou on *Rats* and *Mice* be fed,
And lose thy Bacon, Cheese, and Bread.
May all thy Goods and Furniture,
If thou hast any to secure,
By those vile Vermin be destroy'd;
And may thy House be still annoy'd,
And stink so with them, ne'er to be,
Kept clean by any Housewifry.
Farther, my *Curses* to compleat,
May'st thou at length be sweetly beat,
With *Cat* of *Nine-Tails*, and then swing,
In *Hempen*, or in *Cat-gut String*.[4]

3 'Spake' (an example of contemporary Hiberno-English pronunciation) is amended to 'speak' in the Huntington Library copy of this text, and by Winstanley in the reprinting.

4 i.e. be flogged and then hanged.

PATRICK DELANY
(1685–*c.***1732**–1768)

Patrick Delany, one of Swift's closest friends, was born in Queen's County (now County Laois) and educated at Trinity College Dublin where he became a Fellow and Professor of Oratory and History. He was ordained into the Church of Ireland and eventually became Dean of Down. Delany is remembered for his hospitality at Delville, his elegant house and estate at Glasnevin, north of Dublin and for the fact that his second wife was Mary Pendarves, the famous artist, collector and correspondent. Swift described Delany as 'a man of the easyest and best conversation I ever met with in this Island, a very good listener, a right reasoner, neither too silent nor talkative and never positive.'

In 'Longford's Glyn', Delany echoes Spenser in a blending of Irish and classical mythology. The setting is the long, mysterious 'Lumford's Glen' near the village of Clogher, Co. Tyrone. The story Delany spins – of a nymph named Monimeca who is turned into the waterfall at the end of the glen as she flees the lecherous giant Fionn mac Cumhaill (while her lover, Altus, becomes the willow tree beside the waterfall) – suggests the origins of unusual rock formations in the glen. The poem (like MacPherson's *The Works of Ossian* (1765)) claims to come from a Gaelic original, though this is most unlikely and none has been traced. Delany's modern editor, Robert Hogan, states that this poem was written 'in 1732 or earlier'. See *The Poems of Patrick Delany* ed. Robert Hogan (University of Delaware Press, 2006, p.173).

from: Longford's Glyn:[1]

A true history. Faithfully translated from the Irish Original

In fair *Tyrone*, for fruitful Fields renown'd,
And waving Hills, with various Verdure crown'd,
Where Mountains over Mountains tow'ring high
With pleasing Horror fill the distant Eye!
Not far from where that antient City stood,
Wash'd by Owindo's[2] smooth and sable Flood,
For royal *Ergal*'s palace[3] fam'd of old,
And *Pagan* oracles from Rocks of Gold;
Clogh-ore from thence in antient Records nam'd,
Though since a See for *Christian* Prelates fam'd,

1 <Situate in the County of *Tyrone*, and Manour of *Cecil*, not far from the City of *Clogher*, antiently a royal City. The Name is derived from the two *Irish* Words … the first of which signifies a *Stone*, and the next *Gold*.> cf. Ir. *clogh-oir*, 'golden stone'; there was a famous oracle stone at Clogher in pagan times.

2 <The *Irish* Name for the River now call'd the *Black Water*.> cf. Ir. *abhann* (pronounced 'owin') a river and Ir. *dubh* (pronounced 'duv') dark or black.

3 St Patrick ordered that a monastery ['palace'] be built in Clogher, which was once called Ergal or Uriel.

Where John[4] renown'd for Bounty and for Books,
Peace at his Heart, and Plenty in his Looks,
Guards well the Ways with hospitable Eye,
Nor lets the Traveller pass hungry by:
A nymph, the wonder of the neighbouring swains,
The pride of all the sweet Cecilian[5] plains,
Fair Monimeca dwelt, of race divine,
Offspring of Pan[6] and glory of his line! ...

Contiguous was a Vale, of various Shade,
By arching Rocks and meeting Mountains made!
Here, parallel approach the mighty Mounds,[7]
And there, in hollow Windings part their Bounds;
The Rocks with Woods, the Woods with Rocks o'ergrown,
Protect the shrilling Hawk, and Woodquest's[8] Moan;
Above the Summit of the craggy Steep,
The Eagle, sailing with majestic Sweep,
Smiles on the distant Terrors of the Gun,
Or tries her penon'd Offspring at the Sun![9]
The Goat, with Pain distinguisht from below,[10]
Late browses, pendant, on the horrid Brow,
With dreadful Negligence! The Shepherd sees,
And shouts him down by dangerous Degrees!
Waking the Dissonance of Rooks and Jays,
Whilst blended Echoes bound along the Maze …

4 <Dr Sterne the present Bishop.> John Sterne (1660–1745).

5 i.e. of the area – the manor of Cecil.

6 The classical god of nature.

7 i.e. the neighbouring ranges of hills.

8 pigeon.

9 i.e. or endeavours to get her winged (penoned: pinioned, with wings) offspring to fly high.

10 i.e. the goat [so high up on the rocks that it is] hard to see from below, has recently been browsing on the dreadful edge, almost hanging over the cliff.

… Fast down the Rock, the living Fountain[11] flows,
To bath her Love[12] and bless him as he grows,
Flows fast, and fondly curling round his Root,
Swells to a limpid Bason at his Foot:
Each, Life and Sense, (so *Pan* decreed) retains,
And lasting as their Life, their Love remains:
Is still the same, to the same Scene confin'd,
No change or chance affects the faithful mind.
Altus, still fondly bending from above,
Beholds himself reflected in his Love;
Nor from his Sight, will *Monimeca* part,
But, raptured, feels his Image at her Heart. …

Live faithful *Altus*, *Monimeca* live,
To all the Length of Years the Muse can give.
From you, be fair *Altmonimeca*[13] known,
All other Names disdaining but her own:
Be *Longford's Glyn* no more the Region's Boast,
But in your nobler Name forever lost.

11 The nymph, Minomeca, has now become the waterfall at the end of the valley and her lover, Altus (cf. Latin *altus*, high or tall) a willow tree growing at the foot of the waterfall.

12 i.e. bathe.

13 <The original *Irish* Name of that Valley, now call'd *Longford's Glyn*.>

JOHN LAWSON(?)
(1708/9–**1733**–1759)

Though this poem appeared anonymously, it was almost certainly the work of the accomplished Latinist, John Lawson, to whom it is attributed in two surviving copies (NLI and the University of Michigan). Lawson was from County Monaghan and entered Trinity College Dublin in 1727. He rose through the ranks to become college librarian, lecturer in divinity, professor of oratory and history and finally (1753) professor of divinity. He was a famous preacher and is often credited as one of the founders of the Anglo-Irish oratorical tradition.

Few eighteenth-century poems describe life in the built environment of Dublin – though there are many about jaunts out of Dublin to Ringsend, Templogue, Cabra, Glasnevin, Finglas and Blackrock for instance. However this poem describes an evening in a Dublin theatre, when Lawson was a student. In Dublin – as in the London of Swift's 'A Description of a City Shower' – the streets were noisy and filthy and the disposal of waste was a problem as yet unsolved. We have included the introduction and conclusion of Lawson's poem.

from: The Upper Gallery

Amidst the Town's tumultuous Scenes,
What rises worthy of Poetic Strains?
Say, Muse, wilt thou the baited Bull rehearse?
Shall the stern Savage[1] bellow in thy Verse?
Or in soft Numbers shall the Milk-Maid shine?
And her Cheek blush for ever in the Line?
Say, shall the Streets with warbled Ballads chime?
Or *Thieves, highwav'ring*, die in mournful Rhime?[2]
Shall Flatt'ry guide thy mercenary Quill;
Lawyers impose no more, nor Doctors kill?
In Misses make sincerity be found,
And Beaux in Principles and Body sound?
Delightful Themes, reserv'd for future Odes!
Sing now, O Goddess, those sublime Abodes,
Where rais'd in graceful Pomp, the jovial Throng
Sweeten the Intervals of Plays with Song. …

1 i.e. the bull. (See below the poem 'Lord Altham's Bull' of *c.*1772.)

2 A reference to printed broadsheets containing what purported to be the 'Last Speech' of condemned criminals. These were sold to onlookers at the execution and were occasionally in rhyme.

... When Ev'ning Clouds condensing fall in Rain,
And draggled Crowds the cover'd Pent-house[3] gain:
Tradesmen take in their Goods, expos'd to sale,
And tuck'd-up Hoops the Maiden Leg reveal:
When Politicians into Shops repair,
And settle Nations, till the Sky grows clear,
Then no Walks please: All Nature seems to frown,
Black Kennels[4] swell, and Coaches shake the Town.
If *one fair Splendid*[5] in thy Pocket glows,
Fly to the Theatre's instructive Shows;
There some fam'd Heroe of a distant Age,
Revives in Verse, and pompous awes the Stage;
Or comic Scenes less solemn Joys dispense,
Please, to instruct, and laugh us into Sense.

While the spruce Beaus loll thoughtless in their Chairs,[6]
Wrapt in thick Rug, we whistle up the Stairs:[7] ...

Secure from high we view th'amusing Scene,
Survey their Follies, and forsee their Pain …
Our thick *Hibernian* Drab,[8] at Midnight Hours,
Repels benumbing frosts, and driving Show'rs,
Whilst those who would sublimer Tast[e]s express,
Shine in a useless and a foreign Dress …

But now the Curtain falls, the Musick flies,
From their throng'd Seats the yawning Audience rise;
Whilst with slow Speed the rushing Crowds descend,
The Stairs sound hollow, and the Gall'ries bend …

3 A covered walk, arcade or colonnade in front of a row of buildings.

4 gutters in the street, black with dirt.

5 a slang word for a small coin. cf. John Philips's poem 'The Splendid Shilling' (1701).

6 sedan chairs.

7 The young men are ascending to the highest part of the theatre, the 'gods'. 'Rug' was a coarse woollen cloth, frequently made in Ireland.

8 cloaks or coats of a thick woollen cloth ('drab') made in Ireland.

The Beaus and Fair last quit the thinn'd Abode,
(The brawny Chairman pants beneath his Load)
Gay Creatures, proud of Dress and transient Bloom,
The light Things flutter round, and gold the Gloom.
So[9] where the Sew'rs thro' broken Channels glide,
And stagnant Filth coagulates the Tide,
Lur'd by the Stench unnumber'd Flies resort,
And wanton circling, mix in various Sport;
From Side to Side the humming Insects run,
Wave their gilt Wings, and glitter in the Sun.

But where shall hungry Bard for Refuge fly
From Paths nocturnal, and a wintry Sky?
Aghast I feel the Chairman's Pole behind,
And dread loud Coaches in each rustling Wind!
Thro' my rent Coat the chilling Tempests blow,
And gaping Shoes admit the Tide below![10]
Thus numb'd by Frosts, or drench'd in soaking Rain,
Oft' I explore my empty Purse in vain;
Alas! no Sixpence rises to my Hand,
Whose magick Force cou'd flying Cars command.[11]
At length, I come where 'mid th'admiring Round,
In Verse alternate, warbled Ballads sound,
Ballads my self had fram'd with wond'rous Art,
To gain a Supper, or a Milk-Maid's Heart!
I with the croud, the tuneful Sounds pursue,
What won't the Love of Fame and Musick do?

Now the arch Stripling[12] from some neighb'ring Stand,
Hurles Flames malignant from his lifted Hand;
Whizzing they fly; the Croud aghast retires
From the dread Squib, and future-spreading Fires.
It bounces, bursts, and in a Flash is lost,
From Side to Side the reeling Crouds are tost;
Now heav'd on high, now trampl'd under Feet,
And *Poets* roll with *Coblers* in the Street. …

9 i.e. thus. The next six lines constitute a parodic incursion into epic simile.

10 i.e. the water from the puddles.

11 i.e. I could afford to get a carriage home if I had sixpence.

12 i.e. a mischievous youth from nearby throws firecrackers into the crowd.

JAMES DELACOURT OR DE-LA-COUR
(1709–**1734**–1781)

The Rev. James Delacourt (the name is spelt in several different ways) was born in Cork. He was educated at Trinity College, Dublin where he became embroiled in a battle of wits that involved Charles Carthy and William Dunkin, among others. Delacourt was ordained into the Church of Ireland and returned to Cork where his contemporaries considered him quite mad. He had written poetry from his student days and was a great admirer of the English poet James Thomson (1700–48) author of *The Seasons* (1728–30) to whom he addressed the following poem. Soon after its appearance, the poem was mercilessly parodied in *The London Magazine* in verses beginning: 'Hail gently-warbling Delacourt.' Only extracts from this rambling and eccentric poem are printed here.

from: To Mr Thomson, on his Seasons

FROM sunless worlds, where Phoebus seldom smiles,
But with his ev'ning wheels hangs o'er our isles;
A western muse to worth this tribute pays,
From regions bord'ring on the Hebrides:[1]
For thee the Irish harp new-strung once more,
Greens our rough rocks, and bleak Hibernian shore:
Thou Thomson, bid my fingers wake the strings,
And with thy praise the wild wood hollow rings;
The shades of rev'rend Druids hover round,
And bend transported o'er the brazen sound. …

BLEST bard! with what new lustre dost thou rise,
Soft as the season o'er the summer skies;
Thy works a little world new found appear,
And thou the Phoebus of a heav'n so fair;
Thee their bright sov'reign all the signs[2] allow,
And Thomson is another name for nature now; ...

BENEATH thy touch DESCRIPTION paints anew,
And the skies brighten to a purer blue;
Spring owes thy pencil her peculiar green,
And drown'd in redder roses summer's seen;

1 Delacourt means 'Ireland' – even if his geography is somewhat eccentric.

2 of the Zodiac.

While hoary winter whitens into cold,
And autumn bends beneath her bearded gold.

IN various drap'ry see the rowling year,
And the wild waste in sable spots appear;
O'er the black bog the bittern stalks alone,
And to the naked marshes makes his moan; ...

A sudden flash of lightning turns my eye,
To thunder rumbling in the summer sky!
Beneath thy hand the flaming sheet is spread,
O'er heav'ns wide face, and wraps it round with red;
With the broad blaze the kindling lines grow bright,
And all the glowing page is filled with light;
Thro' the rough verse the thunder hoarsely roars,
And on red wings the nimble light'ning soars:[3]
Here thy Amelia[4] starts, and chill'd with fears,
At ev'ry flash her eye-lid swims in tears;
What heart but beats for so divine a form,
Pale as a lilly sinking in a storm?
What maid so cold to take a lover's part,
But pities Celadon with all her heart.

How precious gems enrich each sparkling line,
Add sun to sun, and from thy fancy shine!
Here rocks of diamonds blaze in broken ray,
And sanguine rubies shed a blushing day;
Blue mining Saphyrs a gay heav'n unfold,
And Topaz lightens like transparent gold;
Of ev'ning tinct pale Amethysts are seen,
And Em'ralds paint their languid beams with green;
While the clear Opal courts the reader's sight,
And rains a show'r of many colour'd light:

3 cf. Alexander Pope's parody of bad verse in 'An Essay on Criticism', II, 365–70.

4 Amelia and Celadon (l.40) are the protagonists in an episode in Thomson's 'Summer': Amelia is struck dead by a bolt of lightning.

Your sky-dipt pencil adds the proper glow,
Stains each bright stone, and lets their lustre flow,
Tempers the colours shifting from each beam,
And bids them flash in one continued stream.

So have I seen the florid rain-bow rise,
In breded[5] colours o'er the wat'ry skies,
Where drops of light alternate fall away,
And fainting gleams in gradual dyes decay;
But thrown together the broad arch displays,
One tide of glory, one collected blaze!...

O! thou that only in this garb could please,
And bring me over to commend thy lays;
Where rhyme is wanting,[6] but where fancy shines
And bursts like ripen'd ore above the mines:
Enjoy thy genius! glory in thy choice!
Whose Roman freedom has Roscommon's voice.[7]

5 spread out.

6 Thomson's 'The Seasons' is in blank, not rhymed, verse.

7 Delacourt is suggesting that Thomson's verse combines the freedom of expression of classical poets with the (nearly contemporary) voice of the (Irish) Earl of Roscommon whose poem 'An Essay on Translated Verse' (1685) was widely read and admired in the eighteenth century.

HENRY BROOKE
(*c*.1703–**1735**–1783)

Henry Brooke was born in County Cavan, the son of a clergyman. He was educated at Trinity College, Dublin and soon became a prolific writer. His daughter Charlotte, famous for her *Reliques of Irish Poetry* (1789), edited his works for publication and they appeared in four volumes shortly before he died in Dublin in 1783.

Universal Beauty is the most significant philosophical poem written by an Irish writer in the eighteenth century. Like Alexander Pope in *An Essay on Man*, Brooke uses the poem to survey God's creation in the universe, and to give an account of the forms of knowledge and of the nature of man. In the last of the six books of the poem, he contemplates the beauty of the design of the universe and, in the section printed below, expresses a typically Augustan wonder at the social order to be seen among bees.

from: Universal Beauty (Book VI)

... Bear, bear my song, ye raptures of the mind!
Convey your bard thro' Nature unconfined,
Licentious[1] in the search of wisdom range,
Plunge in the depth, and wanton[2] in the change;
Waft me to Tempe,[3] and her flowery dale,
Born on the wings of every tuneful gale;[4]
Amid the wild profusions let me stray,
And share with Bees the virtues of the day.

Soon as the matin glory gilds the skies,
Behold the little Virtuosi[5] rise!
Blithe for the task, they preen their early wing,
And forth to each appointed labour spring.
Now nature boon[6] exhales the morning stream,
And glows and opens to the welcome beam;

1 unconfined.

2 play heedlessly or extravagantly.

3 the most delightful spot on earth, according to many poets in classical literature.

4 used here in its poetic meaning, 'a soft or gentle breeze'.

5 learned persons, particularly those skilled in the sciences, in music or in collecting.

6 bounteous. Milton uses the same phrase, 'nature boon' in *Paradise Lost* IV, 242. The couplet means 'Now bounteous nature breathes forth the morning air ['stream'] and glows and opens [herself] to the welcome [sun] beam'.

The vivid tribes amid the fragrance fly,
And every art, and every business ply.
Each chymist[7] now his subtle trunk unsheathes,
Where, from the flower, the treasured odour breathes;
Here sip the liquid, here select the gum,
And o'er the bloom with quivering membrane hum.
Still with judicious scrutiny they pry,
Where lodg'd the prime essential juices lie;
Each luscious vegetation wide explore,
Plunder the spring of every vital store:
The dainty suckle, and the fragrant thyme,
By chymical reduction, they sublime;[8]
Their sweets with bland attempering[9] suction strain,
And, curious, thro' their neat alembicks[10] drain;
Imbibed recluse, the pure secretions glide,
And vital warmth concocts the ambrosial tide.[11]

Inimitable Art! do thou atone
The long lost labours of the Latent Stone;
Tho' the Five Principles so oft transpire,
Fined, and refined, amid the torturing fire.[12]
Like issue should the daring chymist see,
Vain imitator of the curious Bee,
Nor arts improved thro' ages once produce
A single drachm[13] of this delicious juice.
Your's then, industrious traders! is the toil,
And man's proud science is alone to spoil ...

7 The bee is seen as a chemist or alchemist (i.e. one able to turn one thing into another).

8 i.e. they turn what they have gathered from the dainty honeysuckle and the fragrant thyme [i.e. nectar] into something higher, more excellent [i.e. honey].

9 modifying.

10 In these lines, Brooke is describing the transformation of nectar into honey in terms borrowed from alchemy. Alembics were instruments used in distillation.

11 i.e. Imbibed in secret, the pure secretions [from the nectar] glide [through the bees' bodies] and the living warmth digests them and turns them into liquid ambrosia. 'Ambrosia' was not only the food of the gods in classical mythology, but also another name for 'bee-bread', the mixture of honey and pollen consumed by the nurse-bees in a beehive.

12 The 'Latent Stone' and the 'Five Principles' are terms from alchemy.

13 dram, a small measure of liquid.

Hail happy tribes! illustrious people hail!
Whose forms minute such sacred maxims veil;
In whose just conduct, framed by wondrous plan,
We read revers'd each polity of man.
Who first in council form'd your embryon state?
Who rose a patriot in the deep debate?
Greatly proposed to reconcile extremes,
And weave in unity opposing schemes?
From fears inferr'd just reason of defence,
And from self interest rais'd a publick sense;
Then pois'd his project with transposing scale,
And from the publick, shew'd the private weal?
Whence aptly summ'd, these politicians draw
The trust of power, and sanctitude of law;
Power in dispensing benefits employ'd,
And healing laws, not suffer'd, but enjoy'd.
The members, hence unanimous, combine
To prop that throne on which the laws recline;
The law's protected even for private ends,
Whereon each individual's right depends;
Each individual's right by union grows,
And one full tide for every member flows;
Each member as the whole communion great,
Back'd by the powers of a defending state;
The state by mutual benefits secure,
And in the might of every member sure!

The publick thus each private end pursues;
Each in the publick drowns all private views:
By social commerce and exchange they live,
Assist supported, and receiving give. ...

JAMES STERLING
(1701–**1737**–1763)

James Sterling was born in 1701 in County Offaly, the son of a 'gentleman'. He obtained his BA from Trinity College Dublin in 1720. His first play seems to have been performed in Dublin's Smock Alley Theatre in 1723; he contributed three poems to Matthew Concanen's *Miscellaneous Poems, original and translated* (London, 1724) and published several poems in Dublin in the 1720s. Later Sterling was ordained into the Church of Ireland and in 1733 he moved to London, where he wrote many political pamphlets and some more plays. He emigrated to Maryland in 1740 and spent the rest of his life as a minister there. The poem below, addressed to Arthur Dobbs (1689–1765), Surveyor General of Ireland, provides a memorable description of whaling off the coast of County Donegal.

from: Friend in Need is a Friend in Deed:
or, a PROJECT, At this Critical Juncture, to gain the Nation a hundred thousand Pounds per Annum from the Dutch; by an IRISH WHALE FISHERY.

… Say now my Muse, what Numbers wilt thou bring,
Or in what Lines our Benefactor[1] Sing,
Who thus has taught us of his own accord
What Plenty these our fertile Shores afford;
Who first discover'd *Whales* upon our Coast,
Such Quantities as *Britain* cannot Boast;
Ev'n *Donnegal* produces equal Store
To what is found on *Greenland's* foreign Shore;
How great his Merits, who thus taught a Road
To Feed our wants at home, to send abroad
To save our Coin, and daily fetch home more,
Each tending to encrease the Publick store;
Yet farther, when a Stranger to the Coast,
He found the *Fish* which hitherto were Lost
Lost, or at least, they yet unheeded lay,
Tho' on the Shore they sported every Day,
And always undisturb'd enjoy'd the peaceful Sea.

If it be true what *Horace* sagely Notes,
His Heart was shielded in three Brazen Coats,
Who first adventur'd o'er the fickle Main,
And could intrepidly behold the Train

1 Arthur Dobbs.

Of Finny Monsters skim the glassy Plain,[2]
What had he said, to raise his Country's good,
Had he beheld our Fisher stem the Flood,
Of briny Waves, with what a Coat of Mail
Wou'd he have Arm'd him to attack a *Whale*.
On *Doren*'s Towering Mount[3] thus from afar
I view'd the Dangers of the wat'ry War,
No Ruffling Breeze disturb'd the Marble Sea,
Th'unwieldy Monster on the Surface lay,
The daring Fisher silently draws near,
Deep in his Back descends the bearded Spear;
Rouz'd with the Wound, incens'd with pungent Smart,
He plunges down, th'astonish'd Waters part;
Entomb'd in Floods he cuts his private Way,
The veer'd out Lines his private Paths betray,
The hurry'd Barge through yielding Water flies,
Deceives my Sight, deserts my wandring Eyes.
The Monster breathless now thrusts up his Nose,
The Barge emergent at a Distance Rows,
He Sneesing snorts, transparent Floods appear,
Which mounting up Illuminate the Air,
Repelled by Clouds they downward show'r again
In Sluicy heaps like spouts of Winter rain;
Th'enormous Monster thus expos'd to view
Th'audacious Fishers strait the War renew
Courageously against the Foe advance
Repeat their blow and leave the goring Lance;
Enrag'd with double Smart the Monster heaves,
A hoary Foam o'erspreads the curling Waves,
Downward he sinks, and instantly again
Upon the Surface Floats, the Whitening Main
Exagitated[4] with such vig'rous bounds
Assuming rage obstreperously Sounds;
Above, below, the Monster seeks in vain
To loose the Dart, or mollifie his Pain;

2 Horace, *Odes* I, iii, 9.

3 Doorin Point, to the south-east of Killybegs, Co. Donegal.

4 stirred up.

Nor ease, nor Rest, nor Mitigation found,
Inspir'd with Rage and Fiercer through the Wound,
All Efforts try'd, no more prepares to Fly,
Exerts his Strength and vainly beats the Sky;
His spatt'ring Tail whole Seas of Water throws,
The Waters sink and tremble at his blows;
Heated with frequent Strokes they raging boil,
Tumultuously like Pots of Spumy Oil.
With equal Courage but inferiour Force,
Th'undaunted *Fisher s*teers his giddy Course,
Anxious again to wound the bulky Foe,
Rows boldly up and strikes another blow;
Again falls off his Forky Tail t'evade
Each dashing stroke is with a stroke repaid;
Till Sickening by degrees he Faintly heaves,
Whilst spouting Blood infects the Frothy Waves,
Gathering his wasting Strength he vaults the Skies,
Hangs in the Air, Expiring, falls and dies.
With Peals of shouts the hollow Heavens ring
When on the Prostrate Foe they joyful Spring,
Sweating to Land they tow the vanquish'd Prize,
Supine on Waves the Floating Monster lies;
But e'er they reach it, tumid[5] Billows Roar,
Hoarse, hideous Noises fill the sounding Shore;
Stern *Boras*[6] with despotick lawless Sway
Sweeps o'er the land, and Couches on the Sea;
Now spongy, gathering Clouds o'ercast the Light,
The Day serene sinks into gloomy Night,
While Waves on Waves ebullient[7] dreadful rise
And irresisted seem to dare the Skies,
The skilful Fisher tries his Art in vain
To save his Prey in the tumultuous Main;
The lines are cut, the Labours of the Day
Tost at the Pleasure of th'impetuous Sea.
Scarcely the Floods sustain the pond'rous Freight
But sink depress'd and groan beneath the weight,

5 swelling.

6 Boreas, the north wind in classical mythology.

7 agitated, as if boiling.

Till by the assistance of the driving Blast,
The floating Mountain on the Shore is cast.
In vain the Seaman plies the bending Oar,
Tuggs hard and sweats to reach the wish'd for Shore,
Nor Helm, nor Oars, th'unstable Boat obeys,
But whirling drives before the boiling Seas,
Elate on Waves against the Sky she's tost,
Now low in Waters' darksome abyss lost.
Quite spent with Toil, oppress'd with anxious Care,
'Twixt glim'ring Hopes of Living and Despair,
The Seaman, now no more the Torrent braves
And but half dead escapes the gaping Waves.

Such are the Dangers of the faithless Sea
Through such as these the *Fisher* seeks his Prey.
Awake, HIBERNIA, ope thy Eyes and see
The vast Advantage of a *Fishery*;
With Speed prepare t'attack the Finny Foe,
From taking which such Benefits will flow;
Equip your Boats with sharp *Harpoon* and *Lance*,
Let's strive our publick Treasure to Advance;
So shall Returning Gold reward our Toil,
When *London Lamps* shall glow with *Irish Oil*[8]
To the *Undertaker*[9] let us shew Regard,
His Merits Value and his Pains Reward,
Who has a worthy *Publick Spirit* shewn
To raise the *Kingdom's Good* with Hazard of his *own*.

8 Whale-oil for use in lamps.

9 i.e. the person prepared to finance the undertaking.

PART III
1740–1769

WETENHALL WILKES
(1705/6–**1741**–1751)

Wetenhall Wilkes – one of eighteenth-century Ireland's more endearing eccentrics – was born in County Cavan and educated at Trinity College Dublin. Wilkes was a spendthrift who soon found himself heavily in debt and was forced to take up residence in the debtors' prison in Dublin. While in prison, he wrote and published several long, rambling poems including 'The Humours of the Black Dog' which he dedicated to Swift: he later claimed, quite implausibly, to have sold 17,000 copies of this most peculiar poem in two months. He went on to write opinionated but engaging books of advice for young ladies and a book on religion for children.

Around 1740, Wilkes moved to England where he wrote and published a highly entertaining poem entitled *Hounslow-Heath* celebrating angling, coursing and hunting. He also produced a strange volume he called *An Essay on the Pleasures and Advantages of Female Literature. … To this are subjoin'd A Prosaic Essay on Poetry, … The Chace, a poem, and three Poetic Landscapes* (London, 1741). The three poetic landscapes are Irish and the poems are dedicated to three landowners in the Cavan and Fermanagh area from whom, presumably, Wilkes expected some reward. Though not great poetry, the poems are of exceptional interest for their detailed accounts of Irish houses and gardens in the 1730s. Wilkes was also one of the few poets to explore the relationship between cultivated and 'wild' spaces in Ireland and to give some account of the part each played in social life. At some stage, Wilkes was ordained into the Anglican church and, by the time of his death, was rector of a parish in Lincolnshire.

from: Bellville, a poem
Inscrib'd to Thomas Fleming Esq.[1]

On rising Ground,[2] within a Valley plac'd,
With chequer'd Hills at easy distance grac'd,
A Structure stands; built uniform and neat –
With all the beauties of a Country Seat …
Full on the Front the beamy God displays
The chearful warmth of his Meridian Rays.
Soft rising Breezes, gentle and serene,
Salute each Window from the Sylvan Scene:
The well til'd Hall in vary'd Angles spreads
And to a Stocho'd, lofty Stair-Case leads.[3]

1 The Flemings were a military family who spent considerable sums on improving Bellville, Co. Cavan in the 1730s.

2 <About 4 *English* Miles S.S.W. of *Cavan*.>

3 The floors of halls in substantial eighteenth-century Irish houses were usually covered in black and white tiles arranged diagonally, while the walls were stuccoed.

A sumptuous Parlour opens to the Right;
And shews a triple Prospect of Delight.
The Builder's Skill the Chambers all declare;
And do, though plain, a decent Grandeur wear.

This Fabrick does agreeably present
From ev'ry Side, an easy, slow Descent;
But from the Front an unforced Level spreads,
Where various Beauties creep along the Beds.
A spacious Terrass lies before the Door,
Cemented well and smooth as any Floor.
Upon the Borders of a velvet Plain
Both Sides, where various other Beauties reign,
With taper Trees of Box and Yew are grac'd
Of equal Size, at equal Distance plac'd.
To this an Avenue, serpentine, leads,
Adorn'd with Trees above the shelving Meads.[4]
Just at the Enterance of which there stands
A spacious Gate-way built by curious Hands.
Within two fair Parterres appear to view
All sorts of Flow'rs of lovely Form and Hue.
The painted Tulip, Lily, fragrant Rose,
A blooming Wilderness of Sweets[5] compose.
The pale Narcissus, and the bright Jonquil,
With rich Perfumes th'enamel'd Carpet fill.
On th'Eastern Side delightful Plots appear
Diagonally form'd—tall Hedges rear
Their waving Heads in various Figures round.
The Ear's diverted with the murm'ring Sound
Of Waters falling from a small Cascade,
Down to a Bason in the Garden laid.

Before the Front, upon a gentle Height,
A strong Enclosure stops the wand'ring Sight;
In former Times a *Danish* Fort—but now
A Circle where all kinds of Fruit-Trees grow;[6]

4 gradually sloping meadows.

5 'Wilderness' was a term of art in landscape design of the period.

6 The two 'Danish' forts (i.e. ring forts) and their incorporation into the landscaping at Bellville are clearly seen on eighteenth-century maps of the demesne.

Fair to the Eye, delicious to the Taste,
With pleasant Walks, and neat Divisions grac'd.

From this a grand extended Terrass leads,
Along the Hill adorn'd with graceful Shades;
To the End of which another *Danish* Fort
Does most agreeably our Footsteps court.
Off to the left before our straying Eyes,
A fine Decoy[7] within a Deer-Park lies.
With tuneful Notes the Thrushes charm the Woods,
While various Wild-Fowl sport about the Floods.
In safe retreat they on the Surface play,
Till from the Fowler's view they wing their way.
Then clam'rous Plover, Teal and Wild-Ducks rise,
And cackling Flocks, like Clouds, obscure the Skies.
The airy Circles all commence their Flight,
Float on the Winds, and overcome the Fright;
Nor leave their helpless and unfeather'd Care,
But flutt'ring round them hover in the Air.

The western Side is sweetly compast in,
With shaggy Skirts[8] of an embroider'd Green.
A curious Terrass pleasant Plots divides,
And just Diagonals adorn the Sides.
When on this Terrass we our Steps advance,
Our Wonder gay Varieties enhance;
Tall, antient Trees an ample Shade display,
Expel the Sun, and form a doubtful Day.
Between two Walls we gradually descend,
And o'er a wide Canal our Sight extend.
All on a sudden in a sweet Surprize,
A tranverse Terrass courts our ravisht Eyes.
Thrice fifty Yards in length—from End to End,
Two stately Walls the finest Fruits defend.
From this with easy Steps our Feet explore,
A velvet Slope of fifty Foot or more;

7 A pond or pool out of which run narrow arms or 'pipes' covered with network or other contrivances into which wild ducks or other fowl may be allured and there caught. (*OED*)

8 trees or bushes surrounding the space.

Which to th'imprison'd Water's Margin leads,
On a dead level with two spacious Meads.
Round which a Sylvan Scene ascending grows—
Here from its Spring a chrystal River flows:
A winding Vale the peaceful Flood receives,
And here the Stream its glassy Bosom heaves.
Of this thy Skill its native Course depriv'd,
Judicious Owner! This thy art contriv'd.

Swift o'er the Waters glides the nimble Boat,
While on the Surface frothy Bubbles float.
Two smiling Loves adorn the shining prow,
And silken Streamers lightly dancing flow.
When faintly bright descending *Phœbus* gilds
With milder Rays the clover-painted Fields;
When a low Murmur whispers thro' the Trees,
And smiling Flow'rs enrich the balmy Breeze;
The breathing Hautboy and the sharper Flute,
With varying Tones the mellow Fiddle suit.[9]
Then sooth'd by Harmony the Passions rise.
And pleasing transport kindles in our Eyes.
Th'Amusement all with equal Rapture share,
And ev'ry Breast is free from ev'ry Care. ...

Just at the Southern End of this Canal
And at the head of a delightful Mall[10]
A Grotto stands, adorn'd with various Shells ;
In whose deep hollow list'ning Echo dwells,[11]
Here curious Works and Busts amuse; and here.
Large Sheets of pannel'd Looking-Glass appear;
Which to false views the entring Eyes invite,
And most agreeably deceive the Sight
When on the parching Earth in sultry Days,
Apollo darts his most directed Rays;

9 It was not unusual for music to be provided to enhance the pleasurable experience of those viewing Irish estate lakes from the water. Hautboy = oboe.

10 a walk bordered by trees.

11 In Greek mythology, 'Echo' was a wood nymph.

When his Meridian Beams collected beat,
And ev'n the thickest Shades are pierc'd with heat,
Cool as the Fair One's[12] Grotto was of old,
Where the young Stranger his Adventures told,
To that fair Nymph, who sev'ral Years before
Receiv'd his Father on her grateful Shore;
Or ev'n as Thetis Grot[13] —
O'er Head is built a Pleasure Room; and here,
We view the Glories of the rip'ning Year.
Beside the Door a Bowling-Green is spread
Near fifty Foot Diameter—and made
In form a Circle, regular and neat,
Round which is rais'd a decent, mossy Seat.
To this, contiguous from a shelving Wall,
In foamy curls the murmuring Waters fall.
Into this fair Canal—at th'other end,
Superfluous Bubbles o'er a Bank descend.
The gentler Stream from hence a Channel leads,
In wild Meanders by the flow'ry Meads;
And, wand'ring thro' a venerable Wood,
It steals a Passage to its native Flood. ...

Convey me, Goddess, to the Eastern Side,
Where an huge Mountain boasts Romantic Pride;
Whose bulging Brows in wildest order rise
Rude, Chaos-like, and seem to prop the Skies.
Th'unequal, craggy Masses hang; and hence
The spangled Rocks reflect an awful Glance.[14]
Here an high Wall o'er a vast tract of Ground[15]
Performs a winding, long, laborious round.

12 <*Calypso*, Queen of the Island *Ogygia*.> In Homer's *Odyssey*, Calypso kept Odysseus on her island for seven years intending to make him her immortal husband.

13 There was a famous grotto dedicated to the Greek goddess Thetis in the gardens of the palace of Versailles.

14 Glance is a variety of ore with a lustre that indicates its metallic nature: thus the line means that the sparkling rocks show that they contain ore or some awe-inspiring metal. It is possible that Wilkes was playing with the double meaning of 'glance' and with the similarity of sound in 'awe/ore'.

15 <Here I am conscious of transgressing the Rules of Poetry; a Line of Monosyllables being seldom allowable.> In parts of Ireland long boundary walls built up and over mountains in the eighteenth century are still extant.

Here watch the tender Deer, their fearful Fawns
Stray thro' the Shrubs, and browse the Marshy Lawns.[16]
Securely here they first each other chase,
Then couchant lye at Ease in close recess.
Here from the Heath the black-tail'd Moor-cock[17] springs,
And slowly moves his Wet-incumber'd Wings;
Till from an hostile Gun a Show'r of lead
Breaks forth in Fire and Smoak, and strikes him dead.
The shudd'ring Pout[18] with Wings expanded lyes,
His Feet draws to his Breast, and with a spring[19] he dies.

Unto the painful summit of this height
A gay Gazebo[20] does our Steps invite.
From this, when favour'd with a Cloudless Day,
We fourteen Counties all around survey.
Th'increasing prospect tires the wandring Eyes:
Hills peep o'er Hills, and mix with distant Skies.
But, as they sharpen in th'ethereal hight;
Their rudeness lessens to our distant Sight.
Beneath the Shade of this incumbent Hill
The space between embroider'd Valleys fill:
Upon its Sides impending Fragments grow;
Th'expanded Arms of Pleasure lie below[21]
A thousand Beauties still remain behind.
That ask a Taste like *Addison*'s to find.[22]...

16 untilled, grassy land on the mountain side.

17 grouse.

18 young bird.

19 quick, convulsive movement.

20 a belvedere or lookout building.

21 These lines seem to refer to human habitations built in the valleys around Bellville, including those attached to the pleasure grounds at Swanlinbar which would have been visible from the hill.

22 Joseph Addison (1672–1719) whose essays in *The Spectator* were, throughout the eighteenth century, considered authoritative in matters of taste.

WALTER CHAMBERLAINE(?)
(*c*.1706–**1741**–1754)

Though it appeared anonymously, this poem has been ascribed to Rev. Walter Chamberlaine (*c*.1706–54), brother of the playwright Frances Sheridan and one of the wits in Trinity College Dublin in the 1730s. After a shaky start (in which the clergyman-poet complains that he seems 'doom'd to a Country Church remote and Poor'), the poem gathers pace and interest as the muse persuades the poet to 'paint' the 'Eye-enchanting Scene' of the newly reconstructed Powerscourt House and its magnificent demesne. After considering the tasteful 'improvements' and 'classick Landskips', the poet turns his attention to the famous waterfall in the grounds of Powerscourt and gives a fine verse description of one of the main tourist attractions of eighteenth-century Ireland. The poem is dedicated to Richard Wingfield, the owner of the house and estate.

from: A Poem occasioned by a view of Powers-court House, the Improvements, Park etc.,

… O let my rapt Imagination trace
The Site and Sylvan Genius of the Place,
Where Nature varies, yet unites each Part,
And Chance reflects Advantages to Art;
Or let my Eyes in bold Excursions gain
The swelling *Vista*, and the sinking Plain,
(Where a free Heav'n the Sight's wide Empire fills,
Then melts in distant Clouds, and blueish Hills.)
Or gently catch'd by Views more regular
Take in the verdant Slope, and rais'd Parterre.

Hence, from this *Taste*, are Numbers pleas'd and fed,
The Wise have Pleasure, the Distress'd have Bread,
This Taste brings Profit, and improves with Sense,
And through a thousand Channels turns Expence,
Benevolence in num'rous Streams imparts,
And ends in Virtue what began in Arts,
Removes sharp Famine, Sickness, and Despair,
Relieves the asking Eye, the rising Tear,
Such Woe, as late o'er pale *Hibernia* past[1],
And such (ye Guardian Powers) we wish the last.

1 i.e. the great frost and famine of 1739–41.

If publick Spirit shines, 'tis just at least
To give some Glory too, to *publick Taste*,
Which bids proud Art the pillar'd Fabrick raise,
Scoops the rough Rock, and levels vast High-ways,
Plans future Woods for Prospect and Defence,
And forms a Bower a hundred Summers hence,
Ideal Groves, and Beautys just in View—
But such (my Friend)[2] as Time shall bring to you,
Fresh blow your Gardens! intermingl'd Scene!
Soft Carpet Walks, and Green encircling Green,
A chequer'd Space, alternate Sun and Shade,
The Country round, one wide delicious Glade!
Enamel'd Vales with fair Horizons bound,
Here tow'ring Woods, and pendant Rock-work round!
With graceful Sweeps here mazy Windings run,
Or gently meet in Lines where they begun,
Here gushes down steep Steps a ductile Rill,
There spreads in fluid Azure, broad, and still,
So mix'd the Views, so exquisitely shewn,
Each flow'ry Field and Valley seems your own,
While Nature smiles, obsequious to your Call,
Directs, assists and recommends it all.
At last she gives (O Art how vain thy Aid)
To crown the beauteous Work, a vast Cascade.

Say Muse, who listens where the *Shannon* roars,
Which once divided Empires with its Shoars,
Tell in her western Course immense and fair,
Can all the Falls and Cataracts compare?
Let grand *Versailles* her liquid Landskips boast,
Pure Scenes of Nature here delight us most,
Her rudest Prospects bid the Fancy start,
And snatch the Soul beyond the Works of Art—
O would some Master Hand adorn thy Walls
And catch the living Fountain as it falls,
The gay Original would crown thy Dome,
—And you then boast your noblest Scene at Home.

2 i.e. Richard Wingfield.

Lo! down the Rock which Clouds and Darkness hide
In wild Meanders Spouts a Silver Tide;
Or sprung from dropping Mists or wintry Rills,
Rolls the large Tribute of the Cloud-topp'd Hills;
But shou'd the damp-wing'd Tempest keenly blow
With whistling Torrents, and descending Snow,
In one huge Heap the show'ry Whirlpools swell,
And deluge wide the Tract where first they fell
'Till from the headlong Verge of yon black Steep,
A tumbling River roars intense and deep.
From Rock to Rock its boiling Stream is broke,
And all below, the Waters fall in Smoak. …
The Soul from Indolence to Rapture wakes,
'Till on th'unfolding Ear the Water breaks
This Sound when Night has sadden'd all the Skyes,
The Traveller hears [a]far with wild Surprize:
High o'er the waving Landskip dark with Trees,
A distant Murmur swells upon the Breeze:
Now near, now duing varies with each Blast
Then settles in a sullen Roar at last. …

Description flags—let Thought the rest express,
A Theme untouch'd, delicious to Excess,
Profuse of all the Soul can wish or love,
—A Landskip in the Golden Dreams of *Jove*! ...

SAMUEL SHEPHERD
(1701/2–**1741**–1785)

Samuel Shepherd, a graduate of Trinity College Dublin, was rector of the village of Leixlip near Dublin for many years in the middle of the eighteenth century, having been chaplain to two Lords Lieutenant, the Earl of Chesterfield and the Duke of Dorset. His substantial poetic output includes translations from the classics, odes, lighthearted love lyrics and surprisingly outspoken poetic responses to Swift's 'scatological' poems. His best-known poem (the one that follows) is dedicated to William Conolly (1706-54) – not the famous 'Speaker Conolly' of Castletown House, Celbridge (1662-1729), but his nephew who lived in Leixlip Castle before inheriting Castletown in 1752. This poem refers to the great frost of 1739–41.

from: Leixlip

LEIXLIP! thy devious Walks, thy vary'd Views,
Which oft delighted, now call forth the Muse:
Not the proud Glare, which Wealth untaught by Sense
Provides—, the Trophy of a dull Expence;
But Nature well through all her Tracks pursu'd;
Wild without Waste; and beautifully rude;[1]
Where Art (her Handmaid) steps with equal Pace,
Smooths the rough Scene, and brightens ev'ry Grace.

SOME Virgin thus, a tender Mother's Care
Sends out to join th'Assemblies of the Fair;
With watchful Eye surveys her native Form,
And heightens here. And there conceals a Charm;
Fits ev'ry Fold; proportions ev'ry Dress;
Gay, without Pride; and rich, without Excess:
The Shape, the Features are the Damsel's own;
And but improv'd, by being better shewn....

WHERE its high Top the spacious Building[2] rears,
How pleasing is the Form which Nature wears!
Full in its Front the wide-extended Plain
Spreads to the Eye, and swells the golden Grain:

1 rugged.

2 Leixlip Castle, which dates from 1172 and is reputedly the oldest continuously inhabited building in Ireland.

Slow-rising Hills, and Tufts with Verdure crown'd
Vary the Scene, and close the happy Ground.
Here scatter'd up and down the sloping Mead
Stands a wild Oak, and glories in its Shade.
There, form'd but late to taste the Sweets of Toil,
The cleanly Village just begins to smile,
New to the joys which honest Pains entail!
And yonder stretches the delicious Vale;
Till lost in Wildness and confus'd with Joy. …

HERE musing, o'er the Surface as I bend;
And in its Bosom see new Woods depend,
Lost in the various Scene; at length mine Eye
Marks, where the Trout devours the passing Fly;
Nimble, as Thought, he springs: the Circles play,
And curling wear the mimick Grove away.

ROUS'D by the sudden Motion I proceed,
And gladly follow where the Path shall lead;
Till the cool Grotto, or the wave-worn Seat,
Afford my wearied Steps a kind Retreat.
New Wonders wait me here—on yonder Side
Hangs a steep Cliff, and frowns upon the Tide,
Dreadful as Death! one solid Rock embrown'd!
No Trees, no Pastures bless the horrid Ground:
But, here and there, some stunted Shrub appears,
The Dwarf of Nature; the Disgrace of Years;
Curs'd in its Growth; just able to supply
Some wand'ring Goats sufficient not to die.

FOR softer Views my wearied Eye wou'd search,
And, turning, meets yon venerable Arch,
The Remnant of a Bridge: that long withstood
Its Partner's Fate, the Fury of the Flood;
Ragged and rough: around, on either End,
Twines the thick Ivy, and its Boughs depend.
Beside it seems a pensive Ash to grow;
Enough to hold by as you gaze below;
While from its Womb with unresisted Force
The rapid Torrent pours his headlong Course,

Foaming he sweeps along; the frighted Shore
Groans, as he passes; and the Caverns roar. …

And yet ev'n here, such Strength has Love supply'd!
The dauntless Salmon scorns the raging Tide.
Impatient of Restraint, he twines around;
Joins his two Ends;[3] and from the vast Profound
Darts o'er the Steep. As when some Chief in Fight
Strains the tough Eugh,[4] till both its Horns unite,
Then, loos'ning with impetuous Recoil,
Speeds the swift Arrow, and demands the Spoil:
So springs he: so his golden Sides upheaves:
And a new Rainbow gilds the broken Waves.

OFT in some vacant Hour, serenely gay,
Fair *Anna*[5] here beguiles the Evening Ray,
Wrapp'd in sweet Solitude (the Nurse of Thought)
Counts o'er the Rules by virtuous *Sages* taught:
Or thro' th' engaging Paths of Wit pursues
Some fav'rite Author, some well-manner'd Muse;
Or ever by the Silver Spout supply'd
Pours the warm Coffee's aromatick Tide:
The smoaking Fragrance fills the vaulted Room,[6]
And glads old *Liffy* with the rich Perfume.

BENEATH, mine Eye surveys from yonder Wood
The *Liffy* rolling his majestic Flood.
Smooth for a while he laves the neighb'ring Grounds,
Nor seems to murmur at his narrow Bounds:
But, as some Passion, which usurps the Mind,
Wears a deceitful Calm, while close confin'd;
Then bursts at once, and gives a Loose to Rage;
No Force can stop it; and no Art asswage:

3 It was thought that, before they leapt from the water, salmon would take their tails in their mouths.

4 yew (branch) i.e. bow.

5 Conolly's wife was Anne, daughter of the crypto-Jacobite Thomas Wentworth, first earl of Strafford of the second creation (1672–1739).

6 Presumably a tea-house built beside the river. This passage (like many in eighteenth-century writing) echoes Pope's description of the enjoyment of tea and coffee in *The Rape of the Lock* (1712).

So he, with double Fury pouring o'er,
Breaks thro' the Gates; and swells along the Shore:
Where'er the Rocks their craggy Summits shew,
There his Foam thickens; *there* his Surges grow:
Till rolling on, rejoicing in his Pride,
Where the Arch widens and the Shelvings guide
At once th'impetuous Torrent falls; the Steep
Bends with the Weight: new boils the troubled Deep:
The Billows roar: till whitening o'er the Tide
The Foam runs smoother, and the Waves subside;
The softening Surface glads the neighb'ring Swain;
Joy to the Eye, and Plenty to the Plain. …

YET this vast Weight of Waves, this furious Force,
The Hand of Frost can shorten in its Course.
As when, by Wealth's and Nature's Gifts supply'd,
Some thoughtless Youth exults with airy Pride:
If (unsuspicious of th'approaching Dart)
A sudden Damp strikes deep into his Heart;
Stopp'd in his gay Career; amaz'd; aghast;
His Spirits faulter, and he breathes his Last;
Stiff stretch the Nerves, his Cheeks forget to glow;
His Wit to sparkle, and his Blood to flow.
So, when the piercing Rage of *Eurus*[7] roars,
And *Winter* opens his inclement Stores;
Seiz'd by the chilling Blast, the Torrent's Speed
Breaks short; nor tho' it struggles can proceed:
Hush'd is the watry Dinn: the Waves above
Freeze, as they flow; and stiffen, as they move:
Pendent in Air the new-born Chrystals spread;
And Rocks of Ice enclose the dumb Cascade. …

7 classical god of the east wind.

WILLIAM DUNKIN
(1705–**1741**–1765)

William Dunkin, who came from County Louth, was born in 1705. He was educated at Trinity College Dublin, where he was a member of a group of lively young scholars who entertained each other and the Dublin coffee-houses by publishing scurrilous verse satires. He joined the circle around Swift who described him as 'a Gentleman of much Wit, and the best English as well as Latin poet in this Kingdom'.[1] Dunkin's English verse is certainly ebullient, original and witty and he regularly exploited his classical learning by translating his own English poems into Latin or Greek – or both. He became headmaster of Portora Royal School, Enniskillen in 1746. The poem that follows is on the great frost of 1739–41, and was written in both Latin and English – which partly explains its Latinate vocabulary and syntax.

The Frosty Winters of Ireland, in the Years 1739, 1740

Long had the swains with envious eyes beheld
The smiling face of better Heaven, and fields
A-float with golden grain. At length from Hell
A baneful fury twice effus'd her breath
Malign, twice, gliding o'er Hibernia's coast,
Her cities widow'd of their mournful tribes,
And wide the region of laborious hinds.[2]

A fell[3] infection, (whether through the stroke
Of chance, or fate, or vengeful Heaven, (how due
To crimes repeated!) and the treasur'd wrath
Of God offended,) on the rushing wings
Of winds descended, harbinger of death,
And desolation. Bellowing aloft
The sky gave signal: burst the magazines[4]
Of elemental war from pole to pole;
While nature, sick'ning through the frighted globe,
Forgetful of her usual tenour shrunk,
As into chaos: such a shock she felt,

1 *The Correspondence of Jonathan Swift*, ed. Harold Williams, 5 vols, second ed. (Oxford, 1965), V, 86.

2 i.e both cities and fields were deprived of their miserable inhabitants and workers. Wide = empty; hinds = labourers. Dunkin is translating the Latin '… miseris viduavit civibus urbes, Et campos late cultoribus'.

3 destructive, ruthless.

4 storehouse for arms and ammunition.

As when, deluded by the tempter's wiles,
The mother of mankind, amid the gifts
Of life immortal, disobedient pluck'd
Forbidden fruit, and tasted future death.

The vagrant rivers, in their prone career[5]
Congeal'd, arrested, at the voice divine
Horrific stood, and through the liquid lakes
And arms of ocean, watry fields admire[6]
Unwonted burthens. Fiery foaming steeds
Bound o'er the polish'd plain,[7] and human crowds
Securely glide, and glowing chariots fly
With rapid wheels. Beneath the glassy gulph
Fishes benumb'd, and lazy sea-calves[8] freeze
In crystal coalition with the deep.

The hoary winter, beldam of the year
Unteeming,[9] inly binds the frigid womb
Of all-productive earth. In frequent bands[10]
The cattle perish, and the savage kind,
With each his food; not moisture in the plants
Abides, nor verdure in the bladed grass.
The seed, committed to the faithless glebe,
Belyes the peasant's hope, and, chilled beneath,
Dies unprolific: nor through rigid fields
Neglected brambles, horrid, and perplex'd
With bryar-vines, and poison-pointed thorns,
Alone decay: Vertumnus,[11] all thy pride
Falls in the stem: the various families,
Of rose trees, myrtles, and adopted flow'rs
Resign their odour-bearing souls: nor now
The cypress rises into verdant cone,

5 i.e. their normal downhill flow. Vagrant = wandering.

6 are astonished at.

7 i.e. the ice.

8 seals.

9 mother (or nurse) of the unfruitful year.

10 great numbers.

11 Vertumnus was the Roman god of the seasons, change and plant growth.

Nor into head the fashionable box,[12]
Smit by the frost. In gardens, though immur'd,
Or hedg'd, the pear, and apple-tree, late wont
From summer-beams to yield a shady dome
To noon-tide swain, and to the thirsty lip
Nectareous draughts, and blush with orient gold,
Promiscuous[13] dye. The regal oak in vain
Objects[14] its boughy shield, encircled thick
With lesser subjects of the wood, inur'd
To brave the ruins of inclement skies,
The threats of winds, and tempests, big with hail,
Deep through its fibres, and the triple bark
Imbibes the horror keen, and polar bane.[15]

In vain the birds their plumy coats oppose
To Boreal blasts:[16] the penetrative cold
Pervades their downy limbs, and hearts, transfix'd
With lancet-air: those, upward soaring, leave
Their frozen lives beneath the stars: but these
With eager eyes devour the luring bait,
That shines, beneath an icy mirror barr'd,
And mocks with pure deceit their empty beaks:
They pining linger in the rigid gate
Of tardy death, and in their fall expires
The various music of the vernal grove.

In vain the race of animated bees
Maintain their waxen cells, and citadel
Of woven straw:[17] benum'd with cold, they lose
Their inborn ardour, their ethereal stings,
And, slothful, murmur with a dying buzz.
But piteous Famine, the severer scourge

12 i.e. the box tree.

13 indiscriminately.

14 put out its boughs as a shield.

15 ruin and death.

16 Boreas was the north wind in classical literature.

17 Beehives were made of straw in eighteenth-century Ireland.

Of Heaven, advances, as the fruitful means
Of life decrease: haggard, and pale, the fiend
With sullen grief and anguish overwhelms
Afflicted mortals, and with wild amaze
Appalls despairing citizens, aghast,
Dragging with sickly pace a length of limbs.

Mean-while the winds, with rage redoubled, breathe
Death far and wide: with whirling eddy rush
Loud-rending storms: each grove with hideous crash
Re-echoes, and the long resounding waves
Of naval ocean, whitening into foam,
Boil from the nether bottom, and uprol
Successive, fluid mountains to the stars.

Not sandy shores at other times expos'd
More shatter'd prows, or billow-broken keels:
But, if the waves had haply roll'd to land
Some, warm with vital motion, and a-broach
With oozy brine, they stiffen at the breath
Of Boreas, marrow-piercing, and adhere
In senseless union, to the frozy rocks.

But from the tow'ring north, ingend'ring ice,
Impetuous rattle stony show'rs of hail,
And wintry Jove on snowy wings descends.
The vallies, rising into hills, and wide
The plains continuous whiten with a fleece
Condense,[18] nor aught the pathless eye surveys,
But one vast, hoar, interminable waste.

In vain the warrior-horse with neighing smites
High Heaven, and with his hoof the prostrate plain;
While to his pious lord the toilsome ox,
Of honest front, with rueful aspect pours
At empty crib[19] his bellowing complaint.

18 a thick, condensed white mass (of snow).

19 manger.

But fleecy flocks in vain would utter forth
Even doleful bleating: they, through devious paths
Oppress'd with hoary heaps, receive a scant[20]
Of subtil air, and cold, scarce breatheable:
With shrivel'd hides, contracted to the bone,
Against themselves unnatural they whet[21]
Their hungry rage, and, pastur'd on the wool,
Invade their limbs with self-consuming teeth
Rapacious, and enjoy the native pest.[22]

The swain, unbroken with incumbent toils
Through fleaky frost, sharp ice, and cumbrous rain,
Sudden before the genial hearth expires,
Articulately[23] numb'd, and, lo! the wife,
The softer guardian of his falling house,
Sooths with her hand, close pressing to her breast
The tender pledge of love, her infant babe;
When stupid, motionless, as figur'd stone,
She stares: the faultring accents, on her tongue
Stiff, into silence everlasting freeze.

20 scanty supply.

21 sharpen.

22 This line seems to mean that the sheep suffer pestilence because of their cannibalism: the Latin text is '… laceri cognata peste fruuntur.'

23 clearly.

THOMAS HALLIE DELAMAYNE
(1718–**1742**–1773)

This poem is addressed to the famous Irish portrait painter Francis Bindon (*c.*1690–1765), asking him to paint a particular scene and suggesting, in precise detail, what the poet thinks should be included in the painting. The device enables the poet to highlight particular events and so emphasize their political or social significance while appearing to stand back from them. Though the section of the poem that follows concerns the great frost in Ireland in the winters of 1739/41, the poem as a whole was inspired by the portrait Bindon had painted of Hugh Boulter, archbishop of Armagh, for the workhouse 'near Dublin'. The picture, which shows Boulter dispensing charity to the needy, now hangs in the Provost's House in Trinity College Dublin.

Thomas Delamayne was a good classical scholar and a prolific writer. He was educated at Trinity College and spent some years as a barrister in Dublin. He then went to London where he became known as an anti-establishment figure. His poems critical of the Westminster parliament were very popular when they appeared in the early 1770s and are, even today, highly entertaining.

from: To Francis Bindon Esq.
on a picture of his Grace Dr Hugh Boulter,
Lord Arch-Bishop of Armagh ...

… O'er the froz'd North, I'd stretch a sheet of snow,[1]
No native green should chear, no berry blow;[2]
Depending[3] clouds and fogs condens'd should lie
O'er the white surface, and obscure the sky.
No orbs of night should grace the neighbouring pole,
The orb of day a ball of sulphur roll.
Here the rude floods, as from their steeps they fall,
Caught in their course, should stand an icey wall,
And, further, on their glassy bosoms feel
The waggon's weight, and wear the tractless wheel.
The towns, whose situations far divide
Their tongues and mariners, 'cross the dang'rous tide,

1 The froz'd North is Ulster. Throughout this section of the poem, the poet is telling the painter what he would put in the painting himself, or what he thinks the painter 'should' put into the 'piece'.

2 come to perfection, ripen.

3 low-hanging.

In vent'rous intercourse and traffic strange,
Should now their necessary aids exchange.[4]
The wing'd-heel Scater on the surface flie,
The Learner scarce the slipp'ry plain should try,
The sad disasters of the Croud be shewn,
The fall, the death-struck blow, and fractur'd bone.
The Miller, in his garb of sully'd flour,
Opposing entrance, fill his half-shut door,
In seeming arguments and sad descants,
Wailing his own distress, and Neighbours wants:
The fountain-springs now stop'd, which us'd to fill
The current veins, the wheel of life stands still.
The hungry Corm'rant on his faithless pond,
Fetter'd in ice, be to a statue ston'd;
Pinion'd by cold, Air's jocund Chorists lie
Couch'd on the ground, or reach their springs[5] and die;
The Stag invite the Hound;[6] the tim'rous Hare
Seek the smoak'd cottage and implore the spear.
Lost in a sleeting mist, the Trav'ler's sense,
Mock'd of his way, should stand in dead suspence;
Bent to the whirlwind's drift, the Hors'd-man fast
So-journey on, life's stage already past.[7]
The woolly Flock plunge in the treach'rous snow;
The bellowing Ox for food his pastures blow;[8]
And Man, athirst, scarce lift the ax to cleave
A moist subsistence from the hardened wave,
Or force with prongs of steel the marbled ground,
In search of roots, and ev'n those roots unsound.
Hence naked Want and Famine lean should spring,
And pale Disease spread wide her putrid wing,

4 <There are parts or openings of rivers in *Ireland*, called Loughs, of great extent; one, nine miles across.> The lines mean that the inhabitants of towns normally separated from each other by stretches of water can now help each other easily (by walking over the ice).

5 The nooses or snares set to catch small songbirds.

6 i.e. 'the stag attracts the hound to itself' – presumably (like the hare in the next line) wanting to be killed and so escape the cold.

7 This seems to mean that the horseman, lost in the drifts caused by the whirlwinds, travels fixedly onwards, this part of life's journey already being past for him, i.e. he will die.

8 i.e. tries to melt the snow with his warm breath.

The Fever hence, attended by Despair,
Its blood-shot eyes should, fix'd on Pity, glare.
Here the sick Mother fall, and at her breast
The famish'd Infant cling, and drink the pest.
Nor should the rustic Hinds alone regret
The miser frost and bankrupt season's debt;[9]
In cities throng'd should wand'ring Crouds be seen
Fainting with hunger, and with sickness green;
In yards of burial rows of coffins lie,
Fill'd with their dead, implorers to the skie:[10]
Earth, grown unkind, refuses to receive
Her clayey Children in her peaceful grave. …

Prelates and Peers, through furrow'd lanes of snow,
Ask public alms to aid the public woe:
They, whose free purses served Mankind before,
Man's wants increas'd, turn beggars for the Poor.[11]
Each Noble's table, once a sumptuous feast,
Which rich variety and splendour graced,
With all luxuriant meats of pride and cost,
In which their fruitful Country once did boast,
In bounties better multiplied, affords
A frugal banquet to their sparing Lords. …

Nor foreign to the piece[12] would Dangan's[13] flame
Raise adverse horror from the sad extream.
Gay *Dangan! We'sley*'s hospitable seat!
Where ev'ry Merit sure reception met!
With ev'ry ornament of Taste improv'd!
Lamented now, as for its Master lov'd!

9 This odd couplet seems to mean that countrymen ('hinds') are not the only ones to regret the fact that the season is bankrupt so can't pay what it owes – (while the miserly frost won't pay up either).

10 <The ground was so frozen, that for many weeks it could not be dug for common burial.>

11 <The Lords *Blessington*, *Tullamore*, and several of the Nobility and Bishops, publickly walked the streets to raise contributions for the distressed Citizens. And most of the Nobility and Gentry left off their second courses, to lighten the extravagant prices of the Markets, and threw the usual costs thereof into the fund of the charities.>

12 i.e. the painting.

13 Dangan Castle, Trim, Co. Meath. <A beautiful seat then belonging to Richard Wellesley, Esq; now earl of Mornington, was at this time totally burnt, the ponds and adjacent waters being frozen.>

High in the piece her fiery head should rise,
Spreading wide sheets of flame mid way the skies;
Through the wet mist the blaze should red appear,
And tinge the regions of the highest air;
Then far, below, should o'er the frosted white
Shed a broad gleam in circling rays of light.
The gather'd Croud around the flame should wait,
Like Mourners at the pile, and wail its fate.
Some, all confused, a wild of thought express,
Others stand calm'd, yet senseless to redress.[14]
Here the old Servant view with swelling eyes,
Where each rich piece of costly splendour lies,
The tyrant rage; a statue, there a bust,
Half wrapt in flame, part here already dust.
Sad spectacle! what can they do? Though nigh
Around, lakes, streams, and ponds commanded lie,
Those treacherous servants to all help were froze;
Nor now for once were flame and water foes:
A close conspiracy hard Nature lays,
And fierce Destruction unresisted preys.

The Sailor, beaten by th'inclement skie,
His rudder froze, lab'ring to port should plie;
The ropes within their pullies clog'd should stand,
Nor run in office[15] to his gripeless hand:
Yet, thro' kind Providence by pitying gales,
The Wind to port should set his stiffen'd sails,
Candied in frost, the ropes all glist'ring bright:
At once a beauteous and a piteous sight!
Down from the yards the coral'd ice should grow,
The deck and sides a rock of crystal'd snow.
The Pilot at the helm, congeal'd by cold,
Erect in death, should still the rudder hold.
Others, yet dead in part, with feeble pow'r,
Make signs for help to Crouds agast on shore …

14 incapable of doing anything to save the situation.

15 as they should do.

New scenes of new distress—not long to last,
Should shew the greater horrors of the past.
The snows, now runing from each pendant shore,
Rise into floods and into torrents pour;
The Steer and plough together spread the flood;[16]
The loaded flood appear a floating wood;
The bolder Bull, upon his plains rever'd,
Sprung on the stream, should lead the swiming Herd,
To make the distant hills; thick by his side
The feebler flocks should fill the deadly tide.
Now the bared fields a gastly scene disclose
Of Herds and Herdsmen, Flocks and Trav'lers froze;
Who, lost in pathless snows and sunk in death,
Seem still in various attitudes to breathe;
Like monumental statues of the fate,
They and their Race once felt in Nature's state!
Deep in a valley sunk, a cottage low,
Hedg'd in a gather'd heap of drifted snow,
Beset by Nature, and cut off from aid,
And now too late by human help display'd,
Should lie. Here Father, Mother, Son around
Crippled in death, should strew their houshold ground;
The virgin Daughter, with erected hair
Agast, and on her cheek the frozen tear,
Strove, all her cure, their icey roots to raise[17]
O'er the green wood, which still refus'd the blaze,
To feed their quiv'ring lips; the cauldron cleav'd
Hard to its parent Earth; she weakly heav'd
To loose its hold; at length, herself o'ercome,
She in her struggles fasten'd on her doom;
Compleating death in the domestic tomb! ...

16 The meaning of this passage is unclear.

17 i.e. to get a fire going using the icy, green wood.

LAURENCE WHYTE
(*c*.1683–**1742**–*c*.1753)

Laurence Whyte, who was born in County Westmeath, became a teacher of mathematics in Dublin. He wrote a prodigious quantity of verse and described himself on the title pages of his two volumes as 'A Lover of the Muses and of Mathematics'. Several of his poems depict the effect on ordinary people of the drastic economic changes of the early eighteenth century – particularly rising agricultural rents and huge fluctuations in the price of foodstuffs from one year to another. The first poem we have selected is one of a pair; this poem, 'Famine' describes the effect of the great frost of 1739–41 – and was immediately followed, in the 1742 printing, by a poem entitled 'Plenty: a poem on the sudden fall of Corn in Dublin, July 1741; by the vast importation of all kind of Foreign Grain, and the great Prospect of a plentiful Harvest'.

Famine: a poem
On the great DEARTH and SCARCITY of Bread, in the Year 1740 and 1741

How many bards of old have wrote for Bread?
When pinch'd with Hunger, what fine Things they said?
Whether they wrote in Parlour, or in Garret,
Or quench'd their Thirst with Water, Ale or Claret,
Or by their Stars left for themselves to shift,
They were sometimes caress'd like POPE, or SWIFT.
How comes it now, that in this Year of Want,
When Famine reigns, and Bread so very scant,
That Wit, and Humour rather sink than rise,
And seem to tally with the Baker's Size.[1]

The *Rich* complain that *Wine's* excessive dear,
The *Poor* cry out, that *Ale* is but Small beer,[2]
'Tis Strange that *Mault*[3] when sold at double Rate,
Its Juices have no Influence on the Pate,
So thin and weak, our Secrets we may keep,
And late at Night go soberly to sleep,
This is a Secret none but Chymists know,
And for our Health they keep our Spirits low.

1 i.e. get smaller, like the loaf of bread. The size of a loaf of bread was determined by statute – though when wheat was in short supply, bakers reduced the size.

2 i.e. what is being sold as strong ale is, in fact, weak, inferior beer.

3 whiskey.

No Joke, or Fun, no Song or merry Tale,
Goes down as usual, over *Irish Ale*;
While Shoals of Beggars crou'd at ev'ry Door,
Who cou'd some Months before relieve the Poor,
With many others languishing you meet,
Sunk down by Famine, stretch'd along the Street,
More dismal still should we relate you all;
This Evil's grown more epidemical,
The Nation groans, the Poor unnumber'd dye,
And long unbury'd in each Road they lye.

In HUMPHRY'S[4] Days, the DEAN and DUNKIN writ,
And ev'ry Day produc'd some Sketch of Wit,
STERLING[5] with other Authors tun'd their Lays,
Threw in their Mites, and join'd in HUMPHRY'S Praise,
Who in his Mayoralty gave us a Loaf,[6]
That we in Conscience, then thought big enough;
But cou'd he see our Wants in Forty-one,
Our Tradesmen famish'd, and their Credit gone,
With all our Miseries for want of Bread,
He'd wish himself again among the Dead;
With wishful Eyes the Poor gaze at his Sign,
For him they mourn, and for his Loaf they pine.

When Heav'n was pleas'd to visit us with Woe,
With Cold intense, uncommon Frost and Snow:
Each rapid River then was at a Stand,
And greatest Lakes as passable as Land.
Some Authors say that Islands us'd to float,
To change their Stations like a Ship or Boat;
This if we grant them, for a Truth well known,
Ours must have winter'd in the frigid Zone.
The Earth lock'd up her Treasures under Ground,
And Dearth began to spread itself around:

4 Humphrey French, Lord Mayor of Dublin 1732–3.

5 The references are to Jonathan Swift, William Dunkin and James Sterling.

6 I Geo 11, c. 16. This set the size and quality of bread to be sold in Dublin. See Kenneth Milne, *The Dublin Liberties* (Dublin, Four Courts Press, 2009) p. 40.

The Horn of Plenty[7] flew up from the Earth,
And left behind it Poverty and Dearth,
With Evils equal to Pandora's Box,[8]
Contagion, Famine, Death, and deadly Shocks.

The Poor first felt its dire Effects with Cold,
When Coals were at excessive Prices sold;
Then Corn and Cattle rose to such a Rate,
The Rich were pinch'd to purchase Bread or Meat;
Then honest FAULKNER[9] fill'd the City Chair,
Perform'd each Part becoming a Lord Mayor:
To do us Justice, labour'd Night and Day,
To stem the Torrents that came in his Way;
His active Sheriffs seldom were at Ease,
Nor cou'd their *Posse*, raging *Mobs* appease,[10]
Who are the *Pest* and *Hydra*[11] in all Reigns
Like many-headed Monsters without Brains.

In proper Time and Place, the pow'rful Wand[12]
Hath been transfer'd to Cook's[13] unerring Hand,
With all the Honours then on him confer'd
In strongest Terms, and with Attention heard
To him our grateful Thanks are ever due,
Who does with ZEAL ASTRÆA'S[14] Path pursue,
Poises her *Ballance* with a steady Hand,
And stops the Progress of th'extorting *Band*,
Who to convert their Heaps of *Corn* to *Gold*,
Took tripple Value for each Peck[15] they sold;

7 world of plenty, cornucopia.

8 A box which, when opened (as it was, in Greek mythology, by Pandora) releases all kinds of evils onto mankind.

9 Daniel Faulkiner, Lord Mayor of Dublin 1739–40.

10 Since there was no regular police force, the sheriffs enforced the law; the Dublin sheriffs were answerable to the Lord Mayor.

11 The many-headed, deadly serpent of Greek mythology.

12 his rod or staff of office.

13 Samuel Cooke, Lord Mayor of Dublin 1740–41 – when this poem was written.

14 In Greek mythology, Astræa, daughter of Zeus, personified justice.

15 a measure of quantity of grain – about the amount needed to make a loaf of bread.

Forestal'd the Markets, and engross'd the Grain,[16]
Starv'd half the Kingdom to augment their Gain;
This by th'Inspection, Management and Care,
Of Cook our present vigilant Lord Mayor,
Was strenuously oppos'd, and by his Wand,
Allay'd the *Famine* spreading o'er the Land,
And as a Father takes the City's part,
Whose Lamentations penetrate his Heart,
Exerts himself as far as *Law* can reach;
But to our *Farmers* 'tis in vain to preach,
'Till Foreign Corn reduces them to Reason,
And Heaven gives Prospects of a better Season.

16 i.e. purchased the grain before it reached the market to keep the price articially high.

LAURENCE WHYTE
(*c*.1683–**1742**–*c*.1753)

The extract below is from Whyte's most famous poem, 'The Parting Cup or the HUMOURS of Deoch an Doruis', which depicts life in County Westmeath in the early years of the eighteenth century. Whyte describes the world of a substantial Catholic farmer to whom he gives the name 'Deoch an Doruis', which he translates as 'the parting cup' and by which he means a generous and hospitable man. (Ir. *deoch an dorais*: a stirrup-cup or parting drink.) Towards the end of the poem, Deoch an Doruis and his family have been reduced to abject poverty by rack-renting landlords, and Whyte outlines the effects this has on life in rural Ireland.

from: The Parting Cup
or The HUMOURS of Deoch an Doruis alias Theodorus, alias Doctor Dorus, an old Irish Gentleman ...

... Thus Farmers liv'd like Gentlemen
E're Lands were raised from five to ten,
Again from ten to three times five,[1]
Then very few cou'd hope to thrive,
But tug[g]'d against the rapid Stream,
Which drove them back from whence they came;
At length, 'twas canted[2] to a Pound,
What Tenant then cou'd keep his Ground?
Not knowing which to stand or fly,
When Rent-Rolls[3] mounted Zenith high,
They had their choice to run away,
Or labour for a Groat a Day,
Now beggar'd and of all bereft,
Are doom'd to starve, or live by Theft,
Take to the Mountains or the Roads,
When banish'd from their old Abodes;
Their native Soil were forc'd to quit,
So Irish Landlords thought it fit,

1 i.e. rents per acre were raised from five shillings to ten, to fifteen, and finally to twenty shillings (one pound) per annum. These changes took place over the thirty-year period covered by the poem.

2 sold at auction.

3 The rents payable on the rent-roll or landlord's list of rented land.

Who without Cer'mony or Rout,
For their Improvements turn'd them out.[4]
Embracing still the highest Bidder,
Inviting all Ye Nations hither,
Encouraging all Strollers, Caitiffs,[5]
Or any other but the Natives.

Now Wooll is low, and Mutton cheap,
Poor Graziers can no Profit reap,
Alas! you hear them now complain,
Of heavy Rents, and little Gain,
Grown sick of bargains got by Cant,
Must be in time reduc'd to Want,
How many Villages they rais'd
How many Parishes laid Wast!
To fatten Bullocks, Sheep, and Cows,
When scarce one Parish has two Plows,
And were it not for foreign Wheat,
We now shou'd want the Bread we eat.
Their Flocks do range on ev'ry Plain,
That once produc'd all kind of Grain
Depopulating ev'ry Village,
Where we had Husbandry and Tillage,[6]
Fat Bacon, Poultry and good Bread,
By which the Poor were daily fed.
The Landlords then at ev'ry Gale,[7]
Besides their Rent, got Nappy Ale,[8]
A hearty welcome and good Chear,
With Rent well paid them twice a Year.
But now the Case is quite revers'd,
The Tenants ev'ry Day distress'd,

4 Whyte returned to this theme in a poem entitled 'Gaffer and Gammer, with the Humours of a bad Landlord: a Tale' in his 1742 *Original Poems on Various Subjects*, pp. 14–17. In that poem, he tells of an improving farmer who entertains his landlord well and, as a consequence, 'Next Year poor Gaffer was turn'd out/For brewing Ale so very stout,/For being generous and free,/As Farmers whilom us'd to be.' (whilom = once).

5 villains.

6 cf. Oliver Goldsmith's *The Deserted Village*, written a few years after this poem. Goldsmith and Whyte were both brought up in the Irish midlands.

7 a periodical payment of rent.

8 a strong, home-brewed ale.

Instead of living well and thriving,
There's nothing now but leading, driving.[9]
The Lands are all monopoliz'd,
The Tenants rack'd and sacrific'd,
Whole Colonies to shun the Fate,
Of being oppress'd at such a Rate
By Tyrants who still raise the Rent,
Sailed to the Western Continent,[10]
Rather than live at home like slaves,
They trust themselves to Wind and Waves. ...

9 i.e. families evicted when they could not pay the higher rents are now forced to travel from place to place, 'leading' or 'driving' their animals as they seek pasturage.

10 America or the West Indies.

THOMAS MOZEEN
(*fl.*1744–1768)

Thomas Mozeen was an English actor who lived in Dublin for two years in the 1740s. He seems to have spent his time drinking and riding, and was well known to several residents of counties Wicklow and Dublin, including the sixth Earl of Meath and Owen Bray, the hospitable landlord of a public house at Loughlinstown. Mozeen's most famous poem, the song that follows (sometimes known as 'The Killruddery Hunt'), celebrates a fox hunt which took place in 1744. The persons named were all well-known in hunting circles at the time and the places named can be traced today.

A Description of a Fox-Chase
that happened in the County of Dublin, 1744, with the Earl of Meath's Hounds

Hark, hark, jolly Sportsmen, a while to my Tale,
Which, to claim your Attention, I hope, will not fail:
'Tis of Lads, and of Horses, and Dogs, that ne'er tire
O'er Stone Walls, and Hedges, thro' Dale, Bog and Briar:
A Pack of such Hounds, and a Set of such Men,
'Tis a shrewd Chance if ever you meet with again.
Had *Nimrod*,[1] the mightiest of Hunters, been there,
'Fore gad he had shook like an Aspen for Fear.
La, la, la, &c.

In Seventeen Hundred and Forty and Four,
The Fifth of *December*—I think 'twas no more,
At Five in the Morning, by most of the Clocks,
We rode from *Killruddery*,[2] to try for a Fox;—
The *Laughlin's* Town Landlord, the bold *Owen Bray*,
With 'Squire *Adair*, sure, was with us that Day;
Jo Debill, *Hall Preston*, that Huntsman so stout,
Dick Holmes, (a few others); and so we set out.
La, la, la, &c.

We cast off the Hounds for an Hour or more,
When *Wanton* set up a most tuneable Roar:

1 A descendant of Noah and a 'mighty hunter' (Genesis 10.9).

2 The seat of the earls of Meath, in north County Wicklow.

Hark to *Wanton*! cry'd Jo—and the rest were not slack,
For *Wanton*'s no Trifler esteem'd by the Pack:
Old *Bonny* and *Collier* came readily in,
And every Dog join'd in the musical Din.
Had *Diana*[3] been there, she'd been pleas'd to the Life,
And some of the Lads got a goddess to Wife.—
La, la, la, &c.

Ten Minutes past Nine was the Time o' the Day,
When *Reynard* unkennell'd, and this was his Play;
As strong from *Killeagar*, as tho' he could fear none;
Away he brush'd round, by the House at *Kilternan*;
To *Carrick Mines* thence, and to *Cherrywood* then;
Steep *Shank Hill* he climb'd, and to *Ballyman Glenn*.
Bray Common he past; leap'd Lord *Anglesea*'s Wall;
And seem'd to say, 'Little I value you all.'
La, la, la, &c.

He ran Bushes, Groves, up to *Carbury Bourns*;[4]
Jo Debill, and *Preston*, kept leading by Turns;
The Earth it was open,[5]—but *Reynard* was stout,
Tho' he cou'd have got in, yet he chose to keep out:
To *Malpass*'s Summits[6] away then he flew;
At *Dalkey*'s Stone Common, we had him in View.
He shot on thro' *Bullock* to *Shrub Glenagary*,
And so on to *Mount Town*, where *Larry* grew weary.
La, la, la, &c.

Thro' *Roche*'s Town Wood, like an Arrow he past,
And came to the steep Hills of *Dalkey* at last;
There gallantly plung'd himself into the Sea,
And said in his Heart, 'Sure none dare follow me'.
But soon, to his Cost, he perceiv'd that no Bounds
Cou'd stop the Pursuit of the staunch mettl'd Hounds.

3 The mythological goddess of the hunt, normally depicted naked and carrying a bow and arrows.

4 A note in early editions of the poem identifies Carbury Byrne as a carpenter who lived in the area.

5 i.e. the fox's earth or hole had not been stopped up to prevent his returning. stout = brave.

6 What is now Killiney Hill was owned, at this time, by a Colonel Malpass.

His Policy here didn't serve him a Rush:
Five Couple of Tartars[7] were hard at his Brush.
La, la, la, &c.

To recover the Shore, then again was his Drift,
But e'er he could reach to the Top of the Clift,[8]
He found both of Speed, and of Cunning a Lack;
Being way-laid, and kill'd by the rest of the Pack.
At his Death there were present the Lads that I've sung,
Save *Larry*, who, riding a Garron,[9] was flung.
Thus ended, at length, a most delicate Chace,
That held us five Hours and ten Minutes Space.
La, la, la, &c.

We return'd to *Killruddery*'s plentiful Board,
Where dwells Hospitality, Truth, and my Lord[10]—
We talk'd o'er the Chace, and we toasted the Health
Of the Man who ne'er vary'd for Places or Wealth.
Owen Bray baulk'd a Leap; said *Hal Preston*,—'twas odd;
'Twas shameful, cry'd *Jack*—by the great living God!
Said *Preston*, I halloo'd, Get on, tho' you fall;
Or I'll leap over you, your blind Gelding, and all.
La, la, la, &c.

Each Glass was adapted to Freedom and Sport;
But party Affairs we consign'd to the Court.[11]
Thus we finish'd the rest of the Day and the Night,
In gay flowing Bumpers, and social Delight.
Then till the next Meeting, bid Farewell each Brother;
So some they went one Way, and some went another.
And as *Phœbus* befriended our earlier Roam,
So Luna took Care in conducting us Home.[12]
La, la, la, &c.

7 savage animals.

8 cliff.

9 small horse; cf. Ir. *gearrán*, gelding or small horse.

10 Chaworth Brabazon (1686–1758), sixth Earl of Meath and owner of the Killruddery hunt.

11 i.e. we did not discuss politics, which would be discussed at court.

12 Phoebus = the sun; Luna = the moon.

HENRY JONES
(1721–**1744**–1770)

Henry Jones was born near Drogheda and trained as a bricklayer. He began writing poems and was introduced to Lord Chesterfield, Lord Lieutenant at the time. Chesterfield gave Jones considerable support in Dublin and, later, in London where his *Poems on Several Occasions* (London and Dublin 1749) was very successful, as was his play, *The Earl of Essex*. Jones eventually took to drink and died in poverty.

Earlier in the century, in 1705, the distinction between Irishmen who grew peas and beans (i.e. the planters whose farms were on rich soil) and those who grew potatoes (i.e. the native Irish, banished to farming on poor land in hilly regions) had been clarified in Seán Ó Neachtain's poem '*Cath Nearna Chroise Brighde*', 'The Battle of Bearna Chroise Bridhde'.[1]

On a fine Crop of Peas being spoil'd by a Storm

WHEN Morrice views his prostrate Peas,
By raging Whirlwinds spread,
He wrings his Hands, and in amaze
He sadly shakes his Head.

Is this the Fruit of my fond Toil,
My Joy, my Pride, my Chear!
Shall one tempestuous Hour thus spoil
The Labours of a Year!

Oh! what avails, that Day by Day
I nurs'd the thriving Crop,
And settl'd with my Foot the Clay,
And rear'd the social Prop!

Ambition's Pride had spur'd me on
All Gard'ners to excell;
I often call'd them one by one,
And boastingly would tell,

1 The poem tells of a faction fight between the growers of peas and the growers of potatoes that probably took place in County Wicklow in 1705. See Nicholas Williams's edition of the poem in *Zeitschrift für Celtische Philologie* 38 (1981), 269–337.

How I prepared the furrow'd Ground,
And how the Grain did sow,
Then challenged all the Country round
For such an early Blow.[2]

How did their Bloom my Wishes raise!
What Hopes did they afford,
To earn my honour'd Master's Praise,
And crown his chearful Board!

Poor Morrice, wrapt in sad Surprize,
Demands in sober Mood,
Should Storms molest a Man so wise,
A Man so just and good?

Ah! Morrice, cease thy fruitless Moan,
Nor at Misfortunes spurn,
Misfortune's not thy Lot alone;
Each Neighbour hath his Turn.

Thy prostrate Peas, which low recline
Beneath the Frowns of Fate,
May teach much wiser Heads than thine
Their own uncertain State.

The sprightly Youth in Beauty's Prime,
The lovely Nymph so gay,
Oft Victims fall to early Time,
And in their Bloom decay.

In vain th'indulgent Father's Care,
In vain wise Precepts form:
They droop, like Peas, in tainted Air,
Or perish in a Storm.

2 Blossom, flowering.

HENRY JONES
(1721–**1746**–1770)

This poem by Henry Jones commemorates a series of lectures on experimental philosophy given at 'the Great House in Anglesea-Street' in Dublin by John Booth in 1744. The lectures covered gravity and the solar system, and included experiments to demonstrate the mysterious powers of electricity and magnetism. It was not unusual for young ladies to attend such demonstrations.

Philosophy:

a poem address'd to the Ladies who attend Mr Booth's Lectures.

To Science sacred, Muse, exalt thy Lays,
Science of Nature, and to Nature's Praise:
Attend ye Virtuous, and rejoice to know
Her mystic Labours, and her Laws below;
Her ways above with curious Eyes explore,
Admire her Treasures, and her God adore.

Behold ye Fair[1] how radiant Colours glow,
What dyes the Rose, what paints the Heav'nly Bow,
The purpling Shade, the rich refracted Ray,
And all the bright Diversity of Day.
Lo! here the Magnet's Magic charms the Sight,
And fills the Soul with Wonder and Delight,
In her, coy Nature turns her Face aside,
And mocks th'enquiring Sages learned Pride;
Here, less reserv'd she shows her plainer Course
In mutual Contest of Elastic Force,
Saving each vital Frame from crushing Fate,
For inward Act sustains external Weight,
Which holds reciprocal in ballanc'd Strife,
The Shield of Nature, and the Fence of Life:[2]
The ambient Atmosphere, embracing all
The wide Circumf'rence of this circling Ball,
The Vehicle of Life, to those that breathe
On solid Land, or liquid Waves beneath,

1 i.e. the ladies who attend the lectures.

2 These lines reflect the difficulties of mid eighteenth–century philosophers in finding a vocabulary to explain the newly discovered phenomena of the natural world.

The Universe pervading, filling Space,
And like its Maker unconfin'd to Place.

What pleasing Fervours in my Bosom rise,
What fix'd Attention and what deep Surprize,
When quick as Thought th'electric Vigour springs,
Swifter than Light'ning on its rapid Wings,
A Flight so instant to no Space confin'd,
Eludes Ideas, and outstrips the Mind?[3]
Lo! to the Brain the bright Effluvium[4] flies,
Glows in the Heart and flashes from the Eyes:
Here the fond Youth with raptur'd Eye shall gaze,
And proudly warm, enjoy th'extatic Blaze:[5]
See the proud Nymph partake his Flame by Turns,
See! like a Seraph, how she smiles and burns.
Contracted here by wondr'ous Art is seen
A boundless System in a small Machine;
Here human Skill to proud Perfection brought,
The mortal Mimic of Omnific Thought,
Th'Almighty's Model to the Mind conveys
The Universe, and all its Pow'rs displays:
How wander Planets, how revolves the Year,
The Moon how changes, and how Comets glare.
The Sun's bright Globe illumes th'unmeasur'd Space,
While waiting Worlds enjoy by Turns his Face,
From his bright[6] Presence drink enliv'ning Rays,
From him their Seasons gain, from him their Days;
See Wisdom here her brightest Beams display,
To fill the Soul with philosophic Day,

3 This long passage refers to experiments with an electrical machine. These were common at the time and provided much entertainment as electrical currents were passed through various parts of the body. See the article and plates on 'Electricity;' in *Moore's Dublin Encyclopaedia Britannica*, 18 vols (Dublin 1791–1804) VI, 418–545. The electric current generated by the 'machine' of line 40 caused the 'fond youth' of line 35 to enjoy a sensation of warmth and the 'proud nymph' of line 37 to 'smile' and 'burn' like a seraph while her heart glowed and her eyes flashed.

4 discharge. Electricity was thought to be a liquid.

5 The British Library copy of the poem contains amendments to these couplets in a contemporary hand: 'Here the fond Youth with new Rapture shall gaze,/With joy transmitting the extatic Blaze.'

6 amended to 'rich' in the BL copy.

The Springs unfolding of mechanic Laws,
Tracing through known Effects th'eternal Cause,
Whose pow'rful *Fiat*, whose creative Will
First founded Nature, and supports her still.
Here godlike NEWTON's all capacious Mind,
(The Glory and the Guide of Human Kind)
Shows wedded Worlds far distant Worlds embrace
With mutual Bands, yet keep their destin'd Space,
Roll endless Measures through th'etherial Plain,
Link'd by the social[7] strong attractive Chain,
Whose latent Springs exert all Nature's Force,
Inwrap the poles, and point the Stars their Course.
Mysterious Energy! stupendous Theme!
Immediate Mover of this boundless Frame,
Who can thy Essence, or thy Pow'r explain?
The Sons of Wisdom seek thy Source in vain;
Thyself invisible, yet seen thy Laws,
This goodly Fabrick thy Effect, and GOD thy Cause.

Thrice happy few who wisely here attend
The Voice of Science, and her Cause befriend:
Let others, heedless of their youthful Prime,
Squander on empty Toys their fleeting Time;
'Tis yours, with Reason's searching Eye to view
Great Nature's Laws, and trace her winding Clue;
Behold her Book the op'ning Page expand,
Fill'd with the Wonders of her Maker's hand,
In awful Characters, which clearly shine,
Worthy of Wisdom, and of Pow'r divine.
Peruse God's ways, his perfect Workings trace,
In Nature's Mirrour shines his heavenly Face.

To you, bright Nymphs, where Goodness charms us most,
The Pride of Nature, and Creation's Boast,
To you Philosophy enamour'd flies,
And triumphs in the Plaudit of your Eyes.
When Worth like yours her sapient Throne sustains,
The Queen of Science with true Splendour reigns;
By Beauty aided she extends her Sway,
And, won by you, Mankind glad Homage pay.

7 related.

ANONYMOUS
(1746)

Though it has been suggested (by Douglas Hyde and D.J. O'Donoghue in their catalogue of the Gilbert Library [1918]) that this poem is the work of Rev. Samuel Shepherd, rector of Leixlip and prolific poet – for whom see above – this seems unlikely as it was not included by his daughters in their edition of his poems (Dublin, 1790) and it is considerably less accomplished than Shepherd's acknowledged work. In any case, the reference to the author's ridiculous fear that the clergyman of line 39 might object if the poet described Leixlip church reflected upside-down in the river water suggests a non-clerical author.

This servile and obsequious poem is included here not for its poetic merit but because it suggests what contemporary taste might expect in an Irish landscape painting – and specifically because the scene described in the early part of the poem was frequently painted, drawn and engraved in the late eighteenth century. The most surprising of these representation is that of Francis Wheatley whose 'The Salmon Leap at Leixlip with nymphs bathing' (1783) is famous for depicting improbably naked nymphs sporting voluptuously on rocks from which several bathers had drowned. The second part of the poem describes the estate, grounds and gardens of Leixlip castle and proposes totally implausible motives for the improvements carried out in the area by William Conolly (1706–54).

from: Leixlip: a Poem

To a Young Gentleman, on his painting a prospect of the River Liffy at Leixlip

The Muse, tho' conscious of her feeble Lays,
Ventures on thine and *Leixlip*'s further Praise;[1]
Well has thy Pencil touch'd the Canvass o'er,
Where Surges rough in rumbling Torrents roar,
Along St. *Woolstan*'s Rocks and craggy Mead,
To where the Salmon are by Wiles betray'd;[2]
Contemptuously they view th'impending Rock,
Nor dread the headlong-tumbling liquid Shock,
Right up the Foam the scaly Coursers ply,
Disdain to stop, but by disdaining die:
The sounding Cataract's impetuous Weight
Confutes their Pride, and hurls them back to Fate.
So the proud *Gaul*, vain insolence![3] of late
Disdaining Limits to his mighty State,

1 presumably a reference to Shepherd's 1740 poem on Leixlip.

2 The rocks at which the salmon leap was situated were known as St Woolstan's rocks.

3 <This poem was wrote immediately after the Battle of Dettingen.>

Pour'd forth his Troops, his Empire to enlarge,
Where *Britain*'s CHIEF and *Britons* claim'd the Charge;
Tho' firm their Ranks, and Gleams from horrid Steel
Foretold the Fate ten Thousand *Gauls* must feel,
Still they press'd on, till by the *British* Spear
Transfix'd, they learn superior Force to fear,
While Heaps of Carnage moor the slimy Plain,
Or choak the Windings of the purpled *Maine*.[4]

Here roll the Waves precipitately hoarse,
As fond to finish their long-labour'd Course,
'Till within Sight of Anna's Bow'r[5] they flow,
Then stop their Rage, and creep discreetly slow,
Check'd by the River God, in Wonder lost,
To view the Beauties of the neighb'ring Coast:[6]
In wide Expanse they stretch from Side to Side,
Move smoothly on, and with Reluctance glide,
Till quite serene, they seem at once to rest,
To stamp the lively Landskip on their Breast.

Within the Flood[7] see pompous Turrets rise,
Their Heads pursuing the invaded Skies;
The stately Pine, the wide-branch'd swelling Oak,
Chimnies inverted, downward puffing Smoak;
Low in the Wave the lofty Mansion falls,
And sporting Trouts bound o'er the Castle Walls.

Here I cou'd more, but dread the hallow'd Gown,
Should I describe the Church turn'd up-side-down,

4 The Battle of Dettingen, at which the 'Pragmatic' Army of British, Hanoverians and Austrians (led in person by the British King George II) defeated the French, took place on 27 June 1743 on the banks of the River Main in South West Germany. Loyalist references to 'British' victories overseas are fairly frequent in eighteenth-century verse written in Ireland.

5 <Lady Anne Conolly.>

6 The (absurd) idea that the river god persuades the water to slow down at this point – i.e. where Lady Conolly's riverside teahouse is situated – so that it can view the beauties of the river bank, occurs in other eighteenth-century Irish 'prospect' poems describing slow-moving reaches of rivers.

7 i.e. as a reflection in the still water.

The Steeple too, the impious Hands that dare
Subvert the Building, wou'd subvert the Pray'r
Then cease my Muse—

Th'Impression thus receiv'd, with quicker Pace,
The Stream again resumes his angry Face,
Greatly displeas'd he can no longer stay,
And frowns and murmurs as he's forc'd away.

Thus far, young Painter, has thy early Art
Describ'd the Beauties of each single Part,
The Pencil, true to thy instructive Will,
Loudly proclaims the growing Master's Skill:
Yet stronger Beauties call thee forth again,
And claim the Canvass or persuasive Pen.

Then for a while the humble Plain forsake,
The silent Groves, the Meads and curling Lake,
To *Leixlip*'s loftiest Battlements[8] ascend,
Invoke the Muse, or chosen Colours blend;
From thence, extensive may your Eye command
Fair Prospects rising from a barren Land;
Some well dispos'd to please the haughty Mind,
But more for Blessings to the Poor design'd:
Here the rang'd Elms in goodly Order shew,
Exotics there, by Art, are taught to grow;
The flow'ring Lylacks with Syringas wed,
The gay Carnations fragrant Odours spread;
Tulips in rich Brocade of various Die
Tempt the soft Touch, or charm the ravish'd Eye,
New-blown, like Beauties rising into Bloom
In glitt'ring Groups at Birth-day Drawing-Room.[9]
Whate'er your Fancy seeks, behold it here!
The shaggy Precipice or trim Parterre.
Rough Nature first struck out the bold Design,
And softer Art instructs her where to shine.

8 i.e. the battlements on Leixlip Castle, owned by the Conolly family.

9 The reference is to the high point of the Dublin social season – a 'drawing-room' reception in Dublin Castle to celebrate the monarch's birthday.

Now change the Scene, and view more heav'nly Charms,
Where Industry puts forth her nervous Arms;
Th'unwearied Goddess springs from Field to Field,
Forcing the Glebe the golden Grain to yield,
Unknown before, and scented Clover Hay,
Which the great Owner greatly gives away,
Enriching all the Poor; for them he tills,
For them the Barns are built, for them the Mills;
Those costly Piles afford to him no Due,
The Profit's theirs, His only [is] the View;
Content, if he can by Example shew
The Lord to act, the humble Hind[10] to know;
And urge by Reason's Force *Hibernian* Swains
To prove the Culture us'd in *Albion*'s Plains,
Where Sloth, and her Attendant, ghastly Want,
Are rarely known the humblest Cell to haunt,
While in *Hibernia*'s more prolifick Soil,
The Farmer starves thro' an unskilful Toil. …[11]

10 peasant.

11 The (commonly-held) view that England's rural prosperity was the result of its farmers' industry while fertile Ireland's poverty was the result of the laziness of its inhabitants is, in this case, seen as an 'enlightened' rational one.

EDMUND BURKE
(1729–**1748**–1797)

Throughout the seventeenth and eighteenth centuries, there was considerable admiration for Virgil's *Georgics* and their vision of unsophisticated, natural life in the countryside; passages of the text were translated or paraphrased into English by May, Ogilby, Cowley, Creech, Temple, Dryden, Pope, Thomson and many 'gentlemen'. One of the most interesting Irish verse paraphrases is by the young Trinity student, Edmund Burke; the text was printed in Mary Goddard's *Poems on Several Occasions* (Dublin, 1748). The text paraphrased is Virgil *Georgics* II, 458 et seq.

As a young man, Edmund Burke was an enthusiastic reader and writer of poetry. He told his friend Richard Shackleton (a schoolfellow from his time at the Quaker school at Ballitore, Co. Kildare) that this passage of the *Georgics* had always been 'a favourite part'.[1]

from: *O fortunatos nimium, &c.* paraphras'd
By a young Gentleman

OH! happy Swains, did they know how to prize.
The many Blessings rural Life supplies;
Where in safe Huts from clatt'ring Arms afar,
The Pomp of Cities and the Din of War:
Indulgent Earth to pay his lab'ring Hand,
Pours in his Arms the Blessings of the Land:
Calm thro' the Vallies flows along his Life,
He knows no Danger as he knows no Strife.
What tho' no marble Posts nor Rooms of State,
Vomit the cringing Torrent from his Gate;[2]
Tho' no proud Purple hangs his stately Halls,
Nor lives the breathing Brass[3] along his Walls:
Tho' the Sheep cloaths him without Colours Aid,
Nor seeks he foreign Luxury from Trade;
Yet Peace and Honesty adorn his Days,
With rural Riches and a Life of Ease.

1 *The Writings and Speeches of Edmund Burke* ed. T. O. McLoughlin and James T. Boulton (Oxford, 1997), I, 38.

2 Cast out or reject the 'cringing' suppliants from his property.

3 Virgil's original suggests brass or gold objects captured in battle and displayed on the walls of the house. In the next line, the contrast is between clothes made of plain undyed wool and those made of expensive, coloured wool.

Joyous the yellowing Fields, here Ceres[4] sees,
Here blushing Clusters bend the groaning Trees;
Here spreads the Silver Lake, and all around,
Perpetual Green and Flowers adorn the Ground.
How happy too the peaceful Rustic lies,
The Grass his Bed, his Canopy the Skies;
From Heat retiring to the Noontide Glade,
His Trees protect him with an ample Shade:
No jarring Sounds invade his settling Breast,
His looing Cows shall lull him into Rest.
Here 'mong the Caves, the Woods and Rocks around,
Here, only here, the hardy Youth abound;
Religion here has fix't her pure Abodes,
Parents are honour'd, and ador'd the Gods;
Departing Justice when she fled Mankind,
In those blest Plains her Footsteps left behind. …

Happy the Man who vers'd in Nature's Laws,
From known Effects can trace the hidden Cause:[5]
Him not the Terrors of the Vulgar fright,
The vagrant Forms and Spectres of the Night;
Black and relentless Fate he tramples on,
And all the Rout of greedy *Acheron*.[6]
Happy whose Life the rural God approves,
The Guardian of his growing Flocks and Groves;
Harmonious *Pan* and old *Sylvanus* join,[7]
The Sister Nymphs to make his Joys divine. …

The happy Rustic turns the fruitful Soil,
And hence proceeds the Year's revolving Toil;
On this his Country for Support depends,
On this his Cattle, Family, and Friends;
For this the bounteous Gods reward his Care
With all the Products of the various Year:

4 Goddess of corn and the harvest.

5 Dryden's translation of these lines reads: 'Happy the Man, who, studying Nature's Laws, /Thro' known Effects can trace the secret Cause.'

6 In Greek mythology, Acheron was the river of pain.

7 Pan was Greek god of shepherds (and their Panpipes) while Sylvanus was god of forests and uncleared woodlands.

His youngling Flocks now whiten all the Plain,
Now sink his Furrows with the teeming Grain:
Beauteous to those *Pomona*[8] adds her Charms,
And pours her fragrant Treasures in his Arms;
From loaden Boughs, the Orchard's rich Produce,
The mellow Apple and the gen'rous Juice. …

The languid Autumn crown'd with yellow Leaves,
With bleeding Fruit and golden-bearded Sheaves;
Her various Products scatters o'er the Land,
And rears the Horn of Plenty in her Hand.
Nor less than these wait his domestic Life,
His darling Children, and his virtuous Wife:
The Day's long Absence they together mourn,
Hang on his Neck and welcome his Return:
The Cows departing from the joyful Field,
Before his Door their milky Tribute yield;
While on the Green the frisking Kids engage,
With adverse Horns, and counterfeited Rage.
He too when mark'd with White the festal Day,
Devotes his Hours to rural Sport and Play;[9]
Stretch'd on the Green amid the jovial Quire
Of boon Companions that surround the Fire;
With Front enlarg'd[10] he crowns the flowing Bowl,
And calls thee, *Bacchus*, to inspire his Soul.
Now warm'd with Wine to vig'rous Sports to rise,
High on an Elm is hung the Victor's Prize:
To him 'tis giv'n, whose Force with greatest Speed
Can wing the Dart, or urge the fiery Steed. …

8 The goddess of fruit and fruit trees.

9 White clothes and white paint were used to mark days of festival and relaxation.

10 i.e. his face swollen with the pleasures of feasting and drinking.

JAMES KIRKPATRICK
(1696–**1750**–1770)

James Kirkpatrick was born in Carlow and spent time in Dublin as a young man. Presumably he trained as a physician before he sailed to America in the 1720s. Once in America, he became a respected authority on the newly invented practice of inoculation; after his return to England in the early 1740s, Kirkpatrick wrote a textbook on the subject and styled himself 'MD'. *The Sea Piece* (1750), his only published poem, recalls his first voyage from Belfast to America; in the passage that follows, Kirkpatrick contrasts the veniality of the inhabitants of Dublin with the 'superior' natural world of fish and other creatures that live in the sea.

from: The Sea Piece:
a narrative, philosophical and descriptive poem in five cantos

… We pass the Banks where *Carickfergus* stands,
Whose threat'ning Fort defies invading Bands;
But yet her present Ruins scarce declare
What once the Glories of the City were.
In vain her royal Appellation springs
From old *Ierne*'s Race of *Scottish* Kings;[1]
Whilst her young Neighbour[2] late, and new to Fame,
No regal Honours sounding thro' her Name,
Miry and low beside the Lough display'd,
Prevents[3] her Riches, and attracts her Trade.
From the thin Harbour[4] thro' the vocal Town,
The chearful Sailor's *Hail* is rarely known;
Tho' echoing Ruins greedily repeat
Each Clangor straggling thro' the grassy Street;
Whilst on the Quay, where Merchants drove[5] before,
Plato might muse, and Antiquaries pore:
Yet still her Sons some Privileges claim,
And still the Ruins hold a City's Name.

1 Carrickfergus was said to have been founded in the sixth century by Fergus, a king of Ireland and Scotland.

2 <Belfast.>

3 i.e. deprives Carrickfergus of her riches …

4 i.e. of Carrickfergus.

5 carried on their trade.

Two dreadful Rocks[6] contract the opening Port,
Where greedy Ruin holds her frequent Court.
With dazzling Foam her rugged Domes so white
Distract the Vision, and exceed the Light:
Her thund'ring Voice of num'rous Waters roars,
Stuns the wide Deep, and shakes the echoing Shores;

… Yet safe in distant Waves the Rocks we hide,
And from the *Copeland* Islands safely slide.
And when the tedious Empire of the Night,
Slow and reluctant, yields to solar Light,
New Lands we *make*, by various Names expres't,
And *Hoath*'s high Hill discern among the rest.[7]

Pensive and thoughtful on the Poop I stood,
While the swift Vessel cut the yielding Flood.
The Sea-edg'd Mountain to my Mind restores
The sweet Remembrance of the neighb'ring Shores;
Boys Sports and Cares my acted Fancy move,
And earliest Verse inspir'd by earlier Love.
For not far hence, where *Liffy* purls her Way
Thro' numerous Arches to the fishy Bay,
Eblana's Turrets deck the nether Sky,
And with *Augusta*'s only fail to vie.[8]
What pompous[9] Domes their swelling Summits raise!
What gilded Spires amidst the *Æther* blaze!
What Piles antique[10] their rev'rend Beauties show!
Their Fabrics mould'ring as their Honors grow.
What wreathy Spires of curling Smoke appear
Buoyant and floating thro' the heavier Air;
And, hov'ring round the Region whence they rise,
Present a dusky Cloud to distant Eyes!

6 <Call'd the *North* and *South* Rocks.>

7 The ship is travelling down the Irish Sea, leaving the Copeland Islands off Belfast Lough (or 'Carrickfergus Bay' as it was known in the eighteenth century) and passing by Howth Head. Notes in the 1750 text tell the reader that 'make' is a 'Sea-term' for seeing land and that Howth is 'a Mountain at the Mouth of the Harbour of Dublin'.

8 Eblana = Dublin; Augusta = London.

9 splendid, magnificent.

10 stately, old buildings.

But if the Muse descend the misty Sky,
And deign to walk, as now she dares to fly,
What various Themes invite her future Lays!
What various Nations croud the busy Maze!
The bounding Chariots, as they jolt along,
Shou'd range in rougher Ranks the rattling Song.
Here winding Lanes with darker Allies meet,
And a new Scene's display'd in ev'ry Street:
A various Hurry agitates the whole,
Where different Routs pursue a common Goal.
Wou'd you survey the inmost Nest of Trade,[11]
Where Conscience may be sold, or Bargains made;
Wait the meridian Sun, the Hour to thrive,
And listen to the Buzzings of the Hive;
Where num'rous Tones one common Hum compound,
Which floats, unmeaning, on the Waves of Sound.
But if the toiling World delight thee less,
Smit with the tawdry Charms of gorgeous Dress,
Tir'd of the City, ease thy copious Spleen
Amidst the Follies of the fruitful Green.[12]
This is the Region of Grimace, which dwells
Amidst distorted Beaus, and stiffer Belles;
The antic Pow'r no certain Figure knows,
Convuls'd with Grins, or flourishing in Bows: …
So those the Belles impregnate with Grimace
Are *things* so very worthy such a Race,
That one might judge, excluding human Shape,
The reigning Fav'rite were a very Ape.
Tho' some there are, whose Looks would form Pretence
To Thinking, such Hermaphrodites in Sense,
They both beget and bear the Phantom well,
Without the Aid of an affected Belle.

Thou fabled Queller of the tumid Main,
Neptunus hight by *Latium*'s tuneful Train;[13]

11 <The Tholsel or Change.>

12 <St Stephen's Green near Dublin.>

13 i.e. Neptune, god of the sea as celebrated by classical poets.

Indulge the Muse that from thy Realms doth stray,
And o'er the Lands directs her erring Way;
The odious Objects which I trace on Shore
Teach me to love thy happy Realms the more;
Let me inhabit still thy briny Seas,
Thy fishy Bands are Men, and Monsters these:[14]
Yet daily they their Reason quote to prove
Superior Greatness granted from above.
The various Kinds, that in thy Waters play,
Some Rule confess, and never disobey;
Some, who the more exalted Billow shun,
Skip thro' the Surge, and glisten in the Sun;
While their resplendent various Coats receive
A humid Verdure from the cov'ring Wave.[15]
Others there are amongst the finny Throng,
Who through the roughest Torrents shoot along;
Far distant Billows fleetly they pursue,
And seem a massy Fire as sweeping thro';
While those, who sported o'er the gentler Deep,
On shelly Banks in Groves of Coral sleep:
But Men reject the things they just approv'd,
And boast of Reason, while by Caprice mov'd.
Truth reigns amidst the Nations of the Flood,
Prompt to assail their Foes, or seize their Food.
No Shark, whose Jaws his rav'nous Hunger whets,
Feigns to protect the num'rous Shoals he eats;
As Nature meant, the Creature freely preys,
Nor kills from lustful Pow'r, but feeds for Ease. …

14 The peculiar logic here seems to be that the inhabitants of Dublin city are monsters and the inhabitants of the seas are (as good as) 'men'.

15 i.e. the fish look green through the water. The reference is probably to dolphins.

JOHN WINSTANLEY(?)
(1677–*c.***1750**–1750)

Though bathing in sea water was regularly prescribed as a cure for various ailments in the eighteenth century – and indeed became a fashionable recreation celebrated by poets from Blackrock, Co. Dublin to Ardglass Co. Down – there are few references in verse to polluted water. In this poem, the Revd. Mr ------- has clearly been advised to drink sea water to cure his melancholy; but the poet (who may or may not be the John Winstanley of the title of the volume in which this poem appears) warns his friend that sea water tainted with untreated sewage (the source of which might be any privy in the world) could be 'unkind' to his constitution.

To the Revd. Mr ------- on his Drinking Sea-Water

Methinks, dear *Tom*, I see thee stand demure
Close by old Ocean's side, with arms erect,
Gulping the brine; and, with gigantic quaff,
Pledge the proud *Whale*, and from ten thousand Springs
Dilute the hyp,[1] concomitant unkind![2]

For thee th'*Euphrates*, from her spicy banks,
Conveys her healing stream: for thee the *Caspian*
Filters her Balsam; while the fragrant *Nile*
Tinges with balmy dew the greeting seas,
Conscious of thee; whose tow'ring Pyramids
Would pride to lodge thy consecrated Urn.

For thee the sage *Batavian*,[3] from his stern
With face distorted and convulsive grin,
Disgorges eastern Gums, in bowels pent,
And streaks the surge with salutary hue.[4]

1 hypochondria.

2 i.e. at the same time (as you think drinking sea-water will make you healthy), you are being unkind to yourself.

3 Dutchman.

4 The poet probably means 'sanguinary hue'.

For thee the *Thames*, impregnated with Steam
Mercurial,[5] wafts her complicated Dose
From reeking Vaults, full copiously supply'd
By Bums venereal, ruefully discharg'd
By *Ward*'s mysterious Drop, or magic Pill.[6]

5 Mercury was often prescribed as a cure for syphilis.

6 Joshua Ward (1685–1761), a famous English quack doctor, who claimed that his pills and drops (which were in fact a dangerous compound of antimony) could cure almost any ailment.

ANONYMOUS
(1753)

This poem comes from a strange and interesting collection of poems, mostly the work of Church of Ireland clergymen, entitled *The Ulster Miscellany*. Though the book was printed in Dublin, several of the poems in the collection originated in county Donegal; others come from different parts of Ireland. This is more lighthearted than many of the surviving poems about eighteenth-century Irish spas, though it shows a protestant bias common at the time.

A POEM on the *Hot-Wells* at Mallow

Let Irish priests, who bring their faith from Rome,
Strive to support it by their frauds at home;
Of fiends exorcis'd by their charms and spells,
And foul distempers heal'd at holy wells:
All this their poor deluded vot'ries must
(For dare they doubt their clergy?) take on trust.

To such I leave these little tricks of art;
Prompted by truth to act a nobler part:
'Tis solid truth, I, from experience sing,
And can collat'ral proofs abundant bring.

Near *Mallow*, by a range of verdant hills,
A fountain issues forth in plenteous rills,
By nature tepid made, but from what cause!
Let those enquire, who study nature's laws.
Perhaps with sulph'rous particles replete
It may contract this subterraneous heat;
But I shall wave what lies beyond my *ken*,
And only in known truths employ my pen.

This healing fountain far more virtue hath
Than those at *Bristol*, or her sister *Bath*:
But has one fault; too near! ay quite too near,
Else it, for fame, might vie with *Montpelier*.
From the prodigious service it has done
It might be justly stil'd *Catholicon*.[1]

1 <Universal medicine.>

Do any ill-bred humours lurk within,
Or in an itch, or scurvy blotch the skin?
Do growing ulcers on the vitals prey,
Or lungs corrupted hasten a decay?
Do bileous juices make the blood move slow'r,
Or in a jaundice tinge the body o'er?
Do giddy megrims[2] cause the head to swim,
Or sharp rheumatick pains torment a limb?
Or scalding humours oozing from the head,
Afflict the balls of sight, and turn them red?
Then let the patient to this fountain haste,
And find a perfect cure—*probatum est.*[3]

The gravel[4] (not the least of human ills,
For tho' it kills but slow, it surely kills)
Here finds a cure, this diuretick spring
Dissolves the stone, dissolves the pungent sting.

How oft for death did rackt *Hortensius*[5] call,
When sanguine drops distain'd his urinal;[6]
He felt the gravel in its greatest force,
When to this healing spring he had recourse:
But there it vanish'd as it were by stealth,
And left him happy in a flow of health.

Attend ye lovers, while the muse records,
The charming pleasures which the place affords;
Here stands a wood bedeckt with summer's pride,
There the Blackwater rowls his dusky tide;
Here a canal of waters deep and clear,
Whose spouting cascades please the eye and ear;

2 headache, migraine.

3 i.e. it is proved.

4 i.e. stones in the urinary tract.

5 An imaginary name for a man suffering from kidney stones – possibly intended to remind the reader of the Roman orator, Hortensius, who was a great lover of wine and a bon viveur.

6 i.e. when drops of blood stained his urine.

While on the pebble walks fresh air you breath,
Trees nod above, and fishes swim beneath.
Musick in consort, from a side retreat,
Gives life to all, and makes the scene compleat.
At night a gay assembly, and a ball,
Murphy's sweet harp, and dancing closes all.

ANONYMOUS
(1754)

This strange, unsophisticated poem was an attempt by an amateur poet at a Pindaric Ode – a poem on a lofty theme with rhyming lines of irregular length. It was dedicated to 'Secretary Belchier', presumably the author of 'To the Ortolans' above (1726). The poet, appropriately, put as epigraph to the poem the famous couplet from Pope's *Essay on Criticism*: 'Who ever thinks a faultless Piece to see,/Thinks what ne'er was, nor is, nor e'er will be.'

from: The Villa: or Glasnevin, a poem
Written in imitation of Cowley's Pindariques, ...

III

Near to *HIBERNIA*'s grand Metropolis,
Does a small well-built *Village* stand;[1]
It seems another Fairy-land,
Or second Paradise.
Here smoothly flows a dimpling Riv'let by,
There num'rous lovely Gardens lie;
Gardens so charming and so fair,
Those of the fam'd *Hesperides*,
(Fabl'd t'have been a Dragon's care)
Were not more beautiful or rare.[2]
Here *Appollo* strings his lyre,[3]
(Thou God of verse my song inspire)
Here the tuneful Sisters sing,
Here the *Heliconian* spring,[4]
Fills me with poetic ray,
Promp[t]s me to this bold Essay.
The dread Idea horror-strikes my soul,

1 i.e. Glasnevin.

2 The mythical garden of the Hesperides (three beautiful nymphs) was guarded by a dragon, Ladon.

3 Apollo was the god of (among other things) music. The reference is probably to the poet and clergyman Patrick Delany (for whose house in Glasnevin, see above: Thomas Sheridan's 'A Description of Dr Delany's Villa').

4 In Greek mythology, the spring on Mount Helicon was said to be the source of poetic inspiration.

When late the gapeing firmament
Gave the strong imbred struggling Storm a vent;[5]
The livid light'nings flash from either Pole,
Exploding flame the huge concave o'erspreads
And o'er our frighted heads
Hoarse rumbling thunders roll;
Shot from the bursting skie
The vengeful Bolt is seen to fly;
Th'impending clouds a deluge pour,
And seem as they'd again the world devour.
The *Current*[6] swells insuperably strong,
With wrathful force,
And rapid course,
In one promisc'ous throng,
Hurls trees, rocks, herds and cottages along.
Omnipotence this devastation sent,
A prelude to a greater punishment
Of the ungrateful Sons of discontent. ...

IV

Look to the visage of the noon-tide sun:
Dublin's heaven-piercing spires rise;
The distant Mountains stop our eyes;
Westward they circling run;
Into the confines of dull night
Protrude their heads and lose themselves to sight:
They terminate a wide extended plain,
Studded with stately Villas here and there,
Delicious Mansions of content,
Where never harsh intruding Care
Pitches her hated tent.
Now turn the glass[7] towards the realms of day;

5 The Advertisement at the beginning of the poem explains that the storm described 'actually happen'd, and did several considerable Damages…'.

6 <The small River which runs by *Glasnevin*.>

7 Probably a 'Claude' glass – a small mirror, slightly convex in shape, with its surface tinted a dark colour to assist the traveller or landscape artist who wished to view the countryside as if it were a painted landscape. The viewer would turn his or her back on the real landscape and arrange the Claude glass so that what 'struck the eye' in the reflection was 'picturesque' or 'romantique'.

A vari'gated prospect strikes the eye,
It does in sweet romantique contrast lie:
Here we survey the flow'r-enamell'd Meads;
There thought-inviting Groves, and cooling Shades;
Lo where the fleecy Feeders bleat!
The vocal rocks the sound repeat;
Yonder the buxom[8] Heifer roars,
And there we view the lowly Cots, along the stormy shoars.
New beauties the delighted sense surprize,
See where old *Howth* props the incumbent skies!
See the Masons on the *Wall*![9]
Hark! they to the Lab'rers call!
See there the Ships at anchor in the bay!
See others putting out to sea!
Now they unfurl their sails,
And brace them to receive the wanton gales!
Before the wind they steer,
Now they grow less and less! Now wholly disappear!
And there the vast liquid Champain,[10]
Meets with the azure Vault and closes up the scene! ...

8 obedient, meek.

9 <The Wall now building near the south Bull.> The South Bull wall, built to regulate the tides in Dublin Bay, took nearly 50 years to build; it was finished in 1795.

10 expanse.

THOMAS NEWBURGH
(*c*.1695–**1758**–1779)

Thomas Newburgh was born in Dublin, the son of the chairman of the Linen Board. He was educated at Oxford but returned to Ireland when he inherited an estate in County Cavan. The poem that follows is one of very few describing Irish eighteenth-century urban space. It comes from a volume of Newburgh's miscellaneous work entitled *Essays Poetical, Moral and Critical* (Dublin, 1769) which is sometimes wrongly catalogued as the work of his father, Brockhill Newburgh.

In the eighteenth century, the Dublin park of St Stephen's Green was surrounded on each side by tree-lined walks: Beaux Walk on the north (the most fashionable of the walks), Monk's Walk on the east, Leeson's Walk on the south, and French Walk on the west. Between the walks and the central meadow was a ditch, or 'ha-ha', and in the centre of the green was an equestrian statue of George II. Erected in 1758, this statue was blown up in 1937.

The *BEAU-WALK*, in *STEPHEN'S GREEN*

'Mid Trees of stunted Growth, unequal Roes,
On the coarse Gravel, trip the Belles and Beaus.
Here, on one Side, extends a length of Street,
Where Dirt-bespattering Cars and Coaches meet.
On t'other, in the Ditches lazy Flood,
Dead Cats and Dogs lie bloated, drench'd in Mud.
But lo! a Statue from afar salutes your Eyes,
To which th'Inclosure all Access denies.
So distant, whose, or whom, no Eye can ken,
Plac'd in the Centre of a marshy fen.
But know, 'tis Royal George on whom you stare,
Tho' oft mistaken for some good Lord Mayor:
And tho' his Charger foams in ductile Brass,
The Charger for an ambling Pad[1] may pass;
The whole equestrian Statue for a Toy,
A Horse of Hobby, mounted by a Boy.
For shame, ye Cits,[2] where meet th'assembl'd Fair,
Fill up your Dikes and purge th'unwholsome Air.
Let George's royal Form be fairly shewn,
And like his Virtues, be reveal'd and known.

1 A charger is a horse ridden by an army officer in battle, whereas a pad is a slow, steady, reliable one.

2 A (derogatory) term for a town-dweller.

RICHARD BARTON
(1706–**1759**–1759)

Richard Barton graduated from Trinity College Dublin in 1726 and was ordained into the Church of Ireland, spending most of his life as rector of Shankhill, near Lurgan, Co. Armagh. He wrote on religious subjects and also, extensively, on the topography, geology and natural history of Lough Neagh and its hinterland. The poem that follows was designed to encapsulate the substance of his *Lectures in Natural Philosophy* (1751) and was 'for the use of those, who not having the leisure to read the larger work in prose, may by means of verse, not only see, but easily retain in memory, the main truths of that Book'. Barton wrote the poem in both Latin and English, the two texts facing each other. The full title of the work is: *A Physico-Poetical Essay, Concerning the Wonders of Lake Neah, in Ireland. In Imitation of Lucretius. Tentamen Physico-Poeticum, de mirabilibus Lacus Neachi, in Hibernia; Ad exemplar Lucretii; et in gratiam Extraneorum.*

from: A Physico-Poetical Essay,
Concerning the Wonders of Lake Neah in Ireland.[1]

You, who the wonders of this Globe persue,
And, searching deep, its inmost secrets view,
Do not this Rock, judicious POCOCKE,[2] pass,
As deem'd a rude, and indigested mass.[3]

For once a verdant tree, e'er Noah's time,
It grew a Cedar, in some distant Clime,[4]
Brought to IERNE[5] by the gen'ral flood,
Low sunk in earth, long lay the fragrant wood,
Till, losing vegetation's pliant tone,
The stiffen'd fibres harden'd into stone.

1 This poetic abridgment of the prose lectures was (according to a preliminary note) 'drawn up in the form of an Inscription for a Portico, which was built in the rustic form of Architecture, of materials collected at Lake Neah.' These materials are listed in the poem.

2 Richard Pococke (1704–65), protestant bishop of Ossory at the time of this poem. He is best known for his accounts of travels to Asia Minor and up the Nile. He also travelled widely in Ireland.

3 <In the court before the Portico were two Pillars, each supporting extraordinary specimens of Petrification, one like a fragment of a Rock; See its form delineated in the Book of Lectures, etc. mentioned in the Title Page of this; which Book is sold by W. Johnston, Bookseller, in Paul's Church-yard, in London.>

4 The phenonema described in the poem 'afford the strongest argument in favour of the Deluge', i.e. of the universal Flood described in the book of Genesis.

5 Ireland.

Such transformation, in four thousand years,[6]
Amidst the wonders of this Globe appears!

Where Crumlin River[7] runs with rapid rage,
In channel rough, the work of many an age,
And tributary streams in haste conveys,
To Neah's water, rival of the seas,
Masses, which in the banks and channel lie,
Of ligneous-stone,[8] with wonder strike the eye.

Egypt and Italy may boast renown,
For Catacombs a subterraneous town,[9]
And Pyramids; yet not the Curious please,
With natural, rare phenomena like these.

Tell thou, who all hast seen, from this fair Isle,
To the rough rumbling Cataracts of Nile,
Who much of Art, and Nature's Works, canst tell,
From SALEM's city to Saint CANUTE's cell.[10]

View all these specimens, and make it known,
That Neah's Lake transform'd them not to stone;
Though Nennius said it did, eight ages past,
Which still is said, though Truth is shewn at last[11]. . . .

6 The length of time (according to contemporary scholarship) between the date of the flood and 1759.

7 The Crumlin River, flowing into the east of Lough Neagh, the largest freshwater lake in the British Isles, takes its name from the village of Crumlin, Co. Antrim.

8 i.e. stone which has the texture or appearance of wood.

9 <Heraclea, or Herculaneum, buried beneath above 60 feet deep in the Lava of Vesuvius more than 1600 years past, and very lately discovered.>

10 One of the places visited by Pococke in his travels was the city of Salem in Northern India, a geologist's paradise. 'Saint Canute's Cell' is, according to Barton, Kilkenny i.e. Cella Canuti, St. Canute's (or St Canice's) cell.

11 Nennius was a Welsh monk of the ninth century, traditionally said to be the author of the *Historia Brittonum*. The fiction that, over a seven-year period, the waters of Lough Neagh turned wood to stone had been repeated by the Irish bishops George Berkeley (1685–1753) and Robert Clayton (1695–1758) – both of whom, according to Barton, had erred 'in arduous things beyond their reach'.

No change septennial, vainly told, is made,
Of Wood in Neah's spacious bosom laid:
The petrifying virtue could not reach
Two thousand paces from its sandy beach;
Where this stupendous mass, with others, lay,
In elevated ground, of sand, and clay.

The metamorphosis of Cedar wood,
Arises from the Earth and Noah's flood.
If he who doubteth, digs, there will be found
A stony-Cedar-forest under ground,
From Crumlin southward, till the Ban he meets,
Famous for bleaching, and for Colliers fleets.[12]
Thence, soon becoming fossil Coal, it spreads,
A nation's fuel, through all Tir-owen's beds. …

Thus much we know, that here, by Noah's flood,
A forest lodg'd of aromatic wood,
Deeply intomb'd, imbibing subtle fumes,
Of iron, stone, and coal, the form assumes.

Crystalline subtle steams pervade the pores,
And fine effluvia of metallic ores.[13]

Hence Cedar-wood becomes an Iron-stone,
And if it keeps some substance of its own,
A ligno-lapi-ferrous mass, where three
Dissim'lar kinds of matter well agree.

When wood and stone continuous abide,
This side the weapon whets, which cuts that side.

12 The bleaching of linen was carried out on the banks of the rivers Crumlin and Bann; in addition, coal from County Tyrone ('Tir-owen') was carried by barge down the River Bann to the sea at Newry.

13 Here, as elsewhere throughout the poem, Barton inserts a long footnote giving the scientific proofs for what he asserts.

Razors becomes by this so nicely edg'd,
They give no pain to chops of youths new fledg'd;[14]
Nor will they leave on am'rous Thyrsis' chin,
One hair to injure Sacharissa's skin.

Sometimes Bitumen does ingross the whole
Vacuity, and turn it into coal.

And as Tobacco fumes, convey'd with Art,
New qualities to a fluid mass impart,
Peculiar wholesome streams ascend, which make
Collected waters here, a healing Lake;
Strength to the weak, and soundness to the sore,
With Patience bathing near some chosen shore ...[15]

There, Iron-cedar-whetstone masses—Here,
The beauteous Gems in charming light appear.
The hard CARNELION ting'd with blood ne'er fails
The Artist's skill in fashioning of Seals; ...[16]
The Sardin clouds, the Moco stone contains
Forests, and ruins, in well painted scenes; ...
The Opal rich plays on the puzzled sight,
With diff'rent colours, in each diff'rent light.

The PSEUDO-ADAMAS[17] with vivid beams
Shoots from the hexagon, its dazzling gleams. ...
The deep-dy'd RUBY, and the TOPAZ here,
In their unpolish'd, native forms appear.

14 i.e. a razor sharpened on a whetstone taken from Lough Neagh will be so sharp that it will not hurt the skin of a youth who is starting to shave, or leave any hairs of his beard uncut.

15 At this point, the reader is directed to the passages in Barton's lectures where the science underpinning this assertion is explained. Immersion in the waters of Lough Neagh was said to cure various ailments.

16 The references in these lines are to semi-precious stones, the reddish-brown cornelian, the yellowish sard, the mocha stone or moss agate and the opal. Later lines refer to the spinel or Balas ruby and to a yellow 'topaz' form of corundum.

17 pseudo adamant. The reference is to a rock crystal that looks like a diamond. 'Adamant' was the name of a stone with fabulous properties – often confused with the loadstone or magnet, and with the diamond.

The gemmous matter there you also find,
In shells marine, and molds[18] of diverse kind.

View all, and then acknowledge with delight,
Diluvian[19] treasures open'd to your sight,
Truth dug from pits in which conceal'd she lay,
Ages imprison'd from the face of DAY. ....

O! For a MUSE, this Subject to rehearse,
With nervous[20] language, and harmonious verse;
That this fair Island might due praise receive,
And honour him, who all its honours gave;
Whose vengeful anger drown'd this earthly Globe,
Wrap'd in his mercy still, as in a robe;
Who bad the waters to their beds recede,
And from Confusion fair IERNE made.

18 The mould or concave impression left by a fossil in a rock.

19 connected with the biblical (or Noah's) flood.

20 vigorous, forceful.

WILLIAM BALFOUR MADDEN
(*c.*1730–**1761**–1783)

William Balfour Madden was the fifth and youngest son of Revd Samuel Madden (1686–1765), poet, playwright, philanthropist and satirist, a well-known benefactor to Trinity College Dublin and an enthusiastic supporter of the development of Irish agriculture and manufacture. William published only two poems, the one that follows and a scurrilous but entertaining poem on social life in late eighteenth-century Bath (where he lived), entitled *The Bath Macaroni with other Sketches from Nature* (1781).

Bellisle (now Belle Isle Castle Estate) is magnificently situated on an island in Lough Erne in County Fermanagh. The original house was owned by the distinguished soldier, Sir Ralph Gore (later first Earl of Ross), whose military exploits are the subject of the first few pages of Madden's poem. The poet then describes Gore's Irish estate and the activities of his guests.

from: Bellisle: a poem

Inscribed to Sir Ralph Gore, Bart.

... All hail Bellisle, unrival'd Mansion, hail!
Woods, Lawns and circling Waters, Hill and Dale!
On thee has partial Nature pour'd her Store
So fondly lavish Art can add no more. ...

Oh! might I hope with simulating Grace,
To emulate the Wonders of thy Place.
Wide as thy fair Expanse of Waves to flow,
Bright as thy Scenes of varying Tints to glow.
High as thy cloud-capt Mountain to ascend,
Rich as thy flow'ry Vallies to extend.
Then should Bellisle surpass Arcadia's Plains,
Or Cowper's-Hill in Denham's epic Strains;
And e'en aspire with Windsor to engage,
That lives to Fame in Pope's eternal Page.[1]
Now Bellisle's Groves and aromatic Bowers
Appear before me, by Poetic Powers.
Delightful Scenes in quick succession pass,
By Verse reflected in the mental Glass.
We list not[2] to invoke the Pow'rs Divine,

1 The references are to the pastoral poems most popular (and most widely imitated) in the eighteenth century: 'Cooper's Hill' (1642) by Sir John Denham and 'Windsor Forest' (1713) by Alexander Pope. The term 'Arcadia' denotes a world of pastoral peace and perfection.

2 i.e. we do not need to invoke the power of the divinities of the ancient world.

Of laurel'd Phœbus and the tuneful Nine,
Nor borrow Passion from the Cybil's Cell,[3]
Nor drain the Dregs of Aganippe's Well.[4]
More genial Pow'rs our swelling Breast inspire,
And with a warmer, dearer Rapture fire;
Three here with no fictitious Beauties warm,
Beyond the Sisters three times three,[5] in Form;
Amanda, Sylvia, Stella, these we stile
The living Muses of Hibernia's Isle.[6] ...

Peace to the Joys the sportive Country yields,
The gurgling Rivulets, the bleating Fields,
The chirping Hedges and the warbling Groves,
The cooing Eloquence of am'rous Doves.
The whistling Plowman, the resounding Flail,
The rural Sonnet at the milky Pail,
The Star-bespangl'd Eve, the Morning gay,
That breathes the tedded[7] Fragrance of the Hay;
The steepy Forest and the tangled Brake,[8]
The headlong Heav'n, and Landscape in the Lake.
The boundless Verdure dropt with balmy Dew,
The vaulted Canopy of radiant blue,
The fresh Expance of Æther, spread between
The breezy Rapture and the still serene.
Here, here the Joys and Charities[9] unite,

3 <Cybele was the Daughter of Heaven and Earth, and Wife to Saturn; was worshipped by her Priests with the Sound of Drum, Taber, Pipe and Cymbal.>

4 <A famous Well in Bœotia, by Mount Helicon, sacred to the Muses.>

5 i.e. the three young women are three times more beautiful than the three Graces of antiquity – themselves the goddesses of charm, beauty, nature, human creativity and fertility.

6 Footnotes identify the three as 'Lady Louisa Conolly', 'Lady Gore' and 'Miss Frances Conolly'. The last two were daughters of William James Conolly (a nephew of 'Speaker Conolly' of Castletown House, Co. Kildare). 'Lady Gore' was Catherine Conolly who had married Sir Ralph Gore in March 1761 – shortly before the appearance of this poem. Her sister Frances Conolly later married Viscount Howe. 'Lady Louisa Conolly' was sister-in-law to the other two, having married their brother Thomas (known as 'Squire Conolly') in 1758. Her title was hers by right since her father was the Duke of Richmond.

7 spread out for drying.

8 thicket.

9 feelings of benevolence.

Here mental Wisdom weds with Heart Delight;
Here Innocence is Contemplation's Heir,
Here Virtue, turned to Pleasure, laughs at Care,
Frees ev'ry opening Sense from Guilt's Controul,
And ent'ring sinks in Peace upon the Soul. ...

To Boat's the Word, to Boat, to Boat they cry;
The Waters, Woods and echoing Hills reply.
Rouz'd at the chearful Summons, one and all,
At once we issue from the sounding Hall.
Adown the sloping verdant Lawn we run;
Full in our Sight descends the glowing Sun;
The glad Attendants pour obsequious round;
Oars, Nets and ready Tackle spread the Ground.
A sumptuous Pinnace,[10] near the Beach reclin'd,
Spreads her bright Pennants to the curling Wind.
Eager to quit the Firmness of the Land,
Each Hero takes a Goddess by the Hand.
We mount the Deck, the sprightly Clarions sound,
Inspir'd we hear, and look with Rapture round.
Here vivid Levels from the Prospect fly,
There the brown Umbrage bounds the searching Eye.[11]
Aspiring Woods here scale th'æthereal Height,
Here mingling Lawns break chearful on the Sight.
There pendant Forests skirt the winding Shore,
Forests with Moss of former Ages hoar;
Within the Waters, downward, Forests grow,
And touch the Distance of the Sky below.[12]

Far to the Front extends the Lake's Expanse,
The Sun-Beams on the curling Surface dance;
From Shore to Shore a dazling passage glow'd,
And pav'd, with liquid Gold, our watry Road.

Push'd from the Beach, we launch into the Deep;
Respondent Oars a timely Measure keep.

10 An elegantly-ornamented pleasure boat, named 'Hibernia'.

11 Madden uses technical terms drawn from contemporary painting practice.

12 An attempt to describe reflections on the water.

We leave the lessening Objects far behind,
We spread the fluttering Canvas to the Wind.
On ev'ry Hand, to our admiring Eyes,
New Prospects open and new Scenes arise.
Again those Scenes and Prospects die away,
Again those rise to Sight as those decay.
To right, to left, or whither moving round
Our View, a Group of circling Islands bound.
We row, and now again, on either Side,
The Prospects vary, and the Lands divide
With sudden Inlet and with new Delight;
Long watry Vistas stretch before the Sight
Nor give a Limit to the wondring Eye,
Save by black Mountains, or cerulean Sky.
For as Heav'n's Azure boundlessly display'd,
With Starts of thick Irradiance lies inlaid,
Such, and so fair, this inland Ocean smiles,
Gemm'd with an Affluence of disparting Isles.[13]...
For Ev'ry Isle assumes a different Grace,
And claims a Form peculiar to its Place:
These with shagg'd Horrors, and a fearful Steep
Impend and threaten to o'erwhelm the Deep.
These in chaotic Rocks, of monstrous Size,
And Figures of romantic Wildness rise;
In Robes of Russet Tincture these are seen,
These clad in Groves of everlasting green,
While others with Autumnal Foliage glow,
Dipt in the Colours of the show'ry Bow.

And now we ship our Oars, our Anchor cast,
And bind the furling Canvas to the Mast.
We seize our Rods, the circling Links untwine,
And to the Gale let loose the flowing Line.
Destruction to the Finny Race we breath,
And beat[14] the Barb that subtlely lurks beneath. ...

Each Nymph assumes a Rod, the tap'ring Wand
Trembles within the Whiteness of their Hand.

13 There are hundreds of islands in Lough Erne. Disparting = separate.

14 bait.

The Lines fly off, from whose immerging Ends
The dancing Cork and covert Steel depends.[15]
From every Nook the bright-ey'd Perch resort,
And dare the tempting Dangers of the Sport.

The first Success to Sylvia's Art was due;
Light o'er the Wave her glitt'ring Prize she drew;
Stretch'd on the Deck the little Struggler lies
And, panting, spreads its scarlet Finns, and dies.
Amanda bore the second Prize away
And shewed, exulting, her resplendent Prey,
Then swiftly drew; the Scales reflect the light,
And cast a Gleam of Silver cross the Sight.
Fortune the third Success to Stella brought;
By such an Angler who would not be caught?
Again she whirl'd her slender Line, and strait
Another Perch takes down the fatal Bait.
Compassive Sentiments her Bosom fill,
The Virgin sighs, and kindly mourns her Skill.
Back to the Flood the glitt'ring Prey she cast;
Again the Fool returns, again is fast. ...

Now the broad Sun descends the western Steep
And shoots a level Radiance o'er the Deep.
The Gales[16] recline upon their watry Bed,
And ev'ry Wave uncurls its sinking Head.
We now no more the pleasing Task pursue,
One hundred caught, we bid the Lake adieu.

We launch our Oars, To Land, to Land, they cry;
The lusty Boatmen ev'ry Nerve apply.
On either hand the Coasts partake our Speed,
And from our parting Stern with Haste recede.

Soft Flutes and Clarions breathe their sprightly Notes;
Thro' the still Air the wafted Music floats;
Chear'd by the Symphony, smooth Erne smiles,
And Echo answers from the circling Isles. ...

15 hangs.

16 winds.

JAMES EYRE WEEKS
(*c.*1719–**1762**–1775)

James Eyre Weeks was born in Cork and educated at Trinity College Dublin where he was a contemporary of Thomas Sheridan, the actor and elocution teacher. He was ordained into the Church of Ireland and became tutor to the young Marquis of Lansdowne – later, as Lord Shelburne, an unpopular prime minister of Britain. Little is known of Weeks's life, though he was actively involved with the Dublin theatre and may, at one stage, have kept a school in Tralee. He published poems on a variety of topics, a (mildly indecent) play and an irreverent Dublin newspaper as well an oratorio and several school books on geography. He also spent time in London and contributed the poem that follows to *The London Magazine* in December 1762. Weeks spent his later years as a rector in County Cork.

On the late Fog

Lost and bewilder'd in the thick'ning mist,
We stray amid th'irrefragable[1] gloom,
Nor can th'all piercing eye of day himself
Penetrate here; behind a sizy[2] cloud
The rays of light, his orient messengers,
Are intercepted, nor can steer their course
Wreckt on a coast of jet[3]— ev'n beauty's eye,
Compos'd of azure, here is impotent,
And all subduing is herself subdu'd.
We justle each, by eye-sight unappriz'd
Of meeting, in the anarchy of shade.

Nature herself seems in the vapours[4] now,
Sullen is ev'ry prospect,[5] and the trees
As we approach them, seem like hanging webs
Spun by the spider; ev'n the great St Paul's
With his huge dome and cupolas, appears
A craggy precipice, rude, unform'd,

1 stubborn.

2 dark.

3 hard, black rock.

4 in a state of nervous disorder.

5 (1) outlook; (2) view; (3) what can be seen in the prospect glass or spectacles.

Or like the ruins of an ancient fort
Upon a hill, when twilight shuts the day.
Or if Meridian Phœbus shews his face,
He seems a ball of molten copper-ore,
Or like a beacon on a foggy coast.

Absolute shade maintains despotic sway,
Palpable darkness, for we see by touch;
The beams of day refracted in the cloud,
Like birds in storms, are dubious where to fly;
The coach or wagon warns us by the noise
To shun the danger; by our *ears* we *see*
The threat'ning wheels. We strike against each post,
Like ships against a bank, or sunken rock,
For sight is vain, where nature disappears.
The lamps are feeble as the socket snuffs
Of candles just expiring, rush-lights dim
Like those within a cellar's dreary vault.

'Tis universal mourning, colours fade
And ev'n the soldiers, black as undertakers,
Resemble lobsters, black before they're red.
Long streets of houses seem as pencil'd out
In charcoal prospects;[6] the design of boys:
While by no marks directed, oft we miss
Our well-known passage; boats upon the Thames
Appear but as the buoys of distant ships,
Or corks afloat, upon the tawny flood.

Nature's fine liv'ry, fac'd with ever-green,
Is chequer'd o'er with motly spots of ink;
The wheezing lungs are heard in ev'ry street,
And nature seems one universal blank.

6 i.e. as if they are charcoal drawings of the street.

JOHN CUNNINGHAM
(1729–**1766**–1773)

John Cunningham was born in Dublin and educated in Drogheda. While still in his teens he started writing poetry and plays and joined a troupe of actors travelling around Ireland. He subsequently moved to England, continuing to work as an actor: he published several volumes of pastoral poetry and counted Dr Johnson – among others – as an admirer. Charles Peake in *Poetry of the Landscape and the Night* (London, 1967) describes Cunningham as 'a poet of no great distinction' but says also that his work '… suggests how liberating for the minor poet was the shift away from portentous meditation and pastoral machinery to the evocation of a mood through simple but accurate description of the country scene'.

A Landscape.

Rura mihi et irrigui placeant in vallibus amnes.

VIRG[1]

I

Now that summer's ripened bloom
Frolicks where the winter frown'd
Stretch'd upon these banks of broom,
We command the landscape round.

II

Nature in the prospect yields
Humble dales and mountains bold,
Meadows, woodlands, heaths,—and fields
Yellow'd o'er with waving gold.

III

Goats upon that frowning steep
Fearless, with their kidlings brouse!
Here a flock of snowy sheep!
There an herd of motly cows!

IV

On the uplands, every glade
Brightens in the blaze of day;
O'er the vales, the sober shade
Softens to an evening grey.

1 *Georgics* II, 485.

V

Where the rill by slow degrees
Swells into a chrystal pool,
Shaggy rocks and shelving trees
Shoot to keep the water cool.

VI

Shiver'd by a thunder-stroke,
From the mountain's misty ridge,
O'er the brook a ruin'd oak,
Near the farm-house, forms a bridge.

VII

On her breast the sunny beam
Glitters in meridian pride;
Yonder as the virgin stream
Hastens to the restless tide:—

VIII

Where the ships by wanton gales
Wafted, o'er the green waves run,
Sweet to see the swelling sails
Whiten'd by the laughing sun!

IX

High upon the dasied hill,
Rising from the slope of trees,
How the wings of yonder mill
Labour in the busy breeze!—

X

Cheerful as a summer's morn
(Bouncing from her loaded pad)
Where the maid presents her corn,
Smirking, to the miller's lad.

XI

O'er the green a festal throng
Gambols, in fantastic trim!
As the full cart moves along,
Hearken—'tis their harvest hymn!

XII

Linnets on the crowded sprays
Chorus,—and the wood-larks rise,
Soaring with a song of praise,
Till the sweet notes reach the skies.

XIII

Torrents in extended sheets
Down the cliffs, dividing, break:
'Twixt the hills the water meets,
Settling in a silver lake!

XIV

From his languid flocks, the swain
By the sunbeams sore opprest,
Plunging on the wat'ry plain,
Plows it with his glowing breast.

XV

Where the mantling willows nod,
From the green bank's slopy side,
Patient, with his well-thrown rod
Many an angler breaks the tide!

XVI

On the isles, with osiers drest
Many a fair-plum'd halcion[2] breeds!
Many a wild bird hides her nest,
Cover'd in yon crackling reeds

XVII

Fork-tail'd prattlers as they pass
To their nestlings in the rock,
Darting on the liquid glass,
Seem to kiss the mimick'd flock.

2 A mythical bird said by ancient writers to breed in a nest floating at sea at the winter solstice, charming the wind and waves into calm.

XVIII

Where the stone Cross lifts its head,
Many a saint and pilgrim hoar,
Up the hills was wont to tread
Barefoot, in the days of yore.[3]

XIX

Guardian of a sacred well,
Arch'd beneath yon reverend shades,
Whilom, in that shatter'd cell,
Many an hermit told his beads.

XX

Sultry mists surround the heath
Where the Gothic dome appears,
O'er the trembling groves beneath,
Tott'ring with a load of years.

XXI

Turn to the contrasted scene,
Where, beyond these hoary piles,
Gay, upon the rising green,
Many an attic building smiles!

XXII

Painted gardens – grots – and groves,
Intermingling shade and light!
Lengthen'd vistas, green alcoves,
Join to give the eye delight.

XXIII

Hamlets—villages, and spires,
Scatter'd on the landscape lie,
Till the distant view retires,
Closing in an azure sky.

3 Stanzas XVIII and XIX suggest that the scene described could be in Ireland.

JOSEPH ATKINSON
(1743–**1769**–1818)

Eighteenth-century poems on Killarney – and there are many of them – follow a set pattern: the poet calls on the muses to help him tell the reader how awestruck he is at the beauty of the mountains surrounding the lakes of Killarney and then describes them as seen from specific viewpoints. He praises the local landowners and compliments them on their villas and 'improvements' before giving the reader a guided tour of the various sites and an account of their historical significance. He includes a vivid description of the local field sports – hunting, shooting and fishing – particularly the hunting of a stag. He also explains how impressive echoes are created for the enjoyment of visitors being rowed around the lake by the playing of a French horn or the discharge of a cannon. The poem ends with a paean of praise on the sublime feelings aroused by Killarney in the viewer.

One of the earliest of these poems – though it was also revealingly 'corrected, enlarged and embellished' for republication twenty-eight years later – appeared in 1769, the work of Joseph Atkinson, a young army officer stationed at Ross Castle, Killarney. (For a comparison between the 1769 and 1798 printings, see the Appendix.) Atkinson later wrote comic operas and several long poems, including a description of County Wicklow entitled *A Poetic Excursion* (Dublin, 1818).

from: Killarny: a poem[1]

Thou guardian Genius of KILLARNY say,
Through all thy scenes romantic shall I stray?
Guided by thee, the Muse, and Fancy's train,
Thy sylvan shades and heights sublime attain?
Come then, ye Naiads, and ye sportive Fauns
Who guard the waters and the flow'ry lawns,
Aid me, oh, aid me, with poetic fire!
And to thy wonders let my verse aspire!

See from afar the alp-like mountains rise
To fill the mind with grandeur and surprise!
Some, in the clouds their tops Olympian hide,
And by their distance shew superior pride:
Above them all—high MANGERTON appears,
And to the heavens his daring summit rears!

1 Rhetorical (and syntactically unnecessary) commas were inserted in almost every line of the 1769 Dublin printing of the poem. They have been removed here – though they are retained in the version printed in the Appendix.

This tow'ring Atlas of Ierne's shore [2]
With wonders crown'd—as Africk's Atlas bore![3]
Its top a spacious cavern-lake sustains,
Fed by deep springs and never ceasing rains.[4]
See, some beneath, with less aspiring height
Yield a more verdant and enlivening sight:
Oft like the Sun, obscurely veil'd, they lie,
While o'er their heads etherial vapours fly!
But now dispell'd—the gloomy mist o'er blown;
What bright reflections on their sides are thrown!
Now dancing Sun-beams through the forests play,
Gild all the hills and make the plains more gay:—
While thus from far those glorious views extend,
Where fertile isles and spreading waters blend:
These striking objects first prepare the mind
To taste each beauty nature's there combin'd.

Here crouded mountains form a circling chain,
And frown impending o'er the Liquid plain,
Whose lucid surface from their feet expands
Its silver'd edges to more fertile lands,
Where a huge mass of azure hills conceal
An ever-plenteous ever-blooming vale;
Where the blithe shepherd tills the fruitful earth
And culls his riches with a grateful mirth;
Where intermixed the corn, and pasture field,
A pleasing prospect to his wishes yield:
Fill'd with content and rustic-smiling peace
He sees his harvests and his flocks increase;
Pride, nor ambition, can his mind enthrall,
Blest in his cottage he enjoys his all![5]...

2 <This mountain is the highest land in Ireland, its computed perpendicular height from the verge of Mucrus Lake, is near 1200 yards; and on its very summit there is a small Lake, called the Devil's punch bowl, from its being of a rounded deep form.> Ierne is the poetic name for Ireland.

3 i.e. the Atlas mountains in North Africa – named after the Greek god Atlas who held up the world on his shoulders.

4 The lake is called the Devil's Punchbowl.

5 This paragraph describes the 'pleasing prospect' of Killarney so often represented in paintings and engravings – distant, wild mountains, mysteriously veiled in vapour, separated from the viewer by a large, silver lake while, in the foreground, carefully cultivated farmland is overlooked by 'noble' mansions and 'neat' villas.

The craggy heights and wooded hills oppose
The smiling scene, and Nature's bounty shows;
Wild and infertile to the labourers art,
With native wonders greater charms impart:
The sloping-curves we here and there descry,
Afford new changes to the roving eye;
The mingled contrast of the various trees
That deck their sides and fan the summer's breeze;
The cone-like Firr, and wintry-glooming Pine,
And rev'rend Oak which Ivy-wreathes entwine;
The Box, the Holly, and the browner Yew,
With vernal aspect—ever young and new
Here grow luxuriant, to their native size,
And ev'ry artful, mangl'd form despise.
Greatly superior to the rest is found
The Mountain-ash with crimson berries crown'd!
Which nobly shoots, majestic, straight, and tall
As Norway Pines—but far out-soars them all!
Not the great Oak, tho' royal in his name,
O'er tops its beauty or out spreads its fame!
Each tree or shrub which northern climes produce
Here grows spontaneous for the artist's use:
The bright Cascades the Mountain-torrents form
That rush impetuous in a wat'ry storm,
And faintly glimmer through the waving woods
(Which now discover, now conceal their floods,)
Ev'ry restraint from ev'ry object mock,
But tumbling roar against the sounding rock!
Then sudden stop—nor any course pursue,
As if their lately, greater height to view.—
Next spread in streams and softly-purling rills,
With gentle babling through the sloping hills,
To tell their peaceful and less rapid change,
Through meads enamel'd now to glide and range.
This bright assemblage—with their lights and shades,
(Whilst Phoebus glitters through the op'ning glades,)
The diff'rent tints the trembling leaves unfold,
The new born-green and Autumns faded gold,
The pleasing umbrage of the spreading boughs,
Invite fond Lovers interchanging vows!

While circling Woodbines mid'st the branches rove,
Perfume the Air and shade the secret Grove!
While feather'd Songsters chear their billing loves,
And amorous Turtles woo their fellow Doves.
Ah! had kind Nature more propitious been,
And form'd the Climate equal to the scene!
Then might the Tendrils of the curling Vine,
Amid'st the Groves in sweet confusion twine!
The clust'ring Grape might every Tree adorn,
And Flow'rs Exotic shield the pointed Thorn!
The blossom'd Shrubs in Spring-eternal blow,
In shades retir'd and paths bewild'ring grow;
The Lime and Orange mix with Myrtle bow'rs,
And scent the Zephyrs of the temp'rate hours!
Then too, the Lake, with airy breezes curl'd,
Might boast its barges with their sails unfurled,[6]
The smooth expanse in never lost repose,
Might then defy its ruffling squally foes!
Let splendid gallies through the Islands sail,[7]
And stretch their Canvass to the swelling gale!
Board to and fro along the winding coast,
Nor scar'd by Rocks, or sudden Tempests tost.

But since no Wolves the happy Plains controul,
Nor hungry Lions in the Forests howl!
Devouring tear the harmless bleating Lambs,
Who fly for shelter to their flying Dams!
Nor lurking Vipers in the pasture lye,
Whose venom'd bite the cautious Shepherds fly!
Nor croaking Toads with foaming-poison fill'd,
From baneful Herbs and sulphur'd dews distill'd!
Nor dang'rous monster with amphibious powr's,
Nor frights by Land nor in the Lake devours!
And Nature gracious to this favourite Shore,
Hath bid these Reptiles foreign-shades explore!—

6 <Lord Kenmaire has given his barge men positive orders not to carry sail on account of the sudden squalls from the mountains.>

7 <No water could better admit large vessels to sail on, than this, the lower Lake is between seven and eight mile long, and about half that in breath [*sic*], some parts of it have seventy fathom water, and close to the very shore in some places between twenty and thirty.>

Then freed from ills which warmer climes invade;
For what we have—let thanks to Heaven be paid.

Then, while our Climate boasts th'Autumnal change,[8]
The sporting croud to this blest spot may range,
Here, taste successful ev'ry new desire,
Which active pleasure in their breasts inspire:
Whether to climb the Mountains tufted maze,
And from their heights with fearful wonder gaze;
To spring the Grouse the purple heaths conceal,
And their bright plumage to the Sun reveal;
To rouze the Woodquest's[9] or the Pheasant's flight,
And from their terror catch their own delight;
For Sport—to fire the whizzing shot or ball,
And gain new life to see their victims fall!
Or if a nobler Game thy mind pursues,
(Nature has amply giv'n thee here to chuse),
Rous'd by the Concert of the Hounds and Horn;
When the Lark soars to hail the rising morn,
The Stag awaits thee on the mountain side,
The cov'ring brush his spreading-branches hide:—
Now he's in sight—behold the glorious game!
Let the pursuit thy longing Soul inflame.
How echo sighs to hear his panting groans,
And as in sympathy his fate bemoans!
The well-staunch'd[10] Hounds, unmindful of his cry,
With eager speed and bloody anger fly!
See, the Stag trembles—for his conscious fate;—
Where is there rest! or any safe retreat!
In vain below—the furious chase to shun!
Up the steep mountains 'tis as vain to run!
Hurry'd, with terror, and just-fainting toil,

8 <From the beginning to the latter end of Autumn, is certainly the most agreeable season for visiting the Lake, as nature is then in its highest perfection, and the mildness of the weather, suitable to the beauty of the Lake.>

9 wood pigeons.

10 well-satisfied (presumably because they are chasing the stag).

With desp'rate plunge he seeks the cooler soil!—
Now to the boat exulting Hunters take,[11]
See he divides the foamy-spreading lake!
The stretching rowers all their nerves distend,—
Now, thy assistance to their efforts lend;
See he is near—increase your shouting cries,—
Almost with fear—your frighted victim dies!
He swims no more—but panting now for breath,
And pausing, weeps his ignominious death:
Triumphant fling him in the tott'ring boat!
Secure his limbs—nor gash his reeking throat,
Like lawless victors—Epicures of food![12]
No, leave him ranging in his native wood!
Amongst his wild companions free to live;
He to your sons a future chase may give.

Tir'd with the noise of this tumultuous sport,
Some to the Lake for calmer joys resort:
Where contemplation and amusement join'd,
Employ the body and engage the mind.
Now with the Angle and the floating line,
Your mimick flies upon the surface shine!
The scaly-brood perceive the glitt'ring bait,[13]
But ah, what frauds on promised friendship wait!
Pleas'd with the playful skipping of the fly,
Whose gaudy colours catch their piercing eye!
Now fiercely eager to devour their prey,
Voracious leap the pleasing, fatal way!
Too late they find the treach'rous hook is there,—
In vain they plunge to break the twisted snare!
Give line enough—let loose the 'twirling wheel,—
Nor let them sudden all thy fury feel:
Now while they flag—draw in the slack'ning line,
But still the struggling prize must not be thine:

11 <Some people chuse to stay in their boat all the time of the chase knowing that the Stag will necessarily take the water, as there are men ranged on the top of the Mountains, to prevent his going over the proper boundaries for hunting. There was formerly a great quantity of the Stag here, but they are not so plenty [*sic*] of late years.>

12 This unexpected expostulation (which Atkinson removed from the revised text) is hard to explain.

13 <The Lake and adjoining Rivulets, are stocked with every kind of fresh water fish.>

They plunge—they flutter to preserve their life,
Whilst you, experienc'd, rule the cunning strife!
First to indulge and next their flight restrain,
'Till they lie gasping with fatigue and pain.
The speckl'd Trout may to your Net be drawn,
As the set Partridge, on the stubbl'd lawn!
If the large Salmon owns thy powerful art,
When he is near, the keener Jav'lin dart!
Hold him in triumph to admiring eyes;
While all your skill is envyed in your prize.

When Summer Suns withdraw their chearing fire,
And shiv'ring mortals to their hearths retire;
When leafless Trees are spangl'd by the Frost,
And glitt'ring please, for verdant beauties lost!
The Icy chrystals in the night display,
Adawn-like twinkling, and a rival-day!
If, too, the Lake with shining Ice o'er spread,
Can safely bear the coursing sportsman's tread,
To skim the surface on the sliding skaite
And daring venture on the brink of fate![14]
The Duck and Widgeon, now distress'd for food,
Quit frozen ponds and seek the marshy wood;
The restless Woodcocks roving here repair,
From colder climes, to seek a warmer Air!
The long-bill'd Snipe and squeeking Plover too,
Half dead with cold—yet live in dread of you.
Now trace the game through whiten'd tracks of snow,
And make thy frame with Summer ardor glow. …

… Hence waft me quick KILARNY's pride to paint!
Where art keeps nature in a mild restraint:
MUCRUSS,[15]—thou beauteous nearly-floating Isle,
What shelves of Marble round thy borders pile!

14 <There can't be a better place on the globe for a Sportman, than this where every kind of wood and water Game present themselves every instant for his sport.>

15 <The seat of Counsellor Herbert, which he has improved in a most elegant manner; it is a Peninsula, nearly surrounded by Mucrus, and the lower Lake.>

Here changing objects please the ravish'd eyes,
See Hills from Lakes, and Lakes on Hills, arise!
Here mazy walks to op'ning vistas lead:
To views unbounded—or the closing shade!
Each part adorn'd with ev'ry rural grace
That Woods, that Lawns, that Hilly-mounts can trace.
The treasur'd earth with latent riches fill'd,
Can yield up wealth tho' never sown or till'd!
See, a new Lake here unexpected spreads,
What a white torrent from yon mountain heads:[16]
The silver glimm'ring with reflected rays!
Shines on the sides and through the Valley plays:
To thee, high MANGERTON, this sight we owe,
While from thy lak'y bowl the draughts o'er flow.
Th'Arbutus here, a never-fading green,
In all its pride and blooming beauty's seen;
And, like the Citron, can at once display,
The Mellow Autumn and the Flow'ry-May!
What blending colours on the branches vie,
The Leaf, the Blossom and the yellow dye!
Nor is the Shrub luxuriant here alone,
But through each Hill and Isle's promiscuous thrown,
Sprouts from the solid Rocks infertile waste,
With pleasing sweetness to the eye, and taste. …

Now in the Boat, to mount the Rivers stream,
Wrapt in delight of new enchantments, dream!
Whilst roving fancy to each object tost,
And ev'ry sense in ravish'd wonder's lost:—
Behold, yon awful precipice arise,
From thence the Eagle gives his race supplies![17]
From thence stupendous, wings his soaring way,
Or furious darts upon his helpless prey:

16 <The superfluous waters, from the Devil's punch bowl rush down the sides of this mountain, and here and there form a variety of beautiful cascades, particularly one of near 150 feet high, that precipitately falls into Mucrus Lake. …'>

17 <A perpendicular Mountain, called the Eagles nest from their building on its inaccessible height.>

Should he come near—ah, fire thy vengence fierce!
Blest, if thou canst the greedy tyrant pierce:
Then from his bosom all his vitals draw!
No more to keep the feather'd World in awe.—
But hark! what Musick strikes th'enchanted Ear?
Let all be hush'd—with mute attention hear!
What Magic sounds from yonder cliffs respire,
Sure 'tis the concert of some Heav'nly quire!
Th'Aerial Musick[18] on yon Mountain floats,
Now they are louder—now they're softer notes.—
Hark, they are wafted to yon speaking hill,
Fill all the skies, and through our bosoms thrill!
From ev'ry Grove the tell-tale echoes fly,
Nor keep in silence ev'n a lovers sigh!
The listning Birds would imitate the strain,
And flocks to hear, look gazing from the plain.—
Heav'ns what a thunder in yon rattling peal,
How the loud deaf'ning sounds our ears assail!
The quick-explosion darts a wild affright,
What Earthquake terrors swim before the sight!
Our mind astonish'd, in a dread amaze,
Fancies a Chaos on the World must seize:
Nature seems shudd'ring with convulsive rage,
And ev'ry Element in War to wage!
Mountains look tott'ring, with tremendous quake,
Near to be bury'd in the swallowing Lake:
No Birds can sing, nor timid Flocks can graze,—
What cause unknown such great effects can raise?
But there again th'harmonious Air rebounds,
And by the contrast gains much sweeter sounds!
The echoing Hills in one full chorus ring,
And all the Vallies learn from them to sing!
The sound melodious ev'ry sense inspires,
With melting softness and refin'd desires!
All nature smiles th'auspicious hour to grace,
Whilst Musick breathes, the soothing friend of peace. …

18 <The sound of the French Horn or Clarionet, at this place produces the most melodious echo that can be imagined and by the situation of the surrounding Hills, reverberates, seven or eight different times, which is better proved by the unexpected firing of a Cannon, as described above.>

Now art thou not for all thy pains o'erpaid,
To have such transports to thy mind convey'd!
With blissful sounds and heav'nly visions pleas'd,
Midst scenes inchanted, by enjoyment raised!
Where all we ask delights the ravish'd heart,
And all, tho' nature—seems the plan of art:
Where all's improved, tho' all the work of chance.—
Are we awake, or in some magic trance?
In the bright regions of some fairy Queen,
Or blest Elysium—by the Muses seen!
If it be so—stay, dear Deception, stay,
Nor tear our Fancies from the Scene away!—
No! 'tis a heav'n!—'If heav'n on earth there be.'
A blissful Eden!—to be sung by me.

PART IV
1770–1799

OLIVER GOLDSMITH
(1728–**1770**–1774)

Goldsmith, the son of a clergyman, spent his childhood in counties Longford and Westmeath. He attended Trinity College Dublin after which he went to Edinburgh to study medicine. He travelled widely on the Continent, finally settling in London where he earned a precarious living as a writer and became a trusted member of the circle around Samuel Johnson. Among the works Goldsmith completed at this time was his encyclopaedic *A History of Earth and Animated Nature* (1774). Goldsmith's best-known work, however, is *The Deserted Village*, which draws heavily on his memories of childhood in the Irish midlands though, as Katharine Balderston points out, there is probably a considerable difference between 'the coarse Irish reality of the 1730s' and the 'refined and idealized memories' in the poem (*The Collected Letters of Oliver Goldsmith* (Cambridge, 1928), p. x).

from: The Deserted Village

Sweet AUBURN,[1] loveliest village of the plain,
Where health and plenty cheared the labouring swain,
Where smiling spring its earliest visit paid,
And parting summer's lingering blooms delayed,
Dear lovely bowers of innocence and ease,
Seats of my youth, when every sport could please,
How often have I loitered o'er thy green,
Where humble happiness endeared each scene!
How often have I paused on every charm,
The sheltered cot,[2] the cultivated farm,
The never failing brook, the busy mill,
The decent[3] church that topt the neighbouring hill,
The hawthorn bush, with seats beneath the shade,
For talking age and whispering lovers made!
How often have I blest the coming day,
When toil remitting lent its turn to play,
And all the village train from labour free
Led up their sports beneath the spreading tree,
While many a pastime circled in the shade,
The young contending as the old surveyed;

1 Traditionally closely associated with Lissoy, Co. Westmeath, where Goldsmith spent his childhood.

2 cottage.

3 not ostentatious, appropriate.

And many a gambol frolicked o'er the ground,
And slights[4] of art and feats of strength went round.
And still as each repeated pleasure tired,
Succeeding sports the mirthful band inspired;
The dancing pair that simply sought renown
By holding out to tire each other down;
The swain mistrustless of his smutted face,
While secret laughter tittered round the place;[5]
The bashful virgin's side-long looks of love,
The matron's glance that would those looks reprove!
These were thy charms, sweet village; sports like these,
With sweet succession taught even toil to please;
These round thy bowers their chearful influence shed,
These were thy charms—But all these charms are fled.

Sweet smiling village, loveliest of the lawn,
Thy sports are fled, and all thy charms withdrawn;
Amidst thy bowers the tyrant's hand is seen,
And desolation saddens all thy green:
One only master grasps the whole domain,[6]
And half a tillage stints thy smiling plain;[7]
No more thy glassy brook reflects the day,
But choaked with sedges, works its weedy way;
Along thy glades, a solitary guest,
The hollow sounding bittern[8] guards its nest;
Amidst thy desert walks the lapwing[9] flies,
And tires their ecchoes with unvaried cries.
Sunk are thy bowers,[10] in shapeless ruin all,
And the long grass o'ertops the mouldering wall;

4 examples of skill or skilfulness.

5 The group is laughing at someone whose face has been smeared with smuts without his knowing it.

6 a single landowner has replaced several.

7 i.e. The single landowner's action in ploughing only half the land ('half a tillage') brings to an end ('stints') the cheerful appearance of the plain.

8 a large wading bird. Goldsmith elsewhere described the bittern's booming call as 'dismally hollow' (*A History of Earth and Animated Nature*, 6 vols (London, 1774) VI, 1–2).

9 A bird of the plover family which breeds on islands 'where men seldom resort' (*A History of Earth and Animated Nature*, VI, 32).

10 humble cottages – here probably referring to the temporary structures of landless migrant workers.

And trembling, shrinking from the spoiler's hand,
Far, far away thy children leave the land.

Ill fares the land, to hastening ills a prey,
Where wealth accumulates, and men decay;
Princes and lords may flourish, or may fade;
A breath can make them, as a breath has made;
But a bold peasantry, their country's pride,
When once destroyed, can never be supplied. ...

Sweet was the sound when oft at evening's close,
Up yonder hill the village murmur rose;
There as I past with careless steps and slow,
The mingling notes came softened from below;
The swain responsive as the milk-maid sung,
The sober herd that lowed to meet their young;
The noisy geese that gabbled o'er the pool,
The playful children just let loose from school;
The watch-dog's voice that bayed the whispering wind,
And the loud laugh that spoke the vacant mind,[11]
These all in sweet confusion sought the shade,
And filled each pause the nightingale had made.
But now the sounds of population fail,
No chearful murmurs fluctuate in the gale,[12]
No busy steps the grass-grown foot-way tread,
For all the bloomy flush of life is fled.
All but yon widowed, solitary thing
That feebly bends beside the plashy spring;
She, wretched matron, forced, in age, for bread,
To strip the brook with mantling cresses[13] spread,
To pick her wintry faggot from the thorn,
To seek her nightly shed, and weep till morn;
She only left of all the harmless train,
The sad historian of the pensive plain.

11 i.e. the loud laugh of the village simpleton.

12 a gentle breeze, rather than a violent wind.

13 watercress.

JOHN LESLIE
(*c.*1719–**1772**–1778)

John Leslie was born in County Donegal. He entered Trinity College Dublin in 1736, was awarded a scholarship in 1739, a BA degree in 1740 and his MA in 1760. O'Donoghue states that he was tutor to Lord Clanwilliam – which, if true, must have been a difficult task as his lordship was one of the most notorious rakes and spendthrifts of the age. Even the normally equable Mrs Delany was outraged when his lordship, then a boy of six, was allowed to run wild in her drawing room (*Letters of Mrs Delany*, ed. Lady Llanover, II, 597).

Leslie's two surviving publications were substantial poems on Killarney and the Phoenix Park, both of which appeared in 1772. In the short 'Advertisement' to 'Killarney', he observes that a passionate love of the charms of Nature 'chiefly predominates in those of warm and susceptible minds'. His description of the landscape around Killarney was an attempt to represent in words what artists showed in paintings. 'Killarney' is a very long poem only a little of which is reproduced here.

from: Killarney: a poem

THY scenes, KILLARNEY, scenes of pure delight
Call forth my verse, and wing my daring flight:
O form'd to charm, new rapture to Inspire,
To feed the Painter's, and the Poet's fire!
Far other pow'rs than mine, thy praises claim,
Yet, strongly glowing with the sacred flame,
May I, advent'rous, sing thy matchless pride,
Fair nature's boast? Be Nature thou my guide;
Teach me to think, my feeble voice to raise,
Thou safest, best inspirer of my lays;
Where-e'er we rove, thro' forest, lake, or wild,
Bring with thee Fancy, thy creative child,
And gay associate, aptest she to tell
The haunt of Dryad, and the Echo's cell;
Where dwells the mountain's Genius, where the wood's,
And where the Naiads of the silver floods;
Where, seldom seen, the rural Pow'rs retreat,
The Friends and Guardians of thy sacred seat.

But lo! in sylvan majesty arise
The green-wood Mountains, and salute the skies,
Circling the deep, or shelt'ring yonder plains,

Where Ceres smiles, and KENMARE[1] chears the swains.
No Alpine horrors on their summits frown,
Nor Pride, dark-low'ring, on the vale looks down;
No massy fragments, pendant from on high,
With hideous ruin strike the aching eye,
The swelling Hills, in vernant bloom elate,
Smile by their sides, th'attendants of their state.

High o'er the rest, our steps aspiring tread
Exalted MANGERTON'S[2] cerulean head,
Parent of springs, where nurs'd the dews and rains
Timely descend to glad the thirsty plains;
Where spreads the Lake diffusive o'er his crown,
And, like another Caspian,[3] all his own,
While down his bounteous side the Torrent[4] roars,
A richer tide than huge Olympus[5] pours;
Lodg'd in the blue serene, supreme he stands,
And all the region, far and wide, commands:
The less'ning Mountains now no more aspire,
Parnassus' rivals[6] modestly retire:
In guiltless times, perhaps a Druid throng
There strung Ierne's lyre, and wak'd the song,
And still, tho' rude the note, a learned strain,
The simple peasants of the West[7] retain;
The Lakes, the Isles, the Forests shrink below,
And, but in miniature, their glory show.

New objects rise from his stupendous height,[8]
Nor can the tow'ring region[9] bound the sight:

1 Lord Kenmare, the largest landowner in the district.

2 <One of the highest mountains in Ireland.> Cerulean = deep blue.

3 <A sea supposed not to communicate with any other.> The reference is to the Devil's Punch Bowl, the lake near the summit of Mangerton.

4 <A waterfall in view of Mucrus.>

5 <A mountain abounding with springs.>

6 <A remarkable double-top'd mountain.>

7 <In allusion to many of them, who speak Latin.>

8 i.e. the viewer can see new objects from the summit of the mountain.

9 <A range of mountains, called the Reeks.>

Prospect immense! our eyes excursive roam,
To yon tall[10] beach, where rushing surges foam;
Where, ebbing from their shores, the waves retreat,
One blue expanse of majesty sedate.

Now skirting wide, the happy plains are seen,
Where vanquish'd Desmond bow'd to freedom's Queen;[11]
The first that gave them peace, who captive led
Their tyrant Lords, and crush'd Rebellion's head.

Now Kenmare's harbours spreading from the main.
Invite the passing mariner in vain:[12]
Hard fate! shall thousands on Ierne's coast,
Be still to commerce and to Britain lost?
Copious and calm, see BANTRY'S lordly tide,
For all Britannia's fleets a station wide;[13]
A Port secure, long since well known to fame,
And signaliz'd with gallant Herbert's name.[14]
To DINGLE[15] far we stretch, and o'er the main,[16]
Once fatal to the naval pride of Spain;
And where, in fruitless war, conflicting sides
Dash foamy round the SKELLIGS[17] marble sides,
On to the CAPES,[18] where haughty Shannon roars,
And drives th'Atlantick backward from his shores.

10 fine, large or excellent.

11 The reference is probably to the countryside north of Killarney, a stronghold of Desmond power and to the decision of Gerald Fitz Gerald, 14th Earl of Desmond and hereditary lord of Munster, to surrender to the forces of Queen Elizabeth in 1589.

12 <The river.> The line probably refers to the fact that Kenmare and its hinterland were insufficiently prosperous, at this time, for trading vessels to call.

13 The reference is to the port of Castletownbere or Berehaven on Bantry bay, a significant harbour for the British navy from the seventeenth century to 1938.

14 A note in the 1772 edition draws attention to Admiral Herbert's victory over the French fleet in Bantry Bay on 1 May 1689.

15 <The most Westerly port of Europe.>

16 <The Sound of the Blasquets, where some of the Spanish Armada were supposed to be lost, particularly, the Rosary of 1200 Tons.> The Spanish ship, 'Our Lady of the Rosary' ran onto rocks in the Blasket Sound in September 1588 and all but one of the 500 on board were drowned.

17 <Three remarkable islands on thc S.W. of Kerry.>

18 <Loophead and Kerry point.>

Thou, mighty Pharos[19] of Ierne's isle,
Round whom recountless charms, and graces smile,
Proud MANGERTON, whose breast the storm restrains,
A gracious bulwark to the distant plains,
Th'astonish'd soul all fitted to inspire
With silent wonder, and with holy fire,
Let me on wing'd devotion ardent fly
Tow'rd him, who rear'd thine awful head on high.

Descending now from Ether's pure domain,
By fancy borne to range the nether plain,
Behold all-winning Novelty display'd
Along the vale, the mountain, and the shade;
The scenes but late diminutive resume
Their native grandeur, and their wonted bloom;
The woods expand their umbrage o'er the deep.
And with ambitious aim ascend the steep,
Stage above stage, their vig'rous arms invade
The tallest cliffs, and wrap them in the shade;
Each in its own pre-eminence regains
The high dominion of the subject plains,
Smiling beneath; such smiles the people wear,
Happy in some paternal Monarch's care.
Shall we the thicket, hill, or vale explore,
To cull the healing God's[20] salubrious store?
Or climb-th'empurpled summit, there to breathe
Ethereal air, and view a world beneath,
While o'er the steep, the Zephyr's early gale,
And perfume wild, assist us to prevail?

Ye sportive Youth, it is your season now,
At blush of morn, to range the mountain's brow:
The russet Cock,[21] forth from his heathy lawn,
Defiance crows, and challenges the dawn,

19 a beacon for directing mariners rather than a lighthouse.

20 <Apollo.> Apollo was god of (*inter alia*) medicine and healing.

21 <The Grouse.> 'Growsing' is the word used to describe this passage in the 'Argument' that precedes the poem.

Behind, robust and proud, the well-plum'd Pack,[22]
Rambling, pursue their parents mazy track;
The mark is here to win a sportsman's fame,[23]
The Partridge is a poor, domestick game;
Here train'd to distant toil, you learn to dare
The roughest deeds, and steel your nerves for war,
With thund'ring tube prepar'd, disdain to set
The gen'rous brood, you murder with the net;[24]
Let nought insidious tempt your manly hearts,
To poachers leave the circumventive arts :
Now to the covert brown, all closely pent,
The Pointer draws,[25] and stiffens in the scent,
Expectance beats, while each successive springs,[26]
And trusts his safety to the strength of wings,
The well-aim'd gun arrests him as he flies,
He wheels, he falls, he flutters, bounds and dies.

Cheer'd by the rural sport, the active Mind
Flies all abroad, and scorns to be confin'd,
Sweeps o'er the forest, up the mountain springs,
Where to his pendant flock, the goat-herd sings,
List'ning the while, Content that never wants,
And rosy Health reclin'd on balmy plants;
Whitening the verdant steep, the fountains play
In concert with the Sylvan warbler's lay,
Autumn and Spring their diff'ring seasons join.
And, social on the bough, together twine.

The ARBUTUS,[27] array'd in flow'rs and fruits,
The pride of all the shrubby natives shoots,

22 Presumably a reference to the young grouse.

23 i.e. there is enough game here for you to attain the standard of a 'sportsman' in your pursuit of it.

24 To set is to spread out (a net) to catch birds. The distinction is between cowardly poachers who trap young birds with nets ('murder') them, and true sportsmen who shoot them with guns.

25 pent = straining but restrained as the dog 'points' at the game in the brown covert; to 'draw' is to move slowly towards the game after 'pointing' it.

26 i.e. one bird, 'expecting' to escape, flies up with wings beating and is 'succeeded' by others 'springing' into the air.

27 Flowers and fruit appear at the same time on the evergreen arbutus or strawberry tree.

Various their tints, (not more the Prism displays
When show'ring on the eye light's parted rays)
An union rare, and such the pleasing sight,
When Youth and Manhood gracefully unite;
Emblem of him, whose heav'n-attemper'd mind
Is form'd to profit, and delight mankind;
Some proudly upward tend, some lowly creep,
And some, inverted, stoop to kiss the deep,
Narcissus-like, and as the seasons glide,
Blossom, and bear with interchanging pride;
While other tribes, but transient charms assume,
These thro' KILLARNEY'S wilds perennial bloom.

Child of Marsh-elder, next the Guilder-rose[28]
Of humble origin, yet gayly blows,
Silver'd by happy chance, how strange to see
An offspring[29] so unlike the parent tree!
The splendid native of the mountain's side,
Now in the garden lifts its snowy pride.[30]
Graceful and rich the Juniper appears,
Like the Arabian-tree, distilling tears;
Here spreading wide, magnificently dress'd,
In purple rob'd, and by Apollo bless'd.[31]
Deep blushing near, the Service-fruit[32] repays
The woodland warblers wild, and grateful lays;
Allur'd from far, they flock with eager wing,
They feast luxurious, and more tuneful sing.

From one kind stem,[33] behold with wond'ring eyes,
Curious and lordly proud, a forest rise;
No art instructs the various boughs to spread,
Nor from inoculation grows the shade:

28 The marsh elder or guelder rose tree is also known as the snowball tree.

29 <The difference supposed to be accidental.>

30 <Commonly called the snowball tree.>

31 <In allusion to its medicinal virtues.> The purple berries of the juniper tree are used in medicines – and in the manufacture of gin.

32 <This tree is remarkable for its attraction of singing birds.> The *Pyrus domestica* is a small tree that bears edible, pear-like fruit.

33 <A stem of yew, under the mountain Glena.>

The regal Oak, the hardy Ash ascend,
And their umbrageous arms together blend.
The gold-stain'd Holly lifts its prickly spears,
The Quicken-tree[34] its sanguine clutter bears;
Their strength, their bloom, all grateful strive to show,
And grace the parent stock, from whence they grow.
The stranger Vine a friendly mansion finds,
Lodg'd in the cliff, and o'er the summit winds
In purple pomp, while, like a bashful bride,
The Myrtle joins its fragrance and its pride,
Together twin'd, their native union prove
The God of vineyards, and the Queen of love.

Can Flora's self recount the shrubs and flow'rs,
That scent the shade, that clasp the rocky bow'rs?
From the hard veins of sapless marble rise
The fragrant race, and shoot into the skies:
Wond'rous the cause! can human search explore,
What vegetation lurks in ev'ry pore?
What in the womb of different strata breeds?
What fills the universe with genial seeds?
Wond'rous the cause! and fruitless to inquire,
Our wiser part is humbly to admire. …

34 The rowan or mountain ash tree.

ANONYMOUS
(1772)

The text that follows is a rare example of an eighteenth-century Dublin street song that refers to the interaction between humans and animals. It was collected in the nineteenth century but can be dated from internal evidence to 1772.

It is a 'patter song' designed for public performance. As in a pantomime or ballad opera, comic, demotic prose is interwoven with the short, sung verses. The Hiberno-English or Irish-English of the patter after each verse is so obviously exaggerated that it is best characterized as 'stage-Irish'. The notes provide a rough translation.

Bullbaiting was not uncommon in eighteenth-century Dublin. Bulls, which were sometimes stolen from herds being driven into the city for slaughter while they were resting for the night, were baited either in special bull-rings or in the streets.

Lord Altham's Bull

'Twas on the fust of sweet Magay,
It being a high holiday,
Six and twenty boys of de straw
Went to take Lord Altham's bull away.[1]

'I being de fust in de field, who should I see bud de mosey wid his horns sticking in de ground. Well becomes me, I pinked up to him, ketched him by de tail, and rode him dree times round de field, as well as ever de master of de tailor's corporation rode de fringes; but de mosey being game to de back bone, de first rise he gev me in de elements, he made a smash of me collar-bone. So dere being no blunt

1 *Stanza 1*: A rough translation might be: It was on the first day of the sweet month of May, a high holiday, that twenty-six straw-boys went to take Lord Altham's bull away. 'I was first into the field, and who should I see but the bull with its horns sticking in the ground. As befits me, I crept up to him, caught him by the tail and rode him three times round the field, as well as ever the master of the tailor's corporation rode the franchises. But the bull was full of life, and the first time he tossed me up in the air, I smashed my collar-bone. Since I had no money in my pockets, I had to go to Mrs Stevens's hospital where I lay for seven weeks in luxury, flat on my back like Paddy Ward's pig, by heaven!' **Notes on stanza 1**: Magay = May; boys of de straw: It is tempting to see this as a reference to the 'straw-boys', groups of young bachelors dressed in garb made of straw, who were permitted to behave in a riotous manner at certain times of year under the general direction of someone called the 'Mayor of the Bull-ring' (see J. E. Walsh, *Ireland Sixty Years Ago* (Dublin, 1847), p. 94). However, since those involved in the stealing of the bull are transported to Virginia at the end of this poem, the reference may be to boys employed in the Dublin straw-market at Smithfield. Lord Altham = Lord Altamont; mosey was a common name for a bull; de master of de tailor's corporation rode de fringes: every three years, members of the Dublin guilds rode around the bounds of the city in a ceremony known as beating the bounds, franchises or 'fringes'; blunt in de cly = money in the pocket; Madame Stevens was de word refers to Dr Steevens' Hospital; endowed by Dr Richard Steevens (1653–1710) and built by his sister, Grizell (the 'Madam Stevens' of the text), the hospital opened in 1733; Paddy Ward's pig: the meaning of this is obscure. Be de hokey: a slang expression of extreme surprise used in Ireland.

in de cly, Madame Stevens was de word, where I lay for seven weeks in lavendar, on de broad of me back, like Paddy Ward's pig, be de hokey.'

> We drove de bull tro many a gap,
> And kep him going many a mile,
> But when we came to Kilmainham lands,
> We let de mosey rest awhile.

'Oh! boys, if de mosey was keeper of de ancle-spring warehouse, you cud not help pit[y]ing him; his hide smoked like Ned Costigan's brewery, and dere was no more hair on his hoofs dan dere's wool on a goose's gams, be de hokey.'[2]

> We drove de bull down sweet Truck-street,
> Widout eider dread or figear,
> When out ran Mosey Creathorn's bitch,
> Hand cotched de bull be de year.

'Hye, Jock—dat dog's my bitch—spit on her nose to keep her in wind—fight fair, boys, and no stones—low, Nettle, low—shift, shift, my beauty, and keep your hoult'. Oh! boys, your souls, I tought de life ud leave Mosey Creathorn's glimms, when he saw his bitch in de air; 'Oh! Larry Casey, happy det to you, and glory may you get, stand wide and ketch her in your arms—if her head smacks de pavement, she's not worth lifting up—dat's right, yer sowls, now tip her a sup a de blood while it's warm.'[3]

2 *Stanza 2*: We drove the bull through many a gap, and kept him going many a mile. But when we came to the fields at Kilmainham, we let him rest. O, boys, if the bull was the keeper of the stocks, you could not help pitying him. His hide smoked like Ned Costigan's brewery and there was no more hair on his hoofs than there is wool on the legs of a goose, by heaven! **Notes on stanza 2**: de ancle-spring warehouse = the stocks; Ned Costigan's brewery was famous for the smoke it discharged over Dublin, according to Walsh (p. 96).

3 *Stanza 3*: We were driving the bull down sweet Tuck Street without either dread or fear, when out ran Mosey Creathorn's bitch, and caught the bull by the ear. 'Hi, Jock, that dog's my bitch! Spit on her nose to help her to breathe! Fight fair, boys, and no stones! Low, Nettle, low! Shift, shift my beauty, and keep your hold!' O boys, your souls, I thought the life would leave Mosey Creathorn's eyes when he saw his bitch in the air! 'O, Larry Casey, may you have a happy death, and may you get glory! Stand with your legs wide and catch her in your arms! If her head smacks the pavement, it's not worth lifting her up! That's right, now give her a little of the blood while it's warm!' **Notes on stanza 3**: spit on her nose could mean 'blow in her nostrils'.

We drove de bull down Corn-market,
As all de world might segee,
When brave Tedy Foy trust his nose tro' de bars,
Crying 'High for de sweet liberty'.

'Oh! cruel Coffey, glory to you, just knock off my darbies—let me out on padroul of honour—I'll expel de mob—kill five, skin six, and be fader of de scity, I'll return like an innocent lamb to de sheep-walk. Oh! boys, who lost an arm, who lost five fingers and a tumb?' 'Oh!' says Larry Casey, 'it belongs to Luke Ochy, I know it by de slime on de slieve.'[4]

De mosey took down Plunket-street,
Where de clothes on de pegs were hanging,
Oh! den he laid about wid his nob,
De shifts around him banging.

'Oh! Mrs Mulligan, jewel, take in de bits o' duds from de wall, out o' de way o' de mosey's horns—be de hokey, he'll fly kites wid dem, and den poor Miss Judy will go de Lady Mayress's ball, like a spatchcock.'[5]

Lord Altham is a very bad man,
As all de neighbours know,
For driving white Roger from Kilmainham lands,
We all to Virginy must go!

4 *Stanza 4*: We drove the bull down Cornmarket, as all the world might see, when brave Teddy Foy thrust his nose through the bars, crying 'Hey for sweet liberty! O cruel Coffey, glory to you, just knock off my handcuffs, let me out on parole! I'll get rid of the mob in the street, will kill five of them and skin six! I'll be the father of the city and will return like an innocent lamb to the sheep-walk. O, boys, who lost an arm, who lost five fingers and a thumb?' 'O', says Larry Casey, 'it belongs to Luke Ochy; I know it by the slime on the sleeve'. **Notes on stanza 4**: Teddy Foy was a prisoner in the Newgate prison and Coffey was presumably the gaoler there.

5 *Stanza 5*: The bull took off down Plunket Street where the clothes were hanging on the pegs. O, then he laid about him with his head, with petticoats flapping around him. 'O, Mrs Mulligan, dear, take in the bits of clothes from the wall, out of the way of the bull's horns! By heaven, he'll make kites out of them, and then poor Miss Judy will go to the Lady Mayoress's Ball like a spatch-cock.' **Notes on stanza 5**: Plunket Street was a centre for second-hand clothes stalls; a spatch-cock was a fowl killed, dressed and grilled at short notice, so here the phrase means 'naked as a spatch-cock', i.e. with no clothes on.

‘Well! boys!—suppose we go for seven years, an’t dere six of us! Dat’s just fourteen monts a-piece. I can sail in a turf-kish, and if ever I come back from his Majesty’s tobacco-manufactory, I’ll butter my knife in his tripes, and give him his guts for garters. All de world knows I’ve de blood of de Dempseys in me.’[6]

6 *Stanza 6*: Lord Altham is a very bad man, as all the neighbours know. For driving white Roger from Kilmainham lands, we are all to be transported to Virginia! Well, boys! Suppose we go for seven years – aren’t there six of us? That’s just fourteen months each! I can sail in a turf-basket, and if I ever come back from his Majesty’s tobacco-manufactory, I’ll butter my knife with Lord Altham’s intestines and give him his guts for garters. All the world knows that I have the blood of the Dempseys in me. **Notes on stanza 6**: white Roger was the name of the bull.

GERALD FITZGERALD
(1740–**1773**–1819)

Gerald Fitzgerald entered Trinity College Dublin as a sizar (a student who undertook menial tasks and received a free education) in 1759. He became a fellow of the college in 1765, professor of Law in 1783 and of Hebrew in 1790. He retired at the age of 66 and spent the last thirteen years of his life as a country clergyman. The poem which follows recounts the events of a day's expedition from Dublin; the poet and his friend leave Trinity College early in the morning and, after shooting snipe and woodcock in the Dodder valley, climb the Dublin mountains where 'many a shot repays the pleasing toil'. In the late afternoon, the two friends are still in the Dublin mountains; they have a fine view over the countryside and can see the city in the distance, but they are tired and in need of some refreshment.

from: The Academick Sportsman

... The Day advanc'd, and waning to the West,
Demands a thought for respite, and for rest,
Back to the city calls a sudden eye,[1]
Where vary'd beauties all in prospect lie;
The pointed Steeples menacing the Skies,
The splendid Domes, that emulously rise,
The lowly Hamlets scatter'd here and there,
That scarcely swell to breathe refreshing air;
The hedge-row'd Hills, and intermingled Vales,
The distant Villas fann'd by floating Gales;
And Eastward still, along the Bay serene,
Attendant Commerce crowns the solemn scene.[2]

These to behold may please the vacant mind,
More pleasing far the Cottage of the Hind,[3]
That yonder smokes,[4] by russet Hawthorn hedg'd,
By hay-yard back'd, and side long cow-shed edg'd:
Oft have I there my thirst and toil allay'd,
Approach'd as now, and dar'd[5] the dog that bay'd;

1 i.e. the poet suddenly turns his eyes to look at the city.

2 They can see commercial shipping in Dublin Bay.

3 labourer.

4 i.e. smoke from the hearth fire rises either through the chimney or, more probably, through the thatch.

5 challenged.

The smiling Matron joys to see her Guests,
Sweeps the broad hearth, and hears our free requests,
Repels her little Brood, that throng too nigh,
The homely board prepares—the napkin dry,
The new-made butter—rasher's[6] ready fare,
The new-laid egg, that's dress'd with nicest care;
The milky Store, for cream collected first,
Crowns the clean noggin[7] and allays our thirst;
While crackling Faggots, bright'ning as they burn,
Shew the neat cup-board, and the cleanly churn—
The modest Maiden rises from her wheel,
Who, unperceiv'd, a silent look would steal;
Call'd she attends, assists with artless grace,
The Bloom of Nature flushing in her face,
That scorns the die,[8] which pallid pride can lend,
And all the Arts which Luxury attend.

With fuel laden from the brambly rock,
Lo! forward comes the Father of his flock,
Of honest front:[9] salutes with rustic gait,
Remarks our fare, and boasts his former state,
When many a cow, nor long the time remov'd,
And many a calf his spacious pasture rov'd,
'Till rising Rents reduc'd him now to three,
Abridg'd his Farm, and fix'd him as we see;
Yet thanks his GOD, what fails him in his wealth
He seeks from labour, and he gains from health:
Then talks of sport; how many Wild-ducks seen!
What flocks of Widgeon,[10] too, had fledg'd the green!
'Till ev'ry 'Prentice dar'd the city shun,
Range the wide field, and lift the level gun.

While thus amus'd, and gladden'd with our lot,
The hasty Ev'ning calls us from the Cot;

6 thin slices of bacon or ham.

7 a small drinking vessel.

8 i.e. artificial powders and cosmetics.

9 forehead.

10 a particular kind of wild duck.

A small gratuity dilates their heart,
And many a blessing follows as we part.
Nor you, ye Proud! their humble state disdain,
Their state is Nature's, hospitable, plain,
Transmitted pure from Patriarchal times,
Unfram'd, unfashion'd to Corruption's Climes—
To you unknown their sweets from Toil's release—
To you unknown their Innocence and Peace—
Secure from Danger, as remov'd from Fame,
Their Lives calm Current flows without a name.

With limbs refresh'd, with lively tales and gay,
We homeward haste, and guile the tedious way;
Each object view, in wintry dress around,
And eye the Dogs, that wanton o'er the ground;
The pensive Red-breast on the leafless bough,
And, just beneath, the fragrance-breathing cow,
While still more grateful, with her cleanly pail,
The ruddy Milkmaid hears a tender tale
From the lov'd Swain, who swells th'alternate sigh,
Leans on his staff, and lures her side-long eye,
With artless guile, his passion to impart,
With looks that speak the passion of his Heart. ...

... Lo! yonder come—yet distant to the eye,
The vagrant PLOVER wafted thro' the sky;
Swift to the hedge, on diff'rent sides we run,
That skirt the copse, and hide the deadly gun;
Onward they move regardless of their state,
A single Guide[11] conducts them to their fate—
The sudden Thunder bursts upon their head—
The foremost fall and all the rest are fled. ...

At length arriv'd, where DUBLIN's boasted Square
Rears its high domes, yet, spreads a healthful air,
O'er the wide view my willing eyes I cast,
And fill remembrance with its pleasures past,

11 i.e. the bird leading the flight.

Its shady walks, that lure the Noontide gale,
And sweeter breath of Love's enraptur'd tale;
Its sparkling Belles, that, arm'd in beauty's pride,
Wound as they pass, and triumph on each side;
But now no more these glories gild the Green—
Chill night descends, and desolates the scene.
The rising moon, with delegated sway,
Supplies the radiance of the distant Day,
Smiles on our path, directs our weary feet
Thro' all the busy tumults of the street—
With head-long pace, *here*, vagrant *Hawkers* scour,
And *bloody News* from lungs horrific pour,
There, dull, discordant Ballad-Notes annoy,
That mock the crowd, with love's fantastick joy;
The cumb'rous coach, the blazon'd chariot shows
Where lazy pride, or lordly state repose;
While, close behind, and heedless of her way,
We see the friendless, shiv'ring female stray:
She, once, the darling of her mother's arms,
Her father's pride, and blest with blooming charms,
Thro' all the village known for spotless fame,
Fair was her beauty, fairer still her name;
'Till the Tempter urg'd insidious suit,
And lur'd her weakness to forbidden fruit,
There perish'd grace, her guardian honour fled,
And sad remembrance mourns each blessing—dead!
Expell'd from Paradise of native sway,
She wanders now to ev'ry vice a prey—
A prey to yonder terror of the Night,
(Avert, ye Gods! such monsters from my sight,)
The Bully[12] dire! whose front the furies swell,
And scars dishonest mark the son of Hell—
In vain! she shrinks to shun his luckless pace,
Aw'd by the terrors of his vengeful face;
To scenes TARTAREAN,[13] see! the wretches hie,
Where, drench'd in vice, they rave—or rot—or die.

12 one who protects prostitutes and lives on their earnings.

13 hellish. In classical mythology, Tartarus was one of the regions of hell.

Heav'n! how unlike the pure, the tranquil plain,
Where rural mirth, and rural manners reign;
Where simple cheer disclaims the cares of wealth,
And fresh'ning gales diffuse the glow of health;
Where, undisturb'd, unenvy'd, unconfin'd,
Calm reason rules each movement of the mind;
Where mock'd ambition seeks her last retreat,
And proves the world, a bubble or a cheat.

As op'ning streets with brighter aspect smile,
Lo! ALMA MATER[14] rears her rev'rend Pile,
Unfolds the portals of her awful[15] Square,
Where Arts and Science own her fost'ring care;
Struck with the scene that boasts ELIZA's name,
We pause, and praise the consecrated name,
The hallow'd ground, with softer footsteps, tread
Where BERKELEY reason'd, and where USHER read,
Where, born to combat an untoward age,
Indignant SWIFT explor'd the classic page—
Hail! happy Shade!—with griefs that once were thine,
IERNE[16] bends beneath thy patriot shrine;
In times like these, when gath'ring woes impend,
She mourns her Dean, her Draper, and her Friend,
Her exil'd commerce, half-deserted land,
Her harp unstrung, and manacled her hand,
While her pale Artists,[17] ev'ry comfort fled,
Droop in her streets, and die—for want of bread.

Thus past the day, and paid the pious tear
To worth deceas'd—to virtues ever dear,
Each fond Reflection, rising in our breast,
At length subdues, and yields to soothing rest;

14 i.e. Trinity College Dublin, founded in the reign of Queen Elizabeth I ('Eliza') and boasting among its teachers or graduates the philosopher Bishop Berkeley, Archbishop James Ussher and Swift.

15 awe-inspiring.

16 Ireland.

17 artisans, tradesmen. There was a widespread feeling at the time of this poem that Ireland was suffering from a severe economic depression, the effect of British restrictions on Irish trade.

Pleas'd we behold the bright'ning fuel blaze,
And hot repast, that challenges our praise,
While keenest appetites a zest bestow,
Which listless luxury can never know:
The cloth remov'd, with blessing for our fare,
We, next, the Bowl's convivial juice prepare,
Or, the rich Grape's nectareous bev'rage pour,
To raise the heart, and cheer the social hour,
When toil declining claims refreshment's smiles,
And mirthful innocence the time beguiles. ...

ANONYMOUS
(1776)

This unusual poem appeared in *Walker's Hibernian Magazine* in July 1776, two years before the foundation of the Irish Volunteers. Patriotic fervour was building up throughout Ireland as British soldiers were withdrawn to fight in the American War of Independence (1775–83). Landowners and men of property saw the reduction in troops as an opportunity to put pressure on the British government to relax the laws that were stifling Irish trade. From this grew demands for legislative independence for Ireland; this was finally obtained in Grattan's parliament of 1782 and brought to an end by the Act of Union of 1801.

The poet imagines the river god of the river Lagan (which flows through Ulster from south to north) rising up and calling on those freeholders of Antrim who are of an 'independent' mind to support the local candidate for the Irish parliament, Ezekiel Davys Wilson. Wilson, who was mayor of Carrickfergus, was duly elected MP for the county borough in 1785. He voted against the Union in 1799 and 1800.

Lagan upon the Mountain

Hard by those plains where *Lagan* gently flows,
And scenes of wealth in his smooth bosom shews,
As lately walking, by the dawn of day,
To court the Zephyr, or perhaps to pray;
I saw the waves a sudden lustre spread,
I saw old *Lagan* leave his oozy bed,
And lightly skimming up the verdant hills,
Touch the glad founts, and wake the warbling rills;
Then full on *Collan*'s[1] peaky summit rest,
And gaze around and shake his weedy crest.

Rejoice, he cries, you independent train,
Who sacred truth and liberty maintain,[2]
Bold let the gallant sons of *Antrim* rise,
Extol their hero[3] to the bending skies:

1 The southernmost of the main Belfast Hill summits, Colin Mountain dominates the Lisburn side of the Belfast Hills. The Colin river is the main tributary of the Lagan.

2 During the 1770s, Irish political life became polarised between those who sought free trade and political concessions from the British government (who often, following the example of the American colonists, asserted that they were fighting for 'liberty' and some kind of 'independence') and those who supported the Dublin administration.

3 Presumably Ezekiel Wilson of line 22.

Let *Antrim*'s self[4] attend the joyful call,
And ride triumphant from his mossy hall,
Bear the loud pæns to each secret cell,
Along the moor, or down the dusky dell,
Whirl up the mountain, on the valley strain,
Follow the brook, and sweep the breezy plain;
Bid all his people mutually proclaim,
That *Liberty* and *Wilson* are the same.[5]

Fair flow such merit to the latest song,
And catch new incense as it rolls along:
Well, meek *Ierne*! Well it were for thee,
Were all thy people so completely free;
Did all freeholders, spite of lawless sway,
The genial impulse of the mind obey;[6]
Not, as they do, for some vile futile fee,
Stoop to the yoke, and bend the supple knee.
Well wot[7] I then how goodly would appear,
The rural labour and the sylvan cheer:
How would I then my own dear seats[8] survey,
My seats for ever pleasant, for ever gay;
Where lads go lightsome, splendid villas rise,
And hills of linen whiten to the skies;[9]
Where love the heart while honour guides the soul,
And female sweetness dignifies the whole.

This said, down shoots the river God, to gain
The shady coverts of sweet *Ballydrain*.[10]

4 i.e. the famous Randall MacDonnell, First Marquess of Antrim, lieutenant-general of the forces of the Irish confederacy in the 1640s – a figure admired by those striving for Irish independence.

5 Ezekiel Davys Wilson (1738–1821).

6 Carrickfergus was a county borough, which meant that both freeholders and citizens could vote for its member of parliament. The next line refers to bribery and corruption in parliamentary elections.

7 know.

8 Several contemporary poems refer to the beautifully-sited country houses above the Lagan river and its tributaries.

9 Since linen manufacture was a staple industry of the area, large sheets of fresh linen could often be seen spread out to bleach in the sun in 'bleach-fields'.

10 Ballydrain is a small community located outside Comber on the shores of Strangford Lough.

ANONYMOUS
(1777)

Cock fighting was common in seventeenth- and eighteenth-century Ireland. Many towns had permanent cockpits where large sums of money were gambled. The 'sport' was not outlawed until 1837. This poem appeared in the 'Original Poetry' section of *Walker's Hibernian Magazine* for 1777.

The Cock

Stately bird of dauntless courage!
 See him with his cackling train,
Strutting o'er the busy farm-yard,
 Picking up the scatter'd grain.
Should a neighbouring foe, advancing,
 Thro' the fence, invade his right;
Straight, indignant, he attacks him,
 Death the combat ends, or flight.
If victorious, how he triumphs,
 Struts, and claps his wings, and crows,
Woos and chears his merry females,
 Scrapes, and chucks and boons bestows.
But that noble, valiant instinct,
 Oft proves fatal, nature gave;
Safety shields secure the coward
 Danger persecutes the brave.
Men, miscall'd, of brutal feelings,
 Who in barb'rous sports delight,
Joy to make more gen'rous creatures
 Join in fierce, unnatural fight.
Stript of all his brightest plumage,
 Now half-naked he appears,
On his legs steel'd martial weapons,
 Glitt'ring in the sun, he wears.
How unlike to Chanticleer[1] that
 Lately grac'd the farmer's door!

1 The name of the cock in Geoffrey Chaucer's 'The Nun's Priest's Tale'. Chanticleer's favourite wife was Partlet.

Not ev'n Partlet now wou'd know him,
 Whom she knew so well before!
A pit! A pit!—the gaping croud straight,
 In the midst a circle form—
Big with awful expectation,
 Now begins the battle's storm.
Heel meets heel, in bloody conflict,
 Beak meets beak, and wing meets wing,—
'Till or chance or strength superior
 Down the fated hero bring.
Now the echoing shouts of triumph,
 Pierce confus'd the yielding air;
Whilst aloud the madd'ning rabble
 Their disorder'd joy declare.
Fly, my muse, such savage transports;
 Hie thee to some secret cell,
Where secure from frantic folly,
 Wisdom, quiet, virtue dwell.

ANONYMOUS
(1781)

The anonymous author of this poem was determined to present the incoming Lord Lieutenant with a realistic picture of life in the Irish countryside. Though the poet warns that ‘civil broils’ caused by ‘*Faction* mask’d in patriotic guise’ exist in the country, his real concern is with the effects of landlordism. The prose introduction to the poem notes that ‘peasants’ in Ireland are ‘more truly indigent, naturally improvident, more unemployed [and] more miserably circumstanced’ than those in any other civilized nation. The writer continues: ‘Luxury and ostentation may throw the splendid mantle of tinseled riches over our natural poverty, and wretchedness; … It is the interior parts of our country, my Lord, which has [*sic*] sat for the picture I have the honour to present to your lordship…’. The author claims that ‘upwards of £732,000’ is spent every year by absentee landlords living abroad.

from: Ierne: a poem addressed to his Excellency the Earl of Carlisle,

Lord Lieutenant General and General Governor of Ireland on his arrival in this Kingdom …

… Then let our absent prodigals return,
And o’er their rackt estates and tenants mourn,
Bid our rich Landlords and their Agent-train,
Relieve the sufferings of our rustic Swain:
Drive hard Oppression from their litter’d Sheds,
Their cold starv’d Hovels, and their Hurdl’d Beds:[1]
Where *pining Poverty*, her Woes among,
Scarce feeds herself, or cloaths her naked Young.
Where ruthless Want and Indigence extreme,
Implore our Pity, and our Comfort Claim:
Whilst they like Vassals, bound in Feudal chains,
Are ill repaid for all their labouring Gains.
But *Tythes* and *Tallies*[2] grind their wretched lot,
And drive the famish’d Hinds[3] from Cot to Cot.
Then bid our Wandering, gay, voluptuous Great,
Who crush the Nation, and its griefs create,
Bid them no more for foreign Pleasures roam,
But taste more solid Luxury at home:

1 i.e. made of willow sticks woven like hurdles

2 <A custom on most parts of this Kingdom where tenures are held on Condition of working for the Landlord at 5d. per day, paid by Nicks on a Tally.>

3 farmworkers.

No more self-exiled from their Manors rove
Nor let their Tenants or their Farms be drove
At Folly's beck, or Dissipation's call,
To raise their Rents, or bid their Woodlands fall,
Whilst the neglected and desponding Swains
(That source of Riches, which the Proud disdains)
Ne'er see those happy hospitable Days,
When their Lords came their drooping Hopes to raise,
Made the Plains gay with rural Mirth and Cheer,
And bade content in every look appear.
By generous Deeds, their grateful Tenants blest,
Supply'd their losses, and their Cares adrest:
Whilst the leas'd Farms through Generations ran,
And Sons improv'd the Plans their Sires began.
When *Fines*, nor *Proctors*[4] with oppressive Hands,
Neither monopoliz'd nor stript their Lands;
But ev'ry Peasant to his Cottage fix'd
The Fruits of Labour, with Contentment mix'd.
—To such Examples, Policy, and Skill,
Britain her Riches owes, and Yeomen still.

Ah! what avails our long-wish'd Rights of Trade,
Or all the Laws our Legislature made
If cold Neglect and slothful Langour foil
These precious Gifts, and damp ingenious Toil?
If public Spirit to our Welfare's dead,
And Speculation and Invention fled? ...

... Let Cultivation come with smiling Face,
That feeds, employs and populates our Race:
For once our Country and Ourselves befriend,
And busy Toil with Manufactures blend:
Raise other Birminghams and Sheffields here,
And bid new Manchesters and Fromes[5] appear;
With Flocks and Herds our verdant pastures fill,
And the plough'd Glebe with Agriculture till:

4 A fine was a sum of money paid by a tenant at the beginning of a tenancy and proctors were agents for the collection of rents and tithes.

5 <Famous for its Woollen Manufactory>.

Make Art on Nature, new Improvements frame,
Enclose our dreary Wastes, and Swamps reclaim.
Bid Sylvan prospects clothe the naked Land,
And Shady Hedge-rows o'er its face expand:
Erect huge Engines on the teeming Earth,
And give our Mines and new Employments birth:
Bid Navigations intersect the Plain,
Combine our Rivers, and unite the Main:[6]
Bid Towns and Hamlets in our Desarts rise,
And new Creations, novel Works devise. …

… Let Toleration!—human Nature's Friend,
Its peaceful Freedom and Indulgence send:
Let moral Deeds, and philosophic Zeal
O'er Persecution's tyrant Scourge prevail;
That social Concord and celestial Love
May hail the great Omnipotence above!
That ev'ry Worship in Religion's Cause
May groan no more beneath their penal Laws:
Bid ev'ry District feed its helpless Poor
And vagrant tribes of Mendicants secure:
This idle Nuisance from our Country drive,
Nor let such Drones infest the social Hive;
Bid the Police, and Civil Pow'r unite,
Exert the Laws, and guard their sacred Right,
That all the Nation may their Rule obey,
Confess their Justice and corrective Sway;
That lawless havoc, and her savage crew
No more may riot nor their rage pursue.[7]

Bid pastoral Virtue on the Plains revive,
And good Examples with her Precepts strive
To spread the Bliss that o'er Arcadia reign'd,
And make this Land a Paradise regain'd. …

6 A plea for the construction of canals across Ireland.

7 The reference is to the agrarian violence of the time.

JAMES HENDERSON
(*fl.*1777–**1784**)

From 1777 onwards, the 'Original Poetry' section of *Walker's Hibernian Magazine* contained numerous poems from the pen of 'J.H. of Hillsborough', Co. Down. O'Donoghue states that they were the work of a James Henderson but gives no indication where he found this information. Henderson's poems suggest that he spent his childhood wandering the hills above Belfast, but he also knew the Lagan valley and the river Bann well. This poem, like many others published in Irish monthly magazines at the time, expresses contempt for the 'sportsmen' who shoot wild birds in Ireland.

The Woodcock

Look where Kilwarlin rises on the sight,[1]
A verdant country, pregnant with delight!
Whence purest streams in mazy currents flow,
To bless and beautify the vales below;
Where birds delighted, whilst the smiling spring
Scatters her sweets, and through the summer, sing;
Where bearded plenty yellow autumn yields;
And, when wild winter desolates the fields,
Where still the neighbourhood with sports is gay
Whilst hounds and horns awake the dawning day,
Horses and horsemen croud the echoing hills,
And spreading clamour every valley fills.

There, by cool fountain, shaded from the storm,
A Woodcock sported, of the fairest form;
From Lapland never did a fairer fly,[2]
Or back to Lapland cleave the liquid sky,
Though some suppose that birds of passage go
Hence to the moon, thence come to us below.
Certain it is, by night the woodcocks love
To leave the rilly copses,[3] and to rove
Beneath the starry lustre, and to feed
Over the yellow heath, and moonlight mead.

1 The escarpment of the Kilwarlin plateau in County Down overlooks the Lagan valley.

2 The woodcock, a large wading bird with short legs and a very long straight tapering bill, spends the winter in Ireland, but migrates to Lapland and Russia for the summer.

3 i.e. copses beside small rills or streams.

This woodcock, then, what time the night is near
And evening echoes gratify the ear,
Soon as the stars begin, of largest size,
To shew their fires, and sparkle from the skies,
Was wont, attentive to the grateful gleam,
To leave the murmurs of the shaded stream;
Forth from the woods on whirling wings to fly,
Dart from the view, and tumble down the sky;
Then in the stubble was she wont to play,
And watch the passing moon till break of day,
By break of day spring from the sportful plain,
And boldly sink into the woods again.

This saw a youth, who daily with his dog
Pursues the game, and beats the bushy bog;
A youth of spirit, who can ride and run,
Follows the hounds, and famous with the gun!
No youth so well as he an aim could take,
Bring down the pheasant bursting from the brake,
Arrest the mallard in his furtive flight,
Or send the sudden snipe to shades of night.
Kilwardin was his chosen walk, where he
Would slay his thousands in destructive glee;
With every rising, every setting sun,
The woods resounded with his deathful gun.
How would he force the thicket, pass the flood,
Marking his way with feathers and with blood!
To range the mountains and to beat the bogs,
Was all his happiness, and all his dog's.

One evening, weary, as he took his way,
Returning from the slaughter of the day,
He saw the woodcock from the covert spring,
Dart from his view, and wanton on the wing;
Nor could he reach her, though in truth he tried:
Then, disappointed, in revenge he cried,
'Ere twice twelve hours shall run their rapid round,
My shot shall seize thee, and my fire confound,

Devoted bird of passage! Thou shalt fall
Before my glorious gun, which conquers all.'

Soon as the shades of the succeeding night
Began to fall, and make a dubious light;
When stars of the first magnitude appear,
And distant noises sweetly soothe the ear;
Though, for our youth, we rather should remark,
When oxen bellow, and when mastiffs bark:
Then, and so soon, our hero took his way,
True to the signal of declining day;
His piece[4] in order, no piece could be more:
His bag behind him, and his dog before;
With hasty steps thus did he pass along,
To blast the bird, the subject of our song.
Stir not, O woodcock, though the stars appear,
Or fly not that way, for the fowler fear;
Perhaps some gentle genius of the glade,
Some sympathetic spirit, might have said,
Who saw the youth, on a convenient hill,
Now watchful stand, the comely bird to kill.
Out came the woodcock, with a wonted bound,
The skilful savage brought her to the ground;
Beheld her bleeding wounds, with gleeful eye,
Then flung her in his net, without a sigh.

Ill-fated bird! the muse cannot forbear
To mourn thy death with a despondent tear.
Ill-fated bird! thou shalt, alas, no more
The streamy copse, and shaded rill explore;
No more, with vernal suns, ascend the sky,
Look down on mortals and to Lapland fly;
No more from thence, before the solar light
Departs, and winter there is one dread night,
Return to brighter climes, with weary wings,
To sweet Kilwardin, and its limpid springs;
Whatever life thou hadst, whatever joy,
A youth, barbarian, did at once destroy.

4 gun.

There was a time, when with a better grace
Our youth had sported with the winged race;
When, wild in woods, our rugged sires did know
The use of little but the bended bow:
But now the sciences and arts abound,
Now that pursuits far nobler may be found,
Still, still to prosecute the sylvan strife
The woodland war, is plainly losing life,
And giving up the man, and manly joys,
For vulgar pleasure, and the sports of boys.

"Œ.L."
(1790)

This poem is another example of the provincial poetry – in this case from Belfast – carried in Irish monthly magazines in the late eighteenth century. This piece appeared in the *Universal Magazine and Review or Repository of Literature containing the Literature, History, Manners, Arts and Amusements of the Age* for March 1790. Like several other anonymous authors, this poet expresses outrage at human cruelty to animals.

The Lamentation of *Cara Pluma*,[1] a Female Pheasant,

for the Loss of her Husband and Children.
Dedicated to Mr. Robert McCormick, the celebrated Irish Gun-Maker[2]

Retir'd amidst the fading grove,
The muse the widow'd mourner heard,
And, mov'd with grief for injur'd love,
The tale imparted to the bard.

'Shall tyrant man alone complain,
To lose the partner of his heart?
And must I still my grief restrain,
And not my keenest woes impart?

Ah no! my murder'd partner, no!
While love shall warm thy once-lov'd bride,
I'll curse with constant cries the foe
That snatch'd thee from my faithful side.

And still at sober ev'ning's dawn,
(Of cruel guns no more afraid),
I'll court the copse and walk the lawn,
And love the spots where once we've stray'd.

1 Probably intended to be translated as 'beautiful feather'.

2 Advertisements in the *Belfast Newsletter* indicate that Robert McCormick was carrying on business as a gun-maker in Castle Street, Belfast from 1784 onwards. He left Belfast for Dublin in 1794 and continued his business in Abbey Street.

How oft have I, beneath the shade,
When summer deck'd the Sylvan scene,
Thy shining plumage all survey'd,
And mark'd the look that call'd me queen.

When bless'd with home and children dead,
No mortals felt supremer joys.—
But joys like these no more shall cheer
My heart,—for death the charm destroys.

Remembrance brings thee still to view,
And still I see thee fond and fair,
Some flatt'ring phantom bids pursue,
'Till faint, I sink beneath despair.

Now scatter'd wide our children roam,
To 'scape the bloody spaniel's way;
The bush-clad bank we call'd our home,
The sportsman plunders for his prey.

Oh! savage man thy sports restrain,
But hark—a shot!—my heart's alarm'd;
Perhaps the son and sire are slain,
That son so like his father form'd.

'Tis he!—my husband's image!—he,
My fav'rite son, I hear his cries,
The shouting murderers too I see,
They seize my child!—Alas! He dies!

No more can life afford me joy,
My husband and my children slain!
If man was form'd thus to destroy,
Alas!—why is he call'd humane.'

ANONYMOUS
(1790)

Towards the end of the eighteenth century, many songs celebrating particular localities in Ireland – their natural beauty and that of their maidens – made their way into print. Though Cappoquin is in County Waterford, this song was included in a chapbook printed by William Goggin of Limerick to be sold by chapmen at local fairs and assemblies in that area. Many songs like this one were probably dictated by singers whose first language was Irish to compositors themselves uncertain about the syntax, grammar and vocabulary of standard English. The charm of these texts lies in their lack of sophistication.

Cappoquin, a new Song

From Cupid's darts my heart I must release,
I'll sing no more his tragic scenes and plays,
Now I'm inspired with grand and noble lays,
Sweet Cappoquin I am resolved to praise.[1]

The houses ranged in proper order are,
No ornaments are wanting I do declare,
It's situated handsomely and fair,
Never was there known such wholesome air.

A purling stream[2] along the centre glides,
Which decorates the streets on e'ery side,
And I wish with pleasure that I were inspir'd,
To praise the Banks of the Black-water side.

Its verdant plains abound with vernal flowers,
Free from all noxious and destructive showers,
What pleasing grottoes and delightful bowers,
Are formed by the bright celestial bowers.

1 This is a standard trope – that the singer will replace his usual love songs with praise of a locality.

2 The River Blackwater – a celebrated salmon fishery.

The landscape round about with country seats,
Belmount's[3] and Prospect-hall of late,
And many others which I could relate
The assistance of the Muses I do entreat.

A curious Edifice in Belmount's found,
For structure noble and architecture crown'd,
It is by all conjunctively[4] renowned,
Which adds to the encomiums of this town.

The beauteous walks that do this seat surround,
By art reformed and by nature crown'd,
Were you to trace this nation round and round
So fine a place on earth could not be found.

I need not sing the Wooden-bridge[5] most fam'd,
As strangers from all parts do it maintain,
In pleasing raptures they do all exclaim,
A greater wonder never nature fram'd.

Foreign traders thither have recourse,
And noble statesmen from all princely courts,
Along this river gently do they cruise,
In vessels fit adapted for this use.

To angle here these nobles all resort,
And never fail of meeting with good sport,
For cruddy[6] salmon and the silver trout,
No other river does so far abound.

What pleasant objects strike the curious mind,
To see the lads to merriment inclin'd,
Brave, courageous, generous and kind,
All nations range,[7] the like you'll ne'er find.

3 Belmount was rebuilt as Cappoquin House in 1779. The magnificence of the new house is referred to in lines 21-4 (though it is referred to by its old name). Prospect-hall has disappeared.

4 i.e. by everyone.

5 The wooden bridge over the River Blackwater at Cappoquin, built during the late seventeenth century, was replaced by a stone bridge in the nineteenth century.

6 'Crud' or curd is the fatty substance found between the flakes of flesh in boiled salmon.

7 i.e. wherever you travel.

What beauteous damsels blooming young and gay,
Admired by strangers and adored each day,
And more than this I think I cannot say,
For Cappoquin (by Jove) doth bear the sway.

And if the muses all were to unite,
To guide my pen and for me to indite,
I am sure that all that they and I could write,
Would fall far short to praise this town aright.

JAMES CREIGHTON
(1736–**1791**–1819)

James Creighton was born in County Cavan and educated at Cavan Grammar School and at Trinity College Dublin. He was ordained into the Church of Ireland and served as curate of Swanlinbar, Co. Cavan.

Creighton was a man of strong Christian faith who came under the influence of John Wesley and became a Methodist though he continued (as Wesley intended his followers to do) to be an active member of the Established Church. He lived for a while in London and visited America with Wesley in 1784. Creighton was a prolific writer of pamphlets and sermons as well as of verse, the latter collected in his *Poetic Miscellanies* (London, 1791). His strong faith and his love for the Irish countryside come together in the poem from which the following extract is taken.

from: The Prospect of the Lake Erne,
and the country adjacent, from the Hill called Knockninny

The morn invites; come then, and let us climb
Up yonder Hill that rears its crest sublime:
Let us inhale the sweets upon the lawn,
View frisking lambkins, and the sportive fawn:
And when we gain *Knockninny*'s utmost height,
We'll feast our eyes with exquisite delight.
My friend,[1] I know, has taste, and he shall find
A copious subject to expand his mind.
This day we'll spend, and chearfully employ,
In viewing Nature, and our GOD enjoy:
Each blade of grass, each flow'r, each shrub, each tree,
Will point us out the hand of DEITY:
Their various tints, their uses, and design,
Will fully prove the work is all divine!
If things minute, with microscopic eye,
We closely view; an atom, or a fly;
An embryo insect, veil'd within its coat;
Or lighter things, which in a sun-beam float:
If *Vegetation* should our mind engross,
And we should stop to view a bed of Moss;
Or, if the Fluids, rising from the Root,
Producing Leaves, perhaps delicious Fruit;

1 i.e. the friend who accompanied the poet on the climb.

If these, and thousands more, our thoughts engage;
The creeping Ivy, and the Mountain-sage;[2]
The Thistle's Down, the Petals of the Flow'rs,
Where bees sip nectar from ambrosial show'rs:
The heath with crimson crown'd; the slender rush;
The wild-rose op'ning; and the hawthorn bush.
If each of these we study, or the whole,
A sweet astonishment shall seize the soul!
Their beauty, texture, curious parts combin'd,
Afford much matter for a thinking mind:
The more we search, examine, and explore,
More cause we find to wonder and adore:
And, tho' the use of each we cannot scan,
Because beyond the reach of mortal man,
Yet still in all, in each, a God we see,
To whom, with rev'rence, all should bend the knee.

And now, methinks, your mind begins to fill
With pleasing rapture, as we mount the Hill:
Then let this hillock be our seat awhile,
'Till I shall point you first to sweet *Bellisle*.[3]
See there it lies, almost beneath your feet,
A most enchanting, lovely, calm retreat:
Remote from noise, and from the bustling scene,
Where sharpers cheat, and Cits[4] are fill'd with spleen;
Where flattery cringes with a smiling bow,
And perjury succeeds the faithless vow;
Where honest worth but rarely meets a friend,
And Patriots[5] speak but for some *private* end:
Where native blushes (counted now disgrace!)
Would seem a wonder on a female face:
And whilst the husband pores upon the news,
His partner oft frequents the public stews:[6]

2 <*Knockninny* abounds with Mountain-Sage.>

3 <The Seat of the Earl of Ross; in an Island of *Lough Erne*.> See also William Balfour Madden's 1761 poem on Bellisle (above).

4 citizens or those living in towns.

5 i.e. members of one party in the Irish Parliament.

6 brothels.

—But, stop, my thoughts!—with horror now I start!
E'en *thoughts* of Cities might pollute the heart!

Then let us turn our ears to yonder grove,
To hear the black-bird, and the cooing dove!
Behold that meadow, and the new-mown hay,
That lawn, where lambkins sport the live-long day;
That splendid dome; that garden with its fruits;
Its grapes, and green-house, with exotic roots!
See there a clump of trees, and here a brake,[7]
Which seem down-bending in the placid lake!
Then lift your eyes, and for a moment gaze
On those green hills where various cattle graze:
And, what doth much the rural scene adorn,
See interspers'd the waving fields of corn!
The russet mountain next will take your view,
And gently lead you to th'ethereal blue.
Here stop awhile, and take a prospect round,[8]
For, here th'horizon terminates the bound:
And whilst from East to West you cast your eyes,
A thousand objects strike you with surprize. …

7 thicket.

8 i.e. take in the view, perhaps using a 'prospect-glass' or telescope.

ELLEN TAYLOR
(*fl.*1792)

Though she later seems to have kept a school, Ellen Taylor was employed as a maid in a house near Graiguenamanagh, Co. Kilkenny when she wrote this poem. She explained, in the introduction to *Poems by Ellen Taylor, the Irish Cottager* (1792), that it was a guest in the house who encouraged her to write poetry. The same unknown benefactor may have been behind the attempt to raise money for her through the publication of her work. Only forty copies of her *Poems* were printed and it is remarkable that such a slight, cheaply printed pamphlet has survived.

Written by the Barrow[1] side
where she was sent to wash Linen

Thy banks, O Barrow, sure must be
   The Muses' choicest haunt,
Else why so pleasing thus to me,
   Else why my soul enchant?

To view thy dimpled surface here,
   Fond fancy bids me stay;
But Servitude, with brow austere,
   Commands me straight away.

Were Lethe's virtues[2] in thy stream,
   How freely would I drink,
That not so much as on the name
   Of books I e'er might think.

I can but from them learn to know
   What misery's complete,
And feel more sensibly each blow
   Dealt by relentless fate.

1 The river Barrow flows through Graiguenamanagh.

2 Lethe was one of the rivers of hell in classical mythology. Those who drank its waters forgot all that they had done, seen or heard.

In them I oft have pleasure found,
  But now it's all quite fled.
With fluttering heart, I lay me down,
  And rise with aching head.

For such a turn ill suits the sphere
  Of life in which I move,
And rather does a load of care
  Than any comfort prove.

Thrice happy she, condemned to move
  Beneath the servile weight,
Whose thoughts ne'er soar one inch above
  The standard of her fate.

But far more happy is the soul,
  Who feels the pleasing sense;
And can indulge without control
  Each thought that flows from thence.

Since naught of these my portion is,
  But the reverse of each,
That I shall taste but little bliss,
  Experience doth me teach.

Could cold insensibility
  Through my whole frame take place,
Sure then from grief I might be free:
  Yes, then I'd hope for peace.

SAMUEL THOMSON
(1766–**1793**–1816)

Samuel Thomson lived all his life in a small thatched cottage at Carngranny near Templepatrick, Co. Antrim. Unlike most other self-taught 'weaver poets' of his time, Thomson was an educated man and he ran a small school in his house. Though he also wrote in English, Thomson's best work is in Ulster-Scots. He greatly admired Robert Burns whom he visited in Scotland in 1794. Thomson's own verse has a sprightly force and a delight in language frequently equal to that of Burns.

To a Hedge-hog.

Unguarded beauty is disgrace Broome[1]

While youthful poets, thro' the grove,[2]
Chaunt saft their canny lays o' love,
And a' their skill exert to move
The darling object;
I chuse, as ye may shortly prove,
A rougher subject.

1 'The Coquette', line 15, *The Works of the Poets of Great Britain and Ireland*, 8 vols (Dublin, 1793–1804), V, 470.

2 Rather than clutter the text with annotations of unfamiliar Ulster-Scots words and phrases, we provide a rough paraphrase of this text in modern English: When young poets softly sing their clever love songs in the woods, and exercise all their skill to move the object of their affections, I choose a rougher subject, as you'll soon see. What use is it for us to bother ourselves in rhyme about [the beauty of] chin and cheek, and forehead and headdress – whistling like a widowed linnet lurching along the whitethorn ditches? The pains of love are hard to bear, I acknowledge: but let's get to my hedgehog. You are by far the grimmest looking of the rough animals grubbing for your food by thorn-covered walls! Good heavens, you are not short of pikes – sharp, strong ones! You look (Lord save us!) like a creeping flax-comb! Some say you are related to the sow – but I believe you're closer to the devil! And there are few that can say what use you are – but, as wise men say, nothing was made in vain. Sure, in the beginning, it was the devil that fathered you on some cursed old gorse or thorn bush! And some monstrous, horny-fingered old woman nursed you, you ugly urchin! And the Devil himself, laughing fit to burst, called you 'hedgehog'! People say that you're no fool: when windfall fruit lies softly all around, you roll yourself into a ball and carry away, on your back, what you need for a day or two. But whether that's true is more than I'll say here and now; if, as some assert, you squeeze the last drop of milk out of a cow in the field, I'll allow that you are a pretty milkmaid! I've heard superstitious people say that, if we meet you in the morning, we'll have bad luck – some terrible mischance – that day; but I think fools who think that have no common sense. I've seen many hedgehogs early in the morning when I'm setting out and also in the evening when I'm coming home – but my fate that day has not been different. How long will mortals blather nonsense, and souls tie themselves to superstition! For witchcraft and omens are just damned nonsense that now mean little to us or to the Scotch folk. Now creep off the way you came, and look after your squeaking little ones at home. If my dog Collie should overhear them, it might be fatal for you, despite all the pikes you claim, to do battle with him.

What sairs to bother us in sonnet,
'Bout chin an' cheek, an' brow an' bonnet?
Just chirlin like a widow'd linnet,
Thro' bushes lurchin;
Love's stangs are ill to thole, I own it,
But to my hurchin.

Thou grimest far o' grusome tykes,
Grubbing thy food by thorny dykes,
Gudefaith *thou* disna want for *pikes*,[3]
Baith sharp an' rauckle;
Thou looks (L–d save's) array'd in spikes,
A creepin' heckle!

Some say thou'rt sib kin to the sow,
But sibber to the de'il, I trow;
An' what thy use can be, there's few
That can explain;
But naithing, as the learn'd allow,
Was made in vain.

Sure Nick[4] begat thee, at the first,
On some auld *whin* or thorn accurst;
An' some horn-finger'd harpie nurst
The ugly urchin;
The Belzie,[5] laughin, like to burst,
First ca'd thee *Hurchin*!

Fok tell how thou, sae far frae daft,
Whar wind fa'n fruit lie scatter'd saft,
Will row thysel', wi' cunning craft,
An' bear awa
Upon thy back, what sairs thee aft
A day or twa.

3 As Frank Ferguson notes (*Ulster-Scots Writing*, [Dublin: Four Courts Press, 2008] p. 467, n.12) this is a pun on the spikes of the hedgehog and the weapons of the United Irishmen.

4 'Old Nick', the devil.

5 Beelzebub, the devil.

But whether this account be true,
Is mair than I will here avow;
If that thou stribs the outler cow
As some assert,
A pretty milkmaid, I allow,
Forsooth thou art

I've heard the superstitious say,
To meet thee on our morning way,
Portends some dire misluck that day—
Some black mischance;
Sic fools, howe'er, are far astray
Frae common sense.

Right monie a hurchin I hae seen,
At early morn, and eke at e'en,
Baith setting off, an' whan I've been
Returning hame;
But Fate, indifferent, I ween,
Was much the same.

How lang will mortals nonsense blether,
And sauls to superstition tether!
For witch-craft, omens, altogether,
Are damn'd hotch-potch mock,
That now obtain sma' credit ether
Frae us or Scotch fok.[6]

Now creep awa the way ye came,
And tend your squeakin pups at hame;
Gin Colley should o'erhear the same,
It might be fatal.
For you, wi' a' the pikes ye claim,
Wi' him to battle.

6 Though he differentiates himself from the Scots here, Thomson felt close ties with Scotland, with its people and its language. He once said of himself: 'Yet tho' I'm *Irish* all without, I'm every item *Scotch* within.'

JOHN SEARSON
(*fl.* **1795**)

There is a certain innocent charm in John Searson's doggerel descriptions of the north of Ireland in the 1790s. Searson seems to have been at various times a schoolmaster in Coleraine and a merchant in New York and Philadelphia – he was at all times an indefatigable versifier. Among his many self-published verses are 'several entertaining pieces of poetry' descriptive of America, (including a 'rural, romantic and descriptive' poem on Mount Vernon, George Washington's estate, and elegiac verses on Washington's death in 1799) and many poems set in Ireland. He had his verse printed in Coleraine and Strabane as well as in Philadelphia and Baltimore. His Irish verse shows him seeking patronage from the Earl of Bristol and the Marquis of Abercorn.

from: A Poem, or Rural Entertainment;
Particularly Descriptive of the Most Noble the Marquis of Abercorn's Cottage, near Strabane; of Barons Court, the seat of his Lordship: the canal and town of Strabane ...

Romantick scenes, here strike my wond'ring eye,
And still as I walk on, with wonder spy,
How beaut'ous is this calm retirement,
From anxious care, and brooding discontent,
The pond'rous rocks, which here surround the place
And rural verdure still before my face,
The ivy turning round about each tree,
And rural shades, that most delightful be.

The COTTAGE so recluse and wond'rous fine,
My Lord no doubt with friends sometime here dine,
In this most pleasing, sweet retired spot,
The birds harmonious, too, delight this grot;
I've dined with friends in this sweet rural scene,
The Heav'ns our house, our table was the green,[1]
Whilst mirth and joy diffus'd around that day,
Dancing and music help'd to make us gay. ...

1 <Having no house to accommodate the gentlemen who din'd here this day, we made an open field answer this end: and having no table, made the green grass answer this purpose, an Irish Piper was our music, salmon roasted in the field our chief food, mirth, festivity and friendship closed the scene.>

See yon stupendous rocks, and water-fall,
Pour down the mountain, sloping hill and all,
Cascades in winter here must much surprize,
When dreary winter darkens all the skies;
The tuneful birds with all their chearful notes,
Have now no song, the hills are clothed with goats. ...

O, may this Cottage, and the Glen also,
E'er find me innocent, where e'er I go;
Then will I range the flow'ry walks and groves,
And taste the sweets that virtue only knows—
My Lord in this retreat, must pleasure take,
From courts and cities seek this dear retreat;

Here spend with friends, the social hour
Passing the friendly glass, in this sweet bow'r,
For life itself is but a shadow here,
Therefore with joy, we'll pass this present year;
To-morrow may bring forth some wond'rous tale,
For who can future things to us reveal. ...

Walking thro' the Glen, at distance view,
The improving work, of late, to you I shew,
'Tis the Canal, of use to trade, so bright,
That every viewer must in it delight,
See sloops, and boats e'er long come up this way,
And bring much merchandize to our new quay,
Bid merchants flourish in th'town of Strabane,
Which is surrounded by a pleasant lawn. ...
Such Canals may yet spread thro' the nation
As greatly will encrease our navigation,
And much enrich our land, in food and wealth,
Give comfort also in our days—and health.

I turn mine eyes, and peep at Strabane Town,
A place of trade, and now of much renown;
The people happy and the town compleat,
Their market-house, is here so very neat,
The people too is very fine and clean,
To strangers, they are striking to be seen,

Kind providence, dwells here with honest men,
Gives happy days, and peace in latter end.
Their Bridge and Town, is so compleat and neat,
So is their Square, which here is so compleat;
How solemn is their Church, and place of pray'r,
Induces the devout there to repair,
The River here is pleasing to behold,
It's rapid stream delightful is and bold;
The Angler here diverts himself with trout,
And to his pleasure adds, good food thereout. ...

FRANCIS BOYLE
(*c.*1730–*c.***1795**–*c.*1811)

Francis Boyle, one of the earliest poets to write in Ulster-Scots, lived in Gransha, Co. Down and was probably a weaver. He had a boisterous sense of humour which makes his *Miscellaneous Poems* (Belfast, 1811) more entertaining than the work of some other weaver poets.

Address to the Cuckoo

Welcome great songster o' the spring![1]
Its aye glad news which thou dost bring,
Whan thou return'st again to sing,
Thy Maker's praise;
Then a' our groves an' woodlands ring,
Wi' thy sweet lays.

1 Since this text is in Ulster-Scots, we provide a rough paraphrase in modern English: Welcome, great songster of the spring! It's always good news you bring when you return to sing your Maker's praise; then all our groves and woodlands ring with your sweet song. How silently you wait through all the weary time of winter! When suffering birds are in all kinds of distress, kind nature provides a place of rest for you. You can't fly to southern climes, for that's far too long a flight for you; the woods are full of whip-poor-wills – they are on every tree – where the famous hero, Washington, set them free. It's well for you that you sleep so soundly while storms rage around the world; many a beautiful nest has been blown down this very year, and merchants in the bustling town have lost their possessions. Last winter when you were away, we were not too distressed by snow; but we had many a frost and thaw, and wind enough; and heavy rain stopped us from ploughing. A threatening moon appeared at the beginning of the new year – she had a dreadful look about her – and the wind tore the slates and the thatch from farmers' roofs. But it's particularly bad for those who go to sea; they get the worst of it when their fine ships are dashed onto rocks or piles of stones; this causes many wives to cease joking and to weep for their children. The foaming ocean roared loudly and Britain's shipping suffered greatly: large oak trees were torn up by the roots in St James's Park, and wrecks were strewn along the shore at high-water mark. Now the sun has called you out of your grave, or from some dark and dreary cave, to raise your voice higher than all the rest and sing more loudly than all our splendid songbirds. You won't sing on the 'borrowing days' when the Egyptians lent their clothes and their gold rings to their mortal enemies, the Israelites; but you'll sing sweetly enough when the daisies are in flower on the hills. Perhaps, about the middle of April (when nature begins to smile), you'll start singing until the sudden arrival of a short, sharp storm that batters the bushes and strikes us dumb. But in the blooming month of May, you rise early every day to charm the beautifully dew-covered woodlands with your sweet song – even though you have nothing to sing or say except 'cuckoo'. Then comes the pleasant month of June, when barley ripens; your throat grows hoarse, you lose your voice and seem as if you're choking; you slip away to lay yourself down, you poor, weak fool! And after all the noise of your singing, you arc just like the rest of your false race and leave behind a worthless, whinging, whining bastard, without even a feather to protect him from the wet.

In what a silence dost thou bide
Through a' the weary winter's tide,
When grief pours in frae every side,
On birds distrest,
Kind Nature does for thee provide,
A place o' rest.

To southern climes thou canst not flee
For that's owre far a flight for thee,
Wi' whipper-wills on ev'ry tree
The woods aboun'[2]
Whare the great hero set them free,
Fam'd Washington.

It's weel for thee thou sleepst sae sound,
While tempests rage the warl' round;
There's monie a bonie nest blawn down
This vera year;
An' merchants in the bustlin' town
Hae lost their gear.

Last winter when thou wast awa
We werna much distrest wi' snaw,
But we had monie a frost an' thaw
An' win' enough:
An' heavy pours o' rain did fa',
An' stapt the pleugh.

About the first o' the new year
A threatenin' moon did then appear,
A direfu' aspect she did wear,
On her bow't back,
The win' ilk farmer's house did tear,
Baith slates an' thack.

2 The Whip-poor-will is a medium-sized native American bird, known for its haunting, ethereal song. This stanza, with its reference to George Washington (1732–99), suggests that the poem was written for an international audience – or that Boyle believed that the cuckoo winters in North America. It is not clear how Washington set the whip-poor-wills free, unless he is seen to have emancipated every living thing in America.

But wae's me for sea-farin' folks,
Its they that bide the warst o' strokes,
Their bonny ships are dash'd on rocks,
Or staney cairns,
Makes monie wives to quat their jokes,
An' greet for bairns.

The foamin' ocean loud did roar,
An' Britain's transports suffered sore,
Great aiks up by the roots were tore,
In James' park;[3]
An' wrecks were strawn alang the shore,
On the sea-mark.

Now Sol has called thee frae thy grave,
Or frae some dark an' dreary cave.
To raise thy notes aboon the lave,
Wi' highest rant,
An' sing down a' our sangsters brave,
Wi' thy loud cant.

Thou wilt not sing on borrowin' days[4]
When Gipsey bodies lent their claes,
To Israelites their mortal faes,
An' their gowd rings,
But whan the daisies deck the braes,
Thous sweetly sings.[5]

3 There is a St James's Park in Belfast, but this probably refers to the park in London where trees were blown down in a severe storm in 1795.

4 The last three days of March (often characterized by a spell of bad weather) are called the 'Borrowing Days', said to have been a loan from April to March.

5 See Exodus 12:35-6; the Egyptians persuaded the Israelites to borrow their valuables so that they could accuse them of theft and pursue them as they left Egypt. As Frank Ferguson notes (*Ulster-Scots Writing* p. 462), the poet is punning on 'borrowing days' and suggesting that the cuckoo only sings in good weather.

About the middle o' April,
(For nature then begins to smile),
Thou'lt aiblins cry for a short while,
Till gowk's storm[6] come,
An' make the bushes a' recoil,
An' ding us dumb.

But in the blooming month o' May,
Thou risest early ilka day,
To charm the groves wi' thy sweet lay,
On pearly dew,
Though thou hast nought to sing or say,
But aye Cuckoo.

Then comes the pleasant month of June,
When barley-corn shoots up its crown;
Thy throat grows hoarse, thou tinst thy tune,
An' like to choak,
Thou slip'st awa' an' lay'st thee down,
Poor silly gowk.

An' after a' thy rhymin' din,
Just like the lave o' thy fause kin,
Thou lea'st a scabby get behin'
To whinge and greet,
Without a feather on its skin,
To turn the weet.

6 'Gowk's storm' is a Scots term for a brief storm coinciding with the arrival of the cuckoo.

JANE ELIZABETH MOORE
(1738–**1796**–?)

Jane Elizabeth Moore was of English extraction. She gives a vivid account, in her *Genuine Memoirs of Jane Elizabeth Moore* (1785), of her work as a clerk in her father's business. She moved to Dublin where she apparently bored Thomas Moore by insisting on reading her poems to him. In addition to the poem that follows, her volume of *Miscellaneous Poems* (Dublin, 1796) contains a poetic celebration of the opening of Maynooth College, Co. Kildare.

On the Discovery of the Gold Mine in the County of Wicklow[1]

Say why so long in dark oblivion lay
This mystic metal, in it's native clay?
Which millions long in distant climes have sought,
And from it's torrid regions millions brought;
The glitt'ring lore, thus grasp'd with ardent speed,
Has harmless millions doom'd at times to bleed!
And tho' by Poets oft has been despis'd,
By them possest, it's pleasures have been priz'd;
To Nature yielding in her state deprav'd,
Perverted gifts, which they before had crav'd.
Prolific bounties, Wicklow, long thy boast,
May with this golden gleam upon thy coast,
Vie with all Europe, Asia rich defy,
And barb'rous Spanish maxims e'er descry.
No harass'd victims to the torture brought,
To sully true benevolence of thought;
'Tis by true efforts of industry gain'd,
That ne'er by ghastly av'rice was arraign'd!
Replete with hope, shall commerce swell her sail,
And deep the plough in culture fresh prevail;
The tatter'd peasant by such bounty clad,
With joyful toil shall make his children glad!

1 According to G. N. Wright (*A Guide to the County of Wicklow*, 2nd ed., Dublin, 1827, p. 97), a nugget of pure gold was found in a riverbed near Avoca by 'an old school-master' in about 1775. A subsequent find in 1796 led to a 'gold rush'; from 1796 until it was destroyed in 1798, the Wicklow gold mining operation was run by the government.

What happy prospects will in course combine,
Where arts and science in a country shine;
Those well united in a nation's cause,
Shall yield protection to it's pristine laws:
Thus if dispos'd on Reason's solid ground,
Shall gold diffuse it's use to all around!
By Virtue's clue in each department spread,
Shall this pure metal[2] raise each drooping head,
And deck Hibernia with a pleasing grace,
That may allure to home each native face;[3]
Where precept and example may entwine
To strew that blessing in kind Heav'n's design,
In gifts transcendent of superior kind.
Thus draw the line, preponderate success,
And this new blessing shall with blessings bless.

2 <Alluding to the metal being found in a pure state.>

3 <Meant to recommend to the Landholders the spending the income of their estates upon the spot.>

JOHN CORRY
(*fl.*1797)

John Corry was born near Newry and is said to have worked in Dublin as a journalist before moving to London. Many members of the United Irishmen were subscribers to his *Odes and Elegies, Descriptive and Sentimental* (Newry, 1797) – a volume containing some interesting local verse. Corry wrote many novels, several volumes of history and a popular *Life of George Washington* (Dublin 1801).

Air: an Ode

Spirit of Life! Vivific Air!
Thou breath of Heav'n, that Earth surrounds!
Thy presence brightens ev'ry sphere
That beams thro' vast Creation's bounds;
There, pure, thy living ether plays,
And strengthens the tremendous blaze
Of the swift comet, that, with ceaseless flight,
Pervades Immensity's vast fields of light.

'Tis Air sustains the beauteous whole
Of animated beings here—
'Tis Vegetation's secret soul—
It's fost'ring breezes ever chear.
The cheek of Beauty—the fair frame—
That blooms with Life's electric flame,
To vivifying Air perfection owe:—
With ev'ry breath we draw, new spirits flow.

The atmosphere a medium forms
Thro' which the light of Day descends:
And when the cloud, concealing storms,
With horror big, o'er Earth impends,
Oft struggling, 'mid the gloom confin'd,
With dreadful force, expanding wind
From the burst mass the flaming lightning flings,
And bears the thunder on its rushing wings.

Light, o'er the globe-encircling main,
Brisk gales extend their veering flight;
There Commerce, chear'd by hope of gain,
Steers his swift bark, by Learning's light;
But, if condens'd the winds descend,
And with the growing billows blend,
Convulsive Tempest, with resistless wrath,
Sinks the descending ship in caves of Death.

Where subterraneous vapours swell
'Tis the expansive force of Air
Doth the dire Earthquake's rage impel,
Which can in fragments regions tear;
Or, where immense volcanic fires
To the high smoaky Peak aspires,
'Tis Air propels the gushing flood of fire,
That, flaming down, makes man and beast expire.

In scenes where no terrific form
E'er comes to fill the heart with fear,
Where the loud voice of giant Storm
Ne'er sounded dreadful to the ear,
The variegated landscape fair
Is cherish'd by enliv'ning Air;
There, glist'ning groves, elastic, kiss the gale,
That bears the odours of the vernal vale.

Hail, Source of Music! the soft voice
Of Love owes all its pow'r to thee;
Thou bidd'st all Nature's tribes rejoice,
That flourish in the earth and sea:
Pure minister of heav'nly love,
Deputed from the world above,
Thy pow'r, invisible, pervades all space—
Thou active agent of Almighty Grace.

WILLIAM HAMILTON DRUMMOND
(1778–**1797**–1856)

'Hibernia', which first appeared anonymously in the Belfast radical newspaper *The Northern Star*, is normally attributed to William Hamilton Drummond, clergyman, antiquarian and (later) author of the best-known poem on the Giant's Causeway (see below). Like much of the verse that appeared in Irish newspapers and pamphlets during the 1790s, the poem reflects increasing political and social tensions. Union with Britain would, in the poet's eyes, restore Ireland to the state for which Nature had designed her.

from: Hibernia, a poem

Much injur'd Erin! Faction troubl'd isle!
No more the land where Peace and Concord smile!
Rous'd by thy wrongs to patriotic ire,
For thee I tune the bold adventurous lyre: …

Oh why did Nature, with too lavish hand,
Scatter profusion o'er thy smiling land,
Nutritious moisture thro' thy veins infuse,
And pour down plenty in salubrious dews?
If thou must ne'er those tranquil pleasures know,
That from Contentment's source unsullied flow,
Why form'd thee thus replete with ev'ry good,
Bade no dire ills on thy blest soil intrude;
But made thee flourish ever fair and green,
The mart of Commerce, and of isles the Queen?

For this, at her omnific[1] word, arose
Tall rocky bulwarks, terror of thy foes;
And girt thy craggy shores, but pleas'd to form
Thy harbours safe against th'encroaching storm;
Scoop'd them capacious, sandy, deep and wide,
At once thy boast, thy ornament and pride.
And made them point around where ev'ry breeze,
Wafts the bold sons of ocean o'er the seas.
She form'd thy streams majestic, broad and strong,
Where Commerce rolls her richest stores along;

1 all-creating.

Pours wealth and splendour from the torrid zone,
And gluts thy soil with riches not thy own:
Where all the finny tribes abundant stray,
That in the brook or stream deep-rolling play.
Now here she bade the rugged mountain rise,
Swell o'er the vale and tow'r amid the skies.
There rais'd the cliff, whose tall terrific side,
Frowns on the vale below with haughty pride;
Dash'd the wild cascade o'er the cloud-capt rock,
Shaking old earth beneath th'impetuous shock,
And sent it glad'ning, with a thousand rills,
The vales embosom'd in a thousand hills.
She spread abroad the lake's extensive floods,
And crown'd thy vallies with umbrageous woods.
Bade flow'rs spontaneous deck the verdant soil,
Her choicest gifts reward the labourer's toil;
With scenes Arcadian made thy landscapes teem,
And realize each old romantic dream.
She made thy sons magnanimous and brave,
Hardy and just, and ever prone to save,
To succour those tyrannic laws oppress,
And cure the pungent wound of deep distress;
In war impetuous as the tempest's rage,
When North and South on ocean's breast engage.
She gave thy daughters all the charms of youth,
Angelic beauty, elegance, and truth:
And tho' she made them fair, she made them wise,
Such as pure virtue for her own might prize;
Bade ev'ry female grace their minds adorn,
Mild as th'ambrosial breath of orient morn,
Chaste as the pearly drop depending from the thorn.

When all was finish'd with complacent smile,
The Goddess view'd the gay luxuriant isle;
With wonder all the scenes she drew survey'd,
And seem'd astonish'd at the work she made.
And thus with energy divine she cries,
'Thou loveliest isle beneath the concave skies,
Of all the isles that Nature's bounty share,
Thee has she made the most supremely fair.

Let Indian climes rich orange groves produce,
And boast the milky Coco's nectarous juice;
Let those soft realms that view the rising day,
And where fierce Phœbus shoots a downward ray,
Boast the rich soil replete with flaming mines,
The luscious figtree, and the clustring vines;
Let Hebrus[2] wander o'er his bed of Gold,
And seven-mouth'd Ganges richest plains behold;
Rich in their fields by luxury o'er-ran,
And rich in all things but high-minded man:
Such fruitful glebes, such wealth you envy not,
Blest is an humbler and more happy lot.
No storm on thee with polar fury blows;
No Sun with equinoctial fervour glows:
Here no dire blasts pestiferous repair,
No plague e'er taints thy health-inspiring air.
In thee no Lion roars, no Tyger foams,
Nor Wolf voracious on thy mountains roams,
On the soft turf in safety lies the swain,
Nor fears the venom'd reptile of the plain;
Nor dreads forth issuing from the marshy brake,
The monstrous Hydra,[3] or the crested snake:
Rejoiced he sees the real goods you yield,
Where golden harvests wave along the field;
Where lowing herds adorn the sylvan scene,
And flocks lie scatter'd on thy banks of green:
Unnumber'd flocks more white than virgin snow:
Unnumber'd streams with milk and honey flow;
Health, Joy, and Plenty, on thy plains appear,
And all Creation's mildest charms are here.
Let Union only thy brave sons combine,
And every sublunary bliss is thine.'…

2 A Thracian river-god in Greek mythology. The rivers Hebrus and Ganges are considered a source of wealth.

3 The many-headed water-serpent of mythology.

PART V
1800–1819

WILLIAM DRENNAN
(1754–**1802**–1820)

William Drennan – the most outspoken Irish poetic voice of his age – was born in Belfast, the son of a dissenting minister. He was educated at the universities of Glasgow and Edinburgh and settled in Dublin where he practised as a doctor. He was one of the founders of the United Irishmen and was tried for sedition in 1794, though acquitted. He later moved to Belfast and founded *The Belfast Magazine*. Drennan's most famous poem is the harrowing account of the execution of William Orr, hanged for administering an illegal oath. He is also known for 'Glendalloch', a long poem that, while celebrating the natural beauty of the glens of County Wicklow, derides the druids and monks who, over the centuries, spread 'illusive fancy' and superstition from their hideout in Glendalough. The poem moves on to cast vitriolic scorn on those who, in the recent past, have sold Ireland's legislative independence for gold by accepting the 1801 Act of Union. The poem below, 'To Ireland', is equally outspoken, pouring invective on the 'abortive men' who have become the 'soft contented' slaves of Britain, turning the once noble land of Ireland into the 'base posterior of the world'. The poem ends by comparing the land of these 'sterile' Irishmen to that of Arabs whose bravery makes their country – a mere desert of sand and stone – free, happy and 'blest'.

To Ireland

My Country! Shall I mourn or bless,
Thy tame and wretched happiness?

'Tis true! The the vast Atlantic tide
Has scoop'd thy harbours deep, and wide,
Bold to protect, and prompt to save,
From fury of the Western wave:
And Shannon points to Europe's trade,
For THAT, his chain of lakes was made;
For THAT, he scorns to waste his store,
In channel of a subject shore,
But courts the Southern wind to bring
A world, upon its tepid wing.

True! thy resplendent rivers run,
And safe beneath a temp'rate sun
Springs the young verdure of thy plain,
Nor dreads a torrid Eastern reign.

True! thou art blest, in Nature's plan,
Nothing seems wanting here, but—MAN;

Man—to subdue, not serve the soil,
To win, and wear its golden spoil;
Man—conscious of an earth his own,
No savage biped, torpid, prone;
Living, to dog his brother brute,
And hung'ring for a lazy root,
Food for a soft, contented slave;
Not for the hardy and the brave.

Had Nature been her enemy,
IERNE might be fierce and free.
To the stout heart, and iron hand,
Temp'rate each sky, and tame each land;
A climate and a soil less kind,
Had form'd a map of richer mind.
Now, a mere sterile swamp of soul,
Thro' meadows spread, and rivers roll;
A nation of abortive men,
That dart—the tongue; and point—the pen.
And, at the back of Europe, hurl'd—
A base POSTERIOR of the world.

In lap of Araby the blest,
Man lies with luxury opprest;
While spicy odours, blown around,
Enrich the air, and gems—the ground.
But thro' the pathless, burning waste,
Man marches with his patient beast,
Braves the hot sun, and heaving sand,
And calls it free and happy land.

Enough to make a desert known,
'Arms, and the man,' and sand, and stone!

SAMUEL BURDY
(*c*.1758–**1802**–1820)

Samuel Burdy was born at Dromore, Co. Down, and educated at Trinity College Dublin. He was ordained into the Church of Ireland and spent most of his working life as curate at Ardglass, Co. Down. His most famous work was *The Life of the late Revd Philip Skelton* (1782) – an account of one of the more saintly Irish protestant divines of the age and a philosopher of note – but he also wrote histories of Ireland, a travel book and a volume of verse, *Ardglass, or the ruined castles* (1802), which gives interesting insights into Ulster life.

from: Ardglass, or the ruined castles

… The sun, the stars, the high celestial frame,
Point out the existence of a God supreme;
The regions too of the extended sea,
In every clime, his wondrous power display;
Tho' vex'd by EURUS,[1] and his surly band,
Its raging waves he curbs with gentle sand,
Directs th'alternate motions of the tide,
Advancing now in grave majestic pride,
O'er the high rocks with wilks[2] and limpets bound,
And now receding to the vast profound.
Such wondrous works display'd to human sight,
Strike with surprise, or fill us with delight.

When the huge body, and enormous shoal
Of numerous herring quit the frozen pole;
Desert their northern hive for temperate climes,
Like Goths and Vandals in the barb'rous times,
To British seas, long wish'd, at length resort,
And yield our anxious poor a kind support,
Then various birds with wonder we survey
Attend the pilgrims on their watery way;
Of these the gull and gannet are the chief,
Who eat them up as glutton would roast beef.
The gull, like diver, rides the wave secure,
As huntsman rides the courser o'er the moor,

1 the east wind.

2 whelks.

Yet ne'er descends within the briny flood,
But on the surface takes the finny brood.
With vent'rous wing the gannet mounts on high,
And darts straight downward from the vaulted sky,
Pierces to wondrous depth the liquid plain,
Seizes his prey, and then ascends again.
But should the hog[3] with open mouth assail,
Adown his throat they run as thick as hail:
Now here and there, from side to side he'd pass,
And thus collect them to a solid mass.
Then downward dive, and in the middle rise,
Devour, disperse, and raise them to the skies.
Yet boats and men he'd shun with cautious care,
And flimsy texture ne'er disturb nor tear.

Our happy seas no baneful shark annoys,
That human life alas! Too oft destroys;
But on our shore the useful fish abound,
Both those that swim, and those that skim the ground,
The speckled mackrel, and the gornet red,[4]
The haddock firm, and cod with wondrous head,
The gentle whiting, and delicious sole
Ta'en by a net extended on a pole,
The flowk,[5] the ray, the plaise, the bret[6] so nice,
And charming turbot of enormous price,
With lobsters, crabs, and others small and great,
In verse or prose too tedious to relate.
The prime of these are sent to distant towns,
Convey'd by smacks, by cadgers, or by clowns:[7]
There the plump alderman, at city feast,
Devours them greedily, and extols their taste,
Praises our fishers for their skill and care,
In thus providing such delicious fare. …

3 sea-hog or porpoise.

4 bearded gurnard or red mullet.

5 the fluke or flounder.

6 the brill.

7 by fishing smacks, by carriers or carters, or by countrymen.

JAMES ORR
(1770–**1804**–1816)

James Orr, the radical weaver poet, was born in Ballycarry, Co. Antrim and educated at home. As a young man he published poems in the *Northern Star* newspaper and was actively involved in the 1798 rebellion. After the failure of the rebellion, he emigrated to the United States using his experiences of the voyage as the basis for two memorable poems. He returned to Ireland and settled in Ballycarry, making his living as a weaver and writing many poems describing life in the area.

from: Fort-Hill[1]

The sweet rose of June scents your shade,
The peas that you've propp'd are in bloom;
I've moulded my roots[2] with my spade,
And heap'd up my fuel at home.
My fair! Shall we walk by yon hedge?
Or angle a while in the rill?[3]
Nay rather, let's gaze from the edge
Of soft-sloping, stately Fort-Hill.

How lovely the landscape below!—
The boats on the silver lake move;
The conic hay-cocks form a row;
The dome gleams and glows thro' the grove:[4]
The nymphs and the mead-mowing hinds[5]
Toil blithe. Yon stript slave stoops to swill
A draught of the cool stream that winds
From the bosom of beauteous Fort-Hill.

1 Almost certainly a reference to the heights of McArt's Fort (an Iron-age hill fort) on Cave Hill, above Belfast, from which there is a fine view over Belfast and Strangford Lough.

2 i.e. potatoes.

3 i.e. go fishing in the stream for a while.

4 Probably a reference to the dome on St Anne's church, Belfast (1778). The copper-covered Corinthian dome formed 'an interesting and conspicuous object for many miles around' according to Samuel Lewis's *Topographical Dictionary of Ireland* (London, 1837).

5 i.e. the countrymen mowing the fields.

Here, westward, the cateract white,
Roars, roughens, and bounds o'er the steep;
And there, with her ship-saving light,
Sits Copeland emerg'd from the deep:[6]
The bowling-green, here, crowns the height,
A wood-circled scene of blithe skill,
And there, glides some glorious first-rate,[7]
Whose thunders could shake e'en Fort-Hill.

Beneath us the hamlet's street smiles,
The forge chimes, the full school breaks, free;
While home haste the glad lab'ring files,
Dismiss'd by the bell on the tree:
May they soon dance each eve to the fife
That's now only heard at the drill;
And the horrible kettle of strife
Cease to boil in the view of Fort-Hill.

Observe yon proud city, how grand
Her spire seems![8] How dreadful her tow'r!
Grim-rising o'er both sea and land,
Like the stern sprite on wild Patmos' shore.[9]
What smoke from yon found'ry aspires;[10]
Yon safe port what groves of masts fill![11]
Yon tide-crossing bridge, joining shires,[12]
Is at once firm and fair, like Fort-Hill.

6 The reference is to the lighthouse on one of the Copeland Islands, off Co. Down. In 1796, the new British and Irish Lighthouse Board fitted oil lamps in the lighthouse.

7 'First rate' was the designation used by the Royal Navy for its largest ships of the line.

8 Perhaps another reference to St Anne's Church – the only tall ecclesiastical building in Belfast at the time of this poem.

9 Probably a reference to the tower of the old castle of Belfast, since replaced. The stern sprite (= spirit) on Patmos's shore is Artemis, Hellenic goddess of the hunt, wild animals and wilderness whose power (according to Greek mythology) caused Patmos to emerge, as an island, from the sea.

10 The first iron foundry in Belfast was established in 1792.

11 Belfast was a flourishing port at the time of this poem as linen manufacture was at its height.

12 Belfast straddles two counties, Antrim and Down.

Hail! wonted walks! distant shires, hail!
Hail! wide realms, that seas roll between,
Immensity's self draws a veil
On the skirts of the soul-raising scene:
The heaths where, of yore, Ossian warr'd,[13]
The plains famed, poor Burns, by your quill,[14]
And the isle where the Manx tongue is heard;[15]
Conspicuous are all to Fort-Hill.[16] ...

13 Disputes over the authenticity of James Macpherson's 'translation' of the poems of Ossian were raging at this time: Irish scholars were infuriated that Macpherson's version of an old Irish tale was set in Scotland. Irish sagas set many heroic encounters in Ulster.

14 Scotland.

15 The Isle of Man.

16 i.e. they can all be seen from Fort-Hill.

JAMES ORR
(1770–**1804**–1816)

Orr's vivid account of the baiting of a bull reflects growing public concern in Ireland at the suffering of animals.

The Bull-beat[1]

If e'er the poet, pity's child,
Forsakes his spirit-soothing lyre,
And joins the sport with comrades wild,
He oft deplores while they admire;
While they torment, he now wou'd save
The landscape's monarch, bold and brave.

Confin'd amid th'assembling crowd,
Sedate and sad, the victim stands;
The mastiff eyes the man of blood,
And panting, waits his fell commands;
And lo! keen rushing from the slip,
The lordly brute they fiercely grip.

While one obliquely pulls his tongue,
Another tears his ample chest,
A third is at his shoulder hung,
And different posts employ the rest:
Just as we've seen the human herd
Mangle a brave man, singly fear'd.

Unmov'd, he now stands torture-proof,
Now madly on his foes he bounds;
His horn rips some, and some his hoof,
That, archly pawing, foils the hounds:
Heard you that groan?—how vast his pain!—
What noble strife has been in vain!

1 bait (pronounced 'beat' in Ulster).

Firm, tho' forlorn, and bent to make
One glorious effort, ere he yield,
He darts intrepid from the stake,
And falls abruptly on the field;
Huzzas and howls, at once ascend;
Foam, gore and mud, together blend.

And now the butcher aims his piece,
And firing, ends the suff'rer's life—
Can men endure such scenes as these?
Can Christians pride in gore and strife?
Such scenes amuse the slave and sot;
But saints and heroes shun the spot.

WILLIAM WEBB
(*fl.*1805)

Nothing certain is known of William Webb who seems to have published no poems but 'Lakelands' (named after the house he owned at Kilmacud, near Dublin) though it is possible that he was the William Webb who subscribed to Patrick O'Kelly's *Eudoxologist* in 1812. This poem started life as a translation of three lines from Horace that Webb attempted 'for the purpose of inscription on an octagon building in a favourite recess' in his garden. However the poem grew until it was over 200 lines long and it appeared in print in *The Poetical Register, or repository of fugitive poetry for 1806–07* (London, 1811). 'Lakelands' was one of many villas built during the late eighteenth and early nineteenth centuries in the Stillorgan and Kilmacud areas a few miles south of Dublin. In his 1837 *Topographical Dictionary of Ireland*, Samuel Lewis lists 33 of these, with their owners; 'Lakelands' gave its name to the housing estates that have replaced it.

The poem is remarkable for its observant picture of the attractions of the untamed country of the Dublin mountains and for the vivid contrast it draws between Dublin and its suburbs; for Webb, 'Nature's shrine' is his garden in Kilmacud from which he could see the Irish Sea on one side, the Dublin mountains on the other and rolling countryside between. Mr Webb was a commuter, regretfully leaving the peace of 'Lakelands' for the 'diurnal drudge' of travelling into Dublin through crowds and smoke to 'fretful cankering toil'. The poem is rare in its criticism of the urban developments of late eighteenth century Dublin – which Webb dismissed as the 'labour'd whimsies of the sons of gain'.

from: Lakelands: a poem

Originally written for inscription on a country residence in the Vicinity of Dublin.

... What tho' not thine[1] the boast of wide domain,
Nor gorgeous wonder stablish here her reign;
Tho' not for thee Creation's proud array;
For thee nor Ocean waves expand their sway,
Nor o'er thy head in mad disorder wild
And savage waste the eternal granite pil'd;
For thee no sweep of frowning forest near,
No devious wizard haunt of gloom and fear;
Not thine the giddy heights, the headlong steeps,
Nor chasms that shuddering yawn to midnight deeps;
Fantastic scenes! with living force impress
Of mystic influence o'er the human breast!
Nor these high honors thine! oh barely free
From City concourse and from rabble glee!

1 The poet is addressing the seat in his garden for which the inscription was intended.

Free from the clouded dust, the clattering noise
Of City parties and their Sunday joys;
The scenes where ceaseless throng, at wealth's loud call
The brick-red villa and the sad stone wall:
Scap'd too from City taste! whose meddling hand
With cumbrous frippery deforms the land,
Marshals its mimic gauds in dull parade,
Its vamp'd up brick-pool and spruce starv'd cascade;
Bids Chinese bridge or Chinese temple flare,
Or old-new Gothic nick-nack rise in air;
Nor knows the country its primaeval green
While envious masonry usurps the scene!

Yet peace to such! nor heeds thy just disdain
These laboured whimsies of the sons of gain.
Not here intrudes their sad tumultuous care,
Nor frivolous joys thy bosom'd quiet share.
For has not nature's self here rais'd her shrine?
Breathes not around thee all her calm benign?
Her steps of peace serenest raptures trace,
And thrilling airs her living presence grace.
Wide spread, behold! for thee her various stores
With fond munificence profuse she pours;
O'er thy loved home her emerald mantle throws,
While woods sequestering veil its soft repose;
Or bold contrasting swells the russet train
Of uncouth downs or rudely wild champaign,
Where not a tree o'erlooks the expanse austere,
And not a sound breaks on its peace severe,
Save, simplest sounds! the sheep-bell's tinkling call,
Or insect hum, or streamlet's rippling fall;
A world of solitude! whose large control
To thrill extatic wakes the accordant soul.
No envious fence here checks the excursive range,
As gathering round successive glories change,
Far as yon triple cloud-topt rock ascends,[2]
Or lengthening mountain range still onward bends,

2 <Three-rock Mountain.>

O'er wastes where erst my loitering youth has strayed
To trace each wild recess, each devious glade,
Each witching charm of Wicklow's fairy reign,
Each thrilling maze of Powerscourt's proud domain,[3]
Each heath-clad steep that Liffey's fountain crowns,
Each fearful cliff whose lowering menace frowns
O'er the wild lake beneath far shadowed deep,[4]
And guards the horrors of its awful sleep:
Or in fond change, to gaze with searching eyes
Where northern Mourne's bleak forms aspiring rise,
Or thwart the ocean waste, mark Snowdon rear
His hoary mass mid the blue fields of air
Distinct, with mighty nameless summits more,
That watch sublime the British sister shore.[5]...

Blest seat![6] from thee diurnal drudge while borne
And from thy shades of peace regretful torn;
Torn from each joy that glads thy social dome,
Each fond endearing charity of Home; ...
Through crowds, through smoke, through fretful
  cankering toil,
Through all vicissitude of human coil,
Each fever'd throb, each fiercer wish control,
And fix thy empire o'er my willing soul;
Dispel vain fears, all earth-born hope refine,
And raise the mortal to a height divine. ...

3 The Powerscourt demesne lies south of Enniskerry, on the edge of the Dublin mountains.

4 <Lough Bray, Luggellaw, Glandelough, &c.>

5 Webb refers to the fact that it is possible to see the Mountains of Mourne in County Down as well as the peaks of Snowdonia in North Wales from hills near Kilmacud. Further passages describe the countryside closer by.

6 Webb refers to an actual seat in his octagonal garden house.

MATTHEW WELD HARTSTONGE
(1772–**1805**–1825)

Matthew Weld (he added the name Hartstonge later in life) was born in Dublin and educated at Trinity College Dublin. He was a lawyer, but does not seem to have practised in Ireland. He corresponded extensively with Sir Walter Scott and wrote a historical romance entitled *The Eve of All-Hallows; or, Adelaide of Tyrconnell* (1825). *The Minstrelsy of Erin, poems lyrical, pastoral and descriptive* (Edinburgh 1812) – from which the following lines are taken – was his second volume of verse.

Lines written at the rocks of Kilcarrick,[1]
County of Carlow, Ireland

Kilcarrick, isolated vale!
Shelter'd from the boisterous gale;
Romantic, fair, enchanting spot!
Oh, never be thy charms forgot!
Delighted here, the eye may dwell
On hill, or dale, on rock, or dell,
Or hoary moss-capp'd pinnacle.

Behold at distance, grand and wide,
Where Barrow rolls his pond'rous tide.
Majestic Leinster[2] meets the skies,
Here Blackstairs'[3] azure heights arise;
While there the grey-clad mountain lies.
On sullen wing the falcon glides,
On rocky steep, the goat abides;
On heathy couch reclines the hare,
Securely keeps the fox his lair,—

1 Kilcarrick is near Leighlinbridge, Co. Carlow. <The rocks of Scalp-seskin, which are, in fact, a continuation of Kilcarrick rocks, are extremely wild, and still more picturesque in themselves than the latter, though not comprehending so extensive a view; they are in every point worthy of observation; they are in the neighbourhood of Ballymoon-castle, about four miles distant from Leighlin-bridge.>

2 <The mountain called Mount-Leinster is partly in the county of Carlow, the minor part in the county of Wexford; in the former it fronts the south, in the latter the north.> The river Barrow, the principal river in the region described in this poem, rises in the Slieve Bloom mountains and flows for about 190 km to Waterford harbour where it joins the rivers Nore and Suir.

3 <'Blackstairs-heights', a chain of mountains apparently connected to Mount-Leinster, partly in the county of Carlow, and partly in Wexford.>

While in aërial regions free,
The sky-lark hymns his minstrelsy.

No martial sound of trump, or drum,
To silence here the wild-bee's hum:
No hunter's horn, the vales along,
Startles the linnet's lonely song:
But each wild path, since time began,
Each glen is free from restless man.
Most grateful landscapes to my heart,
That eye, that mem'ry can impart.
While nations rage for sov'reign sway,
Contented here I lonely stray,
Where the wild-rose's sweets combine
With the dew-sparkling eglantine.
Grey rocks with plumes of ferns are crown'd,
The tangled ivy creeps around.
The gaudy furze, in yellow bloom,
Here wafts its fragrant rich perfume;
While drooping waves the dark-green broom.
The purple heath from graceful stem,
Might form an artless diadem
For the lone genius of the scene,
Or mountain-nymph,[4] fair freedom's queen.

Serene the sky with balmy gales,
A pleasing stillness here prevails.
Ambition's woes are all unknown,
Hence each corrosive care is flown:
Content and competence are mine,
Oh, spare me these, great Pow'r divine!
Give me the sweet, the pensive vale!
Where no rude sounds the mind assail;
Mild Contemplation here may dwell,
Her silent shrine some rocky cell,
May here from mortal care retire,
And trim the lamp's pale midnight fire.

4 <'And in thy right hand lead with thee/The mountain-nymph, sweet Liberty!' Milton's *L'Allegro*.>

The trickling rill, so soft it flows,
Perchance might lull the mourner's woes,
Or yield to hapless love repose!

Then hail, ye pleasing rural charms,
Unstain'd with blood, or faction's arms;
And ever peaceful may remain,
The rocks that bound Kilcarrick's plain;
Tranquil, green Erin's sea-girt shore,
Though loud the storm at distance roar!

May no base tyrant's ghastly band
Enslave the fertile happy land;
But may it long united be,
In virtue, peace, and liberty![5]

5 The contrast is between an Ireland conquered by Napoleon and one united with Britain.

WILLIAM M'ELROY
(*fl.* 1806)

William McElroy came from Fintona, Co. Tyrone and was, as O'Donoghue puts it, 'a religious enthusiast'. His extraordinary *The experience of manifestation: a poem to youth* (printed for the author, Dublin, 1806) is charged with fanatical zeal and enlivened with copious biblical quotation. One poem, 'To the proprietors of the new BOTANIC GARDEN, in concert with those of the new MOUNT-JOY garden, North-side, Dublin' features a conversation between a gardener in Dublin, the church and Christ. At the end of the book, the reader is told that 'he who reprinteth this book on better paper in the name of Jesus shall receive the reward of Jesus.' McElroy's poem on the bird-blinders, like many in the book, culminates in an apt biblical quotation, the source of which is cited in the text.

The Blind Bird's Mournful Lamentation to the Bird Blinders

When shall that sympathetic tender power
Find entrance in thy cruel bower;
To thee O Man, to thee I speak,
When shall thy feeling powers awake.
That lovely bird that mourns its sight,
Thy cruel dart prolongs its night;
It chirping cries for help in vain,
Its righteous plaints no entrance gain,
Into thy hard unfeeling breast.
With gifts of light heaven's bounty blest,
Can man be just their precious sight,
Their Sun to obscure, God's gift of light;
In plaintive strains their mournful song,
Some human archer did them wrong.
Who formed the eye shall he not see;
They never sinn'd, then let them free,
But like to Samson thou Philistine,
Those ornaments God made, you blind.[1]

Two birds being sold for one farthing sings odd,
Yet none is forgotten, not one, before God
Matthew x. 29.[2]

1 The story of Samson, the strongest of the Israelites, is told in Judges 16. Blinded by the Philistines, Samson gets his (and God's) revenge by pulling down the pillars of the Philistines' temple and killing all those in or around the temple.

2 Matthew 10:29 reads: Are not two sparrows sold for a farthing? and one of them shall not fall on the ground without your Father.

RICHARD ALFRED MILLIKIN
(1767–**1807**–1815)

Richard Millikin was born in County Cork and trained as a lawyer, though he was temperamentally more interested in painting, literature and music than the law. He lived in Cork city most of his life where, in 1797/98, he and his sister ran a literary magazine called *The Casket or Hesperian Magazine*. He wrote several plays and five volumes of poetry. Though he is best remembered for 'The Groves of Blarney', his parody of 'Sweet Castle-Hyde' (see *Verse in English from Eighteenth-Century Ireland*, pp. 520–5), his long poem 'The River's Side' – notable for its elaborately engraved title page and its many, sensitive descriptions of nature – should be better known. In the passage that follows, Millikin describes the almost hidden birth of the river, the course of which he follows through the three books of the poem.

from: The River's Side: a poem

From some cold rock in woody covert hid,
Clear springing forth with pure unsullied drops,
Or bubbling out, with soft and tuneless fall,
From the drear bosom of some barren wild,
Remote, and hopeless of the mower's toil,
Or waving Ceres;[1] where the bending waste
From the bleak summits of two neighbouring hills
Forms a rude plain; the River comes, at first
Distinguished only by the tufted rush,
Or wat'ry cresses, that its course denote
Seen verdant mid the rigid desart brown;
And seldom seen but by the Fowler. He,
With vent'rous foot, the yielding surface treads
From tuft to tuft—he knows the place alone
And shuns the faithless green, that hides below
A treacherous abyss;[2] while, as he toils,
With measured step and slow, his faithful dog
Sedulous amid the marshy covert tries,
And plunges often in—up springs the snipe,
And whirrs on rapid pennon 'gainst the breeze,
Sole habitant of these neglected swamps,
Except the Heron, who perhaps at times
Attracted here for prey, far down the glen,

1 i.e. barren land which has no hope of ever being tilled or producing corn.

2 i.e. the sportsman knows the land well enough to know that green grass betrays treacherously boggy ground.

Beside a clump of flags,[3] silent and still,
Scarcely distinguished by his slender form,
Stands lonely; startled at the deadly sound,
With outstretch'd neck, he rises o'er the fen
With heavy beating wing, unwieldy, slow,
A doubtful burthen on the mountain air,
And then, his lengthened neck into a curve
Contracting, wheels into the middle sky,
And far away he floats, screaming aloft,
Complaining of the bold intruder, man.

As yet a slender urn the River pours;
A little nameless rill, that trickles down,
Obscure amid its rudely channel'd bed;
Divided oft in many a slender vein
By the heaped ruin of the mountain flood,
Through which it drips; 'till with collected stream,
It spouts from ridge to ridge, then sinks again
And chafes and murmurs, 'till a smoother bed
Spreads it abroad a silver current clear,
Dimpling along round many a pointed stone,
And shews a lengthened train of broken light;
Then sudden falls into a yawning rift,
And thence escaping, glances rapid down
Compact and smooth; and now on either side
Receives the offered tributes of the hills,
That trickling fall from many a pendent rock
Mid tangling briers that begin to cloathe
Its mossy sides, and oft discoloured seen
By mineral dross from the adjacent ore,
That in the secret chambers of the hill,
Lies far and deep. …

3 flag (or wild) irises.

SYDNEY OWENSON, LADY MORGAN
(*c.*1783–**1807**–1859)

Sydney Owenson, novelist, poet and literary celebrity, was the daughter of Robert Owenson, the most famous Irish actor of his day. She was brought up in Dublin and in 1812 married the surgeon in Lady Abercorn's household, Thomas Charles Morgan, who was afterwards knighted. Her earliest publication, *Poems: dedicated by permission to the Right Honorable the Countess of Moira* appeared in Dublin in 1801. Throughout her life, and most famously in her popular novel, *The Wild Irish Girl* (1806), Lady Morgan was an ardent champion of her native country, particularly of its natural beauty. By 1807, when this poem appeared, her fame was such that verse she published in Dublin was immediately reprinted in New York and Philadelphia.

The Violet[1]

To her who sent me the Spring's first Violet

'Poiche d'altro honorate
Non possom prendi liete
Guesti negre VIOLE
Dall umor rugiadose'
B. Tasso

I

Oh! say, didst thou know 'twas mine own idol flower
That my heart has just welcom'd from thee?
And, guided alone by sweet sympathy's power,
Didst thou rear it *expressly for me*?

1 <Were I to indulge my fancy as often as I have done my heart in a communion with the sweet and simple *children* of Flora, there is no plant, no blossom, from the venerable aloe to '*the small modest crimson-tipped flower*,' but would have received some poetic tribute from the fancy they had awakened, and the feelings they had touched. Rather a *sentimental* than a *scientific* florist, at 'all times, all seasons, and their changes', a garden has for me an indescribable charm!

Let the philosophic naturalist ascertain the constituent properties of the *plant*: let him deny it sensation, or endow it with irritability; let him limit the nice boundary, or trace the delicate shades of discrimination which divide the animal from the vegetable world, or mark the almost imperceptible degrees of sensation which separate man from the *sea-nettle*. But without being deeply studied in *Linnæus*, or knowing scarcely more of *Bonet*, *Ludwig*, or *Zunguis*, than the titles of their works, the winter's solitary snow-drop, the *spring's early violet*, the summer's first rose, and the autumn's last carnation, speak to my heart a language it understands, which Nature dictates, and Science could scarcely improve: and sure, 'If ignorance is bliss, 'tis folly to be wise.'>

II

Sure thou didst! And how richly it glows through the tears
That dropt o'er its beauties from heaven!
Like those which the rosed-cheek of fond woman wears
When her bosom to rapture is given.

III

And meek, modest, and lovely, it *still* seems to shun,
E'en as though it still blush'd in the vale,
Ev'ry too glaring a beam of the *too* ardent sun,
Ev'ry rudely breath'd sigh of the gale.

IV

Oh! dear is the friend whom the blossom resembles,
Who as sweet, as retiring is found;
In whose eye the warm tear of feeling oft trembles,
Who, unseen, sheds her fragrance around.

V

And thou art that friend! and thy emblem believe
Has now found in my bosom a shrine;
And ne'er did the holiest relic receive
An homage more fervent than mine.

PATRICK O'KELLY
(*c.*1746–**1808**–1837)

Pat O'Kelly, who was born in Loughrea Co. Galway, made a living for himself as a travelling bard, writing verses in praise of (or, if he had been badly treated, in dispraise of) the owners of the various Irish country houses where he begged hospitality. He was well known throughout the west of Ireland – his admirers called him 'blest Laureate of our Isle' and the 'pride of Connacht' – and assembled impressive subscription lists for his books of eccentric and self-congratulatory (but in places interestingly 'local') verse; he is mainly remembered today for having persuaded the Prince of Wales to take fifty copies of *Poems on the Giant's Causeway and Killarney* (1808) and for having written the famous 'Doneraile Litany'. Like Killarney and the Powerscourt waterfall, the Giant's Causeway attracted the attention of many eighteenth-century poets.

from: Description of the Giant's Causeway

HAIL! Architect divine! who giv'st mine eye
To view those scenes, which human art defy:
Rocks 'thron'd on rocks, stupendous work display,
Where awful horrors hold eternal sway;
Where all the group so magically new,
So deep, so wild, and wonderful to view;
Where dreary caverns deep, impress dismay,
And interdictions lour[1] on Phoebus' ray ;
Where countless prodigies thy skill declare,
Whose models Artists to their countries bear;[2]
But vain their efforts, such bold scenes to draw,
And vain is Art to model Nature's law;
Sooner shall Man from scientific lore,
Number the pebbles on the sea-lash'd shore;
Sooner be stars to calculation just,
And graves restore an individual dust,
Than thy great *Causeway*, Architect divine!
In equal splendor by description shine.

Tho' the admir'd Colossus lives to fame,
And Pompey's Pillar full distinction claim[3]

1 i.e. even the rays of the sun look gloomy and forbidding.

2 The best-known representations of the Giant's Causeway were those by Susanna Drury whose 1739 paintings were engraved in 1743 by François Vivares and circulated, in this form, throughout Europe.

3 The reference is to two of the wonders of the ancient world, the Colossus of Rhodes and Pompey's pillar, a Roman triumphal column in Alexandria.

To just renown, and strike Attention's eye,
Here nobler scenes in wild disorder lie.
What height! what gloom! what magnitude! what form!
How prompt each view to live in fame and charm!
Pillars half scatter'd—angles—concave sides;
In whose projection sportive Nature prides.
The cliffs stupendous, wond'rous to behold,
O'erlook the Main, majestically bold:[4]
Its awful heights above th'Atlantic rise,
Burst through the clouds and intercept the skies:
Nature convuls'd this wond'rous work has done,
Proud to compleat a grand phenomenon.
Lo! to PORTRUSH[5] this awful wreck extends,
Where shade with shade, and pile with pile contends;
Horror on horror variagates the scene,
To intersperse th'unequal shade between.
Prismatic columns on each side are here;
In *regular confusion* all appear!

To contemplate the whole, so wild, so vast;
Wonders criterion is, by far, surpast:
Those stately pillars (long by time imbrown'd)
In all that's great and marvellous abound:

In density and form these piles agree,
Still unimpair'd and from disorder free:
Such solid vestiges of liquid fire,
The more we contemplate, the more admire;
One universal standard stamps the whole,
And with amazement fires th'enraptur'd soul.

Reason's bewilder'd, when this work we view,
And leaves Mankind in doubt and darkness too;
Darkness and doubt, at once impress the heart,
So clear th'anology twixt chance and art. …

4 Pleaskin Head, a cliff of volcanic formation rising high above the Giant's Causeway.

5 A seaside town to the west of the Giant's Causeway. awful = inspiring admiration.

MARY (SHACKLETON) LEADBEATER
(1758–**1808**–1826)

Mary Shackleton was born in Ballitore, Co. Kildare, daughter of the Quaker schoolmaster, Richard Shackleton. She was educated at her father's school – where Edmund Burke had earlier been a pupil – and married a local landowner, William Leadbeater. She wrote many books: diaries and prose accounts of her life in the Quaker community at Ballitore, translations from the classics, 'improving' books for the poor (some in dialogue), children's books, history and some verse. Her eye-witness accounts of the events of 1798 are among the most vivid and harrowing to survive.

from: View of Ballitore

In the fresh morning of my early days,
While the gay dreams of fancy floated round,
Seated on this fair hill,[1] with raptur'd eyes,
I trac'd the beauties of the vivid scene,
And fram'd the artless lay.[2] Revolving years
Have somewhat chang'd the scene. Beneath the axe
The stately grove has fall'n, and left expos'd
To publick gaze the graves of those we lov'd.
The village now attracts the passing eye;
The modest village, seated in the vale,
While fair behind ascends the graceful hill,
Crown'd with nine trees, whose summit seen afar
My heart has hail'd, while journ'ying to my home,
By absence dearer made. And there appears
The lov'd paternal roof, embow'r'd in shade,—
The stately ash,—the orchard's twisting boughs,—
And ever-greens, defying winter's frown,—
Deserted now! No more the master dear
'Walks forth to meditate at even-tide,'[3]
Amidst his garden's blooms: to happier climes
His spirit pure has fled. No more his mate
Tends her sweet flow'rs, relaxing thus her mind,
Her careful mind, anxious for gen'ral good.

1 a hill near Ballitore named Mount Bleak.

2 <Alluding to 'The View', a poem written in very early life.>

3 William Cowper, 'The Task' (1783), vi, 948.

Now second childhood has resum'd the reign;
And Innocence, guide of her blameless life,
Gilds the sweet ev'ning with the ray serene,
Escap'd from all the horrors, all the woes,
Which burst upon this valley, since those hearts
So exquisitely feeling ceas'd to feel.
Blest while their noble talents they employ'd;
Blest when their noble talents they resign'd:
For worthily they us'd them. Now we leave
That spot to tender recollection dear;
The eye moves gently onward, where the bridge
Her arches throws across the silver Griese,[4]
Which, oft meand'ring, lingers in the vale.
There thick the clustering habitations stand,
And high amid them tow'rs the ample roof,
Beneath whose shelter oft Hibernia's sons
The lore of science learn'd: Ah, not untaught
The lore of virtue too! Illustrious Burke,[5]
Here dawn'd the beam of thine effulgent day: …

4 the small river that flows past Ballitore.

5 Edmund Burke (1729–97) was a pupil at Ballitore school 1741–44.

WILLIAM TIGHE
(1766–**1808**–1816)

William Tighe, a cousin of Mary Tighe, inherited substantial estates at Rosanna, Co. Wicklow and Woodstock, Co. Kilkenny. He served as an anti-Union MP in the Irish parliament and later as a Whig in the parliament at Westminster. He was the author of an excellent *Statistical Survey of the County Kilkenny* (1802) and of a fascinating long poem, *The Plants* which shows a deep and scholarly interest in the four plants celebrated, the rose and the oak (1808), the vine and the palm (1811). The poem comes with extensive notes and precise lists of the plants mentioned. The 1808 volume also contains occasional poems, including the following.

Lines Addressed to the River at Rosanna in the County of Wicklow

Dear stream, how oft replenished by the rains
Of winter, and by summer heats how oft
Exhausted, have thy lively waters been,
Since first my childhood on thy banks conceived
Its early sports! To chase the dragon-fly
Led by his glittering mail and careless buz;
With vain attempt confine in fairy pools
The eddying foam; or, o'er a mimic fall
Of many-coloured pebbles guide its way;
And on a stone, that mid a shallow bank
Of gravel rose half-dry, with daring feet
Step insecure, and rock the little isle;
Delighted if from thence the speckled trout
Should dart, and turn around the pebbly maze
Fearful of ill; or strive with eager grasp
To entrap the aquatic spider, whose light feet
Scarce touch the elastic surface of the rill,
Mocking, with agile bound, the fruitless aim;
Or often pilot to the further shore
The crazy bark, or strand it on a shoal;
Then with unbalanced step, from off its edge
Down topple; and with dripping vest slink home
Sorrowful, and cautious to elude the eye
Of observation: or the ivied tree
O'erturned by storms, and o'er the water bowed,

Ascend unseen. That living bridge, which more
Than half o'er-arched the stream, the hand of Time
Hath undermined, and torrents borne away:
But not less strong its image lives, portrayed
By Memory's fond pencil; yet, it seems
To wave its dark festoons, and yet, uprear
Its half-discovered root!—Oh! when we die,
(And that must soon arrive!) shall there no trace
Remain of what we were? No portraiture
Be sadly cherished in some friendly breast?
Shall, with a sigh, no pleasing record say,
'Would that his span had been allotted here
A little longer!'—Yes, it were better night
Eternal. And the oblivious shroud of death
Should now enwrap us, than that all around
Should seem to hint that we had lived too long;
Useless and unregarded, as the branch
A playful boy now plucks, now casts away.

Yet live, and long shall flourish, when no more
Our eyes shall measure their expanding shade,
These antique chesnuts; and this tapering lime
Crowning the shelved bank : that well-known yew
Shall still be climbed by many youthful groups
Of generations yet unborn,—as once by us.
How little shall they think, when on the boughs
They ride and shout, or in the central seat
As from a throne, direct the busy sport,
That they but act again the early feats
Their ancestors were proud of once; or that
They ne'er shall reach a scene more gay than this
In life's uninteresting comedy!

Not the rich vale which kings might weep to leave
For Abyssinia's throne; not that where rolls
Peneus[1] his cataracts, with verdant shrubs
O'ercanopied; nor that, whose perfumed flowers
Reflect their waving beauties in the clear

1 A river in northern Greece, the god of which was said, in Greek mythology, to be the father of the nymph Daphne.

Orontes;[2] (though the ever-glowing tints
Of poesy illumine all their haunts)
Mark with a trace so durable, or with
Such pleasing images usurp the soul,
As thou, dear stream, whose current intersects
This tranquil valley: the surrounding groves,
The scattered trees, in quick recurrence wake
The recollection of what once we were,
Careless of future ill, ungrieved at past:
In those no recollections live: from Tempe's rocks,
From Daphne's bowers,[3] we turn refreshed to thee,
And cherish thee the more: nor can be viewed,
Without a grateful sigh, the tufted grove,
Beneath whose pendent boughs a mother's care
First bathed her timorous infant; or the lawn,
O'er whose smooth waving green a father's eye
Solicitous first watched the glad attempt
Of boyish years to urge the tardy steed.
How far from thee, beloved stream, from thee
And peace, my steps have wandered! the rolling years
Leave no impression of an hour, like those
Enjoyed (but ne'er to be enjoyed again!)
Upon thy banks.—With melancholy step
I pace thy margin; now no more by sports
Delighted; nor aroused from anxious thought,
Save, when some friendly voice, or gentle smile,
For one short moment may elude the sense
Of ill; save, when the Muse revisits me,
Singing of other times, and wraps my soul,
Borne from itself, in an enchanted dream:
If any dream can soothe a soul depress'd!
For Time hath scattered all the vernal flowers
Of Hope; and, for the past, a barren waste
Hath left, without one cheering retrospect;
And o'er the future, spread an awful cloud
With dubious portents hung; while life's dull lamp
Wavers, and trembles at each passing breeze.

2 A river in the Middle East, famous in antiquity.

3 A gorge in Northern Greece, favourite haunt of Apollo and the muses. 'Daphne's bowers' refers to laurel trees since the nymph Daphne was turned into a laurel tree to protect her from the advances of the god Apollo.

MARY TIGHE
(1772–**1809**–1810)

Mary Tighe was born and raised in Dublin. She was famously beautiful but became an unwilling bride and an unhappy wife to her hedonistic cousin Henry Tighe, an anti-Union MP in the Irish parliament. Though she and her husband lived partly in London, much of her poetry was written at Rosanna, Co. Wicklow. Her work had very limited circulation during her lifetime, but her major poem, *Psyche*, was much admired by Keats, Shelley and other romantic poets. She died of tuberculosis in March 1810 in County Kilkenny.

Mary Tighe wrote several poems on flowers, often linking the shortness of their life to that of humans.

The Lily

How withered, perished, seems the form
Of yon obscure unsightly root!
Yet from the blight of wintry storm,
It hides secure the precious fruit.

The careless eye can find no grace,
No beauty in the scaly folds,
Nor see within the dark embrace
What latent loveliness it holds.

Yet in that bulb, those sapless scales,
The lily wraps her silver vest,
Till vernal suns and vernal gales
Shall kiss once more her fragrant breast.

Yes, hide beneath the mouldering heap,
The undelighting slighted thing;
There in the cold earth buried deep,
In silence let it wait the spring.

Oh! many a stormy night shall close
In gloom upon the barren earth,
While still in undisturbed repose,
Uninjured lies the future birth;

And Ignorance, with sceptic eye,
Hope's patient smile shall wondering view;
Or mock her fond credulity,
As her soft tears the spot bedew.

Sweet smile of hope, delicious tear!
The sun, the shower indeed shall come;
The promised verdant shoot appear,
And Nature bid her blossoms bloom.

And thou, O virgin Queen of Spring!
Shalt, from thy dark and lowly bed,
Bursting thy green sheath's silken string,
Unveil thy charms, and perfume shed;

Unfold thy robes of purest white,
Unsullied from their darksome grave,
And thy soft petals' silvery light
In the mild breeze unfettered wave.

So Faith shall seek the lowly dust
Where humble Sorrow loves to lie,
And bid her thus her hopes entrust,
And watch with patient, cheerful eye;

And bear the long, cold, wintry night,
And bear her own degraded doom,
And wait till Heaven's reviving light,
Eternal spring! shall burst the gloom.

CHARLES BOYD
(1762–**1809**–?)

Charles Boyd was born in Dublin in 1762, educated at Trinity College Dublin and called to the Irish bar in 1776. He published a translation of Virgil's Georgics and selected eclogues in Dublin in 1808 and this imitation and modernisation of the Georgics in the following year. In his introduction to the translation, he explains that his love of country pursuits has been strengthened by his reading of the Georgics.

The poem is of great interest for its extensive and detailed account of, and recommendations about, life on a working farm in Ireland in the early years of the nineteenth century. The poem is in twelve long sections, one for each month, beginning – as does the farm year – at Michaelmas. It also contains an index listing such items as muck, hogs, turnips, winter, wool etc. The first extract below shows the kind of explicit agricultural and financial advice given throughout the poem while the second is a more reflective passage on the beauty of the settled farmland of County Wicklow. The poem is the only printed Irish verse imitation and modernisation of Virgil's Georgics of its day, though it follows in the footsteps of celebrated English examples such as John Philip's 'Cyder' (1708) and John Dyer's 'The Fleece' (1757). Just as those poems sprang from an intimate knowledge of the English countryside, so this poem reflects a similar knowledge of the countryside of Wicklow.

from: A Georgic of Modern Husbandry

from 'May'

… The twelfth of May is a good time to stock
Your farm with wethers[1] for your yearly flock;
These lean, unshorn, and three years old you'll buy,
The pastures feed them first, you then rely
On turnips for the fatt'ning finish, or
Borecole[2] or rye, as we have said before.
Always in cribs,[3] in yard or pasture, lay
With Winter vegetables, nicest hay.
Nothing more profitable is than this,
You gain a third part, instantly, by fleece,
Of what they cost, and sell for twice as much
At least, and often more; where profit such
As this accrues, you make full cent per cent.[4]
Good farming trade! o'erbalancing the rent.
Ewes in their profits full as high will go;

1 castrated rams.

2 broccoli or kale.

3 the openwork metal basket from which farm animals take their food.

4 i.e. you double your money.

The lamb, the fleece, and, fattened, sold the ewe;
These last at Michaelmas are cheaply bought,
And all in compass of the year is brought.
This of dry land, most fit for sheep, and good,
Must in th'account be always understood;
For spewy clays[5] and Winter's poachy[6] ground,
Unfit for sheep, cannot preserve them sound.
For beasts and tillage use this spongy land,
Drain and sow beans, if you would rent command,[7]
Or cabbage in this soil may well succeed
And, some will tell you, equals turnips' feed. ...

from 'September'

… Mild Autumn now prepares her changing hues
For artist's pencil and for poets muse;
Soon shall the landscape charm the tasteful eye
With the decaying leaf's enrich'ning dye,
The distant mountains, verging on the skies,
Retiring woods and castles dim arise,
The sea confus'd with sky, not blue, nor green,
Almost invisible, yet sea is seen:
Nearer the objects do their shape assume,
Distinguished by more light, more shady gloom;
But the fair fore-ground, rich beyond all thought,
Lawns, mansions, woods with tints of Autumn fraught,
The scatter'd seats and their adjoining groves,
Hills, lakes and vallies; here the riv'let roves
Through the deep glin, hoarse sounding waters fall
And slumb'ring echoes from recesses call.
Mourn not departed crops, for scenes like these
Dispel all grief and sorrow's murmurs ease;
These, Wicklow, are thy scenes; the nearer sea
Shall fleets of trading vessels oft display,
Whose tight-bent canvas, if the day be bright,
Glows with a splendour of unsullied white.
Thus commerce flourishes, art's kept alive,

5 heavy ground tending to be excessively wet.

6 sodden.

7 i.e. have power over the rent.

The hands employ'd in manufactures thrive,
Thus plenty, from the rich, productive south,
Steers to the pop'lous city's harbour-mouth,
In passing gratify the feasting eye
And friendly Agriculture's wants supply. ...

WILLIAM CARR
(*fl.*1810)

William Carr was from Newry. In addition to *Rosstrevor, a moral and descriptive poem* (1810), he published several other substantial poems and a journal of a tour from Edinburgh to the Highlands. The passage that follows is typical of scores of such blank-verse descriptions of the beauties of nature published in early nineteenth-century Ireland. Elsewhere in the poem, Carr describes with considerable enthusiasm the sight of 'enchanting nymphs' bathing naked in the sea, but warns the young reader to beware of the passion aroused by such lovely goddesses. The poem was addressed to the President and Members of the Reading Society of Newry.

from: Rosstrevor

... Now breaking thro' the shades of night, see where
The golden streaks, along the eastern hills,
Proclaim the coming day. From ev'ry copse,
And thicket, shade or grove, the brooding mists,
Which late conceal'd both hill and dale, retire
Before the peeping sun; while far, above
The smooth, untroubl'd surface of the sea,
The mountain tops, in awful grandeur rise.
As from her slumb'ring couch, refresh'd she wakes
See, Nature, to the pow'rful orb of day
Unfolds her blushing charms, and joyful, feels
His vivifying pow'r, her frame pervade.
The softly-swelling hills, and stretching plains,
In pearly moisture clad, as from the scene
Her sable curtain night withdraws, display
The richest verdure of the spring, and glow
With all the charms of cultivating care.
Up-springing from her mossy bed, the lark,
With grateful song, to melody attun'd,
Awakes the slumb'ring grove to raise aloft
To Heav'n the universal hymn of praise.
From ev'ry dew-bespangled shade, the voice
Of harmony resounds. The mellow thrush,
Here perch'd upon the Hawthorn spray, and, there,
The blackbird, whistling from the ferny brake,
In concert chime. ...

... Delightful hour!
Amid the silent glades, or flow'ry lawns,
And with a mind unfetter'd by the cares,
Or shew of life, peruse the ample page
Of Nature's works, disclos'd in ev'ry flow'r,
Or plant; or seen in mountain, hill and dale. ...

... As o'er the boundless scene, th'enraptur'd eye,
From shore to shore in fond succession roves,
How many beauties burst upon the view!
Encircling mountains far on ev'ry side,
Above the green-extending vales and hills,
Around the lake, their lofty heads uprear.
Here Carlingford, with princely brow, array'd
In darken'd hues; Rosstrevor there, o'ergrown
With wild, impendent woods; while farther hence,
O'er intervening glens, and stretching dales,
Ridge, climbing ridge in vast extension stretch'd,
The tow'ring heights of Mourne majestic hide
Their raven-coloured tops amidst the clouds. ...

SAMUEL FENNELL
(*fl.*1811)

Samuel Fennell was a proud native of County Tipperary – a man who, as he stated in his prefatory 'Advertisement' to his 1811 *Original Poems*, had 'never outstepped its borders for Education'. In addition, his book was printed in the County of Tipperary, 'the Frontispiece was painted in it' and 'every line of its contents' was composed in it. The result is an extraordinary, unsophisticated little volume, deeply rooted in the life and lore of the Irish countryside of the early nineteenth century. The only literary influence Fennell acknowledges is that of William Cowper, from whom he borrowed the epigraph for his book: 'The path of sorrow, and that path alone,/Leads to the Land where sorrow is unknown.' ('An Epistle to an afflicted Protestant Lady in France', lines 9-10).

The Hare

SHOU'D the poor Peasant, fed on homely bread,
Far whom no Ox or fleecy Sheep hath bled,
Who scarcely ever tastes (forbidden treat)
Of balmy milk, or nutrimental meat?
Shou'd he, when laboring o'er his daily toil,
In cultivation of the sturdy soil,
Perchance behold, close couch'd within her lair,
That timid creature, the swift-footed Hare,
Temptation strong the pond'rous stone to throw,
She dies, untortur'd at a single blow.
Home to his hut, he bears the welcome prize,
Joy sparkles lively in his children's eyes;
Poor little hungry race, I feel your joy,
And wish your meal may meet with no alloy;
But shou'd ill-nature tell the sporting squire,
How his red orbs will flash with vengeful ire;
Before your Mother has your supper dress'd,
The Gang assails you, and your Father's press'd;[1]
Forc'd from the dear connexions of his life,
His prattling babes, his tender hearted wife;
Plac'd in a moving prison on the wave,
He is condemned to be a weeping slave.
How shall I sing, poor family, your woes,
Or half the sorrows of this hour disclose?
A task too sable[2] for my pen, I yield,
And fly afflicted, the poetic field.

1 i.e. snatched by a press gang and forced into the British navy.

2 dark.

JAMES STUART
(1764–**1811**–1840)

James Stuart was born in Armagh and educated at Trinity College Dublin. Much of the verse in his 1811 *Poems on Various Subjects* is concerned with Armagh and its surroundings, and it is valuable for the light it throws on contemporary Ulster. He subsequently edited the *Newry Telegraph* and the *Newry Magazine*, a journal containing interesting literary and political material. His main historical work was the *Historical Memoirs of the city of Armagh*. (1819). He moved to Belfast in 1821 and continued his connection with newspapers, becoming joint owner of a conservative, protestant newspaper, *The Guardian and Constitutional Advocate*. The 'sadly-pleasing, melancholy joy' of Stuart's description of Armagh was praised by Geoffrey Taylor in *The Emerald Isle* (1952).

from: Morna's Hill

... As round the pine-clad top of Morna's hill[1]
Slowly I wind, what varied scenes appear
In glorious prospect? Whether o'er the plains
Mantled in green, the eye delighted roves,
Or where yon spires peep o'er the sloping hills
And glitter in the sun; or where aloft,
Thy column, Rokeby,[2] lifts its head in air,
High o'er the verdant pines, transmitting down
To latest years, thy friendship and thy name!
Or thine, O Molyneux, that stands sublime,[3]
With form majestick, o'er thy waving woods,
Raised to thy country's glory in the day
Of Erin's fame! How lovely bloom the groves
Whose bending tops play wanton in the gale,
Mingling their varied hues! Bright through the vales

1 <In the neighbourhood of Armagh.> It is now difficult to say where Morna's Hill was 'as so many changes have taken place since 1811' (see William Reeves, 'The Ancient Churches of Armagh …', *Ulster Journal of Archaeology*, Second Series, IV, 4 (1896), 228).

2 <Built by the late Dr Richard Robinson, baron Rokeby, Archbishop of Armagh, by whom it was dedicated to the Duke of Northumberland.> During his period in Armagh (1765–94), Archbishop Robinson (1709–94) rebuilt the cathedral and many public buildings, as well as erecting an archiepiscopal palace and supervising the reconstruction of the town itself. The 'column' referred to was an obelisk, 114 feet high, designed by Francis Johnston and erected by Primate Robinson in 1783 on Knox Hill to commemorate his friendship with the Duke of Northumberland.

3 This (second) obelisk was 60 feet high and was erected on his lands at Castle Dillon by Sir Capel Molyneux in 1782 to commemorate the granting of limited legislative independence to the Irish parliament.

The streams soft gliding, wind their devious course,
Deepening the tender verdure of the fields,
And mantling every blossom of the spring
In robes of humid lustre. Round the hills
Dwell Innocence and rural Industry,
And Peace, and jocund Health, and sinewy Toil,
The sire of Plenty, though the child of want. …

Nor wants the glowing landscape many a charm,
Transmitted down through Time's revolving years,
To dignify the scene. The sacred mound,
Where waves the wild grass o'er the prostrate heads
Of heroes now no more. The convex cairne
That crowns the heath-clad hill, where silent sleeps
The mighty Fion; and the antique rath
Within whose circular intrenchments stood
Secure embattled hosts;[4] ere Science taught
The sons of war to sweep the tented field
With murd'rous cannon. Contemplation loves
To dwell upon these objects; and the soul,
Deep-musing, turns to deeds of ancient days,
And snatches, from the annals of the world,
A sadly-pleasing, melancholy joy. …

4 The reference is to the cairn and mound marking the site of the royal palace of the kings of Ulster at Emain Macha or Navan Fort, near Armagh.

WILLIAM HAMILTON DRUMMOND
(1778–**1811**–1856)

William Hamilton Drummond was born in Larne, Co. Antrim and educated at the University of Glasgow. He worked as a Presbyterian minister in Belfast and Dublin, becoming a strong defender of and advocate for Unitarianism. His many sermons and pamphlets show him to have been a man of strong liberal principles and a defender of the rights of animals. His published verse included translations of Lucretius from Latin and of early Irish poetry for his own book on ancient Irish verse (1852) and for James Hardiman's *Irish Minstrelsy* (1831).

Drummond's *The Giant's Causeway* (Belfast, 1811) is one of the most remarkable and ambitious scholarly poems of the age. Its nearly 2,000 lines are divided into three books, each with a preceding 'Argument' and extensive notes. The lengthy introduction summarizes the geological theories of the day and within the poem itself Drummond covers in detail the history, mythology, folklore and physical appearance of the causeway. There are extended descriptions of the inhabitants of the Antrim coast as well as moral, historical, scientific and theological reflections. The poem caused considerable controversy at the time of its publication as theories of the formation of the earth's crust were being widely debated. The book is adorned with finely engraved views of the causeway and its surroundings.

from: The Giant's Causeway

from: Book II

… Now round the mole,[1] from Giants named of yore,
Thy altar Nature, helm th'obedient prore;[2]
How black, how firm, its adamantine[3] sides
Rise o'er the azure of the heaving tides!
How proud th'indented bound of ocean lowers![4]
What rocky theatres, and spires, and towers!
First bold creation of the plastic hand,[5]
That rolled the billows round the rock-ribbed land!
Nature's primeval forms, whence mimic Art
Saw the first image of her fabrics start,
Th'idea fair of wonders deemed her own,
The breathing canvas, and the quickened stone.[6]

1 massive structure, i.e. the Giant's Causeway itself.

2 i.e. steer the obedient prow of the boat. During this passage of the poem, the poet is observing the Giant's Causeway from the sea and is here instructing the boatman to steer the boat around the Giant's Causeway to give a better view of this 'altar' of Nature.

3 unyielding.

4 i.e. how proud and dark the indented edge of the ocean appears.

5 i.e. the hand that moulded or created the rocks (that of God).

6 i.e. all works of art (painting or sculpture) merely mimic the primeval forms of Nature.

But vain her powers with Nature's pride to vie,
As the gilt dome to match the starry sky;
High be her boast of Tiber's proud arcades.
Her ducts, pantheons, fanes,[7] and colonnades:
See, in these temples of the northern blast,
Their beauty, grandeur, strength and skill surpast. …

High on yon cliff the fisher takes his stand,[8]
The rock's loose fragments arm his brawny hand,
Swift as he marks the glistening salmon glide,
He hurls a rattling stone-shower in the tide.
The patient boatman rocking on the brine,
Elate with hope, beholds the well-known sign:
Swift winds the capturing net, and now in vain,
The fear-struck captive beats the flaxen chain;[9]
Vain is his strength, and vain his dotted mail,[10]
His rapid fin, quick eye, and springy tail:
He sports in Bosca's sable streams[11] no more,
Nor braves majestic Banna's cataract[12] roar;
By hands unpitying, from his native flood
Dragged o'er the pointed crags, defiled with blood,
His scales all ruffled, and his vigour fled,
He gasps—he pants—he lies deformed—and dead.

7 arcades, passages, pantheons, temples and colonnades. i.e. the man-made glories of Rome are surpassed by 'these temples of the northern blast' – the Giant's Causeway.

8 In a note at this point, Drummond describes the methods of fishing for salmon off the Antrim coast, the salmon's reproductive cycle, how painful it is for 'a spectator of humanity' to see salmon attempting to leap from the 'cutts' at Coleraine, and how it is that the salmon gathers energy to leap. (Drummond believed that the fish takes its tail in its mouth when about to leap.) He also quotes lines from Dryden and from Drayton, and ends the note by giving the reasons for the decline of the fisheries (which include poaching), and statistics of catches and of rents paid for salmon fisheries (pp. 153–5).

9 i.e. the net which was made of ropes constructed of long fibres of flax.

10 i.e. his speckled skin – like a coat of mail.

11 This seems to be a reference to the River Bush which joins the sea near the Giant's Causeway – possibly a local name for the river: Ir. *bosca*: a bush of boxwood. The river water would be stained by peat and so 'sable' or dark in colour.

12 The river Bann, which enters the sea at Portstewart. The Bann and the Bush were famous salmon rivers.

What different instinct bids the silvery eel
In countless train up Banna's torrents wheel,[13]
While salmon shoals the downward streams forsake,
And to the stranger brood resign the lake;
In whose clear waves the prickly holly thrown,
Its nature loses, and transmutes to stone?[14]
Unfold it thou, O TEMPLETON, whose view
Has roved creation's peopled regions through;[15]
Thou who can'st speak of all the flowers of spring,
Of fish of every fin, and bird of every wing:
Tell, for thou know'st, how Nature has assigned
Their times and seasons to each tribe and kind,
And how her laws direct, propel, controul,
So wondrous wise, th'instinctive powers of soul.

In shallow streamlets, with th'insidious fly,
Their tiny art let patient anglers try:
Far other sport the hardy natives boast,
Who sweep with long-drawn net this iron coast,
Or o'er the whirling surge the feather spread,
To tempt the Glashan[16] from his oozy bed.
'Tis theirs with storms to urge the bold turmoil,
Where adverse tides in whelming eddies boil;
To hear sad shriekings in the midnight air,
To see the ghastly death-fires of despair
Flash o'er the wreck, and grisly spectres croud
Where floats the wan corse[17] in a foamy shroud;

13 Drummond's long note at this point describes the eel's life cycle and the eel fisheries; to wheel = to go the other way (from the way of the salmon) i.e. to go upstream.

14 For a refutation of the myth that the waters of Lough Neagh turn wood to stone, see Richard Barton's 'Physico-Poetical Essay' above. Drummond covers the matter in a long note.

15 Belfast-born John Templeton (1766–1825) naturalist and botanist. He is often referred to as the father of Irish botany.

16 Ir. *glaisean*. Drummond's note at this point explains that 'The Glashan, coal fish, *Gadus Carbonarius*, is known on the coast of Antrim during the several stages of its growth by the names of Pickoe, Blockan, Glashan and Greylord. When at full size, they weigh from twenty to thirty pounds. There are considerable fisheries of them at Island Magee, Larne, and Glenarm; and they furnish a cheap, wholesome, and nutritious food' (p. 159).

17 corpse. For accounts of fanciful sightings such as these off the coasts of Ireland, see the collections of the Irish Folklore Commission at University College Dublin.

While boding mermaids rising on the swell.
Wring their wet locks, and chant their funeral spell.

… In airy wheels what fowls unnumbered fly,
Dashing the seas, or screaming through the sky;
The Herring's march they follow from the pole;
Millions on millions moves th'enormous shoal;
In gentle undulations as they rise
On the smooth rippling waves, a thousand dyes
Shot from their scales with mingling lustre play,
A field of gems wide-blazing to the day!
Voracious foes their feeble ranks assail,
The Shark, the Porpoise, and devouring Whale;
The keen-eyed Osprey marks the prey from far,
And there th'impetuous Gannet brings the war;
Poised on smooth pinion from his tow'ry height,
With glance more rapid than a shaft of light,
He marks his quarry in the crystal flood,
And plumb-down darting, in the victim's blood
Drives his keen beak.—With rapture-beaming eye
The well-known sign the ready fishers spy
Th'unsparing nets around the prey expand,
And heap with treasure all the yellow sand.

See, as they gambol o'er the hoary brine,
What porpoise shoals with quick reflections shine;
As by the skiff they urge their swift career,
The timid landsman starts with sudden fear;
New to the waves he dreads each novel form,
Shrinks from the spray, and deems the breeze a storm;
But vain his fears—away the monsters sweep,
Like Neptune's coursers plunging through the deep. …

… Prolific Ocean; how thy bounteous flood
From all its sources sends the scaly brood!
For man, dread tyrant, glide their marshaled powers,
From all thy sands, and rocks, and coral bowers;
No scale-fenced ribs against his art avail,
Nor strength, nor bulk, nor shelly plates of mail;

Their swiftest march more rapid he pursues,
Ensnares by cunning, or by force subdues….

from: Book III

SUBLIME LUCRETIUS![18] thou whose daring page
Breathes the high spirit of th'Athenian sage,
With whom high-soaring to the cause of things,
Thy soul quaffed deep the muse's hidden springs;
Come to these capes that brave the northern gale,
And bid, as thou wert wont, blue ocean hail.
Come, hear with me, the big tumultuous waves
Bursting like thunder through a thousand caves,
And see the bark which blackening tempests urge,
Ride o'er the bills of foam, and meet the boisterous surge.

Thrice happy he, whose truth-illumined soul
With Science wanders through the boundless whole;
No angry fiends of night her skies deform,
Or round her roll the lightning and the storm;
Where'er she turns, to earth, or heaven, she sees
The real heralds of divine decrees.
Now plunging downward, see her urge her flight
Through the dark realms of chaos and of night;
Now mid the zones, she spreads her wings afar,
Soars to the sun, and visits every star,
And scanning Nature's universal laws,
Mounts from the second to th'eternal cause.
Here, by overhanging rocks, where Danger keeps
His dreary watch-tower trembling o'er the deeps,
Th' adventurous muse's anxious thoughts explore
What power of Nature formed the pillared shore. …

[The poet imagines the volcanic upheavals that formed the Giant's Causeway.]

… Calm midst the horror of the rueful scene,
Majestic Nature sat, and smiled serene,

18 Drummond's own translation of the first book of Lucretius's *De Rerum Natura* was published in 1808.

Planned on the reeling shores her fair designs,
And built her future palaces and shrines. —
From teeming craters, gushing dense and strong
The black basaltic[19] deluge pours along,
Overtops the chalky cliffs, the valley fills,
Binds the loose soil, and links the severed hills.
Here the red torrent, by the rapid shock
Of frigid waters, changed to pillared rock;
Or pent in caves till thrilled by tardy cold,
Shot into columns of gigantic mould.
Thus in the chymic[20] vase, attraction's law
Bids each fine atom kindred atoms draw;
Close and more close the crouding seeds combine,
Till crystal forms in fair arrangement shine.
For all the various forms which nature breeds
Spring from the union of organic seeds,
Which, by attraction, form their compound frame,
In shape, in nature, and in laws the same:
Hence, in fair crystals falls the flaky snow,
And hence the facets of the diamond glow. …

19 The Giant's Causeway is formed of basalt rock.

20 chemical.

ANNA LIDDIARD(?)
(*c*.1785–**1819**–*c*.1820)

There must be some doubt about the authorship of this poem. Anna Wilkinson was born in County Meath around 1785. She married the Rev. William Liddiard (1773–1841), rector of Knockmark, Co. Meath, a well-known travel writer and poet. Anna published several volumes of poetry, some co-authored with her husband, which show that she had a considerable interest in and affection for Ireland. *Mount Leinster* was published anonymously and was ostensibly the work of a male poet so, not surprisingly, it has been suggested that it was the work of William rather than Anna Liddiard. There is no hard evidence for this though the poem is better written than much of Anna Liddiard's own verse; it also demonstrates stronger anti-British bias as well as being based on a more secure scholarly knowledge of Irish history than Anna's other poems. In addition, the poem contains a surprisingly detailed passage in praise of the cultivation of the potato and a vivid description of a Wexford hurling match. If Anna Liddiard wrote *Mount Leinster* it is, as Julia Wright has stated, 'her best work'.[1]

On the other hand, if the poem is the work of William Liddiard, its anti-British bias is surprising since he had been an officer in the British army during the Napoleonic wars and was chaplain to the Lord Lieutenant of Ireland, the fourth Duke of Richmond. Since Anna Liddiard died at about the time *Mount Leinster* was published, it is possible that William completed Anna's unfinished poem so that it is best described as a joint publication.

The poem celebrates the beauty and fecundity of Ireland while attacking the Union of 1801 and Ireland's treatment at the hands of the British over the centuries, particularly under the Penal laws. Its concentration on the significance of the potato in rural Irish life and its vignette of the poverty of those living near Mount Leinster are particularly poignant given that potato blight and famine were to strike rural Ireland within a generation.

from: Mount Leinster;
or, The Prospect: a poem, descriptive of Irish Scenery

LORD of the landscape, lofty Leinster, hail!
From whose high crown we view the distant sail,
As on the horizon's misty verge it flies,
Where distant ocean mingles with the skies;
With thy majestic beauties varying wide,
As from the base we mount the rocky side,
On an extensive tract the eye first dwells,
Where Erin's shore the rolling surge repels;
Dotted with woods, with villas, and with farms,
A glowing landscape still unfolding charms;
Still, as we rise, sublimer views expand,
In lengthening prospect o'er the sea-girt land;

1 Julia M. Wright, 'J. S. Anna Liddiard' in *Irish Women Poets of the Romantic Period* (Alexandria, VA: Alexander Street Press, 2008).

Where silver streams extend, and hamlets rise
In panoramic view before our eyes:
Ascending yet the hills behind less grow,
And one wide plain appears the scene below;
Till, urging on, all toils and dangers past.
The aerial peak above we gain at last. …

Behold around the countless crops of corn,
Waving in light, brushed by the breeze of morn.
Luxuriant growth! pledge of her grateful soil,
Which cheers the peasant and rewards his toil.
Where late the common savage heath o'erspread,
The o'ercharged wheat-ear rears its yellow head,
And flow'ring clover's verdant tufts arise,
Joy to the flock, and incense to the skies! ...

Hail! Science, hail! thou heaven-descended maid,
Fair Wisdom's glass, man's triumph, pride and aid!
Thy mounting steps the distant spheres ascend,
Or, boldly plunging, to the centre bend:
Whate'er abstruse in Nature's mazes lies,
Thy magic opens to inquiring eyes;
Space, matter, motion, thy decrees control,
And to the mind display the wond'rous whole!
At thy command, the canvass courts the breeze,
And wafts the mariner o'er pathless seas;
By rules defined he gains the distant shores,
And lands remote and unknown seas explores.
Thy presence[2] cheers the cultivator's toil,
And guides his plans to fertilize the soil;
To clear the slope for the productive grain,
Or point the dike[3] to dry the swampy plain,
By signs unerring shews the water's course,
Tracing the latent mischief to its source:

2 i.e. the presence of science.

3 mark out the course for a ditch or field drain. The next few lines concern the drainage of land.

The pliant sallow,[4] branching alder-bush,
Fiorin,[5] flagger,[6] or the spiry rush;
These mark the line, where, boiling from below,
The springs exuding the rank lands o'erflow:[7]
In that nice junction, on the sloping plain,
The skilful farmer excavates the drain. …

Arranged in parallels, with space between,
The young potato-stems, of deepest green,
Their vig'rous heads along their ranks display,
Erect, supported by the moulding clay.[8]
Behold their bloom, while yet the sun is high,
And fervent beams refulgent cleave the sky;[9]
The opening blossoms, decked in vernal[10] pride,
Of varied tints, imbibe the vital tide;[11]
While clouds of sweetest fragrance they exhale,
A grateful off'ring to the passing gale;[12]
As wide below, the branching roots unfold
The swelling clusters, mid the teeming mould.[13]
Who seek large gain their industry to pay,
Make choice of rich, compact, calcareous[14] clay;
For there the root to strength joins large produce,
And floury fracture,[15] when prepared for use.
Ere snows descend, or frost the glebe has bound,
Deep with the share[16] upturn the destin'd ground;

4 willow.

5 Apparently a corruption of Irish *fiorthán*, long coarse grass.

6 <Yellow Iris.> The 'flag' or wild iris grows in marshy ground.

7 i.e. ooze out and flow over the heavy ground.

8 i.e. the earth piled up (moulded) around them.

9 and warm beams of sunlight penetrate the bright sky.

10 springtime.

11 partake of the life-giving season.

12 a light wind.

13 productive earth.

14 containing lime or limestone. These lines on the cultivation of the potato are addressed to those who want their hard work to reward them with 'large gain'.

15 i.e. the cooked potato is 'floury' when broken open.

16 plough-share.

Disposed in ribs then let the fallows lie,
To meliorate beneath the wintry sky.
When early spring brings on the length'ning day,
With caustic lime ferment the unctuous clay:
Rest thence to planting time, while deep its pores
From ambient air imbibe nutricious stores,[17]
Then from the yard its hoard of muck convey,
And o'er the field the smoking spoil display.
The plough arranged, and each his task assign'd,
The joyful work commence, with aid combined;
And, all the seed disposed beneath the soil,
With smoothing roller end the pleasing toil.
When the young buds above the surface bear,
Begins anew the cultivator's care;
The moulding hoe their infant wants supplies,
And gives the plants redoubled strength to rise;
From weed's rank blight the surface keeping clear,
Till their full growth proclaims the harvest near. …

The scene is hush'd; during the sultry hours,
Bees range the meads and sip the blushing flow'rs;
The songsters silent bask upon the spray,
And autumn's opening tints the fields display.
On his high cliff the brooding eagle sits,
And views the plain, and eyes the sun by fits.
Or, wheeling mid the regions of the air,
Descries and pounces on the trembling hare;
On 'sounding pinions'[18] reascends the skies,
And to his callow[19] young resigns the prize.

Amid the calm behold the whirling blast
Rush through the grove, in wild disorder cast;
Skim o'er the mead, and in its eddying sway,
Sweep to the clouds aloft the new-mown hay:

17 i.e. while the land takes in nutrition from the surrounding air.

18 The phrase is first used by Alexander Pope in Book XII of his translation of Homer's *Iliad*.

19 unfledged.

Or from the road the rifted surface[20] bear,
In circling column dancing through the air.
The swains observe, with superstitious fear,
And cross themselves, believing fairies near![21]
Due south beneath his beams, and full in view,
The Blackstair mountain lifts his head of blue,
Stupendous mass! whose length and giant form
Shoots o'er the vales, a rampire[22] 'gainst the storm!
Nor tree nor shrub its granite sides display,
But naked cliffs that frown upon the day:
Blotch'd o'er with moor, the heathcock's[23] wild domain,
Where fox and martin[24] hold divided reign;
Around its breast the dusky vapours lie,
And the loose clouds that range along the sky:
Where oft the hare, pursued with clamour loud,
Breaks on the view descending from the cloud:
Or fowler starts, with detonating sounds,
Which echo with her hundred tongues rebounds.[25]
Here on the steep, of aspect gaunt and strange,
The mountain flocks the heathy commons range,
In shade of rocks, and wrapp'd in fleeces warm,
They bide the 'pelting of the wintry storm':[26]
Where oft the snow entombs them, as they lie,
And, 'neath the drift, the hapless victims die.
Yet these wild tenants of this savage scene
Excel the browsers of the lowland green
In wool, whose fineness rivals silk in feel,
And meat, whose flavour ven'son can't excel.

Freed from the flinty siphons of the hill,
The infant streams on either side distil;

20 i.e. the dust comes from cracks in the surface of the road.

21 <It is a received opinion among the lower classes in Ireland, that whirlwinds are produced by the agency of fairies; who, on occasions, are apprehensive of their malevolent attacks; to which this passage alludes.>

22 rampart.

23 grouse.

24 pine-martin.

25 'Echo' is understood as the Greek goddess.

26 This phrase first appears in a translation from the *Greek Anthology* in the *Monthly Review* for 1807.

And, blending onwards with enlarging tide,
They confluent through the distant valleys glide; …
O first and foremost, Clody![27] Be my theme;
Conduct the Muse along thy wizard[28] stream,
Where, dash'd from rocks you seek the vale below,
While down the hills your lucid waters flow;
'Till clear emerging in your latest scene,
You lave the fairest hamlet of the green;
Romantic spot! array'd in sylvan pride,
Where Slaney's winding streams the vales divide!
Here hanging woods[29] in circling beauty rise,
Extended meads and waters charm the eyes;
And cooling grots, with moss and shells replete,
Exclude the fervour of meridian heat;
The landscape lovely, and the village gay,
A Barry's cultivated taste display.
Happy, thrice happy, dearest Isle! if those
Who drain thy riches did them thus dispose![30]
To mend what Nature, with a lavish hand,
In soil and scenery gives to their command!
Here hills ascend in vain, and rivers stray,
For culture's hand their beauties to display:
To favour'd lands the nutriment is flown,
Which, foster'd, should invigorate our own.
The half-clad peasantry that till the soil,
Find indigence the meed[31] of all their toil.
After the day's fatigue, on meagre fare,
In smoky huts that half exclude the air,
Whose doors but poorly stop the wintry wind,
They seek at night reprief[32] from toil to find:

27 <The Clody, a small river, has its source in Mount Leinster, and falls into the river Slaney, at Newtown Barry, the seat of Colonel Barry; a description of which is here attempted.>

28 enchanted.

29 i.e. trees overhanging the water.

30 This passage is an attack on absentee landlords who spend abroad the rents they receive from Ireland.

31 recompense.

32 relief.

When, dripping thro' the thatch, the chilly rain
Breaks off their rest, and bids them wake to pain.
A cheerless scene, of sylvan honours shorn,[33]
Where hope must pine, creative fancy mourn;
And rebel feeling, spurning such disgrace,
Indignant execrates the vagrant race![34]...

Far right, where Kenny's[35] plains extended lie,
A beauteous landscape opens on the eye: …
Nor to the surface is the view confined,
Where Dunmore's wonders[36] open on the mind:
As through the cavern's depths her vot'ry strays,
Nature her wild, fantastic work displays:
Where, o'er the starry roof's extension bright,
Ten thousand gems reflect the flambeau's light,
In varying tint; and, round the sides, convey
A frostwork semblance glittering in the ray.
But most superb, where from its basis wide,
The massy column rears its polish'd side,
And props the arch on high, diverging round
That sweeps this nether temple's ample bound,
In days of fiction, aptly the abode
Of Cyclops, Genii, or infernal God.[37]

And nearer still, beneath the evening ray,
The ridge of Leinster[38] peers in green array;

33 lacking any of the dignity that should be associated with country living.

34 i.e. rebellious feelings are aroused [in those forced to live in such penury], who scorn the way they are treated and indignantly curse the landlords wandering around the world.

35 <Saint Canericus, or Kenny, from whom the county of Kilkenny takes its name, lived in the sixth century. See Hanmer's Chron. p. 125.> The reference is to Meredith Hanmer (1543–1604) whose *Chronicle of Ireland* was first published by Sir James Ware in 1633.

36 <The cave of Dunmore, of great celebrity as an extraordinary natural curiosity, is situate near Jenkinstown, the seat of Mr. O'Byrne, about five miles from the city of Kilkenny. The writer has been through part of it, the appearance of which he here attempts to delineate.> This note suggests that the writer of this poem is a man.

37 Giants, supernatural beings or gods of the underworld.

38 <Anciently called Slieumargah Mountain; it runs nearly parallel with the Barrow for some miles, and the land rising gradually from the river to its side, which in one part is wooded nearly to the summit, and in a high state of cultivation, presents a landscape which is truly beautiful.>

Due north and south extends the lofty mound,
But late a common, now with culture crown'd.[39]
There fields, by young potato-blossoms died,[40]
And oat enclosures shine in glossy pride;
And whitewash'd cottages, a pleasing shew!
O'erlooking the bright vale that lies below;
Where Carlow's undulating fields extend,
Whose varied shades in sweet disorder blend:
Mid which the raptured eye delights to stray,
And dwells, though oft review'd, 'with fond delay',[41]
On wood, on tillage, or on pastures green;
Or seeks the Barrow through the lengthen'd scene.
    Fair stream! whose placid waters glide,[42]
    In winding course, a gentle tide;
    As through thy own green tales they stray,
    And flow untired their ceaseless way:
    Still, as the parent main they join,
    Drawn from thy streams new rills combine;
    Thence Nature's course unerring keep,
    Thy source the clouds, thy home the deep!...
    O that my humble strain could be,
    As Denham's,[43] emulous of thee:
    That just its beauties being thine,
    It might immortal with thee twine;
    Preserv'd thy stream, would give the lay
    Eternal youth, above decay!
But see! the sun descends, in robes of gold,
Heaven's bright regalia glorious to behold!
The shades advance to greet the coming night,
Warning my steps,[44] from this aerial height.

39 It is not clear if this scene of rural plenty in the valley of the Barrow is intended as a contrast with the earlier description of the poverty of those living high on Mount Leinster.

40 dyed, coloured.

41 The phrase first occurs in William Collins's 'The Passions' (1747).

42 The address to the river Barrow is in four-stressed (rather than five-stressed) lines.

43 <The following well known lines of Cooper's Hill are here alluded to: 'O could I flow like thee, and make thy stream/My great example, as it is my theme,/Though deep, yet clear; though gentle, yet not dull;/Strong without rage; without o'erflowing, full.'> Sir John Denham's 'Cooper's Hill' (1642/1655), the first substantial topographical poem in English, lies behind many of the poems in this anthology.

44 i.e. warning me that it is time to descend.

APPENDIX

The two printed versions of Joseph Atkinson's poem *Killarny* (1769) or *Killarney* (1798) differ from each other in interesting ways. In its first printing, the poem is said to be by 'An Officer in the Army' and is a mere 18 pages in length. The title page of the later 28-page printing, however, gives the poet's name as 'Joseph Atkinson Esq.' and is embellished with an engraved view of the lakes of Killarney. This version also contains a fulsome dedication to the Earl of Moira, 'Lieutenant-General of His Majesty's Forces, &c. &c. &c.' in the course of which Atkinson asserts that 'about half the Poem was written by me, and published without my name, nearly twenty-eight years since.' 'But,' he continues:

> that juvenile and imperfect effort no longer exists on the public recollection, as is now entirely out of print. Since which, having had frequent opportunities of revisiting this terrestrial Paradise, I have lately, during my leisure hours ... endeavoured to correct, enlarge, and embellish the original design to its present more extensive, and, I hope, more pleasing description (p. iv).

Comparison between the two versions shows that the ways Atkinson 'corrected, enlarged and embellished' the text reflects the changing sensibilities of the late eighteenth century in Ireland. 'Romantic' vistas are more fully described in the second text and the language becomes fuller, richer and less immediate. The developments in the text reflect one poet's changing attitudes towards the natural world around him as he grew older and they also show how the increasing influence of the Romanticism which gripped late eighteenth-century Europe filtered through to Irish poetry about the natural world.

For the purpose of comparison, the original version of the first few pages of the poem (TEXT A) is presented on the left side of the following spreads, with a tint behind. The later version of the same material, TEXT B, is presented on the right.

TEXT A

from: Killarny: a poem (1769 printing)

Thou guardian Genius of KILLARNY say,
Through all thy scenes romantic shall I stray?
Guided by thee, the Muse, and Fancy's train,
Thy sylvan shades, and heights sublime attain?
Come then, ye Naiads, and ye sportive Fauns,
Who guard the waters, and the flow'ry lawns,
Aid me, oh, aid me, with poetic fire!
And to thy wonders let my verse aspire!

See from afar, the alp-like mountains rise,
To fill the mind with grandeur and surprise!
Some, in the clouds their tops Olympian hide,
And by their distance shew superior pride:

TEXT B

from: Killarney: a poem (1798 printing)

YE rural powers! ye legendary train,
Who round Killarney's magic circle reign,
Nymphs of the lake! ye dryads, fauns, and fays,
(Which bards inspir'd, by incantations raise,)
Lead me along, each mystic haunt pursue,
Expand each prospect to my raptur'd view;
And whilst my muse the blissful scene surveys,
Which charms my fancy, and invites my lays,
O come, entrance me with poetic fire,
Till equal to my theme my verse aspire.

AND thou, my patron, whose deserv'd acclaim,
Extends our glory and augments thy fame;
Whose proud alliance, and illustrious birth,
Are only equall'd by thy private worth:
In whom our ancient chiefs and nobles blend,
(Who gain'd the rights, thy patriot powers defend)
Around whose brow the laurel'd trophies shine,
Which martial wreaths with classic meeds, entwine;
That on some image shou'd renown engrave,
'As SIDNEY polish'd, and as FAULKLAND brave;'
Whate'er the portrait, or the bust might be,
The public mind must give the palm to thee.

Then MOIRA, come, thy critic taste suspend,
Forget the censor of the lenient friend;
And whilst thy name my humble verse adorns,
(Which like thyself base adulation scorns)
Thy kind indulgence, thy protection grant,
And lend the fancy which my muse may want.

SEE from afar the Alp-like mountains soar,
Like summer verdant, and as winter hoar;
Some in the clouds their tops Olympian hide,
To veil their grandeur with majestic pride.

Above them all—high MANGERTON appears,
And to the heavens his daring summit rears!
This tow'ring Atlas of Ierne's shore
With wonders crown'd,—as Africk's Atlas bore!
It's top, a spacious cavern-lake sustains,
Fed by deep springs, and never ceasing rains.
See, some beneath, with less aspiring height,
Yield a more verdant, and enlivening sight:
Oft like the Sun, obscurely veil'd they lie,
While o'er their heads etherial vapours fly!
But now dispell'd,—the gloomy mist o'er blown;
What bright reflections on their sides are thrown!
Now dancing Sun-beams, through the forests play,
Gild all the hills, and make the plains more gay:—
While thus from far, those glorious views extend,
Where fertile isles, and spreading waters blend:
These striking objects first prepare the mind,
To taste each beauty, nature's there combin'd.

Here crouded mountains form a circling chain,
And frown impending o'er the Liquid plain,
Whose lucid surface from their feet expands,
It's silver'd edges, to more fertile lands,
Where a huge mass of azure hills conceal
An ever-plenteous ever-blooming vale;
Where the blithe shepherd tills the fruitful earth,
And culls his riches, with a grateful mirth;
Where intermixed, the corn, and pasture field,
A pleasing prospect to his wishes yield:
Fill'd with content, and rustic-smiling peace,
He sees his harvests, and his flocks increase;
Pride, nor ambition, can his mind enthrall,
Blest in his cottage he enjoys his all!

EQUAL with all huge MANGERTON[1] appears,
And to the heavens his daring summit rears;
This giant Atlas of Ierne's shore,
A burthen bears, as fabled Atlas bore;
His top a spacious cavern'd lake sustains,
Fed by deep fountains and collecting rains;
And whilst full torrents down his bosom flow,
Reflection gilds them in the lake below.

The humble hills where groves and lawns delight,
Yield a more blooming cultivated sight;
Tho' oft by gloomy exhalations veil'd,
(Like bashful beauty in a shroud conceal'd)
We lose the woodlands and the Alpine blue,
Which recollection longs again to view.

But gradual now the transient mists o'er blown,
What dazzling splendor round their sides are thrown!
Prismatic visions float before our eyes,
Tinge all the lands, and beautify the skies.
When dancing sun-beams thro' the forests play,
The glittering dingles beam with livelier day.

WHILST distant thus such views sublime extend,
Where fertile isles with crystal waters blend;
These glorious objects first prepare the mind
To trace the wonders Nature here combin'd;
Who seems to strip the dreary country round,
That each terraqueous charm might here abound:
As sires, too partial to a favourite son,
Heap all their slighted offsprings' wealth on one.

WHERE crowded mountains form a circling chain,
Frowning impendent o'er the liquid plain;
The lucid mirror from their base expands
Its silver'd edges to more fertile lands;

1 <This mountain is computed at near three thousand feet high, from the verge of Mucrus Lake; and on its summit there is a cavity of water called the Devil's Punch-bowl, a mile and a half in circumference.>

The spacious park, and mansion of KENMAIRE,
Adorn the scene and give a nobler air!
The lordly Owner with exalted mind,
Of access easy, free, polite, and kind,
Here when his choice, permits him to reside,
Maintains a princely old Milesian pride!
Lives an example to the rich and great,
With heart unbounded, as his vast estate.

KILLARNY VILLA, next, the view salutes!
Whose rural neatness with the prospect suits,
Tho' now unnotic'd—From the world apart,
Soon shall thou boast the piling builders art;
When future fame shall spread thy beauties round,
And ev'ry pleasure midst thy wonders found:
Assembling crouds, reviv'd by summer's sun,
From the dull City's gloomy haunt shall run;
Shall here repair;—and bid new structures rise,
While spires with awful grace salute the skies!
Hibernia's Sons, no more their isle shall leave,
But thou, the tributes of their pride receive;
To thee from foreign realms shall nations roam,
And we soon glory in our Bath at home.

The craggy heights, and wooded hills oppose
The smiling scene, and Nature's bounty shows;

Where thy rich manors, and thy parks, KENMARE,[2]
The modern form of fresh improvement wear.
The noble owner, hospitably kind,
(His seat an emblem of his social mind)
Here when his choice invites him to reside,
Maintains a princely old Milesian pride;
Bids his gay fields with novel charms be grac'd,
And plants an Eden in the desert waste.
Here lives a model to the rich and great,
With heart unbounded as his large estate:
And when from transitory scenes remov'd,
His son shall emulate the worth he lov'd;
Whilst his fair consort, deck'd with Paphian grace,
Shall reign the goddess of this heavenly place.

KILLARNEY's villa now the view salutes,
(With grander towns for rising fame disputes;)
How must its comforts its extent encrease,
Since TOLERATION aids the arts of peace;
Since equal blessings with our sister isle,
Bid trade expand and cultivation smile!
Thus, our rude peasants, by example wise,
Shall see new manufactures round them rise:
Then pleased the sympathetic soul may trace,
In their neat cots a renovated race.
Then every foe to sloth, and spurious taste,
To this sequester'd paradise shall haste;
By Nature charm'd, by her attractions won,
From crowded streets to rural scenes shall run.
No longer scrape the flags o'er *Baias* parade,
Or count the piles in *Buxton*'s chill arcade;
Tir'd of the listless, lazy, dull career,
Come, Britain's sons! find healthier naiads here.

THE craggy heights and tufted hills oppose
This cultur'd sight, and wilder scenes disclose;

2 <This part of the poem was written when the person alluded to was living, and fully enjoying the urbanity and politeness for which he was so justly celebrated. The present Lord Kenmare and his amiable Lady deserve equal encomiums, and do every honour to the place and their rank in life.>

Wild and infertile to the labourers art,
With native wonders greater charms impart:
The sloping-curves, we here and there descry,
Afford new changes to the roving eye;
The mingled contrast, of the various trees,
That deck their sides and fan the summer's breeze;
The cone-like Firr, and wintry-glooming Pine,
And rev'rend Oak which Ivy-wreathes entwine;
The Box, the Holly, and the browner Yew,
With vernal aspect—ever young and new!
Here grow luxuriant, to their native size,
And ev'ry artful, mangl'd form despise.
Greatly superior to the rest is found,
The Mountain-ash with crimson berries crown'd!
Which, nobly shoots, majestic, straight, and tall
As Norway Pines—but far out-soars them all!
Not the great Oak, tho' royal in his name,
O'er tops it's beauty, or out spreads it's fame!
Each tree, or shrub, which northern climes produce,
Here grows spontaneous for the artist's use:

The bright Cascades the Mountain-torrents form,
That rush impetuous in a wa'try storm,
And faintly glimmer, through the waving woods,
(Which now discover, now conceal their floods,)
Ev'ry restraint from ev'ry object mock,
But tumbling roar, against the sounding rock!
Then sudden stop—nor any course pursue,
As if their lately, greater height to view.—

Next spread in streams, and softly-purling rills,
With gentle babling, through the sloping hills!
To tell their peaceful and less rapid change,
Through meads enamel'd now to glide and range.

Tho' unembellish'd by laborious art,
Their native wonders greater charms impart.
The swelling curves we interspers'd descry,
Present new pictures to the roving eye;
The grand aspiring wilderness of trees,
Which clothe their sides and fan the summer's breeze;
Th'arbutus, holly, juniper and yew,
With blooming myrtles virent, young and new,
Here grow luxuriant to their native size,
And ev'ry artful, mangled form despise:
The cone-like spruce, the sombrous fir and pine,
Here with deciduous vegetation twine:
From Nature's birth, here all spontaneous blend,
And o'er the lake their twisted arms suspend;
In rival beauty here promiscuous live,
To share the decoration which they give.

THE bright cascades, the mountains torrents form,
Which rush and foam, and down the gullies storm;
Or faintly glimmer thro' the waving woods,
(Now half-discover'd, half-conceal'd their floods:)
The rocks and forests in their rage they sweep,
Roaring impetuous down the delug'd steep.
Thus oft is seen in human life display'd,
Some foreign chief in warlike power obey'd;
Nations are swept before his savage might,
At length he towers to wild ambition's height,
Then down the precipice of fate he's hurl'd,
The scourge and victim of an injur'd world.

Now spread in streams and softly purling rills,
The waters babble o'er the sloping hills,
Thro' meads enamel'd now to glide and range,
And tell in peaceful lapse their tranquil change.
Thus calm in innocence the guileless youth,
(The tenor of whose days is peace and truth)

This bright assemblage,—with their lights and shades,
(Whilst Phoebus glitters through the op'ning glades,)
The diff'rent tints, the trembling leaves unfold,
The new born-green, and Autumns faded gold,
The pleasing umbrage of the spreading boughs,
Invite fond Lovers interchanging vows!
While circling Woodbines mid'st the branches rove,
Perfume the Air and shade the secret Grove!
While feather'd Songsters chear their billing loves,
And amorous Turtles, woo their fellow Doves.

Ah! had kind Nature more propitious been,
And form'd the Climate, equal to the scene!
Then, might the Tendrils of the curling Vine,
Amid'st the Groves in sweet confusion twine!
The clust'ring Grape, might every Tree adorn,
And Flow'rs Exotic shield the pointed Thorn!
The blossom'd Shrubs in Spring-eternal blow,
In shades retir'd, and paths bewild'ring grow;
The Lime, and Orange, mix with Myrtle bow'rs,
And scent the Zephyrs of the temp'rate hours!

Then too, the Lake, with airy breezes curl'd,
Might boast its barges with their sails unfurled,
The smooth expanse in never lost repose,
Might then defy its ruffling squally foes!
Let splendid gallies through the Islands sail,
And stretch their Canvass to the swelling gale!
Board to and fro, along the winding coast,
Nor scar'd by Rocks, or sudden Tempests tost.

Distant from warfare and ambition's strife,
Glides smooth and silent thro' the vale of life.

THIS bright assemblage, with their lights and shades,
Whilst Sol still glitters thro' the mingling glades;
The various tints the trembling leaves unfold,
The new-born green, and autumn cloth'd with gold
While curling woodbines thro' the branches stray,
Scent the mild air, and shade the sultry day:
And thus inviting, as they twine their boughs,
The warbling quire to pledge their mutual vows;
There safe from cruel man to rear their young,
And harmonize the groves from whence they sprung.

AH! had kind Nature more propitious been,
And form'd the climate equal to the scene;
How more luxuriant wou'd those prospects rise,
Nurs'd by the genial warmth of Tropic skies!
Then might the tendrils of the clust'ring vine,
Midst the green hills in sweet confusion twine;
The glowing grape each pregnant bough adorn,
And amaranths conceal the pointed thorn;
Exotic shrubs might here successive grow,
In shades retir'd and paths bewild'ring blow;
The lime and orange blend with plantain bowers,
And scent the zephyrs of the temp'rate hours.

The Lake[3] might then, with gentle breezes curl'd,
Boast its bright barges with broad sails unfurl'd;
The smooth expanse in more secure repose,
Might then escape each ruffling blast that blows;
Let splendid gallies thro' the islands sail,
Stretch their white canvas to the welcome gale;
Devious to board along the winding coast,
Nor fear'd by rocks, nor by strong squalls be lost.

3 <The boats are seldom allowed to carry sail, on account of the sudden squalls from the surrounding mountains. – The lower Lake is upwards of seven miles long, in some parts seventy fathoms deep, and in many places near the shore upwards of twenty.>

But since no Wolves, the happy Plains controul,
Nor hungry Lions, in the Forests howl!
Devouring tear the harmless bleating Lambs,
Who fly for shelter, to their flying Dams!
Nor lurking Vipers in the pasture lye,
Whose venom'd bite, the cautious Shepherds fly!
Nor croaking Toads with foaming-poison fill'd,
From baneful Herbs and sulphur'd dews distill'd!
Nor dang'rous monster with amphibious powr's,
Nor frights by Land, nor in the Lake devours!
And Nature gracious to this favourite Shore,
Hath bid these Reptiles foreign-shades explore!—

Then freed from ills, which warmer climes invade;
For what we have—let thanks to Heaven be paid.

But since, nor earthquakes nor volcanos dire
Convulse our shores, nor burst with liquid fire,
Nor furious hurricanes, which storm the deep,
And o'er the land with desolation sweep;
Nor hungry lions in our forests howl,
Nor wolves voracious in our pastures prowl;
Nor hateful monster, with amphibious powers,
Frights not the shore, nor in the lake devours;
Nor crawling reptile in our meads conceal'd,
With venom'd sting, by antidote unhealed;
Nor clouds of locusts o'er our harvests fly,
Nor noxious pestilence infects our sky:
And Heaven, all gracious, to this isle more blest,
Bade all those horrors foreign climes infest;
Where hateful tyrants bear destructive sway,
And groaning slaves reluctantly obey:
But we, to chartered, lawful Freedom born,
May brave all despots, and their minions scorn.

THEN freed from ills, which richer climes annoy,
Our native pleasures let our sons enjoy.

Sources

Prelude

Luke Gernon
from: C. Litton Falkiner, *Illustrations of Irish History and Topography, mainly of the seventeenth century*. London, 1904, pp. 349–50.

Part I: 1580–1689

John Derricke
from: *The Image of Irelande, with a discoverie of Woodkarne* ... London 1581. Reprinted Belfast, 1985. Extract from 'The First Part of the Image of Irelande', pp. 26–28, 38–42.

Richard Stanihurst
'A Devise made by Virgil ... Englished'. *Richard Stanyhurst, Translation of the first Four Books of the Æneis of P. Virgilius Maro with other poetical Devices thereto annexed*. Leyden, 1582. Reprinted, ed. Edward Arber. Westminster, 1895, p. 136.

Edmund Spenser
from: *The Faerie Queene*, 'Two Cantos of Mutabilitie', canto VI, stanzas 36–55 (written in *c*.1595). London, 1611, pp. 356–8.

Richard Nugent
'Farewell sweete Isle'. *Ric: Nugent's Cynthia. Containing direfull sonnets, madrigalls, and passionate intercourses, describing his repudiate affections expressed in loves owne language*. London, 1604. Reprinted in *Cynthia by Richard Nugent*, ed. Angelina Lynch. Dublin, 2010, p. 75.

Anonymous
A Battel of Birds. Broadsheet, London, 1622. Pepys Ballads, I, 70–71.

Richard Bellings
'The Description of a Tempest'. *A Sixth Booke to the Countesse of Pembrokes Arcadia written by R[ichard] B[ellings] Esq*. Dublin, 1624, sig. P1r-P1v.

Lady Ann Southwell
from: 'An Elegie written by the Lady A: S: to the Countesse of London Derrye. supposeinge hir to be dead by hir long silence', Folger Shakespeare Library MS. V. b. 198, ff. 19v–20v; this text taken from the transcription in *The Southwell-Sibthorp Commonplace Book*, ed. Jean Klene. *Medieval and Renaissance Texts and Studies*, vol. 147. Tempe, Arizona, 1997, pp. 24–7.

Anonymous
'Ye merry Boyes all that live in Fingaule'. British Library, Sloane MS 900, ff. 54–5.

Anonymous
from: *A Looking-Glasse of the World, or, the Plundred Man in Ireland: His voyage, his observation of the Beasts of the Field, of the Fishes of the Sea, of the Fowls of the Aire, of the severall Professions of Men* &c. London, 1644.

Payne Fisher
'On a dangerous Voyage twixt Mazarine and Montjoy'. British Library Add. MS 19863, ff. 23v–25.

John Perrot
from: 'A Song for that Assembly' i.e. the Assembly of Megiddon. *A Sea of the Seed's Sufferings, Through which Runs A River of Rich Rejoycing ... Written in the Year 1659, in Rome-Prison of Mad-Men, By the extream Suffering Servant of the Lord, John*. London, 1661, pp. 10–14.

Katherine Philips
'The Irish Greyhound'. *Poems by Several Persons*. Dublin, 1663, p. 54.

Sir William Temple
'On my Lady Giffard's Loory'. *A Select Collection of Poems* ed. John Nichols. London, 1780. 8 vols. II, pp. 54–7.

Ambrose White
from: *An Almanack and Prognostication for the year of our Lord 1665 .... calculated according to Art and referred to the Horizon of the Ancient and Renowned City of DUBLIN*, by Ambrose White. Dublin, 1665.

Richard Head
from: *The western wonder, or, O Brazeel, an inchanted island discovered: with a relation of two ship-wracks in a dreadful sea-storm in that discovery: to which is added, a description of a place, called Montecapernia, relating the nature of the people, their qualities, humours, fashions, religions, &c*. London, 1674. Part II.

Edmund Arwaker
from: *Fons Perennis: A poem on the excellent and useful invention of making sea-water fresh*. London, 1686.

Part II: 1690–1739

Nahum Tate
'Upon the Sight of an Anatomy'. *Miscellanea Sacra: or, Poems on Divine and Moral Subjects*. London, 1696, pp. 40-4.

George Wilkins
The Chace of the Stagg: a Descriptionary Poem. Dublin, 1699.

Dorothy Smith
The Shepherd's Jubilee. Dublin 1701.

Jonathan Swift
'A Description of a City Shower' (first published in *The Tatler* in 1710). This text from *Miscellanies in Prose and Verse*, second ed. London, 1713, p. 404.

Thomas Parnell
'Health, an Eclogue'. *Poems on Several Occasions written by Dr Thomas Parnell … and publish'd by Mr Pope*. London, 1722, pp. 118–20. Text also in *Collected Poems of Thomas Parnell* eds. Claude Rawson and F.P. Lock, London and Newark, 1989, pp. 156–8 and notes p. 513.

James Ward
'Phoenix Park'. *Miscellaneous Poems*, ed. Matthew Concanen. London, 1724, pp. 379–91.

John Winstanley(?)
'An Elegy on the much-lamented Death of Jenny the Fish'. *Poems Written Occasionally by John Winstanley ... interspers'd with many others ... by Several Ingenious Hands*. Dublin, 1742, pp. 133–37.

John Winstanley(?)
'Upon Daisy being brought back from New Park to Stonybatter'. *Poems Written Occasionally by John Winstanley ... interspers'd with many others ... by Several Ingenious Hands*. Dublin, 1742, pp. 170–74.

James Arbuckle
Glotta: a poem humbly inscrib'd to the Right Honourable the Marquess of Carnarvon. Glasgow, 1721, pp. 3–4. 11–14, 16–18.

Jonathan Swift, trans. William Dunkin
'Carberiae Rupes', translated as 'Carbery Rocks in the County of Cork, Ireland'. *Works of J.S.D.D., D.S.P.D. in four volumes*. Dublin, Faulkner, 1735. II, 479–80.

Thomas Sheridan
'A Description of Doctor Delany's Villa'. *Miscellaneous Poems*, ed. Matthew Concanen. London, 1724, pp. 239–42.

Thomas Sheridan(?)
from: *To the Honourable Mr. D. T., great pattern of piety, charity, learning, humanity, good nature, wisdom, good breeding, affability, and one most eminently distinguished for his conjugal affection.* Dublin 1725. [reprinted as: 'The Case of Man', in *Poems Written Occasionally by the Late John Winstanley A.M.L.D., F.S.T.C.D. Interspers'd with many Others, By Several Ingenious Hands*. Vol II… Published by his Son [George Winstanley] Dublin, S. Powell for the Editor, 1751, pp. 158–62.]

Laetitia Pilkington
'The Petition of the Birds'..., *Memoirs of Mrs Laetitia Pilkington*. 2 vols Dublin, 1749, I, 38–40.

Mr B -------r
'On the Ortolans' by Mr. B -------r. *Poems written occasionally by John Winstanley A.M.L.D., F.S.T.C.D. interspers'd with many others by Several Ingenious Hands*. Dublin, 1742, pp. 119–20.

Murroghoh O'Connor
'The County of Kerry'. First appeared in *Poems, Pastorals and Dialogues …* by Morgan O'Conner [*sic*]. Dublin, 1726. This text is from *The Petition of Morrough O Connor to the Provost and Senior Fellows of Trinity College, near Dublin*. Dublin 1740, pp. 24–28.

Charles Coffey
The Bason: a poem inscrib'd to Samuel Burton Esq. Dublin, 1717.

Mary Barber
'Written from Dublin to a Lady'. Mary Barber, *Poems on Several Occasions*. London, 1734, pp. 99–102.

Matthew Pilkington
'The Bee'. *Poems on Several Occasions*. Dublin, 1730, pp. 39–48.

James Belcher(?)
A Cat may look upon a King. An Epistolary Poem on the Loss of the Ears of a Favourite Female Cat. Dublin, 1732.

Patrick Delany
Longford's Glyn: a true history. Faithfully translated from the Irish original. Dublin, George Faulkner, 1732.

John Lawson
from: *The Upper Gallery. A Poem*. Dublin, 1733, pp. 3–9, 14–16.

James Delacourt
'To Mr Thomson on his Seasons' (*c*.1734). *Poems by the Revd. James De-La-Cour A.M.* Cork, 1778, pp. 55–9.

Henry Brooke
Universal Beauty: a poem. Part VI. London, 1735.

James Sterling
A Friend in Need is a Friend in Deed ... Dublin, 1737.

Part III: 1740–1769

Wetenhall Wilkes
'Bellville'. *An Essay on the Pleasures and Advantages of Female Literature*. London, 1741, pp. 71–7.

Walter Chamberlaine
A Poem occasioned by a view of Powers-court House, the Improvements, Park &c. Dublin, 1741. The attribution of this anonymously published poem is found in a contemporary manuscript note on the copy in the Forster collection in the Victoria and Albert Museum, London. The copy in the Bodleian Library, Oxford, attributes the poem to a John Towers.

Samuel Shepherd
Leixlip: a poem. Dublin, 1747.

William Dunkin
'The Frosty Winters of Ireland in the years 1739, 1740'. William Dunkin, *Select Poetical Works* … 2 vols. Dublin, 1769–70, I; Latin text 'Hyemes Glaciales apud Hibernos' on pp. 430, 432, 434, 436, 438, 440 and 442; translated as 'The Frosty Winters…' on pp. 431, 433, 435, 437, 439, 441 and 443.

Thomas Hallie Delamayne
To Francis Bindon Esq.; on a picture of His Grace Dr Hugh Boulter, Lord Arch-Bishop of Armagh, set up in the Work-house, near Dublin, in Commemoration of his Charities in the Years 1739–40 and 1740–41. London, 1742. The author is given as 'T. H. D.' in the first printing.

Laurence Whyte
'Famine: a poem'. *Original Poems on Various Subjects, Serious, Moral, and Diverting*. Dublin, 1742, pp. 6–9.

Laurence Whyte
'The Parting Cup or The HUMOURS of Deoch an Doruis'. *Poems on Various Subjects, Serious and Diverting, Never before Published*. Dublin, 1740, pp. 68–99.

Thomas Mozeen
'A Description of a Fox-Chase'. *A Collection of Miscellaneous Essays*. London, 1762, pp. 33–36.

Henry Jones
'On a fine Crop of Peas being spoil'd by a Storm'. *Poems on Several Occasions*. Dublin, 1749, pp. 66–68.

Henry Jones
Philosophy: a poem. Address'd to the Ladies who attend Mr. Booth's Lectures. By the Bricklayer. Dublin, 1746.

Anonymous (though ascribed to Rev. Samuel Shepherd by Hyde and O'Donoghue in their catalogue of the Gilbert Library, 1918)
Leixlip: a Poem to a Young Gentleman. Dublin, 1746.

Edmund Burke
'*O fortunatos nimium &c.* paraphras'd'. *Poems on Several Occasions* (by Mrs Goddard and others). Dublin, 1748, pp. 15–22.

James Kirkpatrick, M.D.
The Sea Piece: a narrative, philosophical and descriptive poem. In five cantos. London, 1750.

John Winstanley(?)
'To the Revd. Mr ------- on his Drinking Sea-Water'. *Poems written occasionally by the late John Winstanley, ... interspers'd with many others by several ingenious hands. Published by his son*. Dublin, 1751, pp. 82–3.

Anonymous
'A Poem on the *Hot-Wells* at Mallow'. *The Ulster Miscellany*. Dublin, 1753, pp. 294–5.

Anonymous
The Villa: or Glasnevin, a poem. Written in Imitation of Cowley's Pindariques. Dublin, 1754.

Thomas Newburgh
'The *BEAU-WALK, in STEPHEN'S GREEN'*. *Essays Poetical, Moral and Critical*. Dublin, 1769, p. 215.

Richard Barton
A Physico-Poetical Essay concerning the wonders of Lake Neah, in Ireland. In imitation of Lucretius. Dublin, 1749.

William Balfour Madden
Bellisle, a poem; inscribed to Sir Ralph Gore, Bart. London, 1761.

James Eyre Weeks
'On the late Fog'. *British Magazine*, December 1762, p. 663. Roger Lonsdale prints an amended text (from *The Poetical Calendar*, vi, June 1763) in *The New Oxford Book of Eighteenth-Century Verse*, 1984, pp. 505–06.

John Cunningham
'A Landscape'. *Poems Chiefly Pastoral*. London, 1766, pp. 7–9.

Joseph Atkinson ['An Officer in the Army' was Joseph Atkinson.]
Killarny: a poem. Dublin, 1769. There is no date on the first edition, but Mary Paul Pollard, gives 17 June 1769. *A Dictionary of the Dublin Print Trade*, London, 2000. For Atkinson's heavily revised second edition, Dublin, 1798, see the Appendix.

Part IV: 1770–1799

Oliver Goldsmith
The Deserted Village. London, 1770.

John Leslie
Killarney, a poem. Dublin, 1772.

Anonymous
'Lord Altham's Bull'. John Edward Walsh, *Sketches of Ireland Sixty Years Ago*. Dublin, 1847, pp. 94–98.

Gerald Fitzgerald
The Academick Sportsman, or a winter's day, a poem. Dublin, 1773, pp. 11–13.

Anonymous
'Lagan upon the Mountain'. *Walker's Hibernian Magazine for 1776*. July, pp. 498–99.

Anonymous, ['Banks of Bann'].
'The Cock'. *Walker's Hibernian Magazine for 1777*. June, p. 440.

Anonymous
Ierne: a poem addressed to his Excellency the Earl of Carlisle, Lord Lieutenant General and General Governor of Ireland on his arrival in this Kingdom. Dublin, 1781, pp. vi–vii and 17–23.

James Henderson ['J.H of Hillsborough']
'The Woodcock'. *Walker's Hibernian Magazine for 1784*. Appendix, pp. 791–92.

'Œ.L.', Belfast
'The Lamentation of *Cara Pluma*, a Female Pheasant, for the loss of her husband and children. Dedicated to Mr Robert McCormick, the celebrated Irish Gun-Maker. *Universal Magazine and Review or Repository of Literature containing Literature, History, Manners, Arts and Amusements of the Age*. Vol III, Dublin, 1790. March 1790, pp. 275–76.

Anonymous
'Cappoquin, a New Song'. *The North Country Maid*. Limerick, *c*.1790. pp. 4–6.

James Creighton
'The Prospect of the Lake Erne'. *Poetic Miscellanies*. London, 1791, pp. 57–70.

Ellen Taylor
'Written by the Barrow side ...', *Poems by Ellen Taylor, the Irish Cottager*. Dublin, 1792, p. 8.

Samuel Thomson
'To a Hedge-hog'. *New Poems on a Variety of Different Subjects* ... Belfast, 1799, pp. 126–28.

John Searson
from: *A Poem, or Rural Entertainment; particularly descriptive of the Most Noble the Marquis of Abercorn's Cottage, near Strabane* ... Strabane, 1795, pp. 11–14, 17–19.

Francis Boyle
'Address to the Cuckoo'. *Miscellaneous Poems*. Belfast, 1811.

Jane Elizabeth Moore
'On the Discovery of the Gold Mine, in the County of Wicklow', *Miscellaneous Poems on Various Occasions*, second edition. Dublin, 1797, pp. 88–89.

John Corry
'Air, an Ode'. *Odes and elegies, descriptive and sentimental: with The Patriot, a poem*. Newry, 1797, pp. 61–63.

[William H. Drummond]
'Hibernia, a poem'. The poem appeared anonymously in the radical Belfast newspaper, *The Northern Star*, but is normally attributed to William Hamilton Drummond. This text comes from its reprinting as *Hibernia, a poem*. Belfast, 1797.

Part V: 1800–1819

William Drennan
'To Ireland'. *Fugitive Pieces in verse and prose*. Belfast, 1815, pp. 12–13.

Samuel Burdy
Ardglass or the Ruined Castles. Dublin, 1802, pp. 27–9.

James Orr
'Fort-Hill'. *Poems on Various Subjects*. Belfast, 1804, pp. 64–67.

James Orr
'The Bull-beat'. *Poems on Various Subjects*. Belfast, 1804, pp. 82–83.

William Webb
'Lakelands: a poem'. *The Poetical Register, a repository of fugitive poetry for 1806–07, vol. VI*. London, 1811, pp. 42–9.

Matthew W. Hartstonge
'Lines Written at the rocks of Kilcarrick, Co. Carlow'. *Minstrelsy of Erin*. Edinburgh, 1812, pp. 36–40.

William M'Elroy
'The Blind Bird's Mournful Lamentation to the Bird Blinders'. *Experience of Manifestation: a poem to youth*. Dublin, 1806, sig. B2.

Richard A. Millikin
The River's Side: a poem. Cork, 1807.

Sydney Owenson, Lady Morgan
'The Violet'. *The Lay of an Irish Harp or Metrical Fragments*. Philadelphia, 1807, p. 50.

Patrick O'Kelly
Description of the Giant's Causeway'. *Poems on the Giant's Causeway, and Killarney; with other Miscellanies*. Dublin, 1808, pp. 9–10.

Mary Leadbeater (late Shackleton)
'View of Ballitore'. *Poems by Mary Leadbeater (late Shackleton).* … Dublin, 1808, pp. 351–61.

William Tighe
'Lines Addressed to the River at Rosanna'. *The Plants: a poem*. London, 1808, pp. 152–6.

Mary Tighe
'The Lily'. *Psyche with Other Poems*. London, 1811, pp. 303–05.

Charles Boyd
A Georgic of Modern Husbandry in Twelve Parts; each corresponding with a month, Beginning the year at Michaelmas. Dublin, 1809.

William Carr
Rosstrevor: a moral and descriptive poem. Newry, 1810.

Samuel Fennell
'The Hare'. *Original poems*. Clonmel, 1811, pp. 92–94.

James Stuart
'Morna's Hill'. *Poems on Various Subjects*. Belfast, 1811, pp. 109–30.

William H. Drummond
The Giant's Causeway. Belfast, 1811.

Anna Liddiard(?)
Mount Leinster: or, The Prospect: a poem descriptive of Irish scenery, &c. &c. London and Dublin, 1819–20 (published in two parts, I in 1819, II in 1820).

INDEX OF TITLES AND FIRST LINES

INDEX OF AUTHORS